Detlef Schreiber

Architekt und Städteplaner
Architect and Town Planner

Detlef Schreiber

Architekt und Städteplaner
Architect and Town Planner

Einleitungsessay, begleitende Texte und Textbearbeitung /
Introductory essay, accompanying texts and editing
Christoph Hackelsberger

Herausgegeben von / Edited by Ulrike Schreiber

JUNIUS

Vorbemerkung:

Die mager gesetzten Texte sind Äußerungen von Detlef Schreiber (teilweise gekürzt).

Preliminary remark:

The texts in light typeface are statements by Detlef Schreiber (abridged in part).

Der Verfasser des Einleitungsessays und der begleitenden Texte

Christoph Hackelsberger (geb. 1931), Dr.-Ing., freischaffender Architekt, schrieb fast drei Jahrzehnte Architekturkritiken für die *Süddeutsche Zeitung*, die *Frankfurter Allgemeine Zeitung* und die *Welt am Sonntag* sowie Beiträge zu Fragen des Bauens und der Baupolitik in verschiedenen Fachzeitschriften. In zahlreichen Buchpublikationen und Vorträgen setzte er sich kritisch mit allen Phänomenen des Bauens auseinander.

1980 erhielt er den Kritikerpreis des Bundes Deutscher Architekten, 1983 den Förderungspreis Baukunst der Berliner Akademie der Künste für die kritische Arbeit in der Tagespresse. Seit 1992 ist er Honorarprofessor an der Akademie der Bildenden Künste München und Mitglied der Academia Scientiarum et Artium Europaea.

The author of the introductory essay and the accompanying texts

Christoph Hackelsberger (born in 1931) is a freelance architect and a Doctor of Engineering (Dr.-Ing.). For almost thirty years he wrote about architecture for several leading German newspapers and contributed articles on questions of building and construction policy for specialist periodicals. In numerous books and lectures he has given critical review to a wide range of phenomena related to construction.

In 1980 he was awarded the Critics Prize of the Association of German Architects (BDA), and in 1983 he received the Architecture Prize (Förderungspreis Baukunst) of the Berlin Academy of the Arts for his critical work in the press. In 1992 he was made an honorary professor at the Munich Academy of the Arts and a member of the Academia Scientiarum et Artium Europaea.

Inhalt
Content

7	Detlef Schreiber – Auf der Suche nach der Poetik des Rationalen von Christoph Hackelsberger		7	Detlef Schreiber – seeking the poetics of the rational by Christoph Hackelsberger

17 ARCHITEKTUR   **17 ARCHITECTURE**

18	Wohnsiedlung in der Lilienthalstraße, Oberschleißheim bei München, 1962–69		18	Housing estate in Lilienthalstraße, Oberschleißheim near Munich. 1962–69
24	Verwaltungsgebäude für den Süddeutschen Verlag, Färbergraben, München, 1963–70		24	Office building for the Süddeutscher Verlag, Färbergraben, Munich, 1963–70
42	Privates Schwimmbad in der Harthauser Straße, München-Harlaching, 1967–69		42	Private swimming pool in Harthauser Straße, Harlaching, Munich, 1967–69
50	Pfarrzentrum Heilige Familie, Johannisplatz, Gartenberg, 1969–73		50	Holy Family parish centre, Johannisplatz, Gartenberg, 1969–73
56	Privathaus Im Ginsterbusch 5, Hamburg, 1974–76		56	Private house at Im Ginsterbusch 5, Hamburg, 1974–76
62	Künstleratelier in der Muttenthalerstraße, München-Solln, 1974–76		62	Artist's studio in Muttenthalerstraße, Solln, Munich, 1974–76
68	Laborbau des Landheims Schondorf, Schondorf am Ammersee, 1974–77		68	Laboratory building for the Schondorf boarding school, Schondorf am Ammersee, 1974–77
78	Mehrzweckhalle der Grund- und Hauptschule, Herrsching am Ammersee, 1977–82		78	Multi-purpose hall for the primary and secondary school, Herrsching am Ammersee, 1977–82
88	Büro- und Laborgebäude für die Gesellschaft für Anlagen- und Reaktorsicherheit		88	Office and laboratory building for the Gesellschaft für Anlagen- und Reaktorsicherheit (Reactor Safety Company)
116	Ausstellungs- und Lagerhalle in Herrsching am Ammersee, 1979–81		116	Showroom and warehouse in Herrsching am Ammersee, 1979–81
124	Spielhäuser am Jackl, Westpark, München, 1982–83		124	Am Jackl play houses, Westpark, Munich, 1982–83
132	Ein Bausystem für Stahlhallen und zwei Anwendungen – Lagerhalle in Gundelfingen, 1984–87, und Montagehalle in Stonehouse bei Bristol, 1986–89		132	Two applications of a hall construction system – warehouse in Gundelfingen, 1984–87, and factory shop in Stonehouse near Bristol, 1986–89
150	Kindergarten in der Angererstraße, München, 1988–90		150	Kindergarten in Angererstraße, Munich, 1988–90

158	Wohnanlage in der Lenbachallee, Ottobrunn bei München, 1996–2002	**158**	Housing complex in Lenbachallee, Ottobrunn near Munich, 1996–2002
172	Zweifachsporthalle des Landheims Schondorf, Schondorf am Ammersee, 1998–2001	**172**	Dual sports hall for the Schondorf boarding school, Schondorf am Ammersee, 1998–2001
180	Marienkapelle, Am Vorderen Berg 1, Gundelfingen, 2001–2002	**180**	St. Mary's Chapel, Am Vorderen Berg 1, Gundelfingen, 2001–2002

187 STÄDTEBAULICHE PLANUNGEN   **187 URBAN-DEVELOPMENT PLANNING**

188	Städtebauliche Planungen, regional-, landschafts- und strukturplanerische Arbeiten	**188**	Urban-development planning, work on regional, landscape and structural planning
223	Biographie	**223**	Biography
225	Werkverzeichnis	**225**	List of Works
239	Mitarbeiter	**239**	Staff and collaborators

Detlef Schreiber – Auf der Suche nach der Poetik des Rationalen
von Christoph Hackelsberger

Detlef Schreiber – seeking the poetics of the rational
by Christoph Hackelsberger

Was will diese Überschrift sagen? Wenn Poetik angesprochen wird, dann geht es um das Begreifen, das nachfolgende Verstehen und das aus beidem erwachsende Wissen über das Gestalten und Herstellen von Werken. Poetik ist eben nicht Wissenschaft, sondern Annäherung, sich gänzlich beschäftigen, bestenfalls eins werden mit dem eigenen Tun.

Ohne Begreifen, ohne das In-die-Hände-Nehmen von erspürbaren Gegenständen, Materialien zwischen Luft und Erz, kommt kein Erkennen, kein Verstehen und insgesamt keine Begrifflichkeit und damit auch kein urteilendes Wissen über all das uns Umgebende zustande. Was wir nicht begriffen haben, können wir weder beschreiben noch ordnen und zuletzt auch nicht uns gefügig machen, nicht im abgewerteten, sondern im besten Sinn des Wortes. Genug der Begriffserklärung und nun zum Eigentlichen:

Detlef Schreiber, Baumeister

Detlef Schreiber war ein aufmerksamer, haptisch begabter und erfindungsreicher Mensch. Man könnte ihn einen homo faber nennen. Wo er stand und »für sich« hin ging – das bedeutet Absichtslosigkeit – fiel ihm etwas Unscheinbares auf, geriet ihm in die Hand; eine Wurzel, ein Kiesel, Rinde, ein Nagel, eine Schraube, der Schädel eines Vogelskeletts, ein Knochen, niemals jedoch ein Stück Kunststoff, wohl aber farbige Scherben, Gräser, ein Ast. Was ihm in die Hände kam, wurde aufmerksam gewendet, betrachtet, verworfen oder gewürdigt und von Fall zu Fall in die weiten Taschen seiner strengen Überjacken gesteckt. Unentwegt fand er Dinge im Wald, an Feldrainen, die anzufassen sich lohnte, oft Erstaunliches. Vieles bedeutete ihm etwas, war Anlaß des sich Einfühlens und Nachdenkens.

Der Sammler

Welche Schlüsse er dann zog, in welchen Schubladen und Regalen die Funde abgelegt wurden oder auf welchen Fensterbänken sie überdauerten, war eine Frage des Augenblicks und seines flüchtigen Eindrucks, es würde sich lohnen, auf dieses und jenes oder auch auf eine Verbindung einzelner Teile noch einmal zurückzukommen. Aus der Hand geben muß ja kein Verlieren sein, die Hand kehrt wieder.

What is this title trying to say? If poetics is invoked, then it is about grasping, subsequent understanding and the knowledge about designing and making works that emerge from both grasping and understanding. Poetics is not a science, it is about coming close, thoroughly immersing oneself, perhaps ultimately and in the best case becoming at one with one's own deeds.

Without grasping, without taking tangible objects into one's hands, materials between air and ore, no insight can come into being, no understanding and overall no abstract thinking and thus also no knowledge that can judge everything around us. If we have not grasped something we cannot describe it or order it, and ultimately cannot make it compliant for us, not in the devalued, bad sense of this word but in the best sense. Enough of this explanation of the terminology, and now on to the real matter in hand:

Detlef Schreiber, master-builder

Detlef Schreiber was an attentive and inventive human being with a tactile talent. He could be called the image of a homo faber. Where he stood and walked as he pleased – indicating a lack of clear intention – something unassuming would catch his eye, end up in his hand: a root, a pebble, bark, a nail, a screw, the skull from a bird's skeleton, a bone, never a piece of plastic, but probably coloured shards, blades of grass, a branch. Anything that came into his hands was turned over attentively, considered, rejected or acknowledged and placed in the capacious pockets of his austere outer jackets, taking each case on its merits. He constantly found things in woods, by the edge of fields, that were worth touching, often quite astonishing. A large number of things meant something to him, and caused him to empathize and reflect.

The collector

What conclusions he then drew, which drawer or shelf his finds were then stored in or which windowsill they spent their time on was a matter for the moment and his fleeting impression that it would be worth coming back to this or that or to a link between individual parts. Putting something down does not have to mean losing it, the hand can reach out again.

All diese unscheinbaren Schätze wurden ihm wert durch die Empfindungen, die sie vermittelten. Es war, als gäbe es ein inneres Warten, ein unwillkürliches Übereinstimmen. Da trifft sich einer mit dem, was er für sich schon immer gesucht hat. Es ist nichts Spektakuläres und macht doch reich.

So ist Detlef Schreiber, der Strukturen als die logische Verbindung und Fügung bis hin zum Paradoxon der Mehr-als-Ganzheit höherer Gestaltaussage stets gesucht hat, zu seinem ihm eigentümlichen Ausdruck gekommen. Er dachte ebenso wie Mies van der Rohe: »Das Ganze ist mehr als die Summe der Teile.«

Nichts ist neu unter der alten Sonne

Was ist daran so neu? Nichts und doch so vieles. Die Technik ist nicht neu, die Metaphorik und die Ethik, beides oft nur vorgeblich in der Durchbruchszeit des Neuen Bauens, aber wie bei vielen Kollegen der zweiten und dritten Welle der Moderne genuin frisch, sauber und tief empfunden. Bei vielen tritt dann der meist verquälte Anspruch auf Wissenschaftlichkeit hinzu, als Erweis unumstößlicher Wahrheit und Endgültigkeit, ebenso wie der artistisch-ästhetische Purismus des Nicht-mehr-als-nötig, der eine Unumstößlichkeit des Gefundenen verheißt und gar nicht selten Ödnis verbreitet.

Was die Technik angeht, so hat die ins Unermeßliche gesteigerte Nutzung des Eisens – vom Gußeisen des ausgehenden 18. Jahrhunderts über das stahlähnliche Schmiedeeisen bis hin zum gewalzten Profilstahl, zur Blech-Profil-Niettechnik und zur späteren Rohrverwendung mit der Verschmelzung des Schweißens – das Bauen mit seriellen Elementen, die meist stabförmig, kraftschlüssig verbunden wurden, im 19. und 20. Jahrhundert entscheidend geprägt.

Die architektonischen Verkleidungen der oft bis an die Wagnisgrenzen herangeführten Ingenieurkonstruktionen sind Ausfluss der Konventionen des bürgerlichen Zeitalters mit seinen klassifizierenden Wertordnungen. Die Gerüste der Brücken und neuen Bauaufgaben der Fabriken, Bahnhöfe, Ausstellungshallen und Kaufhäuser, zuletzt auch der amerikanischen Bürotürme, enthielten bereits 90 % aller konstruktiven Gedanken, die später auch die Architektur zu bestimmen begannen. Die strukturellen Neuerfindungen im letzten Drittel des 20. Jahrhunderts basieren auf den Techniken von Rohrverbindung durch Schweißen, auf der Gestaltung von komplexen Knoten und Anschlüssen und auf der Verwendung von Seilen und Membranen bis hin zu gänzlich neu formulierter Textilverwendung, einer sehr alten Kunst.

Wenn man die großen Erfolge der Betontechnik bis hin zum fragwürdigen Geschenk des grandiosen, aber mit der Zeit unversehens gefährlich werdenden Spannbetons als Sonderform ältester Gußtechniken einmal ausklammert, hat das Neue Bauen, aus Amerika zurückgekehrt, nun unscharf »modernes Bauen« genannt, gemessen an den Kühnheiten des 19. Jahrhunderts, im Bereich der Architektur stilbildend eher zu fast archaischen Simplifizierungen geführt, die sich äußerlich seriell und technoid gaben.

Das verwundert nicht. Haben doch ihre mit durchschlagendem Erfolg vor allem in den USA bauenden »Leitwölfe« wie schon deren

All these unassuming treasures were valuable to him because of the sensations they conveyed. It was as though there were a kind of inner waiting, an involuntary agreement. Someone meets something he had always been seeking for himself. It is nothing spectacular, but it does make him rich.

And this is how Detlef Schreiber, who has always sought structures as something logically connecting and fitting together, up to the paradox of more-than-a-complete-whole, found his actual means of expression. He thought like Mies van der Rohe: »The whole is more than a sum of the parts.«

There is nothing new under the old sun

What is so new about that? Nothing, and yet a great deal. The technique is not new, the metaphors and the ethics, both often only allegedly felt in the breakthrough period of Neues Bauen, but as with many colleagues in the second and third wave of Modernism, felt genuinely freshly, cleanly and deeply. In many cases, the usually tortured claim to a scientific approach as a proof of incontrovertible truth and finality, and also the artistic and aesthetic purity of the no-more-than-necessary, which promises the incontrovertibility of the found, and by no means rarely spreads desolation.

As far as technology is concerned, the use of iron, which increased to the point of being almost immeasurable – from the cast iron of the last decades of the 18th century via steel-like wrought iron to rolled sheet steel, to the sheet riveting technique and the later use of tubular steel with welding as a melting process – building with serial elements, usually connected frictionally, like bars, made a considerable impact in the 19th and ultimately in the 20th century.

The architectural of the engineering structures that were often taken to the limits of daring are the product of the conventions of the bourgeois age with its classifying values. The frames of the bridges and the new buildings commissioned for factories, stations, exhibition halls and department stores, and ultimately even the American office towers, already contained 90 % of all the constructive ideas that later started to drive architecture as well. The new structural inventions in the last third of the 20th century are based on techniques of connecting tubes by welding, the design of complex nodes and connectors and the use of cables and membranes, and then on to a complete new formulation for the use of textiles, a very old human art.

When neues Bauen came back from America, in a form now imprecisely called »modern architecture«, if we bracket out the great successes of concrete technology, down to the questionable gift of grandiose prestressed concrete, which unexpectedly started to get dangerous, as a special form of the oldest casting techniques, Modernism then, measured against the boldness of the 19th century, tended to lead to almost archaic simplifications in the field of architecture in terms of shaping style, looking extremely serial and technoid.

This is not surprising. »Big names«, building mainly in the USA with resounding success, but even their predecessors, produced

Vorgänger klassizistische Dogmen variiert. Dies gilt vornehmlich für die Stahlanwender, wenn sie nicht aus den Reihen der Konstrukteure hervorgingen, wie zum Beispiel Jean Prouvé oder Konrad Wachsmann und deren schmale, meist erfolglose Anhängerschaft. Der durchschlagende Erfolg Mies van der Rohes beruhte nicht zuletzt auf der kanonischen Verwendung klassischer Elemente, auf Abbreviaturen von Säule und Balken – modern übereinandergestellten Rahmen. Der klassisch-klassizistische Apparat Säule – Säule, Balken – Architrav wurde purifiziert, entkörperlicht, was vergeistigt bedeutete, und auf Walzprofile des 19. Jahrhunderts reduziert. Vom System her war diese Manier ebenso verwendungsfähig wie der Weltstil des Klassizismus, der seit dem späten 18. Jahrhundert die europäisch beherrschte Welt kultiviert hat.

Kommen wir auf Detlef Schreiber zurück: Er war, oberflächlich verstanden nach seinen Bauten, ein Schüler und Nachfahre Mies van der Rohes, den er tief verehrte. Man kann ihm nachsagen, daß er Mies so verinnerlicht hatte, so genau verstand, daß er ihn durch seinen eigenen Reichtum an Fähigkeiten und Einsichten in vielem überwinden konnte. Schreibers Stahlkonstuktionen waren zwar klassisch in ihrer unbedingten Reinheit und seriellen Konsequenz, aber konstruktiv hatte er das lapidar Klassische des Additiven durch Erfindung geistreicher Strukturen bei Gelegenheit hinter sich gelassen. Es hätte ihm nie gefallen, aus visuellen Gründen überzudimensionieren. Er hätte dies allenfalls auf sich genommen, um die Operabilität seiner Konstruktionen bei der Errichtung zu optimieren. Man kann in seiner Arbeit gut feststellen, daß Artefakte, die sich äußerlich ähneln, aus unterschiedlichen Motivationen auf gänzlich neuen Wegen zustande gekommen sind, zwar dem ersten Anschein nach ähnlich, aber zuletzt sehr unterschiedlich. Seine Artefakte gingen nicht vom fertigen Bild aus, sie waren erlernt beim Denken und Tun.

Aufträge prägen das Werk

Natürlich sind Architekten auftragsabhängig. Detlef Schreiber hätte statt seiner subtilen Hallen oder statt des Süddeutschen Verlags ohne weiteres auch bei einem Hochhausbau bestanden und Besonderes geleistet. Es kommt aber nicht von ungefähr, daß ihm, dem es nie um schiere Größe ging, um hervortretende Signifikanz, Aufgaben unterkamen, an denen er seine umsichtige Gründlichkeit bis hin zum Zufriedensein mit der eigenen Leistung und Durchdringung der Probleme bewähren konnte. Ihm, dem Waldspaziergänger, war es nicht gegeben, irgend etwas unbeachtet zu lassen. Jede noch so bescheidene Merkwürdigkeit berührte ihn, und er konnte in seiner fast scheu wirkenden Bedächtigkeit darüber berichten, mitteilen, was ihm aufgefallen und in die Hände geraten war. Vielleicht mußte man eine gewisse Wesensverwandtheit verspüren und eine Vorliebe für den ländlich-alemannischen Hintersinn haben, der so ganz verschieden ist etwa von der weitschweifigen, zielgenauen Raschheit eines ebenfalls von vielen Phänomenen der Umwelt beeindruckten Konstrukteurs wie Frei Otto. Die Ordnungen, denen der eine und der andere in ihrer jeweiligen Eigenart

variations on classical dogmas. This applies mainly to the steel users, if they did not come from the ranks of the design engineers, like for example Jean Prouvé or Konrad Wachsmann and their small band of largely unsuccessful followers. The formidable success of Mies van der Rohe is based not least on the canonical use of classical elements, on abbreviated columns and balconies – modern frames, placed one on top of the other. The classical-classicist apparatus of column – column, beam – architrave was purified, disembodied, which means spiritualized, and reduced to 19th century rolled sections. In terms of systems, this manner could be used just as well as the world style of Classicism, which the European-dominated world had cultivated since the late 18th century.

Let us return to Detlef Schreiber: he was, understood superficially through the phenomenon of his buildings, a pupil and descendant of Mies van der Rohe, whom he admired profoundly. It can be said of him that he had internalized Mies to such an extent, understood him so precisely, that he could go beyond him in many respects through his own abundance of abilities and insights. Schreiber's steel structures were indeed classical in their unconditional purity and serial consistency, but structurally he had left behind the succinct Classicism of the additive on occasions by inventing inspired structures. He would never have liked making something unduly large for visual reasons. At best he would have taken this upon himself to optimize the operability of his constructions as they were being built. It is very easy to see in his work that artefacts that look superficially similar were produced in completely new ways for a variety of reasons, still looking extremely similar, but ultimately different. His artefacts did not come from a completed image, they were learned by thinking and doing.

Commissions shape the œuvre

Of course architects depend on commissions. Detlef Schreiber would have held his own without difficulty if he had built a high-rise block rather than his subtle halls or the Süddeutscher Verlag building, and achieved something very special. But it is no coincidence that he, who was never concerned with sheer size, with outstanding significance, took on work for which he was able to maintain his prudent thoroughness to the extend of being content with its own achievement and penetration of the problem. As a walker in the woods, he was not prone to failing to pay attention to things. Even the most modest piece of significance moved him, and in his circumspection that could almost seem like shyness he could report and communicate about what had struck him and what had passed through his hands. Perhaps one would have to sense a certain similarity of nature and a preference for deeper, rural-Alemannic meanings that are so very distinctive, perhaps the wide-ranging, precise speed of an design engineer like Frei Otto, who is also impressed by many phenomena in the world around him. The orders that the one and the other served and serve in their own particular ways are very different. One could say that one order, Detlef Schreiber's, is more Pythagorean, while the other,

dienten und dienen, sind recht unterschiedlich. Man könnte sagen, die Ordnung von Detlef Schreiber sei eher die pythagoräische, während die Ottosche der evolutionären Organik, für die man ein ganz besonderes Sensorium braucht, zuzurechnen sei. Doch solche Gedanken gehen ins Uferlose; sie umkreisen etwas, was dann kaum zu werten ist.

Herkunft aus dem Badischen

Detlef Schreiber ist als Sohn eines Architekten im badischen Gailingen-Hochrhein, in einem der verwunschensten Winkel ganz Deutschlands, 1930 geboren und aufgewachsen, wo nur die Einheimischen wußten, ob sie schon in der Schweiz sind oder noch im Reich. 1949 zog die Familie nach München. Dort traf Detlef Schreiber auf Schulen und die große, schon didaktisch aufbereitete gelehrte Architektur dieser damals weidlich zertrümmerten Stadt. Unter den Schulen war für ihn die wichtigste die Technische Hochschule. Nicht daß er dort auf die glänzendsten Lehrer gestoßen wäre, aber einiges wirkte prägend. Es war eine Zeit der Irritation und des Übergangs, und das Gebotene genügte ihm als Anregung. Den Vers auf seine Art der Architektur konnte er sich allemal selber machen, und an Genauigkeit, Originalität und bedächtiger Abwägung hätten seine Lehrer eher von ihm lernen können als umgekehrt, was er sicherlich auch so, ohne eine Spur von Überheblichkeit, gespürt hat.

Studienzeit

Ein Stipendium für Städtebaustudien führte ihn 1957/58 nach London ans University College. Es war die Zeit, als Greater London noch versuchte, was ja auch in unserem Städtebau zu spüren war, Lehren aus dem Luftkrieg zu ziehen und den verfilzten, vielfach zufälligen Stadtteppich durch randständige Subzentren oder Satellitenstädte aufzulockern. So kam Detlef Schreiber mit der angelsächsischen Schule der Städtebaumoderne in Berührung.

Was in München gelehrt wurde, unterlag diversen Einflüssen, war zunächst schweizerisch, also vom Landi-Stil der Landesausstellung 1939 beeinflußt und solides, »währschaftes« Schweizer Bauhaus-Bauen. In der Folge war die nordländische Architektur aus Schweden *en vogue*. Dort hatte man erfolgreich versucht, solide, klassische Traditionen der Provinz mit dem Neuen zu verbinden. Gunnar Asplund war in aller Munde, und es war interessant zu sehen, wie rettend sich ein einziges Beispiel auswirken kann. All das versprach gemäßigte Fortentwicklung, ohne den unterschiedlichen architektonischen Vorlieben des nationalsozialistischen Gestern allzu vehement abschwören zu müssen. Die großen finnischen Architekten Alvar Aalto und Eero Saarinen mit ihrer humanen Moderne halfen dabei, den Krampf zu lösen, der vor allem in Süddeutschland wirkte.

Detlef Schreiber blieb, zumindest aufs erste gesehen, von diesem verquälten Hin und Her unberührt. Er fand bald heraus, wo der eigentliche Kern der Moderne lag, und dies kam seiner Art,

Frei Otto's, has to be classified as evolutionary organics, for which one has to have a very particular sense.

But ideas of this kind tend to become boundless; they circle around something which it is then scarcely possible to evaluate.

Origins in Baden

Detlef Schreiber was the son of an architect. He was born in 1930 and grew up in Gailingen-Hochrhein in Baden, in one of the most enchanted corners of all Germany, where only the locals are sure whether they were already in Switzerland or still in the Reich. The family moved to Munich in 1949, and here Detlef Schreiber met schools and the great, learned architecture, already didactically purified, of this town, which was completely in ruins at the time. The Technische Hochschule was the most important of the schools for him. Not that he came across the most brilliant teachers there, but some things did make their mark on him. It was a time of disturbance and transition, and what was on offer was enough to stimulate him. But he was able to make sense of his kind of architecture for himself, and his teachers could have learned something about precision, originality and careful consideration from him, rather than the other way round, which he certainly sensed himself, without a trace of arrogance.

Student days

An urban development studies scholarship took him to University College, London in 1957/58. It was the time when Greater London was still trying to learn lessons from the air raids, which was also something that applied to our architecture, and loosening up the matted, often random urban carpet with peripheral sub-centres or satellite towns. In this way he made contact with the Anglo-Saxon school of urban development Modernism.

What was taught in Munich was subject to various influences. It was Swiss first and foremost, influenced by the Landi style of the 1939 national exhibition, and solid, substantial Swiss Bauhaus construction. Subsequently, Nordic architecture from Sweden was in vogue. There a successful attempt had been made to combine the solid, classical provincial traditions with the new. Gunnar Asplund's name was on everyone's lips, and it was interesting to see how a single example can seem to come to the rescue. All this promised guarded further development, without having to abjure the various architectural preferences of the National Socialist yesterday too vehemently. The humane Modernism of the great Finnish architects Alvar Aalto and Eero Saarinen then helped to loosen the cramps that still had southern Germany in particular in their grip.

Detlef Schreiber remained, at a first glance anyway, untouched by this tortured toing and froing. He soon developed a sense of where the core of Modernism really was, and this very much suited his way of addressing architecture. A key experience for him was learning from and then working with Franz Hart at the Technische Hochschule. Hart was a sensitive outsider. As a

sich mit Architektur auseinanderzusetzen, sehr entgegen. Ein Schlüsselerlebnis für ihn waren das Lernen und die darauf folgende Zusammenarbeit mit Franz Hart an der Technischen Hochschule. Hart war ein sensibler Außenseiter, der als Bauingenieur eher durch die Umstände der Zeit und weil er sich weder architektonisch noch politisch exponiert hatte, auf einen durch Entnazifizierung vakanten Architekturlehrstuhl gelangt war.

Die beiden bauten 1958 eng verbunden, so daß man nicht recht entscheiden kann, was aus welcher Feder stammt, die an der Arcisstraße gelegene Mensa der Technischen Hochschule, schräg gegenüber dem schreinermäßig klassizistischen Führerbau, einem Leitfossil des NS-Reichstils. Diese Mensa – sie wurde später durch Erweiterung verdorben – war ein Lichtstrahl in die grau-braune Dämmerung des Münchner Baugeschehens, eine herausragend gute, wichtige Architektur, ein durchwegs mit sorgfältiger, aber leichter Hand gestalteter lichter Bau voll neuer Einsicht, daß eine offene Gesellschaft andere Orte braucht als die vor kurzem gescheiterte Volksgemeinschaft.

Eine gültige Aussage

Darauf folgte der Auftrag an die Arbeitsgemeinschaft Herbert Groethuysen, Gernot Sachsse und Detlef Schreiber, das Verwaltungsgebäude der »Süddeutschen Zeitung« am Färbergraben zu bauen. Federführend für dieses Bauwerk war Detlef Schreiber. Für München brachte dies in den Jahren 1962–71 den Anschluß an die weltweite, genauer gesagt, an die moderne Architektur der auch in dieser Hinsicht zur Weltmacht gewordenen USA und für Detlef Schreiber den Durchbruch. Noch heute, 35 Jahre später, zeigt das keineswegs durch Volumen und auch nicht durch städtebauliche Sonderstellung bevorzugte Gebäude, wie eigenständig und sorgfältig auch in München gebaut werden konnte und weiter hätte gebaut werden können, wäre dies nur gefördert und gefordert worden. Indes, der ehemals reichlich vorhandene Architekturwille war dieser Stadt – bedeutende Ausnahmen, vor allem die Olympia-Bauten, bestätigen die Regel – abhanden gekommen, verflacht in Genügsamkeit zur hinlänglichen Bedürfniserfüllung. Es ist bezeichnend, daß Detlef Schreiber in dieser Stadt nach dem Bau für den Süddeutschen Verlag nur noch wenig gebaut hat.

Städtebau und Stadtentwicklung

Vorher arbeitete er 1960/61 ganz zu Beginn am Stadtentwicklungsplan der Landeshauptstadt mit, einer bald in den wechselnden Vorstellungen, was Stadt im allgemeinen und München im besonderen darstelle, versandenden Aktion, welcher von Anfang an kein guter Stern den Weg wies. 1975 folgte indes etwas Neues und Bedeutsames, das noch nirgends versucht worden war, die von der Landeshauptstadt in Auftrag gegebene »Hochhausstudie«. Sie sollte eine Synopse der vertikalen Wertigkeiten erbringen und suchte, oberhalb der Kleinlichkeiten, wieder an die große Münchner Planungsepoche in der Prinzregentenzeit anzuknüpfen.

structural engineer, he had gained an architectural chair that was vacant because of denazification, through the circumstances of the day and because he had exposed himself neither architecturally nor politically.

The two built in very close co-operation in 1958, so that it is not possible to discern what came from which hand, the refectory for the Technische Hochschule, in Arcisstraße, diagonally opposite the cabinet-maker-like classicist Führer building, an index fossil of the National Socialist style. This refectory – it was later spoiled by being extended –, was a ray of light in the grey-brown twilight of Munich building, outstandingly good, important architecture, a light building, designed throughout by a careful, but not a heavy hand, full of insight that an open society needed places that were different from those of the community that had just failed so utterly.

A valid statement

What then followed for Detlef Schreiber, Herbert Groethuysen and Gernot Sachsse, who were commissioned jointly, was the headquarters for the Süddeutscher Verlag in Färbergraben. For Munich in 1962–71, this meant a connection with the worldwide, or put more precisely the Modern architecture of the USA, which had now become a world power in this respect as well. This represented a breakthrough for Detlef Schreiber. Even today, 35 years later, this building, which is favoured neither by its volume and also not by a special urban site, shows how independently and carefully it was still possible to build even in Munich, and how people could have continued to build, if this approach had only been promoted and demanded. However, this city had lost the architectural will it used to possess in abundance, frugally degenerated to merely meeting needs – important exceptions, above all the Olympic buildings, prove the rule. It is significant that Detlef Schreiber subsequently built very little in this city after the Süddeutsche Zeitung building.

Town planning and urban development

But he did work in the very early stages, in 1960/61, on the Bavarian capital's urban development plan, a campaign that soon petered out among changing ideas about what city in general and Munich in particular meant, a campaign that was not under a good star from the outset. In 1975 came something new and significant that had never been tried anywhere before, Munich's commission for the »Hochhausstudie«. This study was intended to produce a synopsis of vertical values and tried, above all the trivia, to link up with Munich's great planning epoch at the time of the Prince Regents again.

This study, exploring the development of urban space, a binding set of guidelines for the future, full of relations to respected sightlines and topographical assessments, was almost essential at that point, after serious mistakes had been made by placing high buildings unduly pragmatically.

Diese Studie, ein Nachspüren der stadträumlichen Entwicklung, ein bindender Leitplan für die Zukunft, voller Beziehungen beachteter Sichtachsen und topographischer Feststellungen, hatte sich damals fast aufgedrängt, nachdem schwerwiegende Fehler bei der allzu pragmatischen Plazierung hoher Gebäude begangen worden waren.

Rasch begriff man indes in dieser nur mehr administrierten und kaum noch gesamthaft gestalteten oder auch verstandenen historischen Stadtlandschaft, daß man, wenn man sich erst an die Satzung gewordene »Hochhausstudie« würde halten müssen, nicht mehr beliebig nach Gusto und raschem Einfall bauen könne. Soweit wollte man nicht gehen. Deshalb verschwand die Studie zunächst für fast zwei Jahrzehnte in den Schubladen.

Tiefschürfenden, landesplanerisch-städtebaulichen Arbeiten Detlef Schreibers im Raum Ingolstadt, die Auswirkungen bis in einzelne Gestaltungsbereiche der Innenstadt gehabt hätten, erging es nicht anders.

Planung stand politisch damals im Westen nicht hoch im Kurs, da im Ostblock von nichts anderem die Rede war. Übergreifende Planung bedarf zumal des langen Atems, und das verträgt sich nicht mit den kurzen Perioden kommunaler Parteienherrschaft, deren eigentliches Elixier der schnelle Erfolg und nur selten die Zukunft der Stadt ist. Hat eine Opposition im Parteienkampf eine bedeutende Lösung erst einmal abgewertet, dann kann sie, an die Regierung gelangt, sich nicht plötzlich um die langfristige Fortschreibung dieser Lösung bemühen.

Die Fortentwicklung seiner subtil genauen Architektur hat Detlef Schreiber zu letzterer Nutzen in der sogenannten Provinz betrieben. Dort hatten Bauherren und Behörden Einsicht, Verstand und vor allem Vertrauen genug, ihn arbeiten zu lassen, und das nie zu ihrem Schaden.

Besondere Bauaufgaben

Seine Spezialität wurde mehr und mehr der Hallen-, Instituts- und Gewerbebau. Aber auch der Wohnbau beschäftigte ihn, nicht das Bauen Stein um Stein, sondern die Möglichkeit typisierten, modularen und vorgefertigten Bauens. Schon in der Zeit nach dem Ersten Weltkrieg träumten Architekten davon, das tayloristische System mit seiner Zerlegung der Arbeit in die einzelnen Arbeitsschritte auf das Bauen zu übertragen. Ebenso war Henry Fords geniale Einführung der Fließbandmontage faszinierend, weil erst durch sie die Massenmobilität in den Vereinigten Staaten erreicht werden konnte; das wirkte stimulierend. Am Bau gelangte man indes nicht annähernd zu ähnlichen Erfolgen. Die Industrialisierung des Bauens gelangte nie über das getaktete Bauen mit groben Elementen hinaus. Die Ergebnisse waren meist weniger als drittklassig.

Für den Wiederaufbau Europas nach dem Zweiten Weltkrieg kam es zunächst in Frankreich und daraus abgeleitet und ideologisch garniert in den Ostblockländern, vor allem in der Sowjetunion und am fortgeschrittensten in der DDR, zur Anwendung von modularen Plattenbausystemen; auch in der Bundesrepublik gab es hierzu Versuche. Nur auf diese Weise war dem akuten Fachar-

However, people soon understood that this historic urban landscape, now merely administered and hardly designed or even understood as a whole, could not longer be built on at random according to personal taste and instant ideas, if the »Hochhausstudie«, which had now become statutory, was to be adhered to. But that seemed a step too far. So the study disappeared for almost two decades, to the point of being lost in a drawer.

Profound work by Detlef Schreiber on local planning and urban development in the Ingolstadt area that could have made an effect right down to specific design areas in the inner city suffered a similar fate.

At that time, planning was not a high political priority in the West, as the Eastern block was talking about nothing else. Interdisciplinary planning in particular needs to work over the long term, and this is not compatible with short periods of local party rule, where the real elixir is rapid success and rarely the future of the town. If an opposition has spoken firmly against a major solution in the struggle between the parties, it cannot suddenly throw itself behind the long-term continuation of that solution when it comes to power.

Detlef Schreiber was driven into the provinces to continue to develop his precise and subtle architecture, to the benefit of the latter. Here the clients and local authorities had enough insight, understanding and above all trust to allow him to work, which, as has been said, never did any harm.

Special building commissions

He started to specialize increasingly in constructing halls, institutions and commercial buildings. But he also addressed housing construction, not building stone by stone, but exploiting the possibilities offered by standardized, modular and prefabricated building. Even in the period after the First World War, architects were dreaming of applying the Taylorian system, which broke work down into steps, to building. Henry Ford's brilliant introduction of conveyor-belt assembly was also fascinating because it had been only through this that the United States had achieved mass mobility, and that was a stimulus. Nothing like success on this scale was achieved in building. The in-dustrialization of construction never got beyond synchronized building with rough elements. The results were usually less than third class.

France was the first country to start using the modular slab construction system for the rebuilding of Europe after the Second World War. This was then followed, derived from this and with an ideological garnish, in the countries of the Eastern block, above all in the Soviet Union, and in its most advanced form in the GDR; attempts were even made at this in the Federal Republic. It was the only way of coping with the acute shortage of specialist workers and achieving a result in sufficient quantities; but the quality left something to be desired almost everywhere. The slabs were difficult to handle, made heavy demands on transport and were ultimately viable only for major high-rise building projects. The method

beitermangel zu begegnen und überhaupt ein Mengenergebnis zu erreichen; die Qualität ließ aber überall mehr oder weniger zu wünschen übrig. Die Platte war unhandlich, aufwendig zu transportieren und letztlich nur für Großmaßnahmen des Stockwerksbaus vertretbar. Der Entwicklung von Architektur war sie nicht förderlich, es sei denn, man war fasziniert vom Massenaufmarsch verödender Gleichheit.

Was aber Architekten wie Detlef Schreiber interessierte und beschäftigte, war das modulare, Vielfalt versprechende Bauen mit kompatiblen Teilen. Aus diesen Gedanken entstanden in den 1960er Jahren Wolfgang Dörings »Formprogramm 300«, 1972 Richard J. Dietrichs »Metastadt« sowie Arbeiten von Günther Domenig und einer beachtlichen, einschlägig arbeitenden Internationale. Das alles wurde aus wirtschaftlichen, aber auch sozialpolitischen Gründen nicht weiterverfolgt.

Modulare Architektur

Dieses modulare Bauen schien – das zeigten die Entwürfe – durchaus architekturgeeignet. Trotzdem kamen die Bemühungen, auch wenn die Systeme bestens ausgedacht waren, nie über Nullserien oder über den Prototypenstatus hinaus. Während in den sozialistischen Planwirtschaftsländern des Ostens – sie waren sämtlich Schwellenländer, welche keine Kapazitäten für differenzierte Bausysteme mit hoher Fertigungspräzision und Komplexität besaßen – das Plattenbauen Rekorde feierte, liefen der Wiederaufbau und Ausbau im Westen weitgehend traditionell ab. Die Leistungsfähigkeit der handwerklich mittelständischen Baubetriebe aller Gewerke, ihre Flexibilität und ihre Bedeutung für den Arbeitsmarkt waren derart überwältigend, daß der Staat, welcher bekanntlich ins Wohnbaugeschehen überall finanzierend eingriff, kein Interesse am fabrikmäßigen Bauen haben konnte. So gab es zwar traditionell, schon aus den 1920er und 1930er Jahren stammend, eine ständig fortgeschriebene Normung des Wohnbaus, aber keine Industrialisierung.

Als die Bundesrepublik unter Willy Brandt sozialdemokratisch regiert wurde, schrieb das Bauministerium 1972 den groß angelegten »Elementa-Wettbewerb für modulares, elementiertes Bauen« aus, und einschlägig interessierte Architekten hätten meinen können, nun käme es zum Durchbruch. Man war vor allem aus Kostengründen auf diesen Ausweg verfallen. Die guten Absichten versandeten aber sofort und erwiesen sich als sozialistische Utopie, da sie mit den Realitäten des westdeutschen Bauwesens, des Arbeitsmarktes und der üblichen kleinweisen Baufinanzierung kollidierten. Detlef Schreiber hatte von einer Gruppe von Bauherren den Auftrag erhalten, in München-Oberschleißheim 39 ebenerdige Häuser in Fertigbauweise möglichst variabel und individualisierbar, dazu mit geringsten Kosten, zu errichten. Seit 1962 bemühte sich diese Bauherrengemeinschaft um ein Partizipationsmodell zur Erreichung bezahlbarer Bauten, ohne voranzukommen.

Diese an sich interessante Aufgabe schien für einen Konstrukteur-Architekten vom Rang Detlef Schreibers geradezu ideal, zumal den

did not promote the development of architecture, unless people were fascinated by the mass accumulation of barren equality.

But what interested and concerned architects like Detlef Schreiber was modular building, promising diversity, using compatible parts. In the 1960s, these ideas led to Wolfgang Döring's »Formprogramm 300«, to Richard J. Dietrich's »Metastadt« in 1972, and to the work of Günther Domenig, and a considerable number of architects working internationally in the relevant field. All this was not pursued for financial reasons, but also for reasons of social policy.

Modular architecture

This modular construction seemed – as the designs showed – to be entirely suitable for architecture. Nevertheless, the efforts made, even when the systems were excellently worked out, never got beyond pilot series or prototype status. Slab construction celebrated record levels in the socialist command economies of the East – these were all newly industrialized countries that did not have the capacity for sophisticated construction systems with a high degree of manufacturing precision and complexity – while reconstruction and development in the West proceeded largely on traditional lines. The ability to deliver shown by middle-sized, craft construction companies including all trades, their flexibility and their importance for the employment market were so overwhelming that the state, which as is well known, intervened in construction finance everywhere, could not possibly show an interest in building using production line methods. So the traditional standardization of construction, dating from as early as the 1920s and 1930s, continued consistently, but there was no industrialization of the process.

When the Federal Republic was under Willy Brandt's social democrat government, the building ministry announced the wide-ranging »Elementa« competition for modular, component-based construction in 1972; architects who were specifically interested could have thought that the breakthrough would now come. This route had been taken above all on grounds of cost. But the good intentions faded away immediately, turning out to be a socialist Utopia, as they clashed with the realities of West German building, the labour market and the customary approach to construction finance. Detlef Schreiber had been commissionned by a group of clients to build 39 prefabricated dwellings at ground level in the Munich district of Oberschleißheim. They were to be as variable and open to individual modification as possible, at minimum expense.

This building co-operative had been trying since 1962 to find a participation model for affordable construction, without making any headway.

This potentially interesting commissionned seemed ideal for an engineer-architect of Detlef Schreiber's calibre, especially as it seemed that the clients had now realized that their wishes could be realized only through a highly professional approach.

So he devised a flexible steel construction system with a broad range of variations, also applying to the buildings' appearance.

Bauherren inzwischen anscheinend klar geworden war, daß ihre Wünsche nur mit hoher Professionalität verwirklicht werden konnten.

Er erarbeitete also ein flexibles Stahlbausystem mit breiten Variationsmöglichkeiten auch für das Erscheinungsbild der Bauten. Sogar Selbstbau wäre möglich gewesen. Als es aber um die Modalitäten der Partizipation Unstimmigkeiten gab, zerstreute sich die Gruppe, und der ursprüngliche Ansatz wurde aufgegeben. Wenige versuchten den Selbstbau, andere ließen sich helfen, aber das Gros der Anlage wurde konventionell von einem Bauträger errichtet. Das Schreibersche System war überhaupt nicht zur Anwendung gekommen, wohl auch weil es bei der kleinen Stückzahl der Bauten – selbst 39 Häuser wären zu wenige gewesen –, gemessen an konventioneller Billigbauweise, zu aufwendig war.

Diese traurige Erfahrung mußten die konstruktiv begabtesten Architekten landauf, landab machen. Hätte für das industrialisierte Bauen tatsächlich eine Chance bestanden, dann hätte Detlef Schreiber mit seinem sorgfältig durchdachten und bei großen Stückzahlen erschwinglichen System bestimmt Erfolg gehabt.

Vielen Architekten eignen große Vorlieben für Utopien. Mancher erinnert sich gut an diese Jahre, als fast alle am sozialen Fortschritt, am Wohnungsbau und an menschenwürdiger Unterbringung möglichst vieler Interessierten davon überzeugt waren, die gewaltige Weltautoindustrie werde mit ihren raffinierten Fertigungsverfahren endlich Erlösung von der handwerklichen Minderqualität und Unzulänglichkeit bringen, und auch die Bedürftigsten könnten in anständiger Architektur untergebracht werden. Dies war naiv und zeigte wenig Verständnis für wirtschaftliche Prozesse und Verfahren. Die Sparte Industrialisierung des Bauens durch Großserienfertigung ist überhaupt nicht vorangekommen. Die Entwicklung ging rechnergestützt einen ganz anderen Weg. Die »Fließbandfertigung« war nicht mehr aktuell.

Detlef Schreibers eigener Weg

Detlef Schreiber hat sich, wie schon angesprochen, konsequenterweise auf andere, seiner Begabung mehr Aussichten und Spielraum gebende Bauaufgaben verlegt. Viele hoher Qualität verpflichtete Architekten haben in den 1970er Jahren auch aus wirtschaftlichen Gründen dem Wohnungsbau den Rücken gekehrt, was dazu führte, daß der Qualitätsgedanke weiter gelitten hat und die Beliebigkeit vorankam. Dieser Exodus der Qualität führte dazu, daß in den Folgejahrzehnten die Postmoderne offene Türen einrennen konnte, das Wohnbauen zu einer Farce verkam und die Reste an sozialer Verantwortlichkeit und Sorgfalt samt fachlichem Wissen über das Wohnen formalen Platitüden und Spielereien geopfert wurden. Außer einigen Renegaten, die nun als Formalisten hohen Ranges ihre Philosopheme beweihräucherten und dabei aufsehenerregende Karrieren machten, tummelte sich nur noch der architektonische Nachtrab bei all den Zuckerbäckereien und dem allgemeinen Stilverschnitt.

Detlef Schreiber hat an solchen Verwirrtheiten, überflüssig dies zu betonen, nie teilgenommen. Er hielt sich an seine strengen Leit-

Build-it-yourself would also have been an option. But the group split up when it had to address the precise conditions for participation, and the original approach was abandoned. Very few people tried build-it-yourself, others brought in help, but most of the complex was built conventionally by a contractor. Schreiber's system had not been used at all, probably also because there were so few dwellings – even 39 would have been too few – which meant they cost too much compared with conventional affordable construction.

The most talented structural architects, and the most selfless ones, were compelled to come to terms with this sad experience all over the country. If industrialized construction had ever stood a chance, then Detlef Schreiber would definitely have been successful with his carefully devised system, which would certainly have been affordable for greater numbers of dwellings.

Many architects are very fond of Utopias. Many of them will remember these years well, when almost everyone interested in social progress, in housing construction and in humane accommodation was convinced that the mighty world motor-car industry with its sophisticated manufacturing processes would finally release us from all the poor-quality craftsmanship and inadequacy, and that even the neediest would be able to live in decent architecture in this way. This was naïve, and showed little understanding of economic processes and procedures. The branch of industrialized building using large series production never made any headway at all. Development moved in a different, computer-aided direction, »conveyor-belt production« was no longer up to date.

Detlef Schreiber's own way

So Detlef Schreiber moved, as has already been suggested, to other construction tasks that offered more prospects and scope for his talents. In the 1970s, many artists who were committed to high quality turned their backs on housing construction for financial reasons, which also meant that the idea of quality suffered further, and a random approach asserted itself. This exodus from quality opened up the doors to Postmodernism in subsequent years, making housing construction into a farce and sacrificing the last vestiges of social responsibility and care, along with expert knowledge about housing, to formal platitudes and gimmickry. With the exception of a few renegades, who now trumpeted their personal philosophies abroad as formalists of the highest calibre, and thus made sensational careers for themselves, only the architectural rearguard romped around with all the over-elaborate confections and general stylistic muddle.

Needless to say, Detlef Schreiber absolutely never involved himself in all this mess and confusion. He clung to his strictly held values, to clear thinking about structure, to well-judged, lucid resources and austere materials that would create order, things whose performance he esteemed and acknowledged in a disciplined way, and to the aesthetic that arises from the correct implementation of two-dimensional quality in a space with the

werte, an die Sauberkeit des konstruktiven Denkens, an die ordnungstiftenden, wohlabgewogen kargen Mittel und spröden Materialien, deren Leistungsfähigkeit er achtete und diszipliniert würdigte, und an die Ästhetik, welche aus der stimmigen Umsetzung von Zweidimensionalität im Raum mit dem durchdachtesten und materiell geringsten Aufwand entsteht.

Daß einer, der sein Werk ernst nimmt und in Strukturen denkt, zum Fügen von Stäben, zum Erfinden von Verbindungen gelangt, nicht in intellektueller Dürre, sondern gescheit und spielerisch, ist kein Wunder und auch nichts Neues.

Holz wurde, wo es irgend verfügbar war, seit Urzeiten so genutzt, und die Zimmerer, die Stämme und Balken zu Häusern und riesigen Dachstühlen fügten oder zu den damals gängigen Maschinen, den Hebeln, Räderwerken und Wasserkünsten und vor allem zu den Kunstwerken der Schiffe, waren die Meister im geordneten Spiel mit den Stäben.

Dieses Erschaffen und Gestalten aus Vorgegebenem, nicht aus amorpher Plastizität oder durch Abarbeiten aus dem Vollen – dies ist Bildhauerarbeit –, birgt die Faszination solchen Begreifens, Fühlens und Denkens.

Das Konstruieren und Fügen in Stahl, in Walzprofilen, Blechen und Rohren unterscheidet sich nur durch eine gewisse Endgültigkeit der Materialien vom Holz, durch größere Schlankheit und gänzlich andere Verbindungen, welche die leidigen Schwierigkeiten, ja Untauglichkeiten des Holzes beim Übertragen von Zugkräften so glänzend überspielen. Und gerade in den Knoten, in der Ausnutzung der Querschnitte, im Erreichen des Filigranen liegt die ästhetische Herausforderung. Hier kann sich Meisterschaft zeigen, aber nirgends ist auch die konstruktive Banalität so nahe – sieht man einmal von den plastischen Deformationen beim Bauen in Beton ab – wie bei der ungefügen Verwendung stählerner Stäbe.

Und ein Weiteres kommt hinzu: die strikte, verständige Beachtung der Manipulierbarkeit vorgefertigter Teile bei der Montage und im Bauunterhalt. Gerade das hierfür erforderliche, vorwegnehmende Verständnis, das Vermeiden jeglichen unnötigen Aufwands und überschüssiger Kraftanwendung war für Detlef Schreiber ein Hauptvergnügen. Das erfordert Phantasie und Genauigkeit. Man muß vom Endergebnis her rückwärts denken können und sich von Effekthascherei freihalten, die beim Bauen eine so verderbliche Rolle spielt, seit alles, wenn auch mit unsinnigem Aufwand, erreichbar ist.

Unterhielt man sich mit Detlef Schreiber über seine Arbeit, so nahmen die Beschreibungen, wie etwas im Detail gemacht sei, breiten Raum ein. Besonders wichtig war für ihn, auf welche Weise er unnötigen Aufwand, zum Beispiel durch genau überlegte und gerechnete Dimensionierung, verfeinerten Kraftfluß und veränderte Auswahl von Profilen und tonnenweise Stahl gespart hätte und nun auch noch mit kleineren Hebezeugen auskäme. Großes Augenmerk richtete er auch darauf, wie die Primärkonstruktion zur Montage alles weiteren genutzt werden konnte. Dabei ging es wohlgemerkt nie vordergründig um materielle Erwägungen. Diese gehörten immanent ebenso wie das Gestalten zum intelligenten Spiel.

most carefully considered expense of money and effort, using a minimum of materials.

It is no wonder, and also nothing new, that someone who takes his work seriously and thinks in structures, comes to fitting rods together and inventing connections, not in a spirit of intellectual aridity, but skilfully and playfully.

Wood has been used for this purpose from time immemorial wherever it is available, and the carpenters, who made the trunks and beams in to houses and enormous roof timbering, or into the machines that were customary at the time, the levers, gear systems and water drives, and above all into the works of art that were ships, were masters of the ordered handling of rods.

This creation and design from what is already there, not through amorphous plasticity or working down from a full shape – that is work for a sculptor – contains within it the fascination of this understanding, feeling and thinking.

Construction and assembling in steel, in rolled sections, sheets and tubes, is different from wood only in a certain finality of the materials, in a greater slenderness and totally different joints, which so magnificently eliminate the moderate difficulties, indeed inadequacies of wood in transferring tensile forces.

And the aesthetic challenge lies particularly in the nodes, in the exploitation of cross-sections, in achieving a filigree effect. Mastery can be shown here, but nowhere is structural banality so close – if one ignores the three-dimensional distortions caused by building in concrete – as when steel rods are used clumsily.

And there is another factor too: paying strict, sympathetic heed to the way prefabricated parts can be manipulated in assembly and in maintaining the building. It is precisely the understanding that is needed for this, which should be taken for granted, the avoidance of any unnecessary effort and excessive use of force that was one of the main pleasures for Detlef Schreiber. This needs understanding and precision. It must be possible to think backwards from the final result, and to avoid any hint of the showing off that can be so damaging to building, since everything can be achieved, though with nonsensical expense of effort and money.

In conversation with Detlef Schreiber about his work, descriptions of how something was achieved in detail took up a lot of time. It was particularly important for him to establish how he could have saved unnecessary effort and tons of steel, for example through precisely considered and calculated dimensions, improved flows of forces and a different selection of sections, thus being able to manage with much smaller lifting devices. He paid particular attention to the way in which primary construction could be exploited for the assembly of everything else.

But it must be said that he was not just superficially concerned with material considerations. Like design, these were an inherent part of his intelligent game.

He would have found it a reproach that was particularly difficult to come to terms with if someone had been able to show that he could have got away with less effort and expense in some way or another. He always anticipated this. He thought his way through

Der Nachweis, daß er auf diese oder jene Weise auch mit weniger Aufwand hätte zurechtkommen können, wäre für ihn ein schwer zu verwindender Vorwurf gewesen. Dem kam er stets zuvor. Er dachte sich durch jedes Detail, jede Situation hindurch, und dem Denken folgte die zuverlässige und unermüdliche Gründlichkeit der Arbeit. Detlef Schreiber war das Beispiel eines gründlichen Arbeiters. Vielleicht helfen einem dabei viele Generationen auf sich selbst gestellter bäuerlicher Menschen. Die gingen ehemals, vor raiffeisenversicherten Zeiten und vor allem, als sie aus dem Schatten der Grundherren und der Klöster in die gänzliche Eigenverantwortung traten, gnadenlos unter, wenn einer nicht gründlich war und sich nicht auf »sein Sach« verstand. Man tüftelte solange, bis das Problem gelöst war. Wer davon nichts weiß, hätte manchmal meinen können, Detlef Schreiber sei umständlich, einschichtig, wo er doch nur alles genau und sachgerecht bedachte und es dann ins Werk setzte. Dieses innere Umkreisen nach selbstgefundenen Regeln und eigener Verpflichtung zur Werkgerechtigkeit führt nicht zu rascher Geschwätzigkeit, wie sie heute gängig ist. Man lernt zu schweigen. Einer, der so beschaffen ist wie Detlef Schreiber, braucht seine Zeit für sich. Eben fürs Umkreisen seiner sich selbst gestellten Anforderungen und nicht, um unentwegt selbstreferentiell sein Innerstes nach außen zu kehren wie einen alten Handschuh.

Seine Art und Haltung machte Gespräche mit ihm ebenso wertvoll wie kurz. Entweder man verstand ihn, dann war das Ausschmücken und Ausbreiten nicht nötig, oder man hatte keinen Sinn für seine freundliche Sprödigkeit, dann traf man zwar auf einen angenehmen und gescheiten Menschen, aber es entging einem vieles, was er zur Architektur zu sagen hatte. Daß er ein feinsinniger Mensch war, hat aber wohl jeder gespürt.

Wie er das Leben mit Ernst und Würde, aber auch heiter, bisweilen geradezu festlich zelebrierte, erfuhr man, wenn man in Widdersberg in seinem schönen, fast shakerhaft anmutenden, sorglos-sorgfältig inszenierten Haus und Anwesen zu Gast war. Seine Frau Ulrike Schreiber-Lohan, fein und lebhaft, doch leis im Schatten des Zeremonien- und Essensmeisters, und dieser selbst, beim Entkorken besten Weins oder bei Erläuterungen, wie diffizile Speisen zuzubereiten seien, auch beim Rauchen wunderbarer Zigarren, das war ein unvergessliches Bild.

Man erfuhr nebenher, wie einer, der es mit seiner Kunst und seinem Tun genau nimmt, Gastlichkeit, Essen und Trinken mit der gleichen Sorgfalt bedenkt und ebenso ernsthaft feiert, wie er arbeitet. Das war schön zu sehen, zu schmecken und zu erleben.

»Mach alles so gut du irgend kannst und nichts halb, weil alles Halbe weniger ist als Nichts und nur Unverstand verrät.« Was soll man noch über so einen besonderen Mann sagen? Daß er aufmerksam, liebenswürdig und auch verletzlich war, steht wohl schon zwischen den Zeilen.

Daß man ihn nicht vergessen wird, so lang man eben kann und daß er in seinem Wesen ein gar nicht aktueller Mensch war in seiner Suche nach der Poetik des Rationalen, ein besonderer unter all den Aufgeregten des Alltags ist wohl auch klar geworden. Es ist gut, ihn gekannt zu haben. Man freut sich an der Erinnerung.

every detail, every situation, and this thinking was followed by the reliable and tireless thoroughness of his work. Detlef Schreiber was a fine example of a thorough worker. Perhaps many generations of peasant folk who had to rely on themselves are helpful here. Formerly, before the days of social safety nets, and above all when they came out from the shadow of the landlords and monasteries to take full responsibility for themselves, they failed inevitably if people were not thorough and did not properly understand what they were doing. And they racked their brains over things they had to think out over and over again; not all of them were so talented, but many in fact were. Anyone who knows nothing about it could sometimes have thought that Detlef Schreiber was laborious and limited when he relied utterly on himself to think everything through precisely and appropriately, and then to put it into practice. This internal mental circling around rules he had invented for himself and his own commitment to working in absolutely the right way did not lead to the kind of quick-fire loquacity that is expected today. People learn to be silent.

Someone who is made like Detlef Schreiber needs time to himself. Precisely to think his way carefully around the demands he is making on himself and not to turn his innermost thoughts inside out all the time, like an old glove.

His nature and approach made conversations with him as valuable as they were short. Either one understood him, in which case decoration and expansive explanation were not needed, or one had no sympathy for his friendly aloofness, in which case one was meeting a pleasant and clever man, but missed a great deal of what he had to say about architecture. But everyone was aware that he was a man of refined sensibilities.

People who were invited to his beautiful, almost Shaker-like home in Widdersberg, carefree and careful in its presentation, experienced how he celebrated life with seriousness and dignity, but also light-heartedly, sometimes even festively. His wife, Ulrike Schreiber-Lohan, was refined and lively, but also slightly in the shadow of the master of ceremonies and of dining. He himself made an unforgettable picture when opening a bottle of wine or explaining how to prepare difficult foods, and also when smoking excellent cigars.

And you discovered on the side how someone who treats his art and his activities precisely will take the same care with hospitality, eating and drinking, and celebrate them just as seriously as his work. This was all wonderful to see, to taste and to experience.

Do everything as well as you possibly can and don't only half do it, as half is always less than nothing, and only betrays a lack of understanding. What else is there to say about such a special man? That he was attentive, charming and also vulnerable can probably be read between the lines.

That one will never forget him for as long as possible and that in his nature he was not an up-to-date person in his search for the poetry of the rational, a special person among all the everyday over-excitement has probably also become clear as well. It is good to have known him. One is delighted with the memory.

Architektur
Architecture

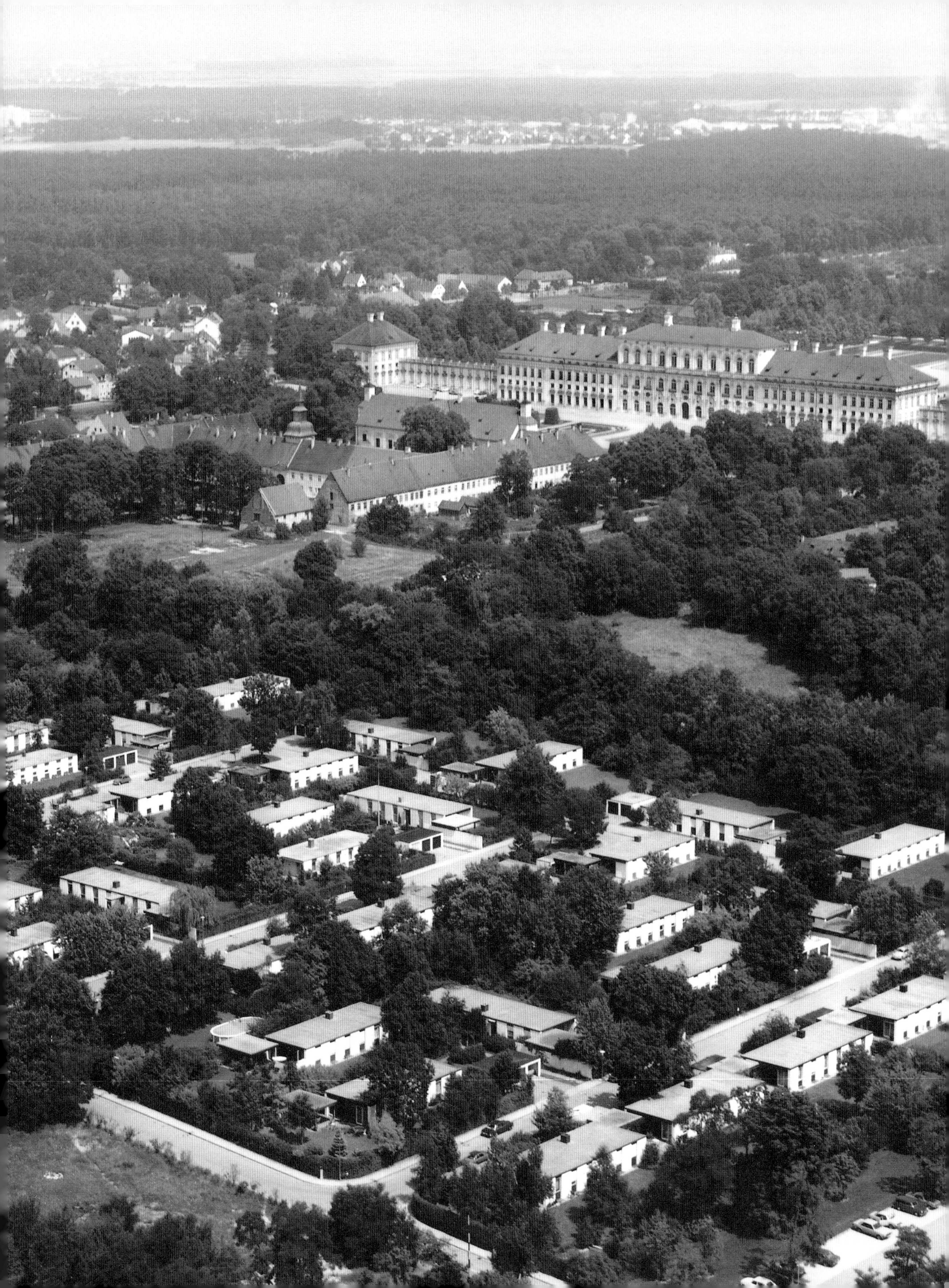

Wohnsiedlung in der Lilienthalstraße, Oberschleißheim bei München, 1962–69
Bauherr: privater Verein

Housing estate in Lilienthalstraße, Oberschleißheim near Munich, 1962–69
Client: private association

Der Wohnungsbedarf der Nachkriegszeit war gewaltig. Merkwürdigerweise bestand, trotz einschneidender sozialer Veränderungen, kein dringliches Bedürfnis nach diesen Einschnitten entsprechenden Wohnformen. Die Stockwerkswohnungen zeigten mit wenigen Ausnahmen dieselben, nur schubweise etwas großflächiger werdenden bürgerlichen Grundrisse, die jenen damals gemäßigten Fortschritt bedeutenden Erarbeitungen der späten 1920er Jahre entsprachen und vor allem an den Vorgaben der in der letzten Hälfte des Zweiten Weltkriegs wirkenden, sogenannten »Wiederaufbaustäbe« ausgerichtet waren. Die von fast allen Bürgern erträumten und für eine große Zahl Wirklichkeit werdenden Einfamilienhäuser hatten das peinliche Flair von Miniaturvillen, die, an der vorderen Baulinie gehalten, vom üblichen Baurecht dort festgeschrieben, mittig auf ihren kleinen Grundstücken hockten. Dazu gab es als praktikable Neuerung den weitverbreiteten Typus des Einfamilien- oder Doppelhauses mit jeweiliger Einliegerwohnung.

Vor solchem kaum erfreulichen Hintergrund waren Siedlungen wie jene in Oberschleißheim seltene Lichtblicke und sind es, nunmehr über Jahrzehnte bewohnt und ganz hinter dem Begleitgrün verschwunden, auch weiterhin.

Housing was in desperately short supply in the postwar period. Strangely enough, despite radical social change, there was no urgent demand for this appropriate dwelling style. With a very few exceptions, high-rise buildings had the same bourgeois ground plans, simply a little greater in their area here and there, corresponding with ground plans devised in the late 1920s, and above all with the requirements of the socalled »reconstruction squads« working in the last half of the Second World War. The detached homes that most citizens dreamt of and that became reality for large numbers had the embarrassing look of miniature villas, sitting in the middle of their little building plots, keeping to the front building line as required by the usual building regulations here. As well as this, as a practicable innovation, there was the frequently encountered type of the detached or semi-detached house, each with a granny flat.

Housing estates like the one in Oberschleißheim were all too rare glimpses of light against this kind of less than pleasing background, and continue to be so, now that they have been lived in for decades and have disappeared completely behind the accompanying green.

Baubeschreibung des Architekten

»Südwestlich der Schleißheimer Schloßanlage, zwischen Bahnlinie und Würmkanal, erstreckt sich ein traditionsreiches Feld, ehemals Standort der königlich-bayerischen Feldfliegerabteilung, zuletzt Airbase eines amerikanischen Hubschraubergeschwaders. Der Streifen, welcher die neue Siedlung aufnehmen sollte, war früher mit Militärbauten bestanden, welche im Zweiten Weltkrieg zerstört worden waren. Die Bundesrepublik Deutschland als Grundstückseigentümer stellte dieses Teilgrundstück einem Verein von Bauwilligen zum Errichten von Einfamilienhäusern mit der Auflage zur Verfügung, so zu bauen, daß sich die Häuser ins Ortsbild einer zukünftigen ›Entlastungsstadt Oberschleißheim‹ einfügen würden. Die Bebauung müsse, so hieß es, ›locker, niedrig und strauchhoch sein‹. Das Grundstück bildet den Übergang zwischen zwei Grünräumen. Der west-östliche grenzt die zukünftige Entlastungsstadt von der Schloßanlage, der nordsüdliche die Siedlung von der Bahnlinie ab.

The architect's description of the building

»South-west of Schloss Schleissheim, between the railway line and the Würm canal, is a field with strong traditions, formerly the site of the Royal Bavarian Air division and finally an airbase for an American helicopter squadron. The strip of land that was to accommodate the new housing estate had previously contained military buildings that had been destroyed in the Second World War. As the owner of the plot, the German Federal Republic made this section of land available to a consortium of people wanting to build for de-tached homes, with the proviso that the design of the buildings should fit in with the image of a future ›Oberschleißheim overspill town‹. The conditions stated that the buildings had to be ›not too close together

Links: Luftaufnahme der Wohnsiedlung, im Hintergrund Schloß Schleißheim

Left page: aerial photograph of the housing estate, in the background: Schleissheim Palace

Es war besonders erwünscht, beide Grünzüge durch ein die geplante Siedlung erschließendes Fußwegesystem zu vernetzen. Der Fahrverkehr sollte getrennt davon geführt werden.

Die städtebauliche Aufgabe bestand einmal darin, längs der Fußwege Raumfolgen zu schaffen und andererseits den Häusern Freiräume so zuzuordnen, daß ungestörte Privatbereiche entstehen konnten. Dieses Konzept wurde nur unwesentlich verändert, während die Gebäudeplanung immer neuen Anforderungen antworten mußte.

Die Bauherrschaft, ein Verein mit 39 Mitgliedern, beabsichtigte zunächst, verschiedene Gebäudetypen mit größtmöglicher Variabilität eines einheitlichen Bausystems errichten zu lassen. Das Ziel war, 39 individuelle Häuser so preiswert wie möglich und geeignet für spätere Veränderung zu bauen und durch das Konstruktionssystem eine gewisse verbindliche Ästhetik vorzugeben. Diese Absicht scheiterte an mangelnder Übereinstimmung der Vereinsmitglieder. Die Bauherrschaft übertrug nun die Durchführung und Trägerschaft einer Wohnbaugesellschaft, welche durch drastische Einschränkungen der angestrebten Vielfalt, vor allem aber der Mitsprache der Bauherren, die Probleme vereinfachte und die Häuser nach einem einheitlichen, reduzierten Schlüssel finanzierte.

Vier Planungsstufen

Das konstruktive System der 1. Planungsstufe war ein außenliegendes, weitgespanntes Stahlskelett. Das Ausbausystem bestand aus nichttragenden Holzelementen.

Die 2. Planungsstufe sah vor, die Außenwände aus tragenden, in engen Abständen angeordneten, mehrschichtigen Wandelementen zu erstellen; die Innenwände waren versetzbar.

Für die 3. Planungsstufe wurde ein Stahlbeton-Fertigteilsystem angewandt, das in der Längsrichtung doppelschalige, tragende Wände mit Abstandsbereichen für Fensteröffnungen hatte. Innenwände und Schrankwände, Fensterelemente und die Stirnwände bestanden ebenso wie die innere Wandverkleidung der Betonaußenwände aus vorgefertigten Holzelementen. Dem Bauträger war auch dies an sich preiswerte und brauchbare integrierte Bausystem zu kompliziert.

Nun wurde beschlossen, Planungsstufe 4 völlig konventionell auszuführen. Nur noch die Innenwände waren nichttragend und versetzbar.

Der Bauträger errichtete 35 Häuser, weitere vier wurden von Selbstbauern verwirklicht. Die Systemerarbeitung war lehrreich, aber nutzlos.«

low and bush-high›. The plot forms the transition between two green spaces. The one running east–west separates the future overspill town from the Schloss complex, and the one running north–south the estate from the railway line.

It was a particular request that the two strips of green should be networked by a footpath system giving access to the housing estate. Vehicular traffic was to be handled separately.

The urban development plan involved first of all created spatial sequences along the footpaths and then allotted open space to the houses in such a way that genuinely private areas could be created. This concept was altered in minor ways only, but the building planning had to respond to constant new demands.

The building clients, an association with 39 members, intended first of all to construct various building types with the largest possible variability afforded by a uniform construction system. The aim was to build 39 individual houses suitable for later change as cheaply as possible, and to provide a certain binding aesthetic through the construction system. This plan fell through because of lack of agreement among the association members. The clients then transferred implementation and responsibility for the project to a housing company, which simplified the problems by drastic reductions of the desired variety, but above all of the extent to which the clients had a say, and built the houses to a uniform, reduced scheme.

Four planning phases

The structural system for the 1st planning phase was an external, long-span steel skeleton. The completion system was made up of non-load-bearing timber elements.

The 2nd planning phase provided for exterior walls in load-bearing, laminated wall elements arranged close together; the interior walls were adjustable.

A prefabricated reinforced concrete system was used for the 3rd planning phase, with double shell load-bearing walls running longitudinally, with spaces for window apertures. Interior walls and room dividers, window elements and the end walls also consisted of prefabricated timber elements, like the interior cladding of the concrete outer walls. This integrated construction system, as such reasonably priced and viable, was also too complicated for the housing company.

It was now decided that planning phase 4 should be carried out conventionally. Now only the interior walls were non-load-bearing and adjustable.

The company built 35 houses, and another four were realized by clients building themselves. Devising the system had been instructive, but in vain.«

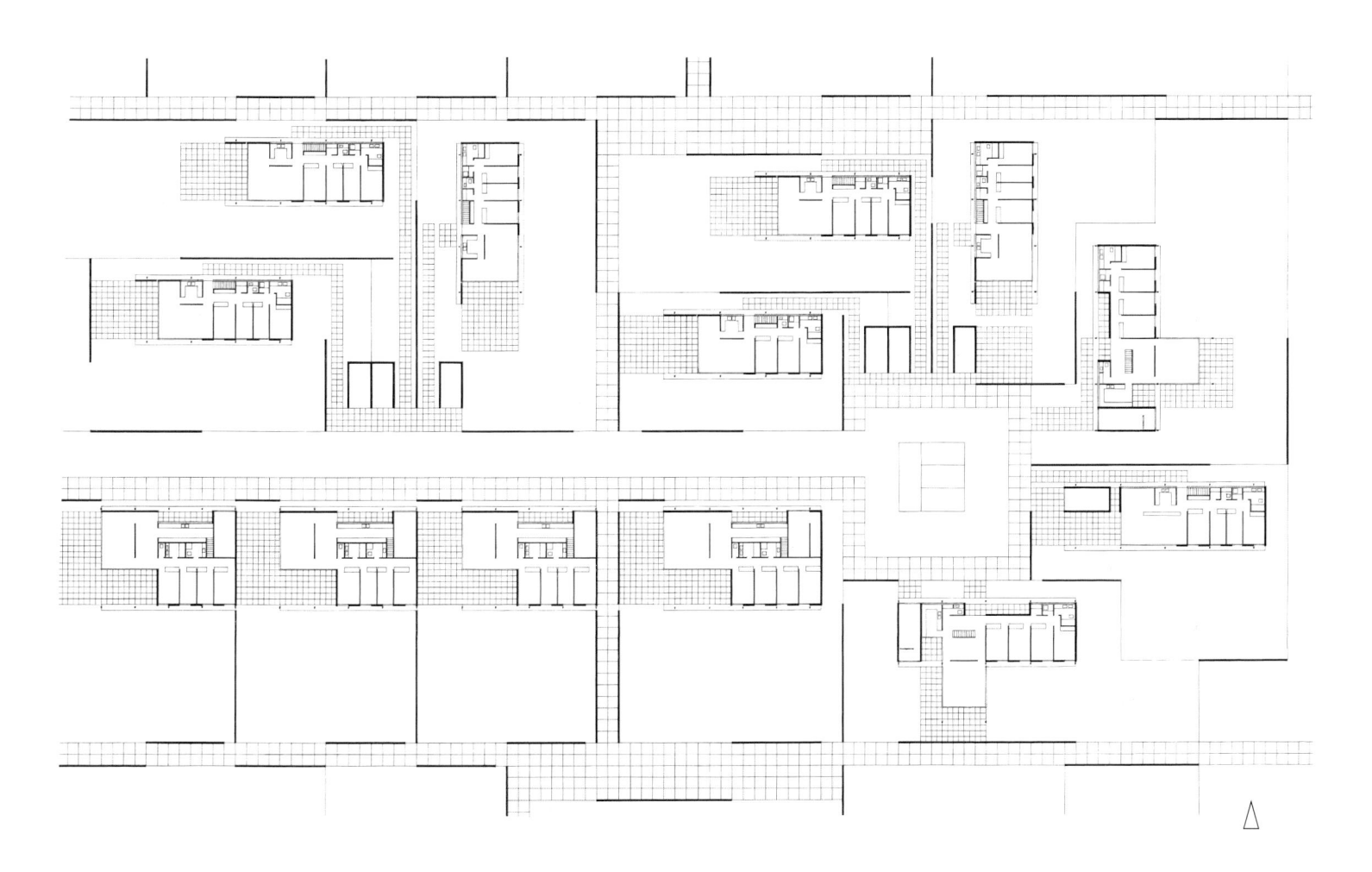

Oben: Ausschnitt einer Häusergruppe aus dem Modell
Unten: Planausschnitt einer Häusergruppe an einer Wohnstraße mit Grundrissen

Top: part of a group of buildings in the model
Bottom: extract from the plans for a group of buildings in a residential road with floor plans

Blick in einen Wohnweg

View of a residential path

Wohnhaus zur Straßenfront mit
Abtrennungsmauer zum Nachbarn

Residential building facing the street,
separated from the neighbouring
plot by a wall

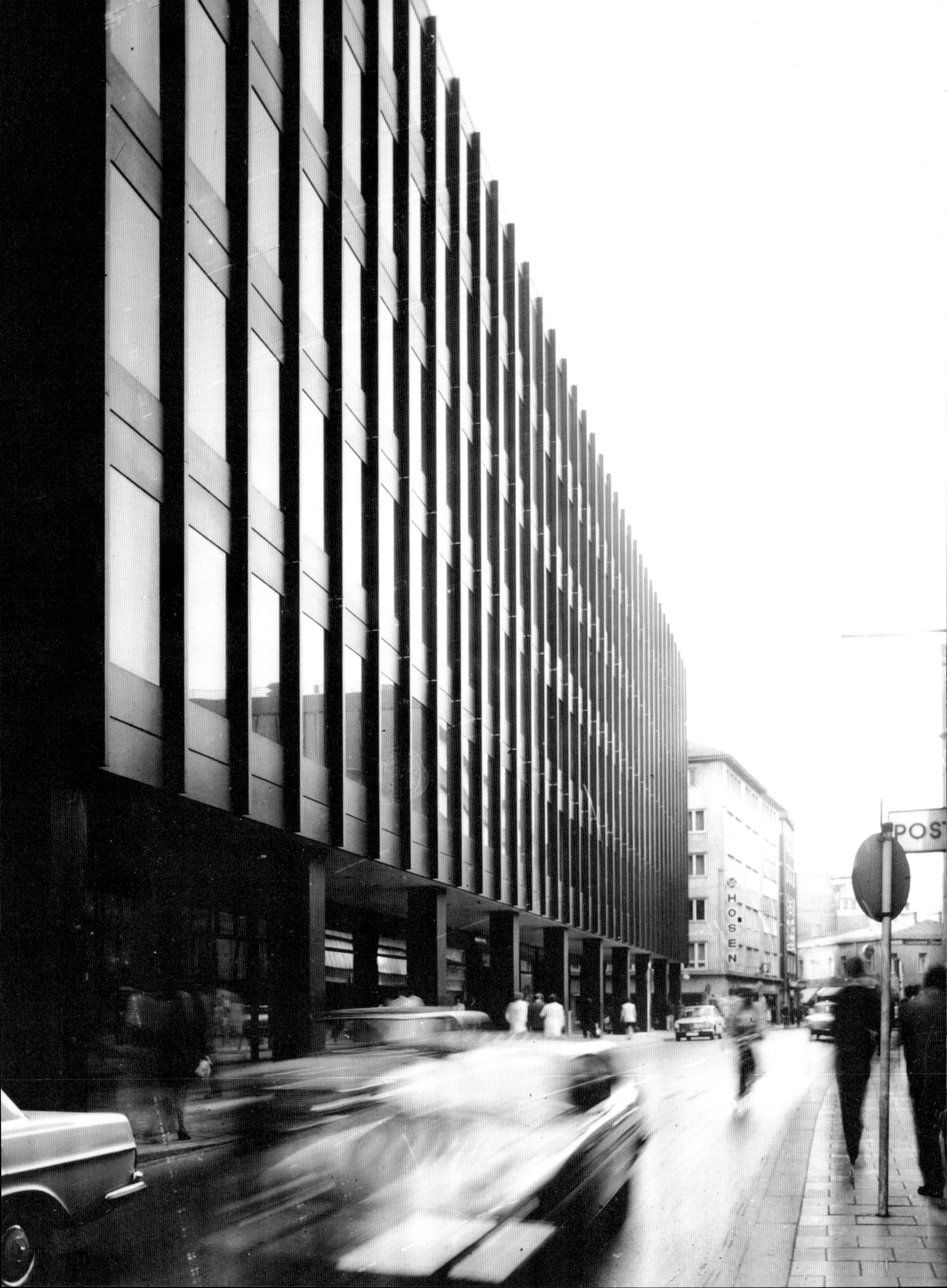
HOSEN

Verwaltungsgebäude für den Süddeutschen Verlag, Färbergraben, München, 1963–70
Bauherr: Süddeutscher Verlag GmbH

Office building for the Süddeutscher Verlag, Färbergraben, Munich, 1963–70
Client: Süddeutscher Verlag GmbH

Der für München ungewöhnliche, einmalige Bau am Färbergraben kann ohne Zögern als das Hauptwerk Detlef Schreibers bezeichnet werden. Zugleich stellt das Bürohaus das wohl beste Beispiel der von Mies van der Rohe beeinflußten Architekturmoderne aus den 1960er Jahren dar, nicht nur in München, sondern in der damaligen Bundesrepublik. Auch wenn man davon absieht, daß die Größe eines Bauwerks oft auch ihren erheblichen Anteil zur Gesamtqualität leistet und der Bau am Färbergraben mit seinen sieben Geschossen, seiner Gebäudetiefe von 22 Metern und einer Frontlänge von 64 Metern eben nicht so groß ist, weil er den bescheideneren Münchner Alt- und Innenstadtverhältnissen Rechnung tragen mußte, gibt es vermutlich in ganz Europa kein besseres Beispiel dieser speziellen, längst zu den wertvollen Beständen der Baugeschichte gehörenden Architektur.

Das Gesamtareal des ehemals im Innenstadtbereich liegenden Süddeutschen Verlags und damit auch dieses besondere Gebäude wurde inzwischen an eine Terraingesellschaft veräußert. Sie mußte schon hinnehmen, daß das 1905/06 von Max Littmann an der Sendlinger Straße errichtete Verlagsgebäude und das sogenannte Technikgebäude aus den 1920er Jahren unter Denkmalschutz stehen. Detlef Schreibers Meisterwerk am Färbergraben, welches dies einmalige Münchner Ensemble des 20. Jahrhunderts so wertvoll komplettiert hatte, steht noch nicht unter Denkmalschutz und ist deshalb disponibel. Noch ist die Gefahr eines Abbruchs nicht endgültig gebannt.[1]

The unique building in Färbergraben, unusual for Munich, can be described unhesitatingly as Detlef Schreiber's major work. At the same time, the office building is probably the best example of architectural Modernism influenced by Mies van der Rohe dating from the 1960s, not just in Munich, but for the whole of the Federal Republic at the time. Even if one disregards the fact that the size of a building often makes a considerable contribution to the overall quality, and the building in Färbergraben, with its seven floors, depth of 22 m and a façade length of 64 m, is not so big because it had to take the more modest circumstances of the Munich old town and city centre into account, it is still permissible to assume that there is no better example anywhere in Europe of this special architecture, which has long been part of architectural history's most valuable stock.

The entire Süddeutscher Verlag site, which used to be in the inner city area, and thus this special building as well, has been sold to a property company in the meantime. This company had to accept that the publishing house built by Max Littmann in Sendlinger Straße in 1905/06 and the socalled technical building dating from the 1920s were listed. Detlef Schreiber's masterpiece in Färbergraben, which completes this unique Munich 20th-century ensemble so valuably, is not yet listed, and thus dispensable. There is still the danger of demolition.[1]

[1] Was der über 25 Jahre für Münchner und weitere bedeutende Tageszeitungen als Architekturberichterstatter und Kritiker tätig gewesene Autor nicht begreift, ist, wie eine nach dem Zweiten Weltkrieg für den deutschen Sprachraum und international tonangebend gewordene Zeitung ihr angestammtes, innerstädtisches Quartier voller guter, bereits weitgehend adaptierter Bausubstanz »verhökern« konnte, als seien 60 Jahre Tradition nichts. Der Gewinn wird das Linsengericht eines neuen, geleasten und keineswegs typischen Büroturms am Ostrand von München sein, irgendwo im Nirgendwo, Architektur von der Stange mit dem Hauptkriterium einer maximalen Höhenentwicklung von 98 Metern. Statt den Mitarbeitern im weiterhin belebten, unverwechselbaren Kern der so einmaligen Münchner Altstadt Milieu zu bieten, wirken diese künftig am Stadtrand, als gälte es nicht, Zeitung zu machen, sondern irgendeine beliebige Ware zu verkaufen.

[1] The author has been working as an architecture reporter and critic for major newspapers in Munich and elsewhere for over 25 years, but cannot understand how a newspaper that ultimately helped to set the tone after the Second World War for the Germanspeaking countries and internationally could sell off its birthright, its innercity quarters full of good building stock that had already been largely adapted as though 60 years of tradition were nothing. The gain will be a mess of pottage in the form of a new, leased and by no means typical office tower on the eastern outskirts of Munich, somewhere and nowhere, off-the-peg architecture whose main criterion is a maximum height of 98 metres. Instead of offering employees a milieu at the heart of old Munich, still lively and unmistakable, they will in future have to work on the periphery, as though they were not making a newspaper but just selling any old commodity.

Fassadenfront zum Färbergraben

Façade facing Färbergraben

Bezugsfertig 1970

Als das Gebäude im Herbst 1970 an die Bauherren übergeben wurde, feierte die »Süddeutsche Zeitung« das Ereignis durch eingehende Schilderung auf den Seiten ihrer berühmten und einzigartigen Beilage »Zeitgemäße Form«. Hans Eckstein, der unvergessene Direktor der Neuen Sammlung, war zu dieser Zeit noch federführend für jene Beilage, die längst wegen vermeintlicher »Lesekurzatmigkeit« der zum »Publikum« mutierten ehemaligen Leserschaft eingestellt worden ist. Er und Detlef Schreiber sollen hier verkürzt zu Wort kommen, so wie sie diesen außerordentlichen Bau in der »Zeitgemäßen Form« vom 1.10.1970 beschrieben haben.

Hans Eckstein: Aus der Schule Mies van der Rohes. Ein meisterliches Werk der Moderne

»In einer ›Wanderung durch die Stadt‹, die Hans Karlinger für bau- und kulturgeschichtlich Interessierte in einem München-Führer bald nach Ende des Ersten Weltkriegs verfaßt hat, [...] erwähnt er das 1905/06 von M. Littmann erbaute Haus der ›Münchner Neuesten Nachrichten‹, hebt dessen ›reiche plastische Ausstattung‹ von J. Seidler und die Inneneinrichtung von Bruno Paul hervor. Vom Färbergraben ist nicht weiter die Rede.

Heute könnte in einer baugeschichtlichen Wanderung durch München der Färbergraben nicht unerwähnt bleiben. Denn da steht jetzt, unübersehbar, ein Bau, den man noch in Jahrzehnten zu den nicht gerade dicht gesäten Meisterwerken der bundesdeutschen Nachkriegsarchitektur wird zählen müssen. Er verdeckt ein für den Uneingeweihten nicht leicht zu entwirrendes Konglomerat von Gebäuden, die für die Bedürfnisse des wachsenden Betriebs des Süddeutschen Verlags großenteils erst in den letzten zwei Jahrzehnten errichtet worden sind. Das neue Gebäude am Färbergraben dient ebenfalls verschiedenen Betriebsfunktionen dieses Verlages. Mit seiner Gestaltung wurde das Architekturbüro Herbert Groethuysen – Detlef Schreiber – Gernot Sachsse betraut, gewiß in der Erwartung, es werde seine Aufgabe in den Formen der modernen Architektur mit derselben künstlerischen Gewissenhaftigkeit erfüllen, mit der in den dekorativen Formen eines versachlichten Jugendstils einst Bruno Paul die Redaktionsräume ausgestattet hat, in denen heute die ›Süddeutsche Zeitung‹ redigiert wird.

Der neue Bau setzt in eine mehr chaotische als einheitliche ›Altstadt‹-Struktur einen kraftvollen Akzent. Frei von jeder possierlichen Altstädterei, wie sie in der Neubebauung um den Marienplatz in Erscheinung tritt, bringt er einen neuen, dem modernen Wirtschaftsleben angemessenen Maßstab in den Färbergraben – frei auch von jener Brutalität, an der es der gegenüberliegende Garagenbau am wenigsten fehlen läßt. So verdient zuerst hervorgehoben zu werden, was an Neubauten in kleinteiligen älteren Stadtteilen nur selten zu rühmen ist: Dieser lange, sechs – mit dem zurückgesetzten Dachpavillon sieben – Geschosse hohe Verwaltungsbau des Süddeutschen Verlags ist städtebaulich ein nicht hoch genug zu schätzender Gewinn für München.

Ready for occupation 1970

When the building was handed over to the clients in autumn 1970, the Süddeutsche Zeitung celebrated the event with a detailed description in the pages of their famous and unique supplement »Zeitgemäße Form« (1.10.1970). Hans Eckstein, the director of the Neue Sammlung, a man unforgotten by friends and connoisseurs, was still responsible for the supplement at that time. It ceased publication a long time ago because of an alleged »short reader attention span« among the former readership, who have now mutated into an »audience«. Now Hans Eckstein and Detlef Schreiber will have their say, unfortunately in somewhat abridged form. This is how they described the extraordinary building on 1 October 1970.

Hans Eckstein: From the school of Mies van der Rohe. A masterly work of Modernism

»In a ›Walk round the city‹ written by Hans Karlinger for readers interested in architectural and cultural history in a Munich guide shortly after the end of the First World War, [...] he mentioned the ›Münchner Neuesten Nachrichten‹ building constructed by M. Littman in 1905/06, drawing particular attention to its ›lavish sculptural decoration‹ by J. Seidler and Bruno Paul's interior design. Nothing else is said about Färbergraben.

Today it would be impossible not to mention Färbergraben on a walk around Munich. For now a building stands there that cannot be overlooked, that will decades later still count as one of the masterpieces of post-war West German architecture, which are not exactly thick on the ground. It conceals a conglomerate of buildings that is not easy for the uninitiated to disentangle, built largely in the last two decades to meet the needs of the Süddeutscher Verlag's growing business. The new building in Färbergraben is also intended to perform various functions for the publishing house. The Herbert Groethuysen – Detlef Schreiber – Gernot Sachsse architecture practice was entrusted with the design, in the certain expectation that it would fulfil its commission using the forms of modern architecture with the same artistic surefootedness Bruno Paul once showed in handling the decorative forms of an objectified Jugendstil to decorate the editorial rooms in which the ›Süddeutsche Zeitung‹ is now edited.

The new building strikes a powerful note in an ›old town‹ structure that is chaotic rather than uniform. Free of the kind of droll old-townery that appears in the new development in Marienplatz, it brings a new scale appropriate to modern commercial life into Fär-

Oben: Ansicht zum Färbergraben (Entwurf)
Mitte: Grundriß Chefetage 5. OG
Unten: Grundriß Erdgeschoß

Top: elevation from Färbergraben (draft design)
Middle: floor plan; managerial storey, 5th floor
Bottom: floor plan; ground floor

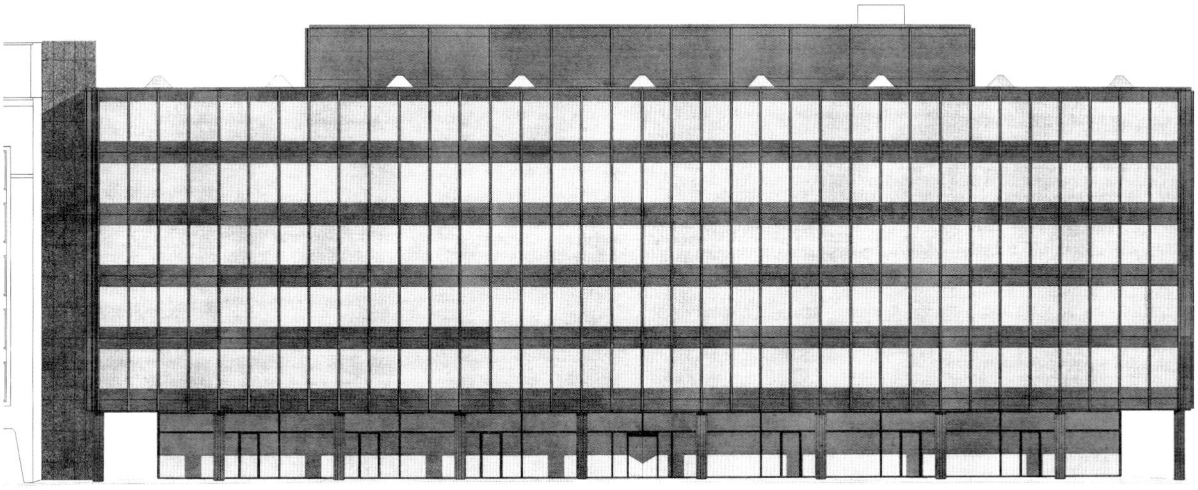

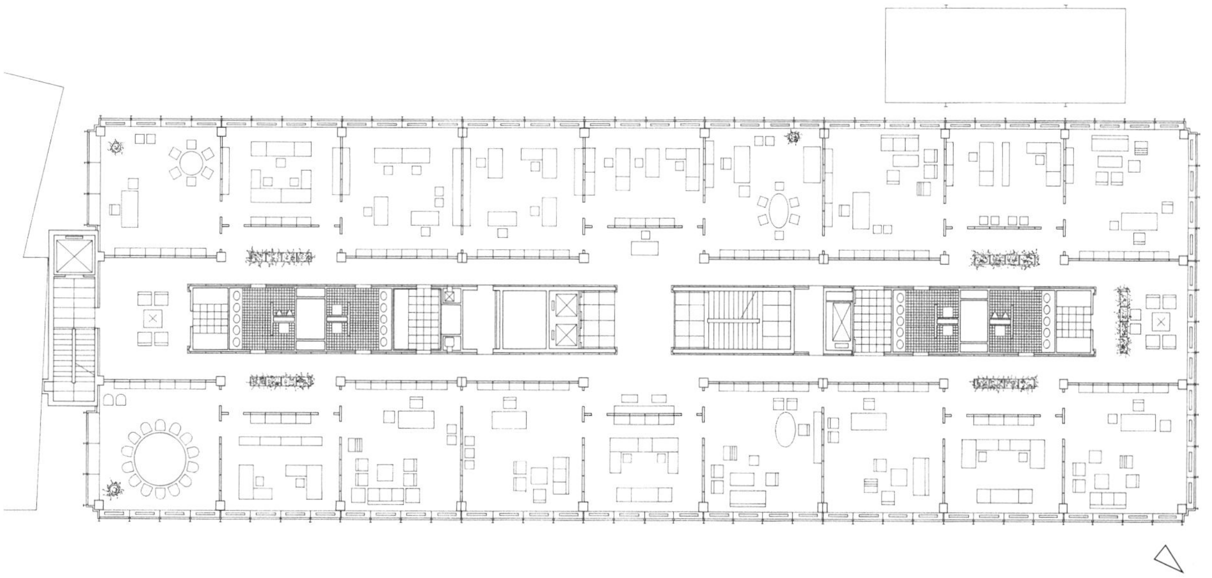

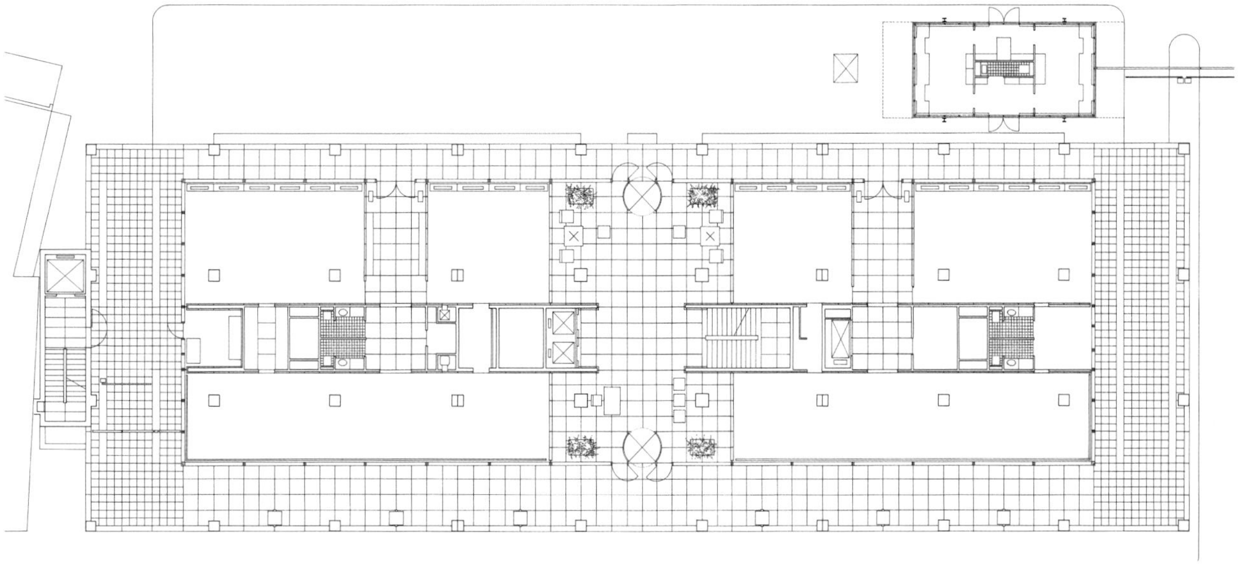

Steht man vor der Fassade, so beeindrucken zunächst die sorgsam ausgewogenen Proportionen. Sie lassen nichts von jenem Unbehagen aufkommen, das sich bei so vielen modernen ›Rasterbauten‹ einstellt. Dabei ist dieser Bau ein Rasterbau *par excellence*. Ja, seine Schönheit verdankt er nicht zuletzt der Sichtbarmachung des Raster-Systems, das seiner Konstruktion zugrunde liegt. Versuchen wir zu ergründen, worauf diese uns im ersten Anblick ergreifende Schönheit beruht, so wären auszuführen:

1. Die Feingliedrigkeit des Sprossenwerks der der Tragkonstruktion vorgehängten Außenwand.
2. Das ausgewogene Maßverhältnis zwischen Wandfachwerk und Fensterfeldern und zwischen den breiten horizontalen Bändern vor den Decken und Brüstungen und den außen aufsteigenden dünnen vertikalen Pfosten, die die Fassade versteifen.
3. Zu der Feingliedrigkeit trägt wesentlich die Trennung der Deckenverkleidung und der Brüstungen durch eine Fuge bei, die diese breiten geschoßteilenden Bänder weniger massiv in die Erscheinung treten läßt.
4. Die schwarze Färbung der eloxierten Aluminiumplatten und der Pfosten strafft die Formen und läßt das Sprossenwerk in einen wohlberechneten farbigen Kontrast zu den Fensterfeldern treten. Zugleich aber ist die Schroffheit dieses Kontrasts gemildert durch eine leichte Grautönung der Thermopane-Glasscheiben, die zugleich eine funktionale Bedeutung hat: Sie verhindert die Blendung und mindert die direkte Sonnenstrahlung ab.
5. Der Verzicht auf eine besondere Fensterrahmung, die durch ein in Zusammenarbeit mit der Firma Gartner, Gundelfingen, entwickeltes Konstruktionsprinzip ermöglicht ist: Das Glas wird über Neopreneprofile mit dem Metall des Gerüsts verbunden. Dadurch wird die Präzision sowohl der Konstruktion wie der Form bedeutend gesteigert. (Im übrigen werden durch dieses Verfahren, die Glas- und Metallteile miteinander zu verbinden, die in diesen Materialien entstehenden Bewegungen gleitend aufgenommen und Kälte- und Wärmebrücken vermieden, da die außenliegenden Metallteile von den inneren getrennt sind.)
6. Die Transparenz der Fassade macht die Konstruktion schon von außen ablesbar und überschaubar, was nicht nur einen optischen Reiz bewirkt, sondern auch die Konstruktion mit der sie interpretierenden Form eng und überzeugend verbindet. Hinter der Glaswand wird die erste Stützreihe sichtbar und dadurch ein weiterer Farbkontrast wirksam: In den Obergeschossen erscheint das Weiß der Stützen hinter dem Schwarz der Pfosten. (Im Erdgeschoß sind die Stützen schwarz verkleidet wie die frei stehenden des Laubengangs.)
7. Bei der beträchtlichen Fassadenlänge von rund sechzig Metern ergibt sich in der perspektivischen Verkürzung eine mit der Entfernung zunehmende scheinbare Verengung der Intervalle der Vertikalgliederung. Das bewirkt, daß der mächtige Baukörper in der ziemlich engen Straße mit zum Teil schmalen Hausfronten nicht als bedrückend empfunden wird.

bergraben – and it is also free of the brutality that the garage building opposite has entirely failed to avoid. So something should be emphasized first of all that is seldom to be praised in new buildings in intricate older city areas: this long office building for the Süddeutscher Verlag, six storeys high – seven with the recessed roof pavilion – is an urban gain for Munich that cannot be esteemed too highly.

If one stands in front of the façade, the first thing to impress is the carefully balanced proportions. They do not cause any unease of the kind usually generated by modern ›grid structures‹. And yet the building is a grid structure par excellence. Indeed, it owes its beauty not least to the fact that the grid system its structure is based on is made visible. If we try to find out what this immediately striking beauty is based on, then these factors could be listed:

1. The delicacy of the bar structure in the outer wall suspended in front of the façade structure.
2. The balanced proportions of scale between the wall framework and the window fields and between the broad horizontal bands in front of the ceilings and parapets and the vertical posts rising outside that reinforce the façade.
3. The major contribution to this delicacy is made by the separation of the ceiling cladding and the parapets by a gap that makes these broad bands dividing the floors seem less solid.
4. The black colouring of the anodized aluminium sheets and posts stiffens the forms and allows the bar structure to enter into a well-judged colour contrast with the window fields. But at the same time the abruptness of the contrast is mitigated by the light grey shading of the thermo-pane glass panes, which also has functional significance: it prevents dazzle and reduces direct insulation.
5. The lack of special window framing, which is made possible by a construction principle developed in co-operation with Gartner of Gundelfingen: the glass is attached to the metal of the frame by neoprene sections. This increases the precision of both the construction and the form. (This procedure of joining the glass and metal parts together also means that any movements in these materials are absorbed by sliding and heat leaks avoided, as the exterior metal parts and separated from the interior ones.)
6. The transparency of the façade means that the construction is intelligible even from the outside, which is not only visually attractive, but also links the construction with the form interpreting it closely and convincingly. The first row of supports is visible behind the glass wall, thus creating another colour contrast: the white of the supports shows up behind the black of the posts in the upper storeys. (The supports are clad in black on the ground floor, like their freestanding equivalents in the exterior corridor.)

Eckausbildung des Gebäudes
Corner of the building

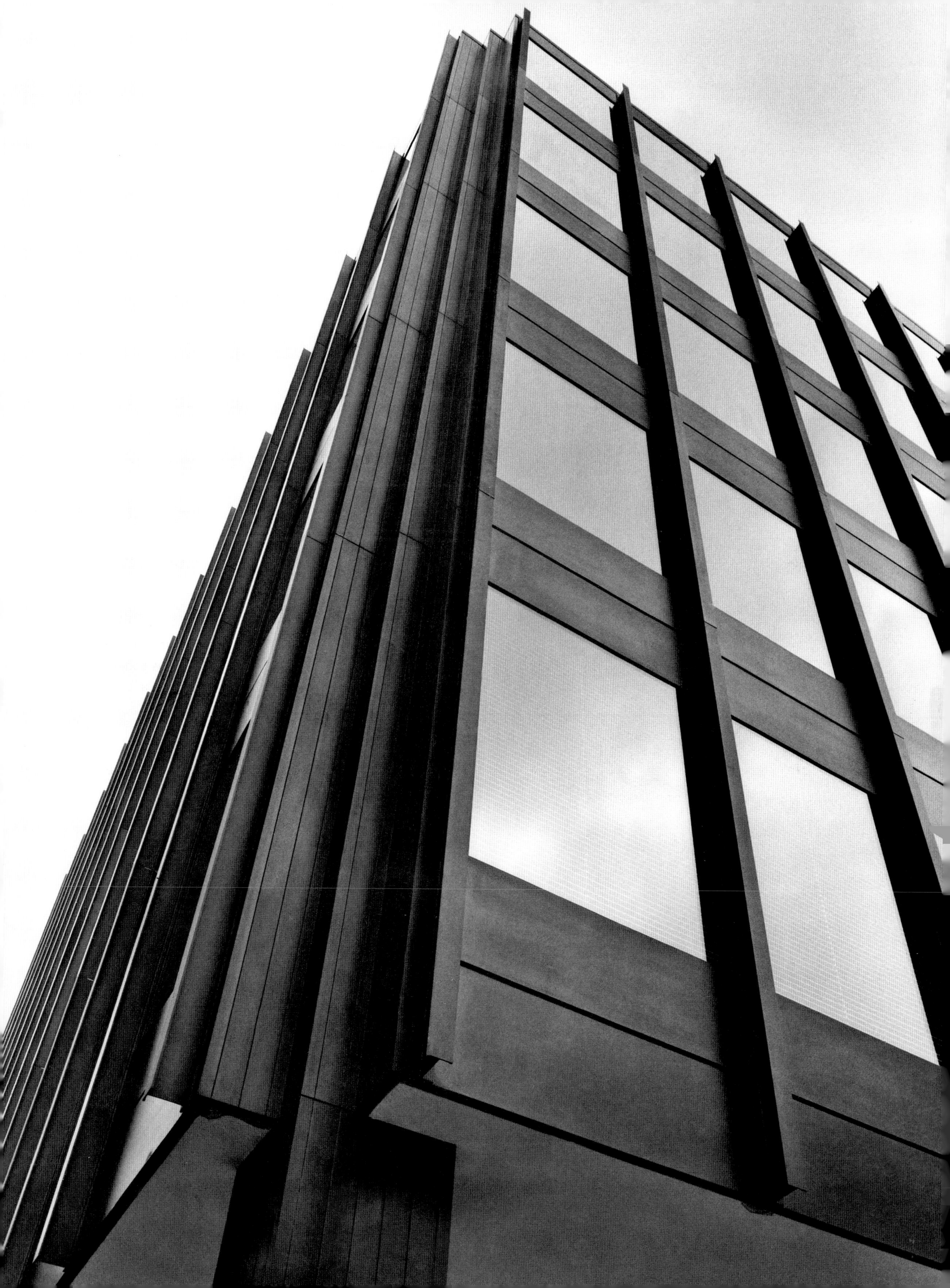

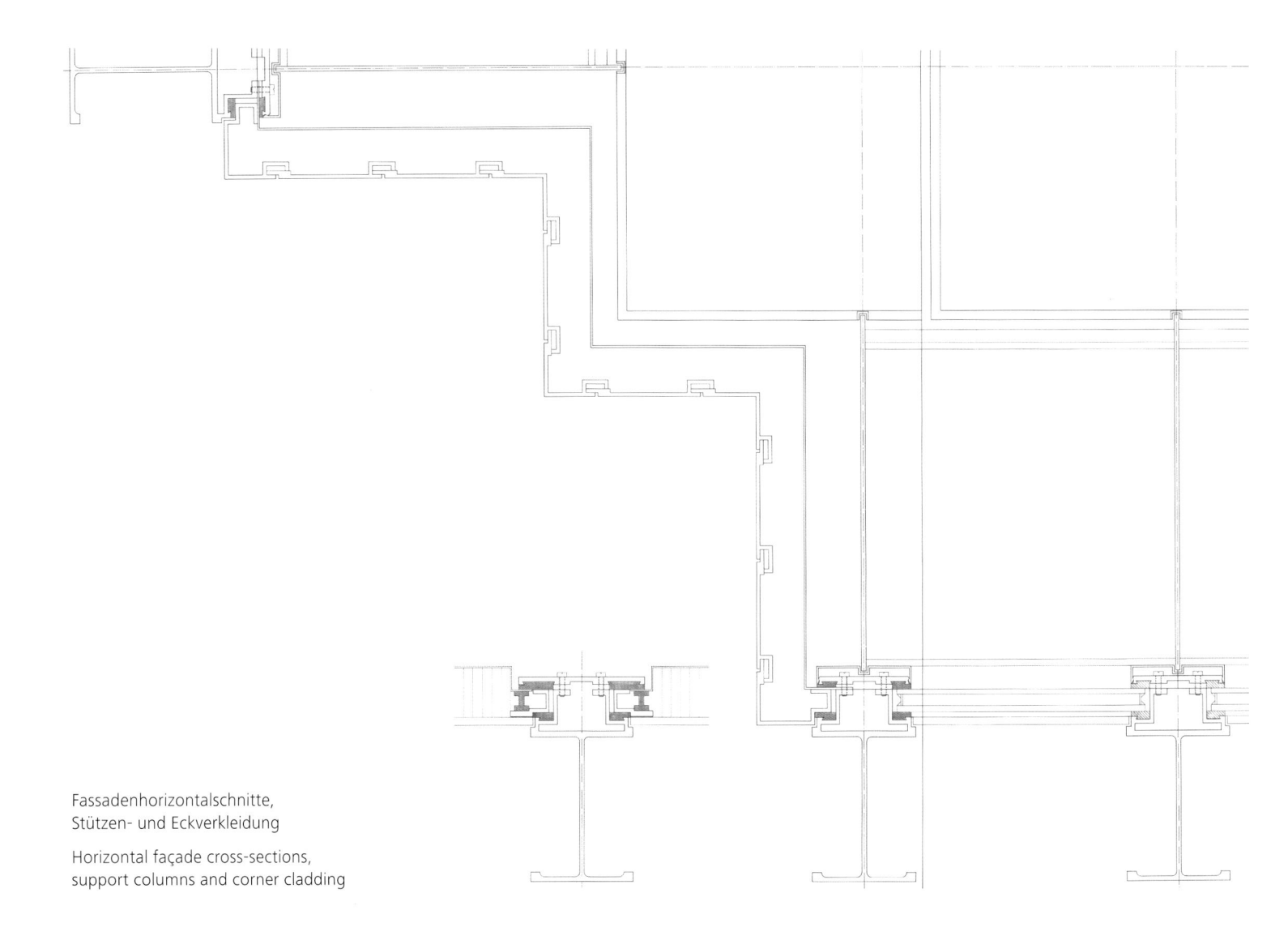

Fassadenhorizontalschnitte,
Stützen- und Eckverkleidung

Horizontal façade cross-sections,
support columns and corner cladding

8. Der durch Aufbauten über dem Dach nicht gestörte gradlinige obere Abschluß der Fassade zeigt die ihren strukturellen Aufbau bestimmenden Elemente: Ein Band von der Breite der Brüstungsbänder und eine Leiste von der Form und Stärke der Pfosten.

9. Die so klare Gliederung der Außenhaut wird durch keine zusätzlichen funktional bedingten Elemente wie Sonnenschutzvorrichtungen beeinträchtigt. Die Jalousetten sind nach innen genommen, und auf weitere Sonnenschutzmittel und Vorrichtungen zur Öffnung der Fenster konnte verzichtet werden, da das Haus eine perfekte Klimaanlage hat.

10. Ein Detail, das sich dem Betrachter weniger augenfällig darbietet, darf nicht unerwähnt bleiben: die Ausbildung der Gebäudeecken. Durch zusätzliche Winkel, negative Ecken, wird ein konstruktiver Sachverhalt formal sinnfällig interpretiert: daß die vorgehängte Wand lediglich eine raumabschließende Funktion, keine tragende erfüllt. Mit dieser Eckausbildung wird ein von Mies van der Rohe zuerst entwickeltes konstruktives und formales Detail in abgewandelter Form übernommen.

7. Given the considerable length of the façade, about sixty metres, the perspective foreshortening produces an apparent compaction of the vertical articulation intervals, increasing with distance. This means that the massive building does not feel oppressive in a fairly cramped street with some narrow façades.

8. The straight line of the top of the façade, unbroken by structures above roof level, displays the elements determining its structural composition: a band the same width as the parapet bands and a moulding of the same shape and thickness as the posts.

9. The lucid articulation of the outer skin is not impaired by any additional functionally determined elements. The louvred shades are placed internally, and there was no need for other sun-shading or window-opening devices, as the building has a perfect airconditioning system.

10. One detail that will not strike observers quite so immediately should not remain unmentioned: the structure of the building's corners. Additional angles, negative corners, interpret one structural state of affairs with formal lucidity: the suspended

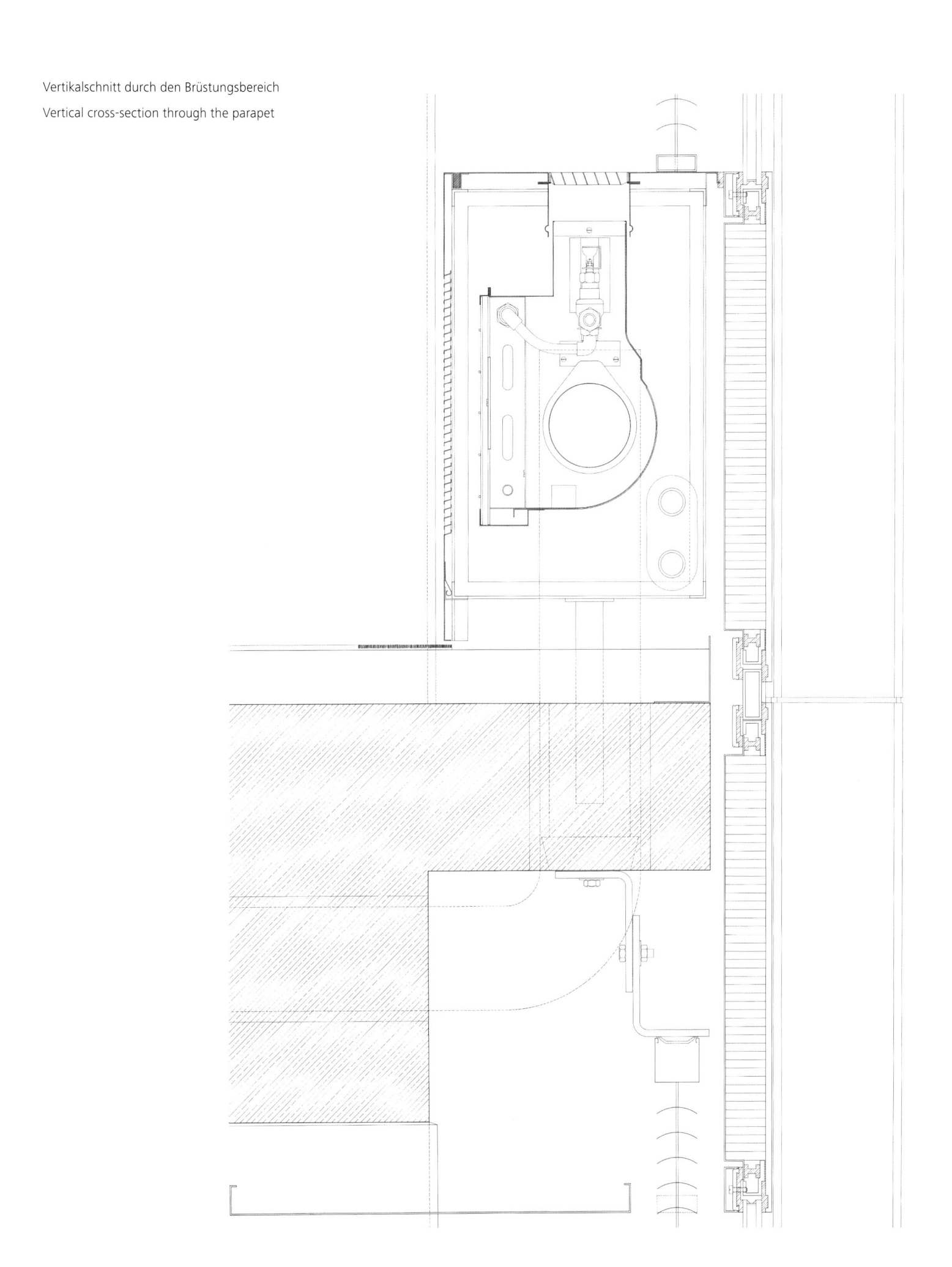

Vertikalschnitt durch den Brüstungsbereich
Vertical cross-section through the parapet

Dieselbe sowohl technische wie formale Perfektion und Präzision, die sich in der Struktur der Außenhaut zeigt, tritt auch im Inneren des Baues, der räumlichen Ordnung eindrucksvoll in die Erscheinung. Hier finden wir dieselbe Beschränkung auf wenige Materialien und Farben. Auf alles bloß Dekorative ist verzichtet. Der konstruktive Aufbau bleibt überall spürbar. Alle technischen Versorgungsleitungen liegen in der mittleren Stützenachse und in den Decken. Der Ausbauraster ist ein Viertel des Rohbaurasters mit einer Seitenlänge von 1,75 m und ist zugleich der Büromodul, der sich durch Schreibtischfläche, Sitztiefe und notwendigen Bewegungsraum zwischen den Tischreihen ergibt. Die Büroräume werden allen Ansprüchen an Flexibilität gerecht. Die Brüstungshöhe ist so niedrig gehalten, daß man auch von jeder Stelle im Raum freien Ausblick hat.

Es gibt wenige Bauten einer so einheitlichen Durchbildung des gesamten Baukörpers sowohl in technischer und konstruktiver Hinsicht als in ästhetischer. In dem Streben nach einer unserer rational-technischen Welt gemäßen objektiven Form ist dieser Bau bewundernswert und erfolgreich radikal und mehr darin als in Anbetracht einiger Details ein meisterliches Werk aus der Schule Mies van der Rohes.«

Detlef Schreiber in der »Zeitgemäßen Form«

»Planen und Gestalten sind in erster Linie rationale Vorgänge, bei denen ein komplexes Bündel von Sachverhalten technischer, ökonomischer, psychologischer und formaler Art analysiert und bewertet wird. Entscheidungen reifen auf dieser Grundlage des analytischen Entwickelns, sie werden ihrer jeweiligen Bedeutung gemäß zu treffen sein. Die Freiheit, zu gestalten, findet in diesem Prozeß in allen Phasen der Gedankenarbeit ihren selbstverständlichen und bedeutungsvollen Platz. Nur auf dieser Grundlage kann das Ergebnis jene sinnvolle Einheit werden, in der Herstellungsmethode, Bedürfnis und Erscheinung übereinstimmen und das Werk als Gestalt sich ausdrückt. Dieser Ausdruck, das kann man mit Sicherheit erwarten, wird allgemeinverständlich und objektiv sein, und er wird auch gefeit sein gegen den Versuch, ihn und die Architektur überhaupt als bloßes Spiel mit Formen, Farben und Materialien zu sehen. Damit soll keineswegs gesagt werden, daß der Entwurfsprozeß in seiner Objektivierung zu einer primitiven Ableitung von Ergebnissen, d. h. aus gegebenen und geforderten Tatsachen wird. Es ist vielmehr so, daß gerade durch die Einschränkung der Wahlfreiheit beim Gestalten oder, besser gesagt, bei ihrer Relativierung, das zu Schaffende in allen seinen Teilen und Aspekten mitgestaltet wird.

Flexibilität oder variable Nutzungsmöglichkeit war ein Planungsgrundsatz für dieses Gebäude. Er beeinflußte seine Konstruktion, die technische Ausstattung und nicht zuletzt seine innere und äußere Form. ›Die Form folgt der Funktion‹, sagt Sullivan, und Mies van der Rohe ergänzte dieses Wort: ›Die Funktion unserer Gebäude heute heißt Flexibilität‹. Welche Konsequenzen hat nun die Erfüllung der Forderung nach Flexibilität?

Die lastentragende Gebäudekonstruktion, die Primärstruktur, die unveränderbar bleibt, muß auf ein Minimum beschränkt werden,

wall is there simply to close off the space, and has no load-bearing function. This corner structure takes a structural and formal detail first developed by Mies van der Rohe and adapts it for this building.

The same technical and formal perfection and precision shown in the structure of the outer skin is also impressively demonstrated in the formal order of the interior of the building. Here we find the same restriction to a few materials and colours. Anything merely decorative is avoided. The structural development can be discerned everywhere. All the technical service pipes are in the central support axis and in the ceilings. The interior finish grid is a quarter of the shell grid with a side length of 1.75 m, and this is also the office module, based on desk area, seat depth and the necessary room for movement between the rows of tables. The office spaces are as flexible as they could possibly be. The parapet height is kept low enough for there to be an open view of the outside world from every position in the room.

There are few buildings with such a uniform overall structure, both from a technical and structural point of view as from an aesthetic one. In this aspiration to an objective form appropriate to our rational and technical world, this building is admirably and successfully radical, and more in this respect than in terms of particular details a masterly piece of work from the school of Mies van der Rohe.«

Detlef Schreiber in »Zeitgemäße Form«

»Planning and designing are first and foremost rational processes in which a complex bundle of technical, economic, psychological and formal matters are analysed and evaluated. Decisions mature on this basis of analytical development, and they will have to be made appropriately to their particular importance. Freedom to design creatively finds its natural and significant place in this process in all phases of the intellectual work. It is only on this basis that the result can achieve meaningful unity expressing production method, agreements about requirements and appearance and the work as form. This expression, once achieved, and this can be expected with certainty, will be generally comprehensible and objective, and it will also be immune to any attempts to see it and the architecture in general as a mere game with forms, colours and materials. This is by no means intended to say that the design process when objectified becomes a primitive act of derivation from results, i. e. from given and required facts. On the contrary, it is the case that it is precisely by reducing the freedom of choice in designing, or better, by relativizing it, that what is to be created becomes an integral part of the design process in all its parts and aspects.

Flexibility or variable possibilities for use was a planning principle for this building. It influenced its structure, the technical equipment and not least its interior and exterior form. ›Form follows function‹ says Sullivan, and Mies van der Rohe completes this by adding: ›today the function of our buildings is called flexibility.‹ So what are the consequences of meeting the demand for flexibility?

um der nichttragenden Ausbaukonstruktion, der Sekundärstruktur, ein Maximum an Veränderbarkeit zu ermöglichen. Für die Primärstruktur eignet sich deshalb das Skelett mit großen Spannweiten, für die Sekundärstruktur ein System möglichst leichter und nicht zu großformatiger Flächenelemente, die in den Rohbau eingefügt, eingehängt oder ihm vorgehängt werden. Es sind dies die Fußbodenkonstruktion mit dem Versorgungskanalsystem, die untergehängte Decke, die nichttragenden Trennwände und die vorgehängte Fensterwand. Die Primärstruktur sagt also noch nichts über die Erscheinungsform des fertigen Gebäudes aus. Erst die Sekundärstruktur bestimmt die Form- und Raumqualität, wobei die Gesetzmäßigkeit für sie bereits in der Primärstruktur als Vielfaches des Rastermaßes vorbestimmt ist.

Das Gebäudevolumen wurde fast ausschließlich durch äußere Einflüsse bestimmt. Baulinien, Abstandsflächenvorschriften und Höhenbeschränkungen bestimmen die Maße für die Länge, Breite und Höhe – sogar für die Tiefe der Unterkellerung war eine Grenze gesetzt – das Grundwasser. Es stand ein Grundstück zur Verfügung, das teilweise mit überalterten, aber dem Betrieb noch zugeordneten Gebäuden bebaut war, die erst abgebrochen werden konnten, nachdem Teile des Neubaus Ersatz dafür geschaffen hatten. Der Zwang, in Bauabschnitten zu bauen, deren erster bereits in sich funktionsfähig – Versorgung und Erschließung – sein mußte, hatte verständlicherweise einen wesentlichen Einfluß auf die Grundkonzeption des Gesamtgebäudes. Das tragende Konstruktionssystem mußte ein Rastermaß haben, dessen jeweiliges Vielfaches in die zur Verfügung stehenden Flächen der Bauabschnitte einfügbar war. Außerdem mußten die Aufzüge, die Treppe, die Hauptversorgungsschächte und die Versorgungszentralen im ersten Bauabschnitt unterzubringen sein.

Die so vorbestimmte Grundflächenform des Gebäudes erlaubte eine Gebäudetiefe von rund 22 m bei einer Länge von rund 64 m. Daß auf dieser Fläche keine optimale Bürogroßraumlösung bei größeren Flächendimensionen zu entwickeln ist, wurde schon frühzeitig bewußt. Die abschnittsweise Errichtung, die im ersten Bauabschnitt nur zwei Drittel der Grundrißfläche ermöglichte, und der Programmwunsch des Bauherrn, die Büroflächen auch in Einzel- oder Gruppenbüros zu unterteilen, verlangte den mittig in der Längsachse angeordneten Kern. Es mußte also eine Lösung gefunden werden, auf beiden Seiten des Kerns eine Zone zu schaffen, die sowohl geeignet ist für aneinandergereihte Einzelbüros als auch für einen durchgehenden Großraum. Daß dieses Problem nur mit Hilfe eines Kompromisses gelöst werden konnte, wird dann klar, wenn man bedenkt, daß für einen Bürogroßraum Raumtiefen von mehr als 20 m gefordert werden, dagegen die Tiefe von Einzelbüros 5 bis 7 m nicht überschreiten sollte. [...]

In diesem Gebäude werden auf engstem Raum über vierhundert Menschen arbeiten und zahlreiche Besucher empfangen. Die Umweltbedingungen sind aus mannigfaltigen Gründen künstlich. [...]

Ein zweiter Planungsgrundsatz für diesen Bau war deshalb der, dem Menschen angemessenere Bedingungen für diese künstliche Umwelt mit Hilfe der Technik zu schaffen. [...]

The load-bearing structure of a building, the primary structure, which cannot be changed, has to be kept to a minimum to make maximum change possible for the non-load-bearing secondary structure, the interior and exterior finish. Thus a skeleton with long spans is suitable for the primary structure, and for the secondary structure a system of surface elements, as light as possible, and not too large in area, that can be fitted into the shell, or suspended in or in front of it. These are the floor construction with the service duct system, the suspended ceiling, the non-load-bearing partition walls and the curtain wall with windows. So the primary structure says nothing about the appearance of the complete building. It is only the secondary structure that determines the formal quality and the quality of the spaces, though the rules that will govern it are predetermined in the primary structure as a multiple of the grid dimensions.

The building volume was determined almost exclusively by external factors. Building lines, regulations about the distance between buildings and height restrictions determined the length, width and height – and a limit was even set on the depths of the cellars – by the ground water. The available site was partially covered by obsolete buildings that were still used by the company, and they could not be demolished until parts of the new building were there to replace them. The necessity to build in phases the first of which had to function as a self-contained unit – services and access – understandably influenced the basic concept of the building to a considerable extent. The load-bearing construction system had to have grid dimensions whose multiples could be fitted into the available areas in the building phases in each case. As well as this, it had to be possible to accommodate the lifts, stairs, main service shafts and control rooms in the first building phase.

The predetermined area available for the building permitted a building depth of about 22 m with a length of about 64 m. It became clear at a very early stage that this area would not make it possible to develop an ideal open-plan office solution with larger area dimensions. The phased construction, which meant that only two thirds of the ground plan area could be realized at first, and the client's programme request that the office areas should also be broken down into individual or group offices, required the core to be arranged centrally on the longitudinal axis. So a solution had to be found that provided a zone on each side of the core that was both appropriate for rows of individual offices and also for a continuous open-plan space. It is obvious that this problem could be solved only by compromising if one considers that room depths of over 20 m are required for an open-plan office, while individual offices cannot be deeper than 5 to 7 m. [...]

Over four hundred people are to work in this building, in a very restricted space, and need to receive numerous visitors. The environmental conditions are artificial for a variety of reasons. [...]
So a second planning principle for this building was to use technology to create conditions for this artificial environment that were more appropriate for the people involved. [...]

Der dritte Planungsgrundsatz war die Forderung nach einer der industriellen Vorfertigung angenäherten Methode der Standardisierung und Typisierung der Bauelemente. Die Anpassungsfähigkeit an veränderte Nutzungen erfordert, wenn man nicht immer wieder neu bauen will, die unversehrbare Demontage der Bauelemente und damit auch ihre Montage. [...]

Die Bestimmung des Moduls, des Grundmaßes für das Rastersystem, war eine der schwierigsten und schwerwiegendsten Entscheidungen, weil damit für das Gebäude ein bindendes Ordnungssystem gesetzt wurde [...] Das Grundmaß beträgt 1,75 m, seine Halbierung erlaubt das Maß von 87,5 cm, seine Verdopplung 3,50 m, und das Vierfache ergibt 7,00 m, die Grundeinheit der Primärstruktur – des Skeletts [...]

Für das Gelingen dieser umfassenden Planungs- und Gestaltungsarbeit war die ausdauernde und begeisterte Mitarbeit vieler die wichtigste Voraussetzung. Der Dank an sie alle verbindet sich mit dem Wunsch, daß auch sie überzeugt sind, daß die Arbeit erfreulich und interessant war. [...]

Das Gebäude mit allen seinen Bauabschnitten ist fertiggestellt und kann jetzt auch in seiner Gesamtheit genutzt werden. Ist das sich darstellende Ergebnis nun identisch mit den getroffenen Grundannahmen? Diese Frage wird die zukünftige Geschichte des Hauses beantworten – es wird die Geschichte seiner Nutzung durch die Menschen, die in ihm arbeiten, sein.«

The third planning principle was the requirement for a method for general and type standardization of the building elements that approximated to industrial prefabrication. Adapting to changed uses means, if one does not want to keep putting up new buildings, that the building elements can be dismantled, and thus also assembled, without wear and tear. [...]

Determining the module, the basic dimensions for the grid system, was one of the most difficult and momentous decisions, because it imposed a binding system of order on the building as a whole. [...] The basic dimension is 1.75 m, halving allows the dimension 87.5 cm, doubling it gives 3.5 m and multiplying it by four 7 m, the basic unit for the primary structure, the skeleton. [...]

Tenacious and enthusiastic co-operation by a lot of people was the most important requirement for the success of this comprehensive piece of planning and design work. Thanks to them all are combined with the wish that they too are convinced that the work was rewarding and interesting [...]

The building is complete in all its phases, and can now be used as a whole. Is the result that presents itself now identical with the basic assumptions made? The future story of the building will answer this question – this will be the story of how it is used by the people who work in it.«

Blick aus dem Eingangsfoyer zum Färbergraben
The entrance foyer looking towards Färbergraben

Flurbereich im Bürogeschoß
Corridor on the office storey

Einzelbüro

Individual office

Bürogroßraum

Open plan office

Sanitärraum

Sanitary room

FOLGENDE DOPPELSEITE:
Blick aus dem Betriebsrestaurant auf die Münchner Frauenkirche

NEXT DOUBLE PAGE:
The company canteen with a view of Munich's Frauenkirche

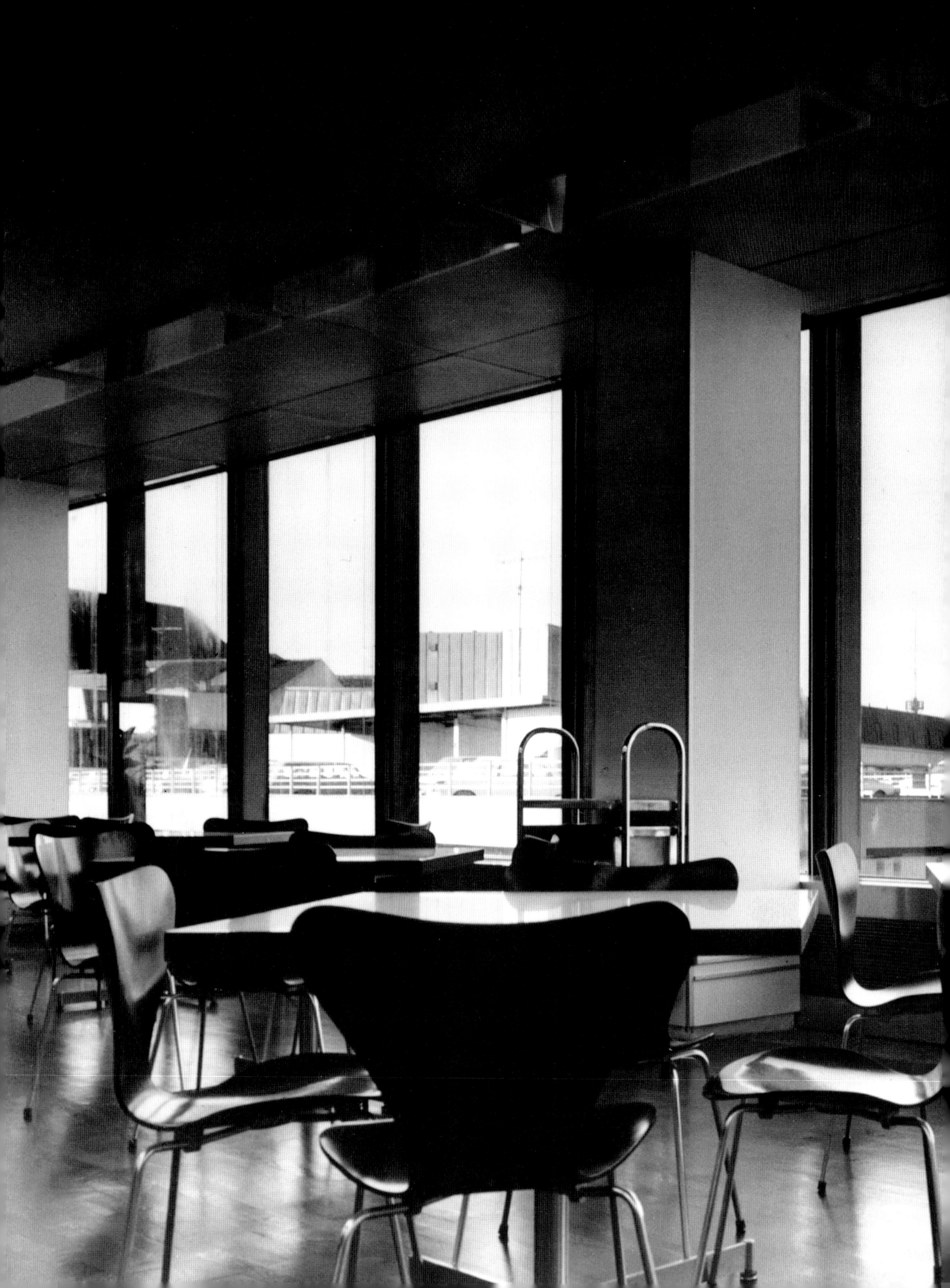

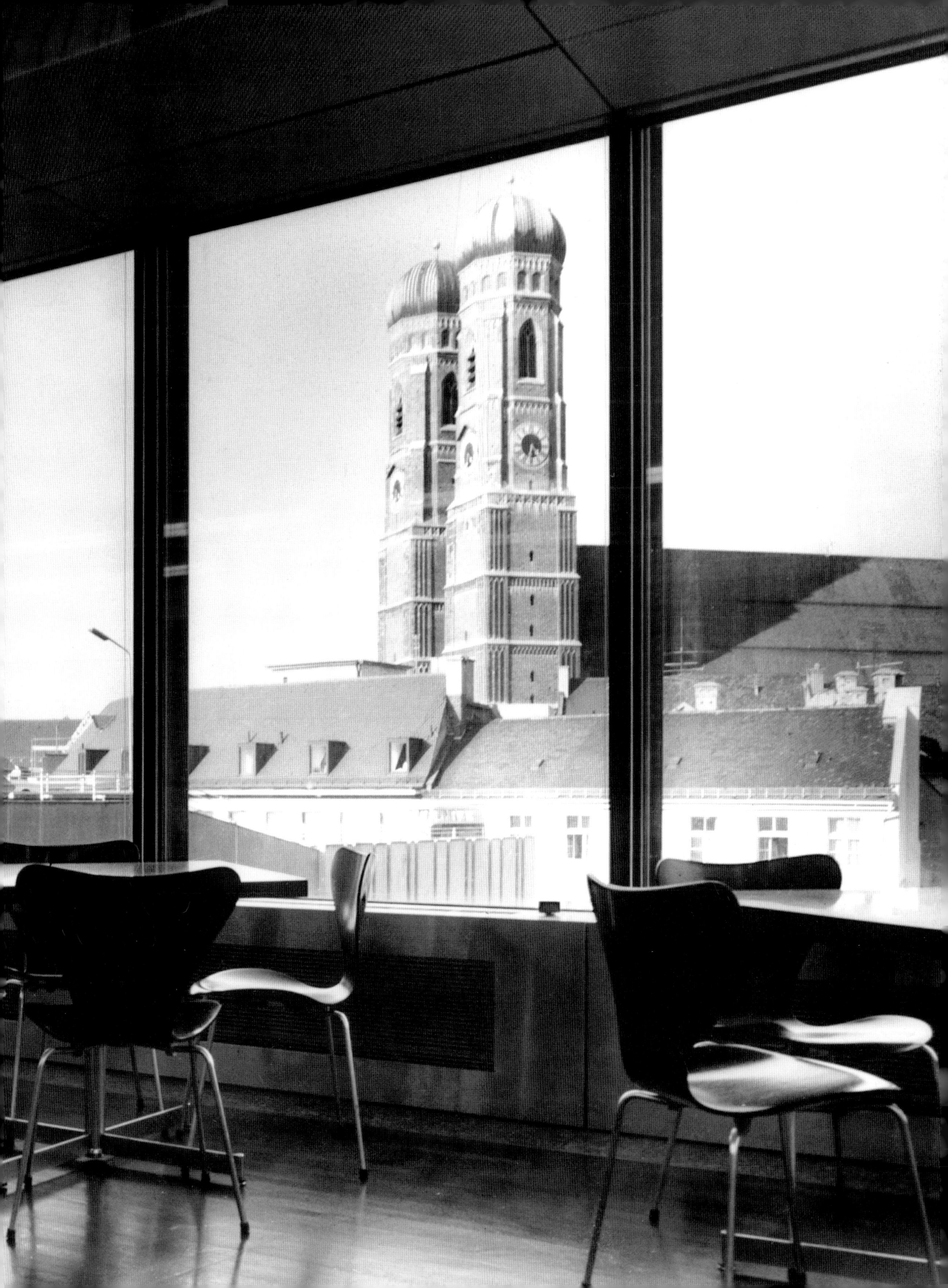

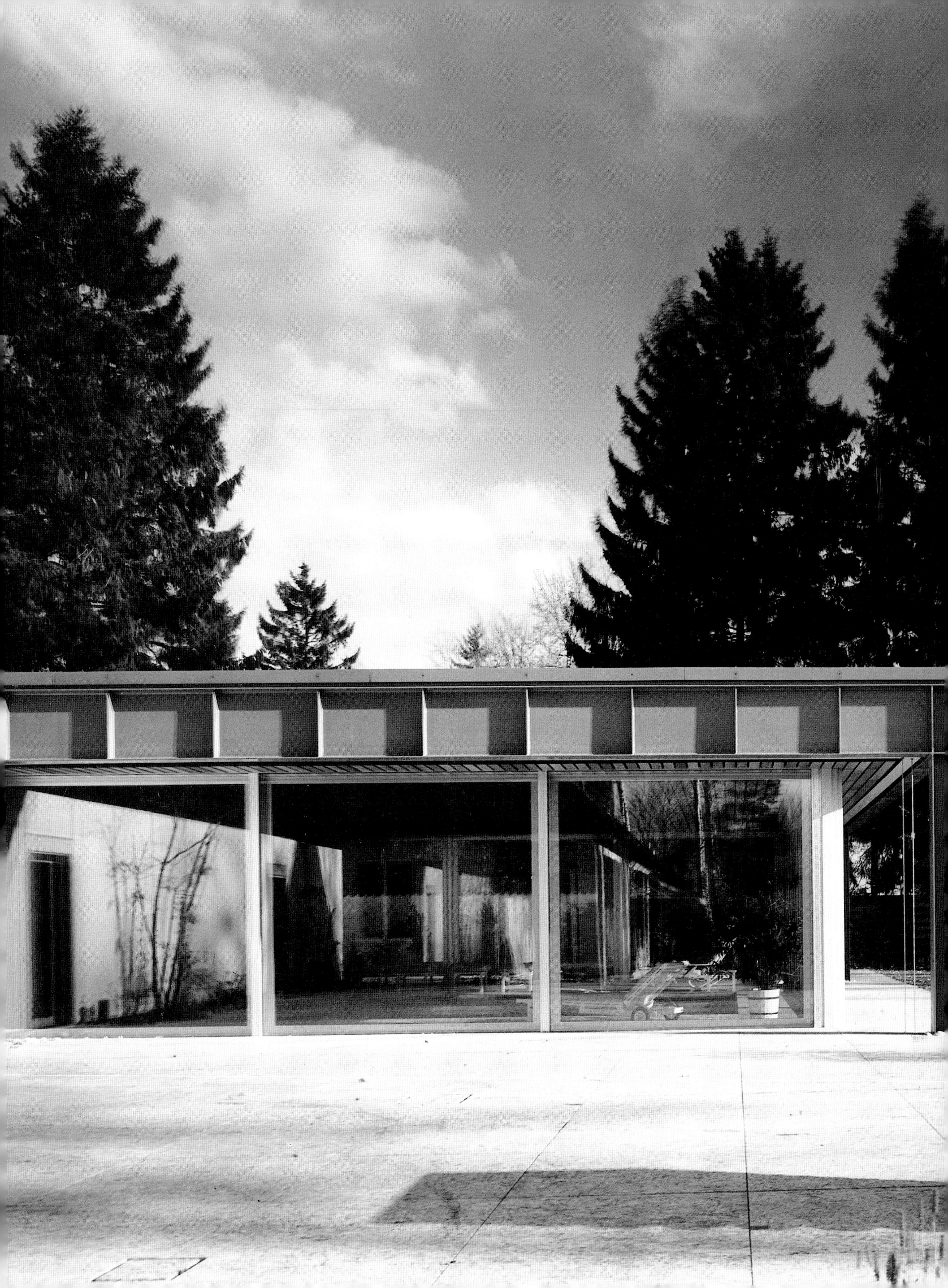

Privates Schwimmbad in der Harthauser Straße, München-Harlaching, 1967–69
Private swimming pool in Harthauser Straße, Harlaching, Munich, 1967–69

Dieser sorgfältigen Stahlbau zeigende, elegante, sich gänzlich vom landläufigen Wohngebäude, dem er zugeordnet wurde, abhebende hochtechnisierte Bau dürfte in solcher oder ähnlicher Konstellation wohl einmalig sein. Seine Errichtung ist eigentlich nur dann verständlich, wenn man mutmaßt, die Bauherrschaft hätte unausgesprochen die Absicht gehabt, mit dem Schwimmbad zu beginnen und später mit dem Wohnhaus nachzuziehen.

Leider ist diese Ergänzung, welche für München Ähnliches hätte bedeuten können wie einst die Errichtung des Hauses Tugendhat in Brünn (1930, Mies van der Rohe), niemals verwirklicht worden. Im Gegenteil: Das schöne Badehaus wurde, mit einem Walmdach verunziert, der trivial anspruchslosen Vorstadtvilla angeglichen. Dieses Pferd wurde sichtlich von hinten aufgezäumt. Die Reiter scheinen die Lust verloren zu haben; vielleicht aber standen auch die Zeitläufte einer Vollendung, die längeren Atem gebraucht hätte, entgegen.

Baubeschreibung des Architekten

»An eine Villa mit Garten in einer der bevorzugtesten Wohngegenden Münchens wurde ein Hallenschwimmbad angebaut. Das Bauvolumen des Anbaus entsprach etwa jenem des Wohngebäudes. Der Schwimmbadbau bedeutete zunächst einen beträchtlichen Eingriff in das Gartengrundstück. Um den Garten nicht zu zerstückeln, vor allem aber, um die Schwimmhalle mit dem sie umgebenden Garten zu verbinden, schlug der Architekt ein vom Wohnhaus abgerücktes durchsichtiges Gebäude (Dach auf vier Stützen) vor, welches mit der Villa durch einen geschlossenen Gang verbunden sein sollte. Die für das Schwimmbad (6 x 12 Meter) notwendigen Nebenräume wurden diesem durch Lichtkuppeln erhellten Gang zugeordnet.

Um die Verbindung zwischen Schwimmbad und Garten noch intensiver und erlebnisreicher zu gestalten, wurden alle Glaswände so konstruiert, daß sie bodeneben versenkbar waren. Diese gänzliche Öffnung war jederzeit möglich, da Klimaanlage und Warmluftanlage so leistungsfähig konzipiert wurden, daß das Bad bei jeder Witterung, vor allem auch nachts, wenn Bäume und Buschwerk beleuchtet waren, geöffnet werden kann.

Normalerweise bildet der Garten mit seinem jahreszeitlich sich verändernden Bestand an Bäumen und Büschen den eigentlichen

This elegant, highly technical construction, showing careful steel work, standing out completely from the conventional home it belongs to, must be unique in this or any similar combination of circumstances. It is actually only possible to understand how it came to be built if one conjectures that the clients had an unspoken intention of starting with the swimming pool and following it up with the house.

Unfortunately this sequence, which could have meant something similar for Munich as the building of the Tugendhat house in Brno (1930, Mies van der Rohe), was never realized. On the contrary: the beautiful pool building was made to conform with the trivially undemanding suburban villa and marred by the addition of a hipped roof. Here the cart was clearly put before the horse. The riders seem to have lost their enthusiasm; or perhaps the temper of the times ran counter to a perfect completion that would have needed a lot of staying power.

The architect's description of the building

»A covered swimming pool was built on to an existing villa in a garden in one of Munich's most desirable residential areas. The building volume of the extension was roughly the same as that of the house. The pool building entailed an considerable intervention into the garden plot in the first place. So that the garden was not broken up completely, but above all to tie the swimming pool in with the garden around it, the architect proposed a transparent building (roof on four columns) shifted away from the villa, and to be linked with it by a closed passageway. The ancillary rooms needed for the swimming pool (6 x 12 m) were placed along this corridor lit by domed skylights.

To create an even more intensive connection, providing a richer experience, between the pool and the garden, all the glass walls were constructed so that they could be lowered flush with the ground. This total opening was possible at any time, as both the heating and cooling plants were so powerful that the pool could be

Links: Ansicht Schwimmbad

Left page: view of the swimming pool

Raumabschluß der Schwimmhalle. Sind aber die in den Stützachsen liegenden Jalousien herabgelassen und entsprechend verstellt, so schließt sich der Raum. Wasser und Glasspiegelungen in Verbindung mit vielfältig steuerbarer Lichtführung ermöglichen dann ein Spiel mit illusionären Raumdimensionen.

Besonderer Wert wurde darauf gelegt, alle sich anbietenden technischen Möglichkeiten der Baukonstruktion und Gebäudetechnik voll auszunutzen, um für das Bad größtmögliche Behaglichkeit zu erreichen.

Das Schwimmbecken hängt frei in den Raum des Kellers und wird dort von heißer, unter Druck stehender Luft umspült. Diese erwärmt das Becken und damit das Wasser, den Fußboden und strömt nach oben in die zweischaligen Wände aus Granit und in die Zwischenräume der doppelten versenkbaren Glasfenster. Wände und Fenster werden auf Körpertemperatur erwärmt und geben die Wärme gleichmäßig an den Raum ab.

Die aufgeheizte Luft füllt auch den Raum zwischen der konstruktiven Dachdecke und der untergehängten Holzdecke. Über ein zweites unabhängiges Be- und Entlüftungssystem wird die Luftfeuchte geregelt. Eine angenehme Raumakustik wurde mit Hilfe von Schallschluckeinlagen in der massiv gearbeiteten Holzdecke erreicht. Alle direkten und indirekten Beleuchtungseinrichtungen sind stufenlos und zentral steuerbar.

Als Materialien kamen grau gestrichener Stahl, weißer Sichtbeton und für die Böden, Wände und den Deckenrand Granit aus Montana zur Verwendung. Die Fenster bestehen aus Aluminium, Edelstahl und Holz. Die massive Decke ist aus Wenge gearbeitet. Alle Einbauten sind mit Wenge-Furnieren belegt.

Die umfangreiche, komplizierte technische Ausstattung und deren Integration in das Bauwerk erforderten gänzliche Neuentwicklungen, deren Gestalt auch entworfen werden mußte (versenkbare Fensterwände, Jalousieanlage, Lichtkuppeldecke, Doppelwände für Heißluft und Beleuchtungskörper). Handwerkliche Leistungen von Schreinern, Steinmetzen und Metallbauern waren in ungewöhnlicher Sorgfalt und Präzision erforderlich, hinzu kamen die Arbeiten an den Innenausbauten.

Den Brunnen im vorgelegten Gartenhof gestaltete der Bildhauer Blasius Gerg, für die Bar konzipierte Karl Gerstner eine elektronisch gesteuerte Licht- und Farbprojektion mit 24 Kleinprojektoren.«

opened in any weather, but above all even at night, when the trees and shrubs were illuminated.

Normally the garden with its seasonally changing stock of trees and shrubs provides the actual spatial conclusion for the swimming pool. But if the blinds in the support axes are lowered and adjusted appropriately, the space is closed off. Then reflections in water and glass combined with considerably variable lighting make it possible to play with illusionary spatial dimensions.

Special attention was paid to exploiting all the technical possibilities afforded by structural techniques and building technology to the full, to make the pool as comfortable and appealing as possible.

The actual pool is freely suspended in the cellar space and is surrounded by hot air under pressure. This warms the pool and thus the water, the floor, and also flows upwards into the twin-shell granite walls and the gaps in the double glass windows that can be lowered. Walls and floor are heated to body temperature and also provide even heat for the interior space.

The heated air also fills the space between the structural roof and the wooden ceiling suspended below it. A second, independent ventilation and extraction system controls air humidity. A pleasant acoustic is achieved with the aid of sound absorbers in the solid wooden ceiling. All the direct and indirect lighting fittings can be controlled centrally and with continuous variation.

Steel painted grey and white exposed concrete were used, with Montana granite for the floors, walls and the edge of the ceiling. The windows are made of aluminium, stainless steel and wood. The solid ceiling is in wenge wood. All the fittings have wenge veneer.

The lavish, complex technical equipment and its integration into the building required completely new developments whose form also had to be designed (window walls that can be lowered, blind fittings, skylight-dome ceiling, double walls for hot air and light fittings). Work by cabinet-makers, stonemasons and metalworkers had to be executed with unusual care and precision, as well as work on the interior finish.

The fountain in the garden courtyard at the front was designed by the sculptor Blasius Gerg, and for the bar Karl Gerstner devised electronically controlled light and colour projections using 24 small projectors.«

Eingebaute Bar
Integrated bar

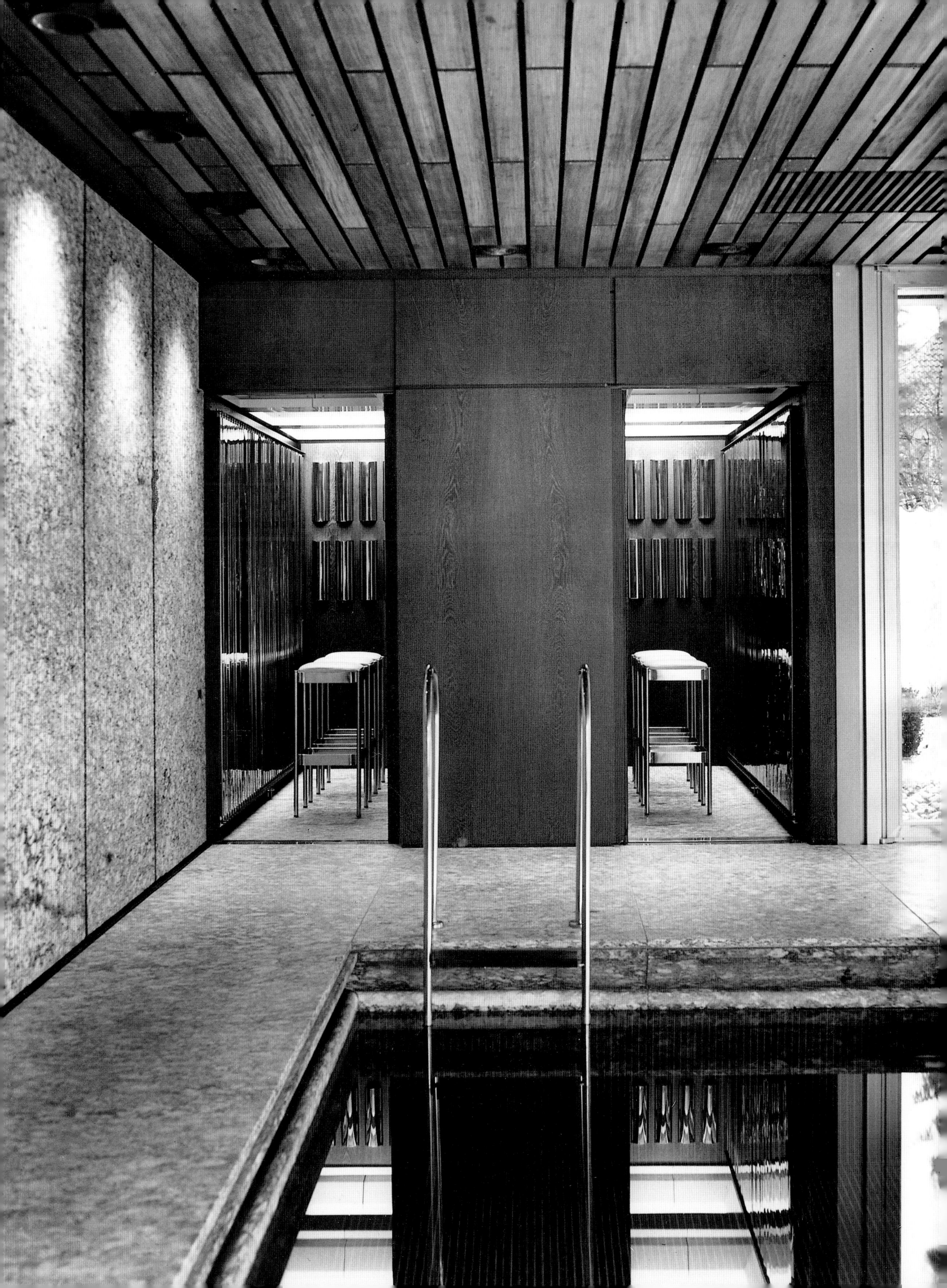

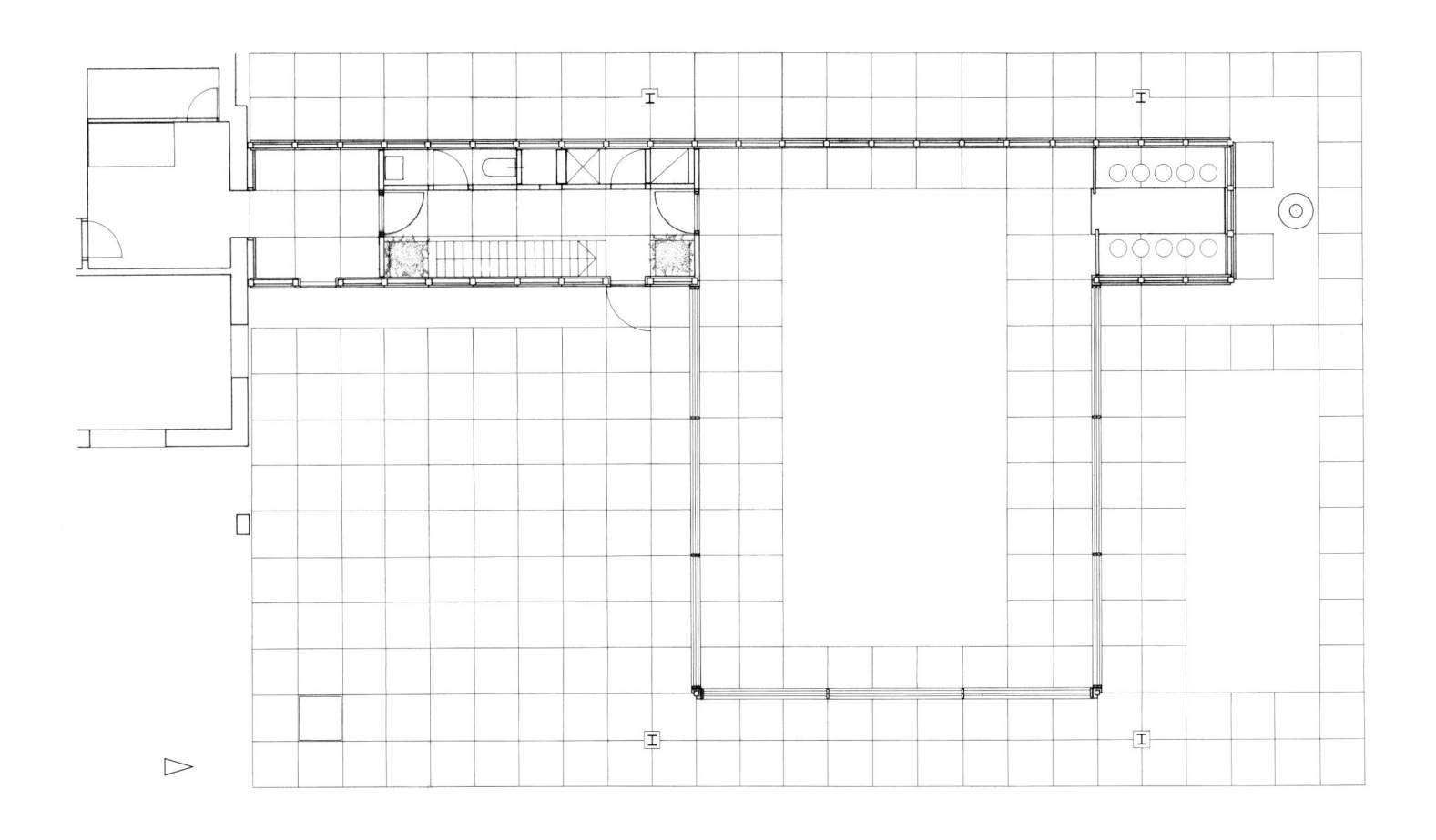

Grundriß Erdgeschoß

Floor plan, ground floor

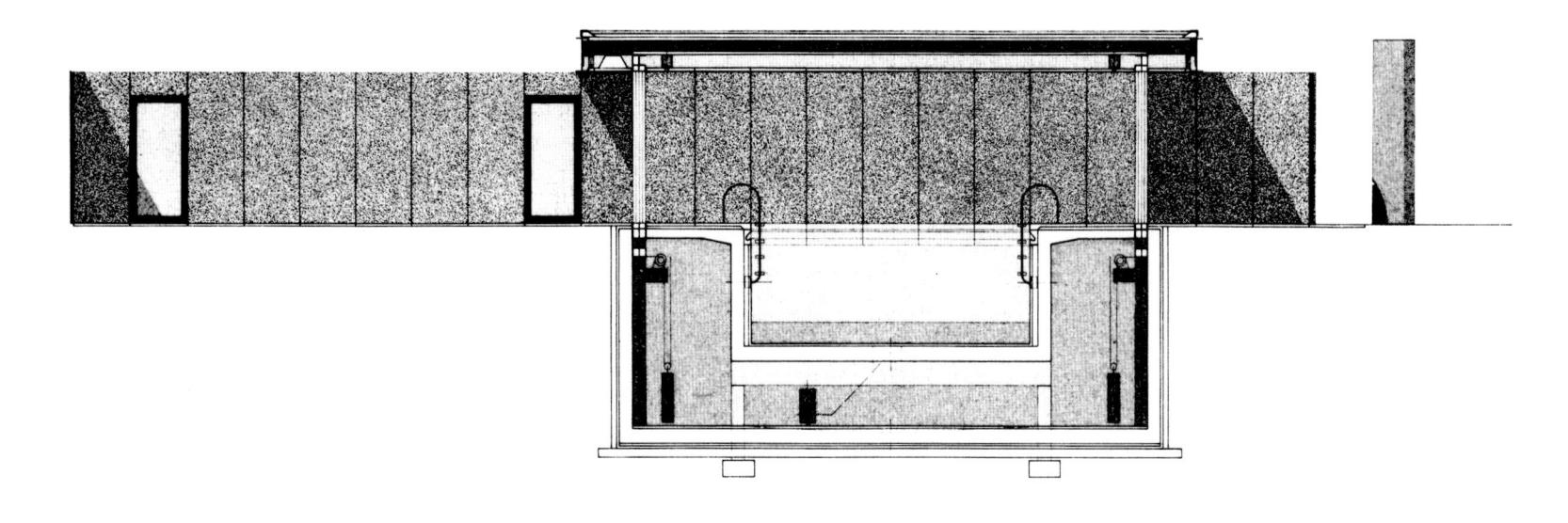

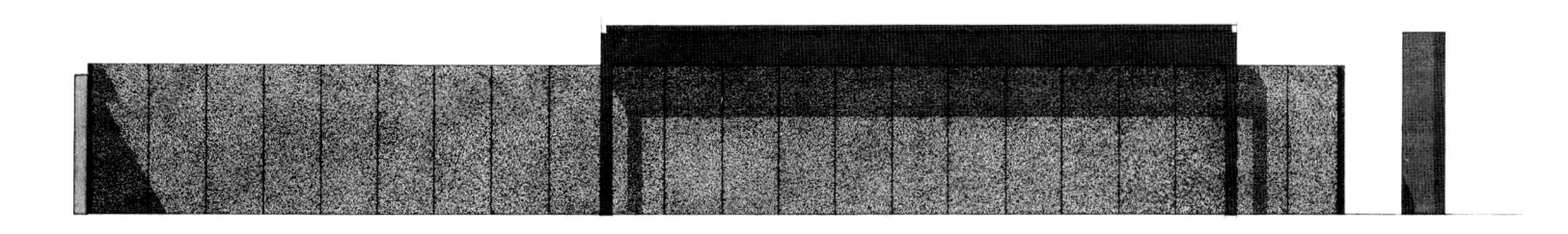

Oben: Ansicht Schnitt
Unten: Ansicht

Top: elevation, sectional view
Bottom: elevation

Innenraum Schwimmbad

Interior of swimming pool

Blick aus dem Schwimmbad in den Garten

View of the garden from the swimming pool

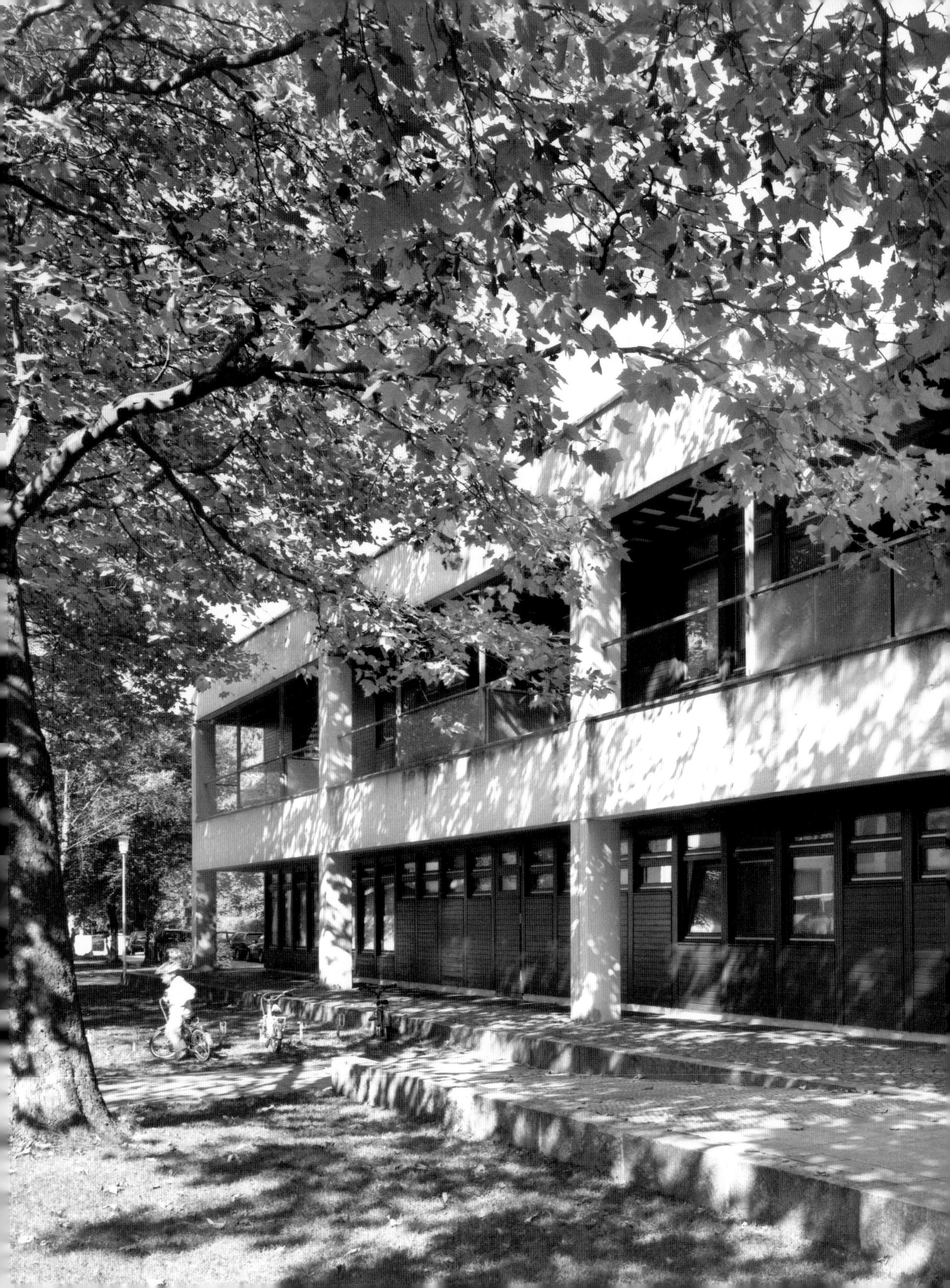

Pfarrzentrum Heilige Familie, Johannisplatz, Gartenberg, 1969–73
Bauherr: Erzbischöfliches Ordinariat München

Holy Family parish centre, Johannisplatz, Gartenberg, 1969–73
Client: Archiepiscopal Ordinariate Munich

Inmitten einer kräftig gegliederten, plastisch ausgeformten neuen Wohnsiedlung sollten an einem dem eigentlichen Kirchengrundstück vorgelegten Platz, in den die Fußwege der Siedlung münden, die Kirche und die weiteren zu einem Pfarrzentrum gehörenden Einrichtungen entstehen.

Daraus eine der üblichen Gebäudegruppierungen zu bilden hätte der städtebaulichen Situation nicht entsprochen. Ein möglichst einfacher, ruhig in sich geschlossener, großer Baukörper schien die beste Lösung. Die Kirchengemeinde teilte überzeugt diese Auffassung, welche ihrer eigenen Bestrebung, das bauliche Programm in konzentrierter Form zu verwirklichen, entsprach. So wurde das Pfarrzentrum zum Haus der Gemeinde, zum Ort verschiedenartiger, bei Bedarf auch veränderbarer Nutzung.

Im Zentrum des Hauses findet sich, über zwei Geschosse reichend, der von oben belichtete, quadratische Kirchenraum. Seine Dimension bestimmt die konstruktive, unveränderliche Primärstruktur eines Sichtbetonskeletts mit großen Spannweiten.

Eine Sekundärstruktur umgibt diesen Kern. Sie ist veränderbar. Die nichttragenden Wände sind bei Bedarf versetzbar. Auch die Außenwände, Holzkonstruktionen, können unschwer veränderten Nutzungen angepaßt werden.

Die Gestalt des Bauwerks ist wesentlich geprägt vom Gegensatz der regelmäßigen Erscheinung der dominanten Primärstruktur und jener der bewegten, unterschiedliche Nutzung anzeigenden Sekundärstruktur. So teilt sich das Gebäudeinnere sprechend durch das Erscheinungsbild nach außen mit.

Das Pfarrzentrum Gartenberg ist ein gutes Beispiel für den nachkonziliaren Kirchenbau im Aufbruch. Der Gedanke an ein neues, sich um den Altar zur gemeinsamen Feier versammelndes Gottesvolk geht mit der sich selbst erklärenden Funktionalität des viele Möglichkeiten bietenden, indes das Geschehen nicht durch Vorgabe bestimmenden Bauwerks eine sachliche Bindung ein. Inzwischen ist diese Haltung schon Geschichte geworden.

The church and the other facilities needed for a parish centre were to be built in the middle of a powerfully structured, sculpturally designed housing estate, on a square in front of the actual church plot to which the estate footpaths led.

It would not have been appropriate to the urban situation to create one of the customary groups of buildings here. The best solution seemed to be a single large building, as simple as possible, and quietly complete in itself. The parishioners were convinced by this view, which fitted in entirely with their own desire to realize the building programme in concentrated form. So the parish centre became the community building, a place that could be used in a variety of ways, and could be changed if need be.

At the centre of the building is the square space for the church itself, rising through two storeys and lit from the top. Its dimensions were determined by the structural, unchangeable primary structure, an exposed concrete skeleton with long span widths.

This core is surrounded by a secondary structure. This can be altered. The non-load-bearing walls can be moved if wished. And the outside walls, timber structures, can easily be adapted for different uses.

The form of the building is largely determined by the contrast with the regular appearance of the dominant primary structure and that of the mobile secondary structure, which indicates different uses. Thus the interior of the building is eloquently conveyed to the outside world by its appearance.

The Gartenberg parish centre is a good example of post-conciliar church building in its early stages. The idea of new people of God assembled around the altar for common worship enters into a material bond with the self-explanatory functionality of the building, which offers many possibilities without determining events prescriptively. This approach has since become history.

Außenansicht
Exterior elevation

Detlef Schreiber: Gedanken zum Bau des Pfarrzentrums Heilige Familie aus einem Abstand von zwanzig Jahren

»Das Baukonzept von Gartenberg ist zweifellos von den unmittelbaren Zeitströmungen, aber in noch stärkerem Maße von den Ergebnissen des Zweiten Vatikanischen Konzils geprägt. Die Diskussion über die bisher geübte Praxis des Kirchenbaus, der sich in reichen Formen und fürstlichen Dimensionen machtvoll darstellte, war 1972/73, der Entstehungszeit der Gartenberger Planung, auf einem Höhepunkt angelangt. Es wurden Kirchenbauten gefordert, die nach Inhalt und Form sich auf die wesentlichen Aussagen der Kirche in unserer Zeit beschränken und deren Baukosten gemessen an traditionellen Repräsentationskirchen weniger als die Hälfte betragen sollten. [...] So setzte sich die Zielvorstellung durch, keinesfalls auf die bisherigen Traditionen des Kirchenbaus, vor allem auf formale Distanz im Stadtbild, zurückzugreifen. [...] Die Programmvorhaben eines Pfarrzentrums blieben allerdings dieselben wie in den letzten vorkonziliaren Jahren.

Auf der Suche nach einem neuen Leitbild für Inhalt und Form des Baus mußten zunächst vor allem die Bedenken ausgeräumt werden, daß nicht billige Einfachkirchen oder nur neue, modische Verkleidungsformen für altbewährte Inhalte zu erfinden waren. Vielmehr galt es, ein Gestaltungsprinzip zu entwickeln, bei dem sich einerseits Inhalt und Form und andererseits Zweck und Sinn zu einem übereinstimmenden Ausdruck des Bauwerks vereinigen. [...]

Das Leben in einer Gemeindekirche wirkt sich nach zwei Seiten hin aus. Einmal ist es das aktive, ziel- und zweckbestimmte soziale Engagement für das Leben in der Gemeinschaft, und zum anderen ist es das in sich ruhende Dasein der versammelten Gemeinde im liturgischen Gebet und der Eucharistiefeier. [...]

Aus dieser Dualität entwickelten sich auch Gestaltungsprinzip und Leitbild folgerichtig. Die Kirche vereinigt alle Bereiche des kirchlichen Lebens der Gemeinde in einem einzigen, zentral geordneten Haus. Dessen äußerer Ring beherbergt die nach außen in die Welt wirkenden Aktivitäten und die einladenden Eingangsräume. Er umschließt aber auch mit schützender Gebärde den im Innersten des Bauwerks liegenden Raum für die Versammlung der Gemeinde zum liturgischen Gebet und zur gemeinsamen Feier der Eucharistie. Es ist der innerste Kern – ganz vom Gesetz des Betens, der Liturgie und vom Gesetz des Glaubens, vom Wahrheitsgehalt der Offenbarung erfüllt –, der dem Außenring stützenden, geistigen Zusammenhalt verleiht. [...]

Der Bau einer Kirche hat weniger mit formal-ästhetischen Kategorien zu tun als vielmehr mit ethisch-moralischen. Es gilt in erster Linie die Frage nach der Wahrheit und der Güte zu stellen und erst dann die nach der Schönheit. Denn wer eine in sich ruhende Schönheit will, der darf nichts anderes wollen, als wahr und gut zu sein.

Das Bauwerk ist sowohl durch seine universelle Charakteristik als auch durch seine Unverwechselbarkeit geprägt. Noch wirkt das damalige, längst schon historisch gewordene Gestaltungsprinzip fort, und noch immer wird das Bauwerk teilweise kontrovers diskutiert.«

Detlef Schreiber: Thoughts about building the Holy Family parish centre after an interval of twenty years

»The Gartenberg building concept is undoubtedly shaped by the immediate trends of its day, but to an even greater extent by the results of the Second Vatican Council. Discussion about previous church architectural practice, powerfully presented in lavish forms and princely dimensions, had reached its climax in 1972/73, the time when the Gartenberg plans were made. Church buildings were required whose form and content was limited to the essential statements the Church could make in our day, and their building costs were to come out as half that of traditional, prestigious church buildings. [...] So it was accepted that the aim would be not to go back, whatever happened, to previous church architecture traditions, and above all not to resort to formal distance in the cityscape. [...] But the programmatic intentions for a parish centre remained the same as in the later pre-conciliar years.

When looking for new guidelines for the building's form and content, scruples had first of all to be addressed about not inventing cheap, unduly simple churches or simply finding new, fashionable guises for tried-and-tested content. On the contrary, a design principle had to be developed that would bring form and content, and then purpose and meaning, together to join in expressing the building's spirit coherently. [...]

Life in a parish church evolves in two directions. On the one hand it is about active social commitment, determined by aim and purpose, to life in the community, and secondly it is the poised existence of the assembled community in liturgical prayer and celebration of the Eucharist.

Design principle and a model to follow also developed logically from this duality. The church brings together all spheres of the community's ecclesiastical life in a single, centrally placed building. Its outer ring contains the activities that impinge on the outside world and the inviting entrance spaces. But it also offers a protective embrace to the space at the innermost heart of the building where the congregation assembles for liturgical prayer and the common celebration of the Eucharist. This is the innermost core – filled entirely with the law of prayer, of the liturgy and with the law of faith, with the truth contained in divine revelation – and this lends the outer ring a supportive, spiritual coherence. [...]

Building a church has less to do with formal and aesthetic categories than with ethical and moral ones. The first concern is to ask the question about truth and goodness, and only then the question about beauty. For anyone seeking the poise of beauty may wish for nothing other than to be true and good.

The building is defined both by universal and its own unmistakable qualities. The design principle found then, now long since historical, continues to make its impact, and the building is still an occasional source of controversy.«

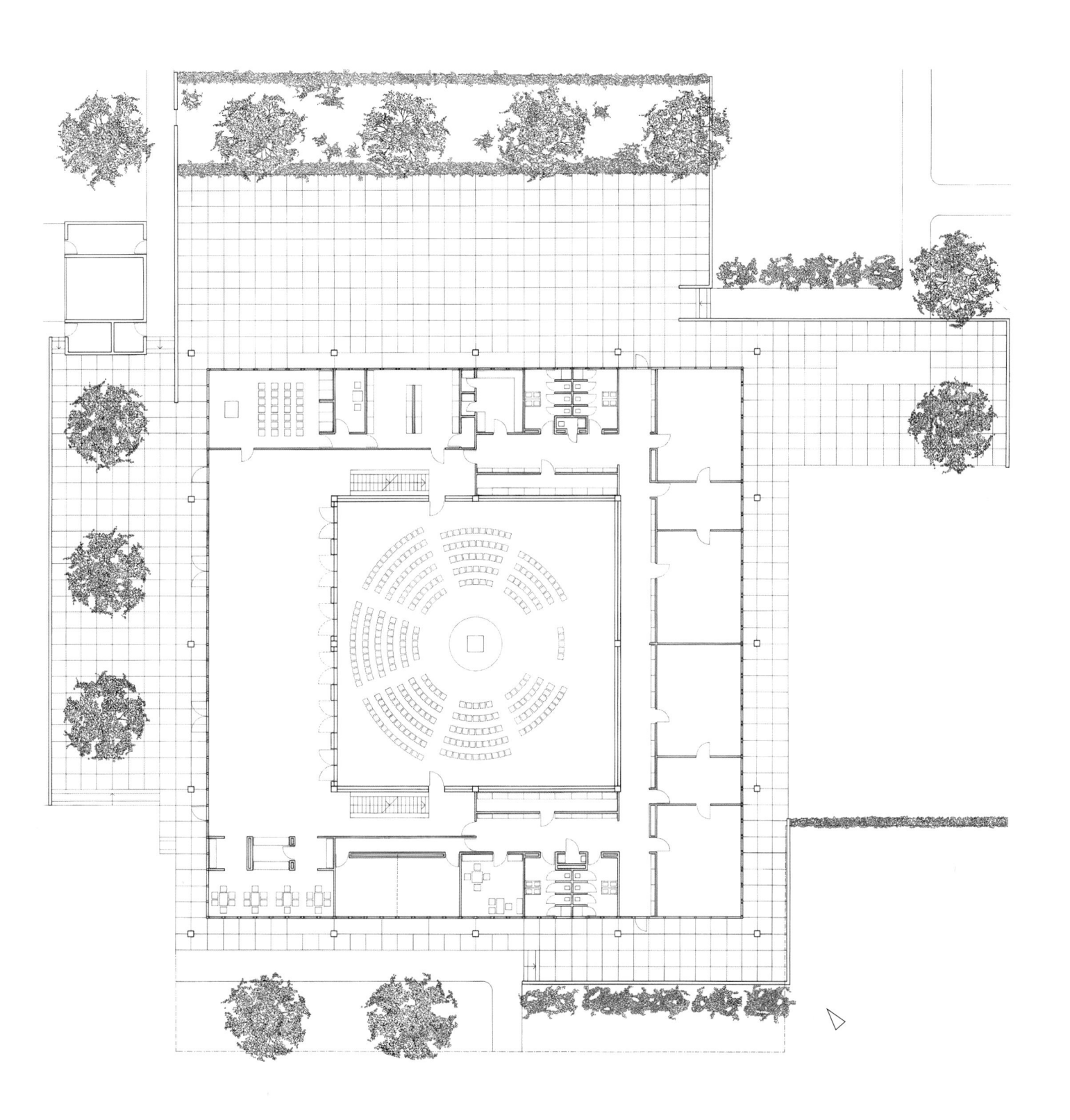

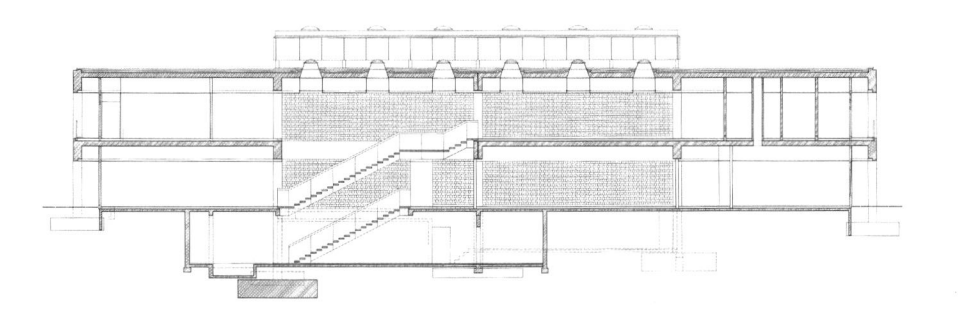

Oben: Grundriß Erdgeschoß
Unten: Schnitt

Top: floor plan, ground floor
Bottom: sectional view

FOLGENDE DOPPELSEITE:
Kircheninnenraum

NEXT DOUBLE PAGE:
Interior of the church

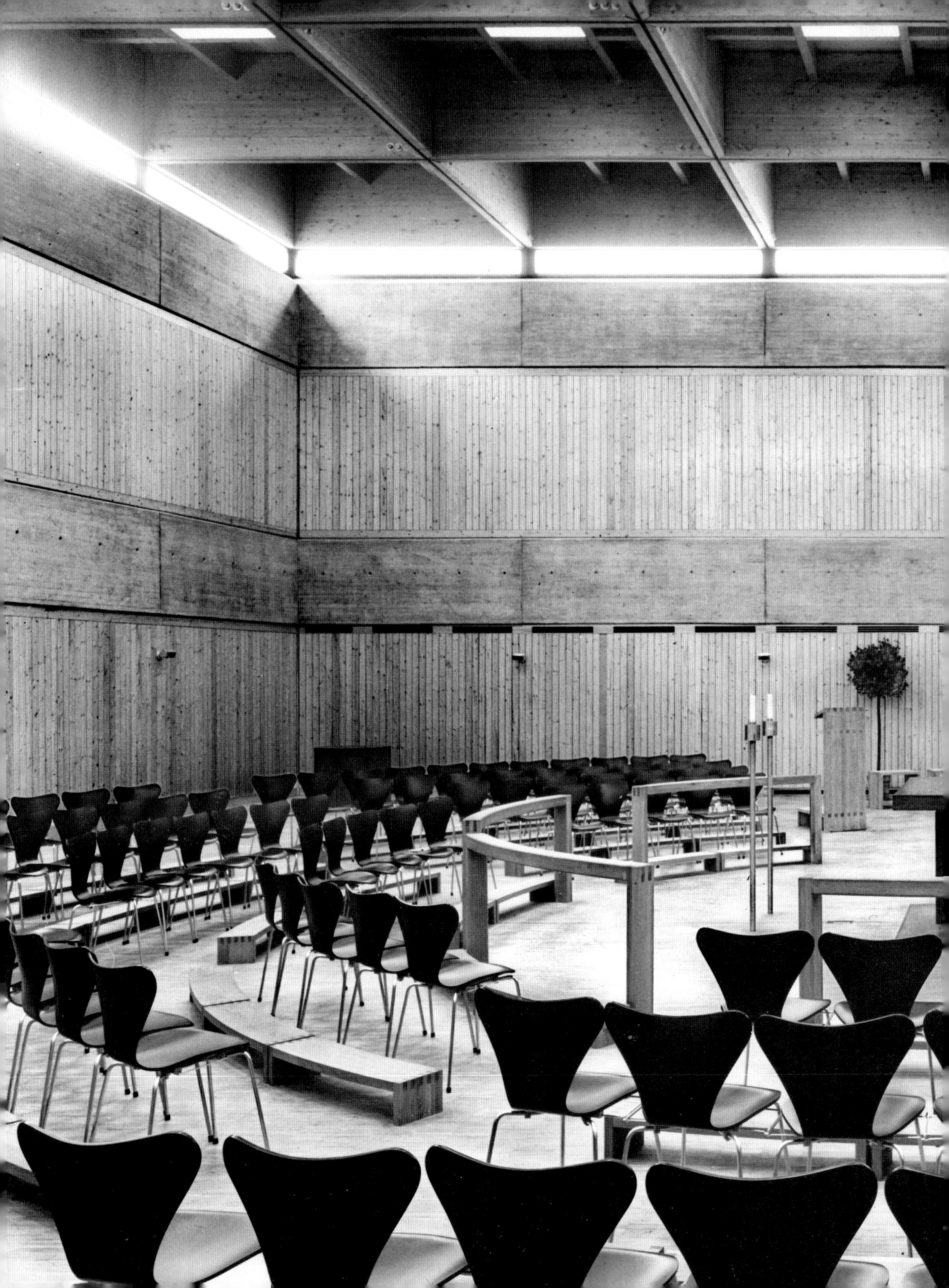

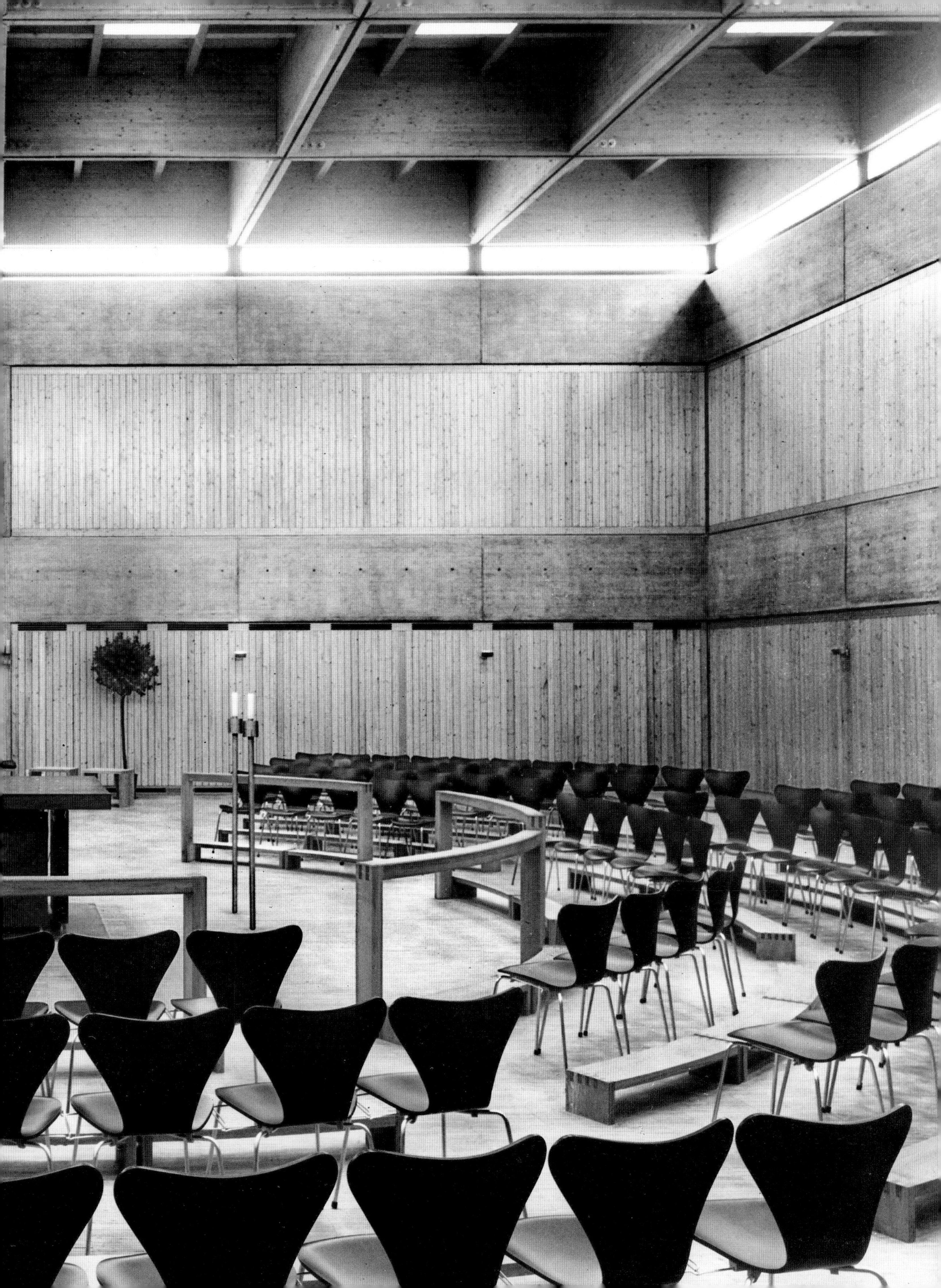

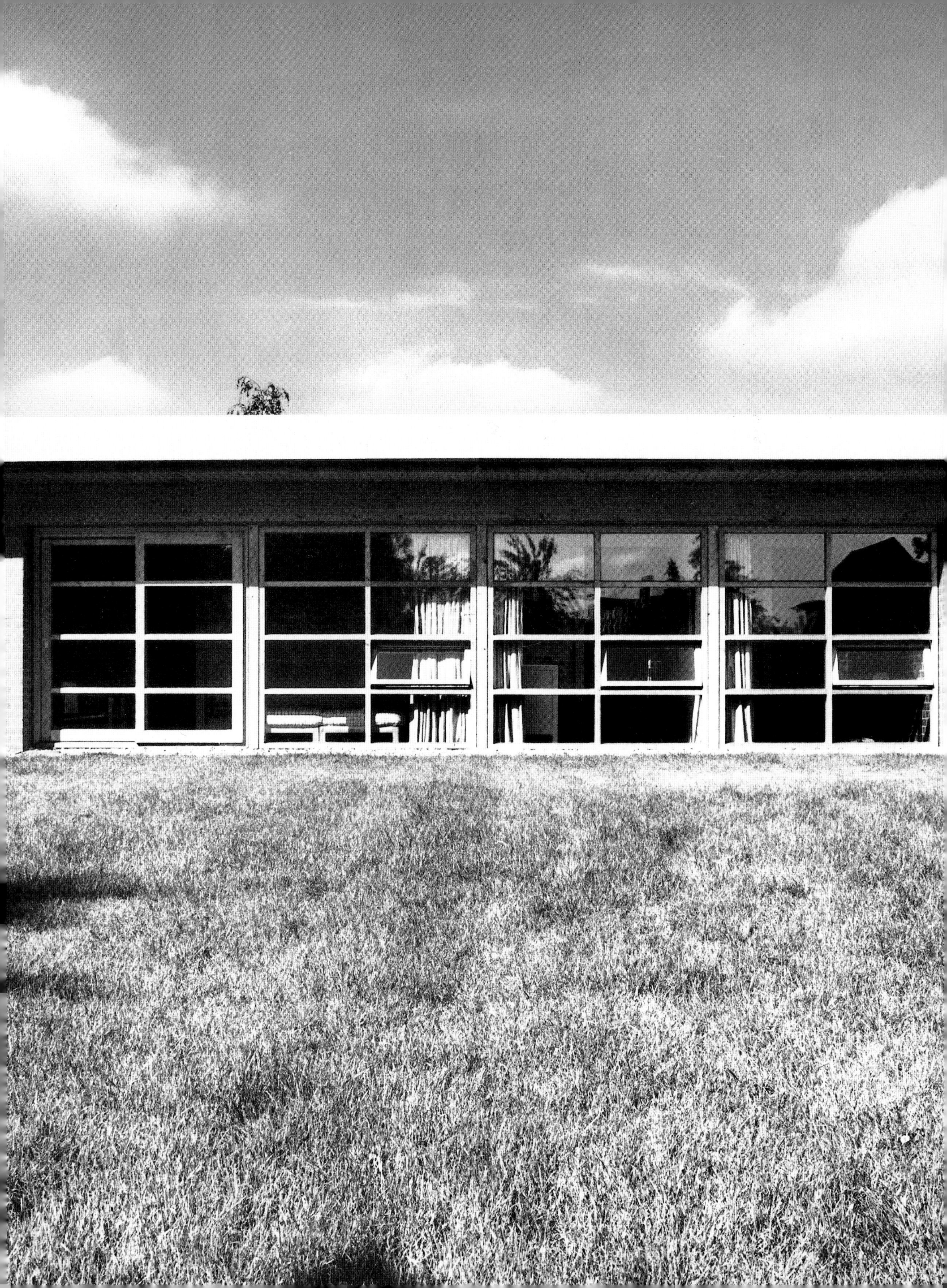

Privathaus Im Ginsterbusch 5, Hamburg, 1974–76
Bauherr: Wolfgang Nolde

Private house at Im Ginsterbusch 5, Hamburg, 1974–76
Client: Wolfgang Nolde

Aus Amerika zurückgekehrt, wünschte sich der Bauherr, ein Physiker, der dort als Professor gearbeitet hatte, ein räumlich großzügiges, zugleich aber preiswertes und rasch zu errichtendes Haus. Das Gebäude sollte zudem eingeschossig sein, ein flaches Dach haben, um im Kern liegende Räume über Lichtkuppeln belichten zu können. Die Größe des Hauses richtete sich nach den Vorgaben des damaligen Wohnbauförderungsparagraphen 7b, der als Obergrenze für die steuerliche Abschreibbarkeit eine Wohnflächenbegrenzung auf 156 Quadratmeter vorschrieb.

Transatlantischen Gepflogenheiten entsprechend, sollte im weitestgehend offenen Grundriß möglichst türlos gewohnt werden. Die zwei eingeplanten, wie damals üblich, nicht sehr großen Kinderzimmer sollten später, wenn die Kinder erwachsen und aus dem Haus wären, ohne viel Umstände veränderbar sein. Der um drei Stufen tiefer gelegte, 64 Quadratmeter große *living room* war direkt an den Mittelbereich, die offene Diele mit Küchenzeile und Eßplatz, über zwei kleine Treppen angeschlossen. Ein gut bestückter Sanitärblock wurde überwiegend dem etwas abgesetzten Schlafbereich zugeordnet.

Den klaren Vorstellungen des Bauherrn entsprach Detlef Schreiber mit einem ebenso klaren und überzeugenden Grundrißkonzept und Bausystem. Der erdgeschossige Flachdachbau mit Teilunterkellerung für Technik und Hobbyraum ist 24 Meter lang, 12 Meter breit und 2,67 Meter hoch.

Zwei parallele Wandscheiben im Achsabstand von 12 Meter bilden die Tragwände. Darüber liegen Leimbinder, welche Sparren samt Schalung und die Flachdachkonstruktion tragen. Drei der Leimbinderpfetten sind 20 m lang und an ihren Enden auf Gartenmauern abgestützt. Sie tragen eine Überdachung, die nördlich als Carport mit Hauseingang und südlich als überdachte Terrasse dient.

Das von der Straße zurückgesetzt inmitten eines relativ großen, 20 Meter breiten und weit in die Tiefe reichenden Grundstücks angeordnete Haus wirkt vor allem durch seine klaren Proportionen, die horizontale, präzise Gliederung seiner gesproßt verglasten Flächen und die sparsame, fast asketische Verwendung von Backstein und Holz. Die Horizontale wird besonders betont durch die hohe, umlaufende Attika des Flachdachs, welches als kräftiger »Deckel« in Erscheinung tritt und die differenzierte, geschichtete Dachkonstruktion an den Rändern zusammenfaßt.

The client was a physicist returning from America who had worked as a professor there. He wanted a spacious house that would at the same time be reasonably priced and quickly built. The building was also to have a single storey and a flat roof, so that the rooms in the middle could be lit from light domes. The size of the house was laid down by the requirements of the then housing promotion paragraph 7b, which prescribed 156 squaremetres as the maximum area for a dwelling that could be set against tax.

In accordance with transatlantic practices, there were to be as few doors as possible in the largely open ground plan. The two planned children's rooms, which were not very large, as was customary at the time, were intended to be easily modified later, when the children had grown up and left home. There were three steps down to the 64 squaremetres living room which was accessed directly from the central area, and the open hall with long kitchen and dining area was reached via two small stairs. A well-equipped sanitary block was largely related to the somewhat offset bedroom area.

Detlef Schreiber met the client's clear wishes with a ground plan concept and construction system that were equally clear. The one-storey flat-roofed building with partial basement for services and hobby room is 24 m long, 12 m wide and 2.67 m high.

The load-bearing walls are a pair with an axial distance of 12 m. Above them are glued trusses supporting rafters together with shuttering and the flat roof structure. Three of the roof truss purlins are 20 m long and supported at the end by garden walls. They carry roofing that serves as a carport and porch on the north side and as a roofed terrace on the south side.

The house is placed set back from the street in the middle of a relatively large plot, 20 m wide and extending well back. It is effective above all because of its lucid proportions, the precise horizontal articulation of its glazed areas with bars, and the frugal, almost ascetic use of brick and timber. The horizontal is particularly emphasized by the high, continuous attic storey created by the flat roof, which looks like a substantial »lid« and pulls the sophisticated, layered roof structure together at the edges.

Links: Ansicht Gartenfront

Left page: garden elevation

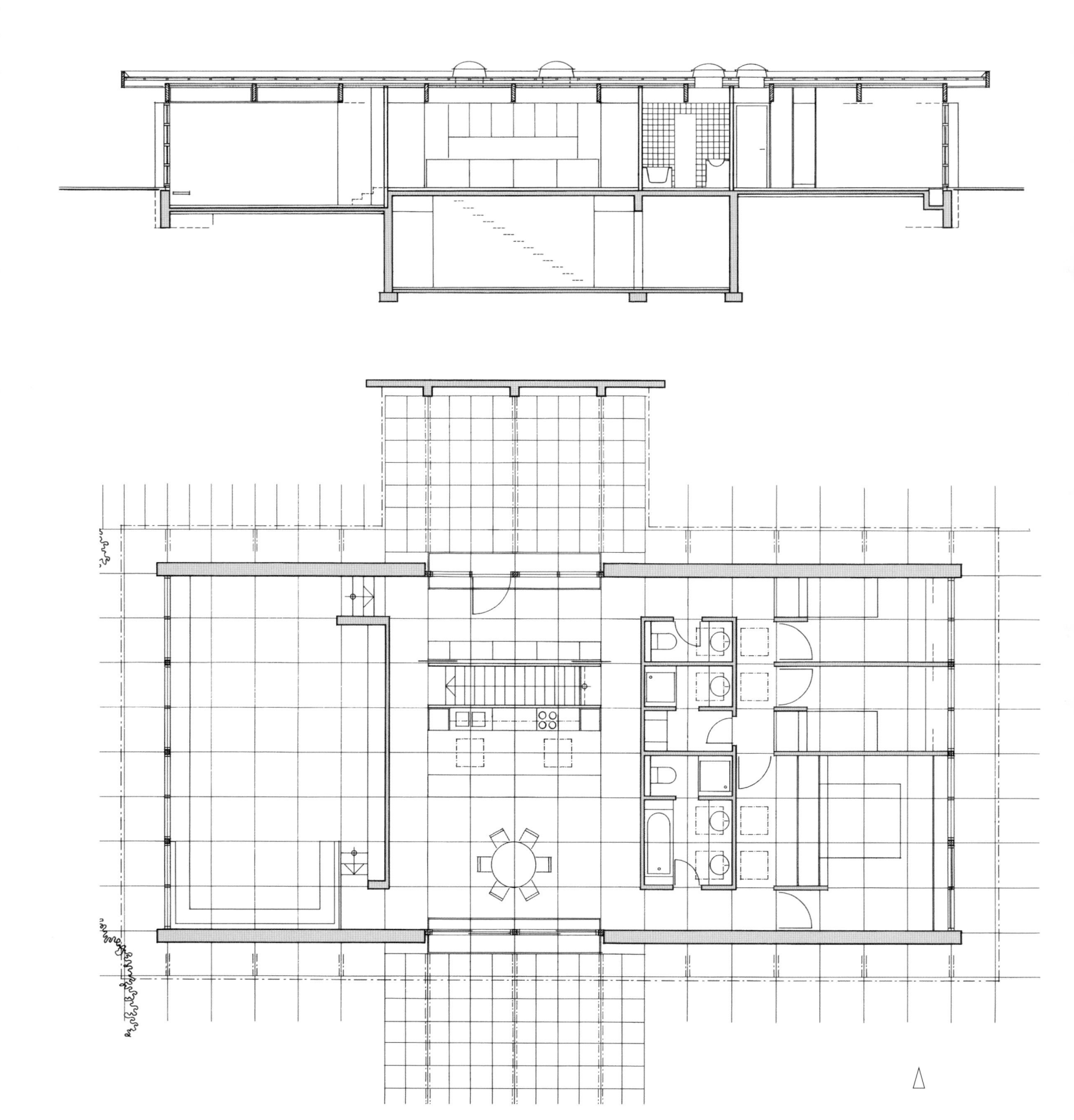

Oben: Schnitt
Unten: Grundriß Erdgeschoß

Top: cross-section
Bottom: floor plan, ground floor

Rechts: Blick vom Wohnraum durch das Haus

Right page: view through the house from the living room

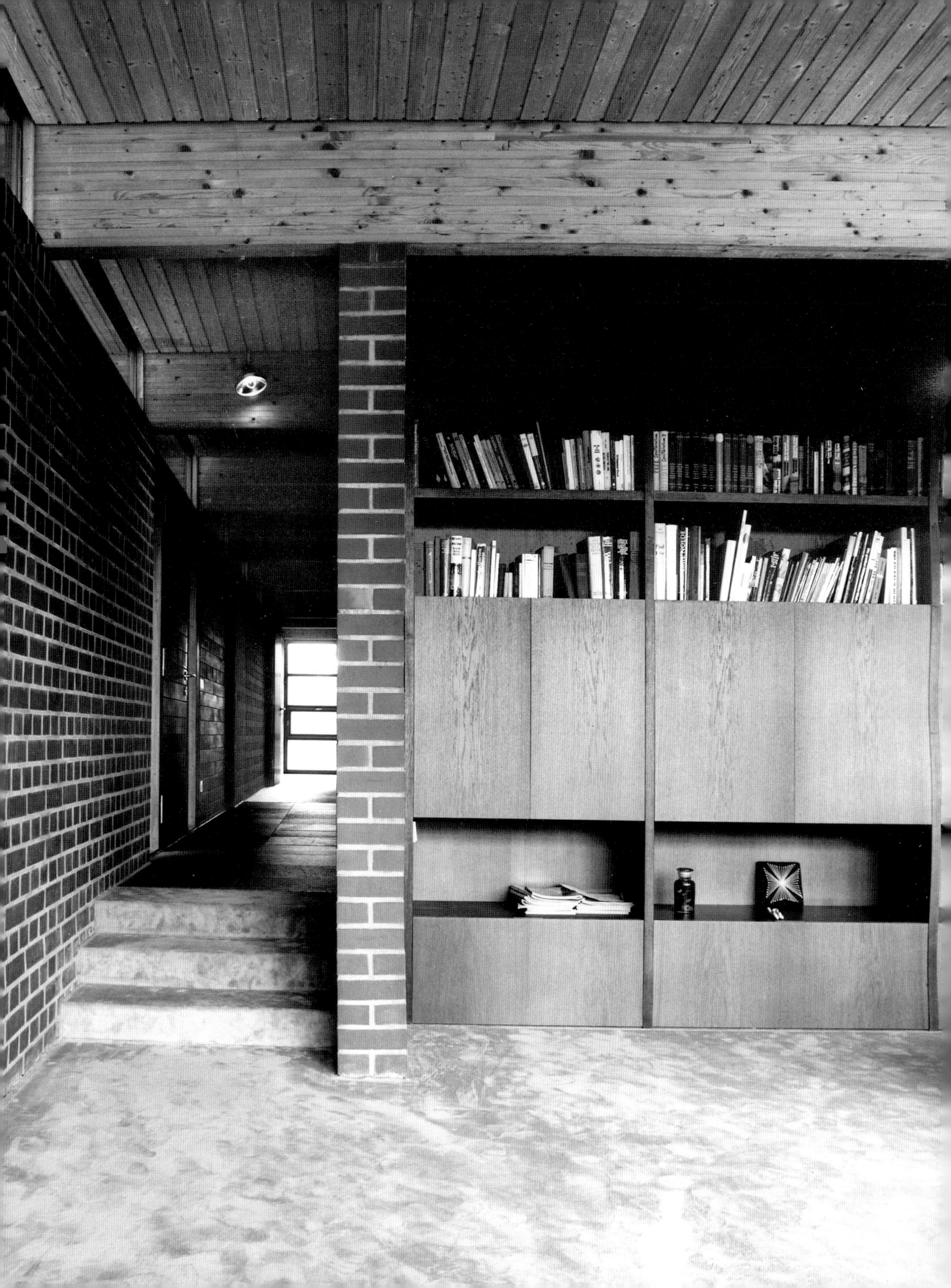

Küche
Kitchen

Wohnraum

Living room

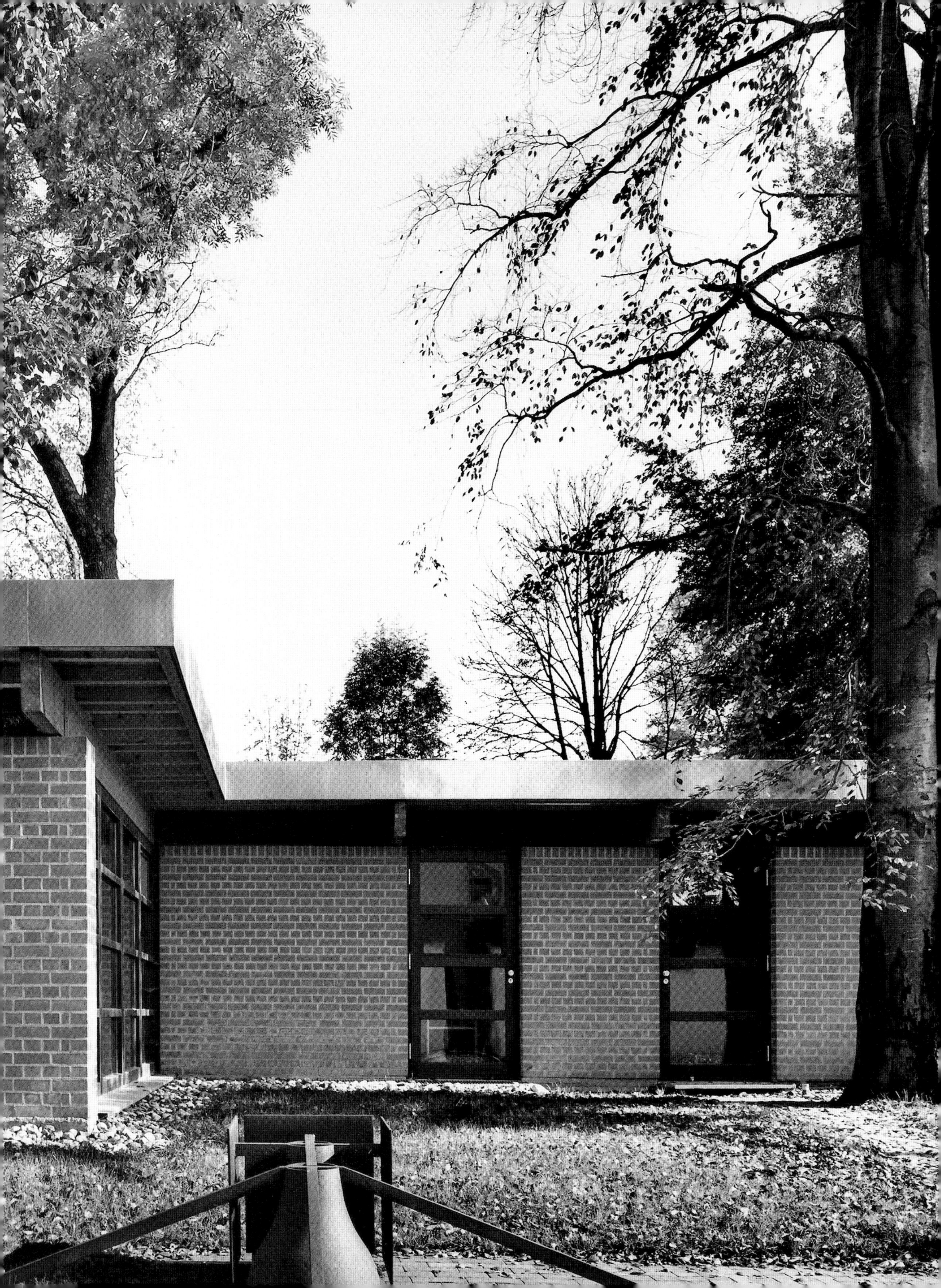

Künstleratelier in der Muttenthalerstraße, München-Solln, 1974–76
Bauherr: Rupprecht Geiger

Artist's studio in Muttenthalerstraße, Solln, Munich, 1974–76
Client: Rupprecht Geiger

Schon Ende der 1940er Jahre war Detlef Schreiber auf Rupprecht Geiger, den heute weltbekannten Maler, aufmerksam geworden. Seither verfolgte er dessen Arbeiten und freute sich über Geigers steigendes Ansehen. 1960 erwarb er ein großes Bild, wurde zu einem frühen Geiger-Sammler und auch zum Freund des Malers. So kam es, daß er für ihn das Atelier baute.

Zunächst sollten auf dem Grundstück an der Sollner Muttenthalerstraße zwei nebeneinanderliegende Wohnhäuser errichtet werden, doch dazu kam es nicht. Statt dessen entstand dort ein Ateliergebäude für den Maler Rupprecht Geiger.

Der übersichtliche Grundriß dieser Werkstatt ist auf einem Quadratraster von 6 x 6 Meter aufgebaut. Eine dreißig Meter lange Mauer aus Sichtziegeln schließt den Bau nach Osten ab. Das Atelier, der größte Raum des Hauses, reicht über zwei Geschosse vom Untergeschoßboden bis unters Dach. Er ist über eine Galerie und Treppe erschlossen. Von der Westseite her gesehen, besteht die Raumabfolge aus Garage, Windfang, Arbeitszimmer und Atelier. Aus dem Arbeitszimmer gelangt man über die Galerie ins Atelier.

Die Abfolge entspricht dem Äußeren des nur wenige prägnante Gestaltungsmerkmale aufweisenden Sichtziegelbaus mit seiner horizontal gesproßten Befensterung. Das Dachtragwerk besteht aus sichtbaren Pfetten, einer Sparrenlage mit oberseitiger Schalung und darüberliegender Dämm- und Dichtkonstruktion des Flachdachs.

Seit 1976 entstehen alle Kunstwerke Rupprecht Geigers in diesem klaren, nüchternen Gebäude.

1987/88 wurde an die Ostseite des Ateliers noch ein kleiner, unterkellerter Anbau in gleicher Bauweise angefügt.

Detlef Schreiber had been aware of Rupprecht Geiger, now a world-famous painter, since the late 1940s. He followed his work from then on, and was pleased that Geiger's reputation was rising. In 1960 he bought a large picture, became an early Geiger collector, and also a friend of the painter. This is how he came to build his studio.

At first, two adjacent homes were to be built on the plot in Muttenthalerstraße in Solln, but this came to nothing. A studio for the painter Rupprecht Geiger was built there instead.

The manageable ground plan for this workshop is built up on a square grid of 6 x 6 m. A 30 m long wall in exposed brick concludes the building on the east side. The studio, the largest room in the house, rises through two storeys from the basement floor to the attic. It is accessed via a gallery and stairs. Seen from the west the sequence of rooms consists of garage, porch, study and studio. The gallery leads from the study to the studio.

This sequence corresponds with the exterior of this exposed brick building with horizontal window bars, which has only a few succinct design characteristics. The roof structure consists of visible purlins, a run of rafters with shuttering above and the insulating, waterproof structure of the flat roof above that.

All Rupprecht Geiger's works since 1976 have been created in this lucid, restrained building.

A small extension with a cellar, constructed in the same way, was added to the east side of the studio in 1987/88.

Ansicht vom Garten, Eingang
View from the garden, entrance

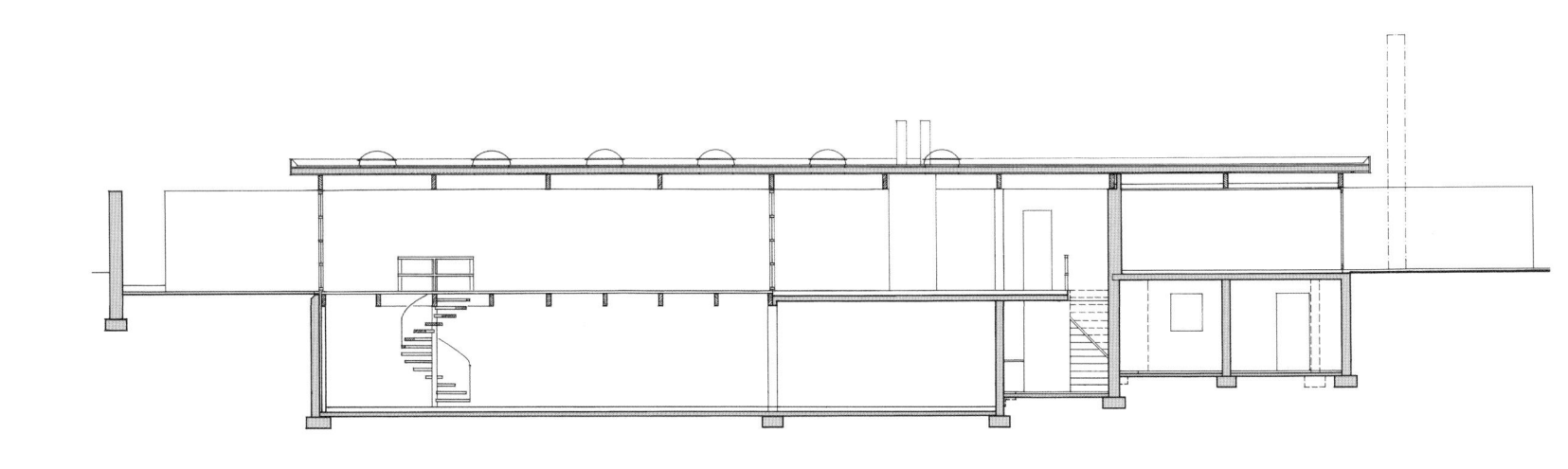

Oben: Schnitt
Unten: Ansicht vom Garten

Top: cross-section
Bottom: view from the garden

Außenfront Atelier

Exterior façade of the studio

Atelier innen

Interior of the studio

Blick von der Galerie in das Atelier

View of the studio from the gallery

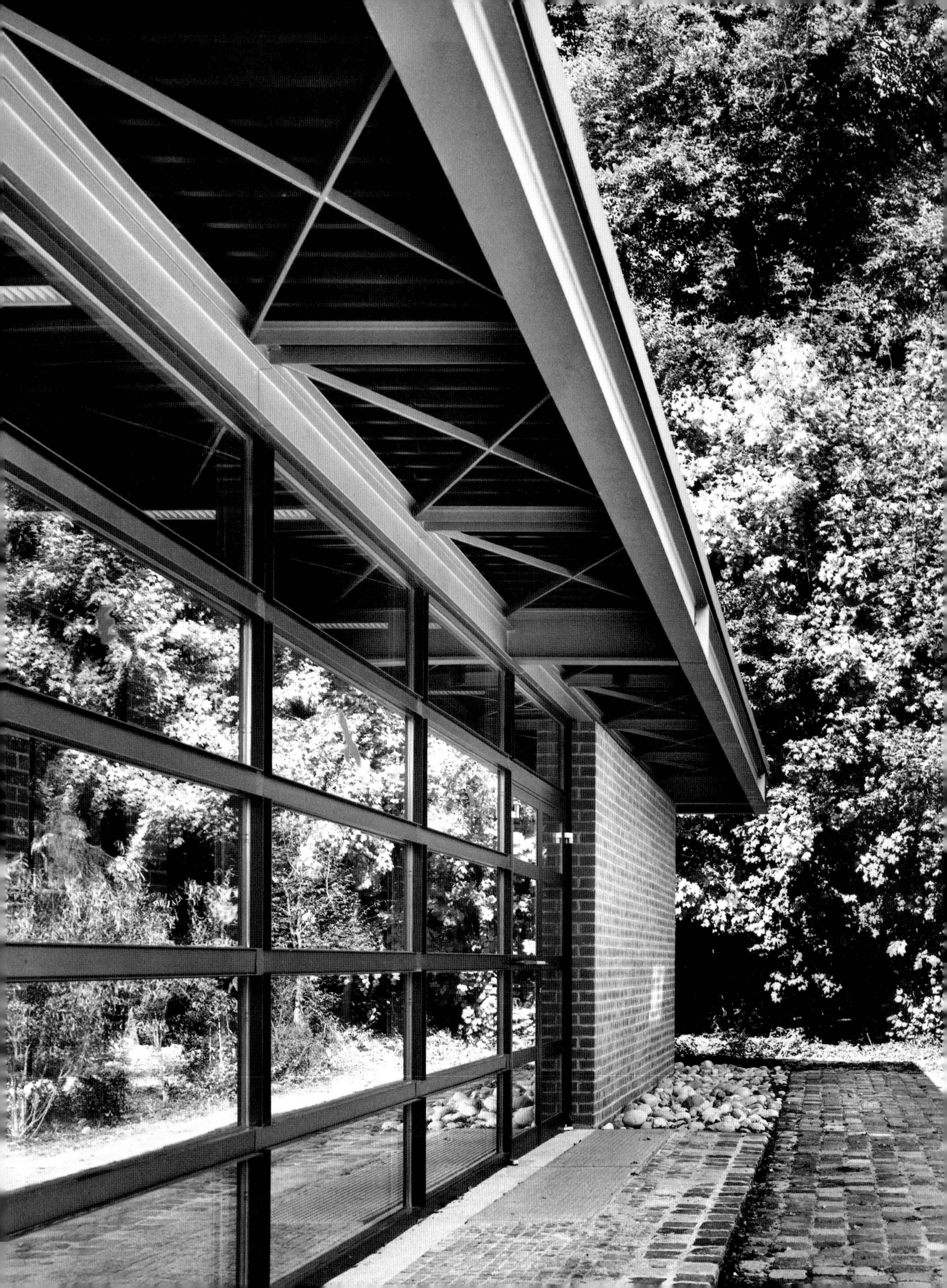

Laborbau des Landheims Schondorf, Schondorf am Ammersee, 1974–77
Bauherr: Stiftung Landheim Schondorf

Laboratory building for the Schondorf boarding school, Schondorf am Ammersee, 1974–77
Client: Landheim Schondorf Foundation

Dieser geradezu klassische Pavillonbau mit seiner aus Konstruktions- und Materialdisziplin erwachsenden Gestalt, gehört zu den Arbeiten Detlef Schreibers, die er selbst sehr schätzte, nicht zuletzt deshalb, weil sie so viel über seine Art zu denken und zu fühlen aussagen. Auf der Suche nach gültigem, in sich logisch gesetzmäßigem Ausdruck duldete er keine Halbheit, keine Kompromisse. Gerade bei seinen dem Umfang nach bescheideneren Bauwerken zeigt sich dieses Suchen nach Integrität des Gedankens und Tuns.

Baubeschreibung des Architekten

»Die Schul- und Internatsbauten des Landerziehungsheims Schondorf – aus unterschiedlichen Epochen formal verschieden geprägt – begegnen sich zwanglos, ohne Vergleiche herauszufordern, in einem herrlichen Park. Die Vielfalt der Bauformen ihrer jeweiligen Entstehungszeit (1904 baute Friedrich Thiersch, 1929 Robert Vorhölzer, und 1960 folgten Helmut von Werz und Johann Christoph Ottow) macht das Ensemble mitten im Grün besonders wertvoll. Dem Prinzip, eigenständige Einzelgebäude in den Landschaftsraum einzugliedern, folgten auch grundlegend Disposition und Entwurf des Laborpavillons. Die Dominanz der Vegetation und der großen Freiräume wurde durch bescheidene Höhenentwicklung gewahrt, aber auch durch ruhige, größtenteils durchsichtige Wandflächen des Gebäudes unterstützt. Die vielfältige Transparenz des Gebäudes und die mannigfachen Spiegelungen der umgebenen Bäume auf den Glaswänden bewirken fließende Übergänge von Artefakt und Natur.

Gestaltung

Die äußeren und inneren Erscheinungsformen des Bauwerks vereinigen sich aufgrund der Transparenz und der unverhüllten Konstruktion zu einer zusammenhängenden und übereinstimmenden Aussage. Die Gestaltungsprinzipien bauen auf der Logik von konstruktiven, funktionalen und wirtschaftlichen Erfordernissen auf.

Die Wahl des Konstruktions- und Ausbaurasters, der Abstimmung untereinander und mit den verschiedenen Konstruktionsgliedern, war von Überlegungen zur Raumfolge, zur Proportion, zum Profil und Detail bestimmt. Mit dem Verzicht auf Verkleidung und Dekoration wird das bauliche Gefüge aus Stahl, Glas und Ziegelstei-

This almost classical pavilion structure with its form derived from structural and material discipline is one of Detlef Schreiber's works that he particularly liked himself, not least because it shows so much about how he thought and felt about things. He would not tolerate any half-measures, any compromise, in his search for valid, logically coherent expression. This search for integrity of thought and deed shows particularly in his buildings that are modest in terms of their scale.

The architect's description of the building

»The school buildings and boarding houses for the Schondorf school – formally different as they were built at different periods – come together in a splendid park, relaxed because they do not invite any comparisons. The numerous building forms from various periods (Friedrich Thiersch built in 1904, Robert Vorhölzer in 1929, then Helmut von Werz and Johann Christoph Ottow followed in 1960) make this ensemble in a green setting particularly valuable. The disposition and design of the laboratory pavilion fundamentally follow the principle of integrating individual buildings into the surrounding landscape. The dominance of the vegetation and the large open spaces was maintained by restricting height, but also supported by the building's calm, largely transparent wall areas. The varied transparency of the building and the many reflections of the surrounding trees in the glass walls created fluid transitions between artefact and nature.

Design

The external and internal appearance of the building are drawn together by its transparency and unconcealed structural approach to make a coherent and unanimous statement. The design principles are built on the logic of structural, functional and financial demands.

The choice of dimensions for the primary and secondary grids, the way they matched and the various structural elements, was determined by considerations about spatial sequence, profile and detail. Omitting cladding and decoration makes the architectural

Links: Fassadenansicht zum Wald

Left page: façade elevation facing the wood

nen einsichtig und selbstverständlich. Diese objektivierte Gestaltung der Baustruktur ermöglicht einen räumlichen Rahmen, in dem noch Platz und Spielraum bleiben für individuelle Entfaltung.

Funktion

Der Laborbau enthält alle Lehr-, Übungs- sowie die Sammlungsräume für den naturwissenschaftlichen Unterricht (Chemie, Biologie, Physik) am Gymnasium. Wichtig war die variable Nutzungsmöglichkeit der unterschiedlichen Räume und die Schaffung von besonderen Übungs- und Experimentierplätzen für Lehrer und Kollegiaten im Leistungskurs.

Die umfängliche, zentral angeordnete Sammlungs- und Vorbereitungszone mit Bibliothek ist durch die Parallelanordnung sowohl von den beiden großen Lehrsälen als auch vom dreifach teilbaren Übungsraum aus günstig erreichbar. Der umgebende Flurbereich erschließt alle Räume zusätzlich von außen und gewährt über Ausstellungsfenster Einblicke und Durchblicke in die Sammlungs- und Vorbereitungszone. Dort wurden auch die besonderen Experimentierarbeitsplätze und Versuchsanordnungen mit Sichtbeziehung nach außen eingerichtet. Die zweckmäßige, funktionale Zuordnung der einzelnen Raumgruppen legte einen großen, quadratischen Grundriß nahe, der zwar den Vorteil der Ebenerdigkeit und einer kompakten, unauffälligen Zusammenfassung des großen Raumvolumens brachte, aber großflächige Innenzonen zur Folge hatte. Über durchlaufende Shed-Fenster wird dieser Innenbereich einwandfrei belichtet und besonnt. Die Glasbänder ermöglichen auch Sicht in die Baumkronen der angrenzenden Waldkulisse, eine besondere Verbindung zur umgebenden Natur.

Konstruktion und Material

Die Baugrundverhältnisse forderten eine leichte, elastische und setzungsunempfindliche Konstruktion. Deshalb bot sich ein Stahlskelettbau mit Betonunterkellerung an. […]

Die tragenden Konstruktionselemente (Stützen und Träger) bestehen aus dunkelgrau gestrichenen, mit Kopfplattenstößen sichtbar geschraubt verbundenen Normstahlprofilen. Innen- und Außenwände, ebenso die Brüstungen sind aus unverputzten Ziegelsteinen gemauert. Die Dachdecke besteht aus einer unverkleideten Trapezblechschale mit Wärmedämmung, Feuchtigkeitssperre und Kiesschüttung. Die Fußböden der Labors sind mit PVC-Bahnen und in den Fluren mit Granitplatten belegt, die Zugänge zum Gebäude mit Granitsteinen gepflastert. Die Innentüren haben Oberflächen aus Naturholz (Teak), die Laboreinbauten aus hellem Kunststoff. Die Außentüren, die Fenster und die festverglasten Glaswände bestehen aus thermisch getrennten Aluminiumprofilen mit wärmedämmenden Glasscheiben. Auf die Kontrolle der einfallenden Sonnenstrahlung wurde durch bauliche Verschattungseinrichtungen großen Wert gelegt.«

structure of steel, glass and brick cogent and natural. This objectified design of the building structure makes a spatial frame possible that still leaves space and scope to develop individually.

Function

The laboratory building contains all the teaching, practical and also collection rooms for science teaching (chemistry, biology, physics) at the school. It was important that the different rooms could be put to various uses, and to create special practical and experiment areas for teachers and advanced students.

The extensive, central collection and preparation area with library is easily accessible through a parallel arrangement both via the two large teaching rooms and also via the practice room, which can be divided into three. The corridor area also provides additional access to all rooms from the outside and provides glimpses into and views through the collection and preparation area through exhibition windows. In the preparation area the special workstations for experiments and research projects were arranged with views outside the building. The practical, functional arrangement of the individual groups of rooms suggested a large, square ground plan. This did bring with it the advantage of being at ground level and also lent the large spatial volume a compact, unassuming coherence, but led to extensive internal zones. This interior area is perfectly lit and insulated by continuous shed windows. The glass bands also give a view of the treetops in the adjacent woodland scenery, a special connection with the nature around the building.

Structure

The subsoil conditions demanded a light, elastic structure that was not susceptible to subsidence. For this reason the best solution seemed to be a steel skeleton building with concrete cellar. […]

The load-bearing structural elements (columns and beams) are normal steel sections painted dark grey, connected with visibly screwed head plate joints. The interior and exterior walls, and also the parapets are built of unrendered brick. The roof covering is an unclad trapezium sheet shell with heat insulation, waterproofing and gravel filling. The laboratory floors are covered with PVC strips, with granite slabs in the corridors, and the entrances to the building with granite stones. The interior doors have natural wood surfaces (teak), the lab fittings are in light-coloured plastic. The outer doors, the windows and the glass walls with fixed glazing are made up of thermally separated aluminium bares with heat-insulating glass panes. Considerable attention was paid to controlling insulation by means of structural shading.«

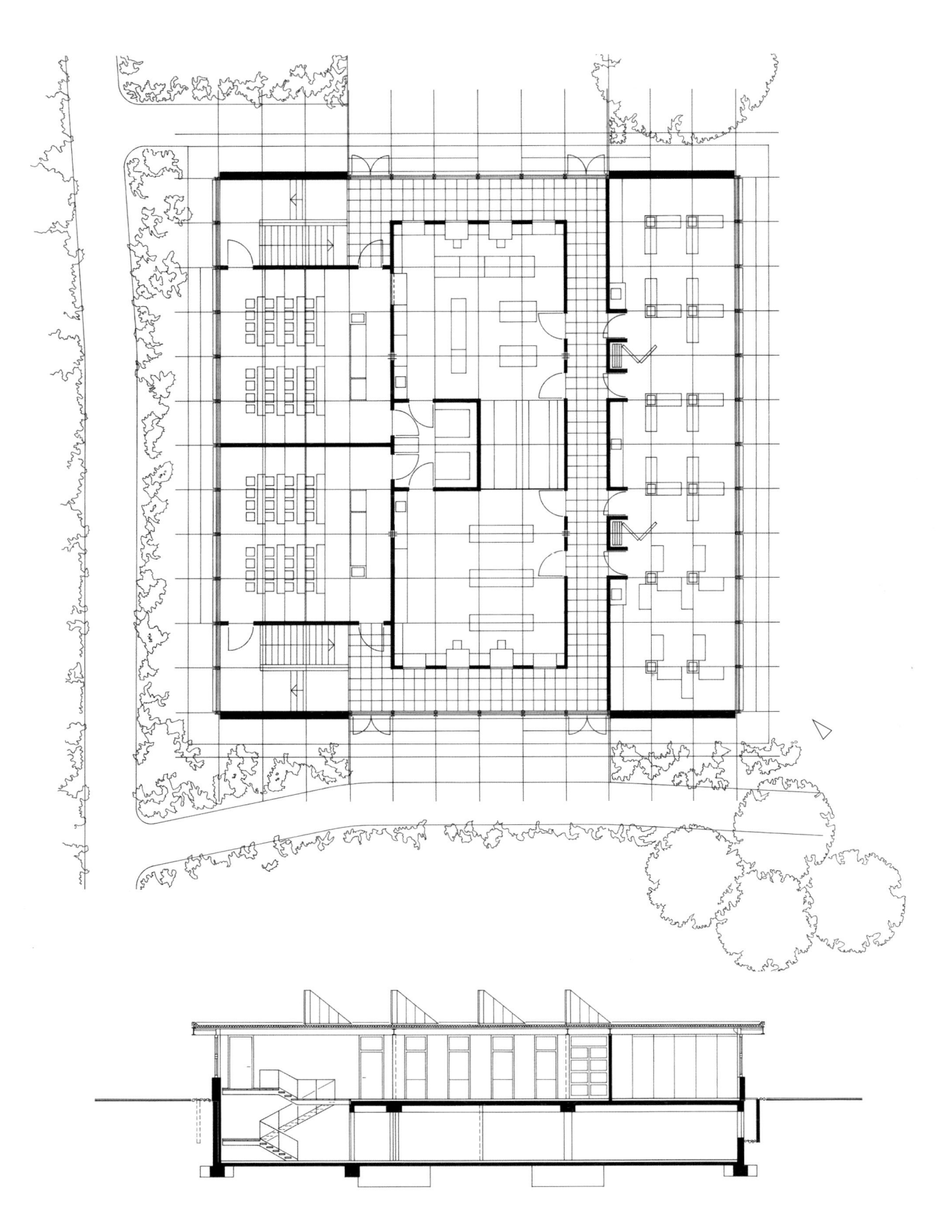

Oben: Grundriß Erdgeschoß
Unten: Schnitt

Top: floor plan, ground floor
Bottom: cross-section

Lehrsaal

Lecture room

Eingangsbereich

Entrance area

FOLGENDE DOPPELSEITEN:
S. 74: Gang zwischen Sammlung und Übungsraum
S. 75: Übungsraum
S. 76–77: Fassade vorm Wald

NEXT DOUBLE PAGES:
P. 74: Corridor between the collection and
the practical room
P. 75: Practical room
P. 76–77: Façade facing the wood

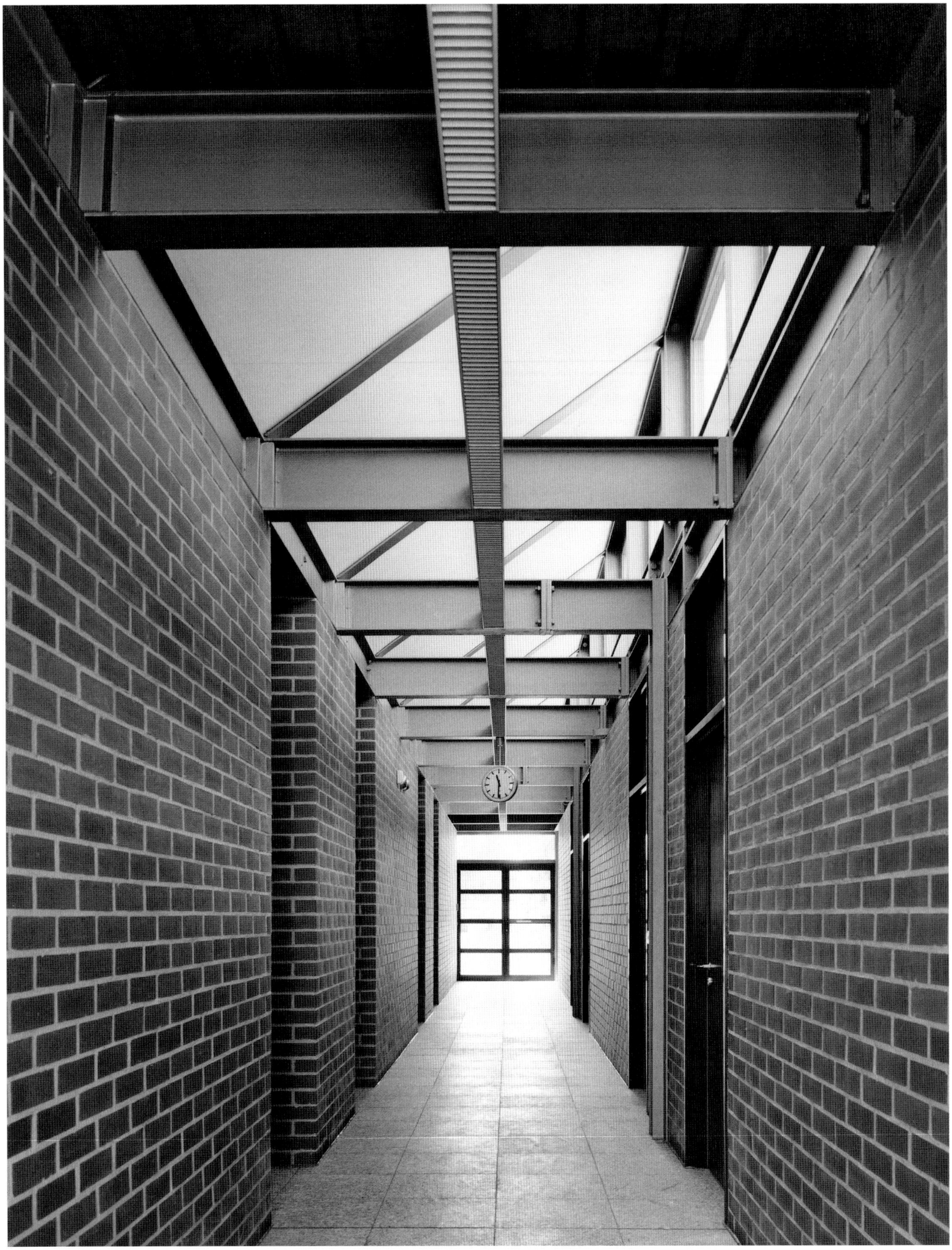

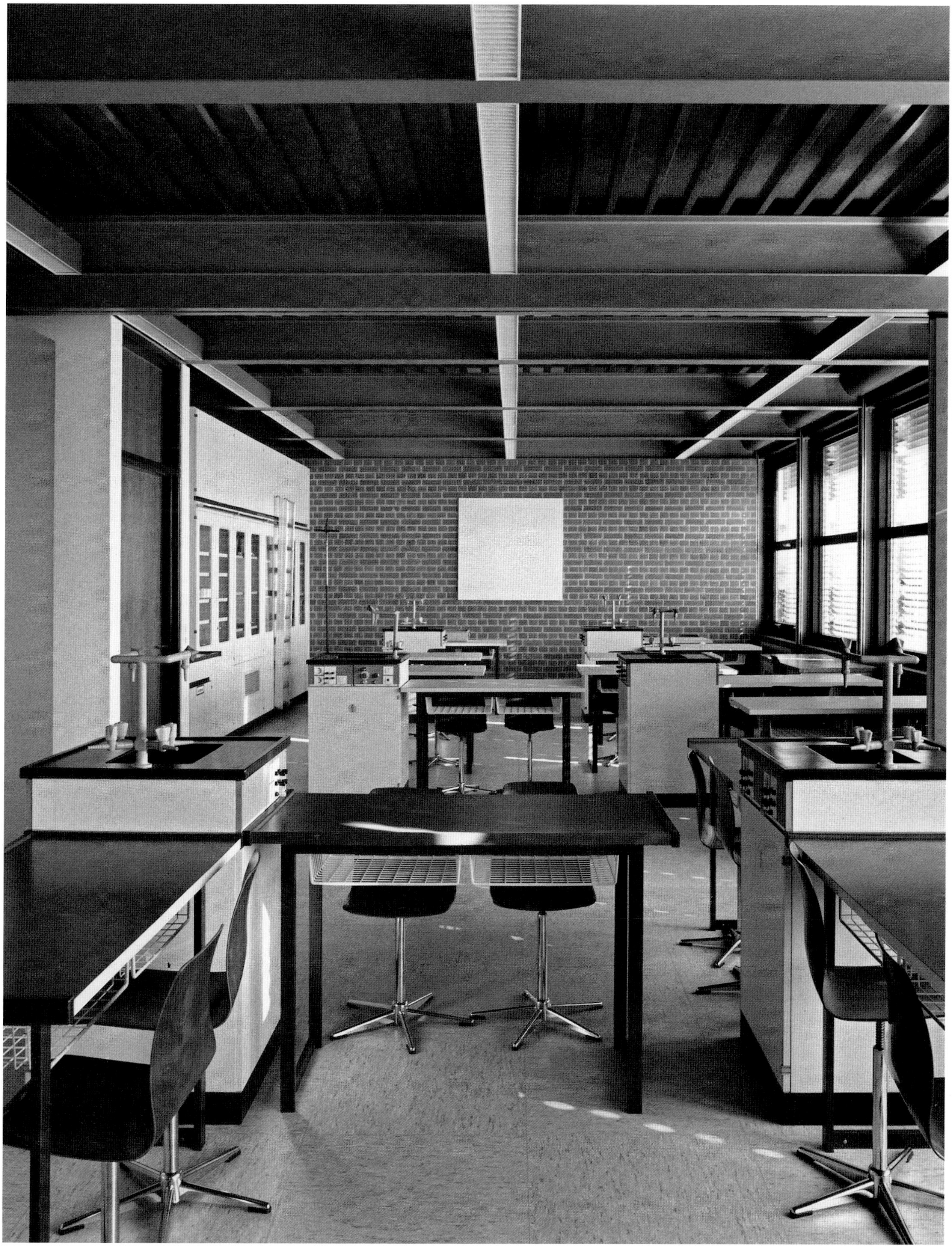

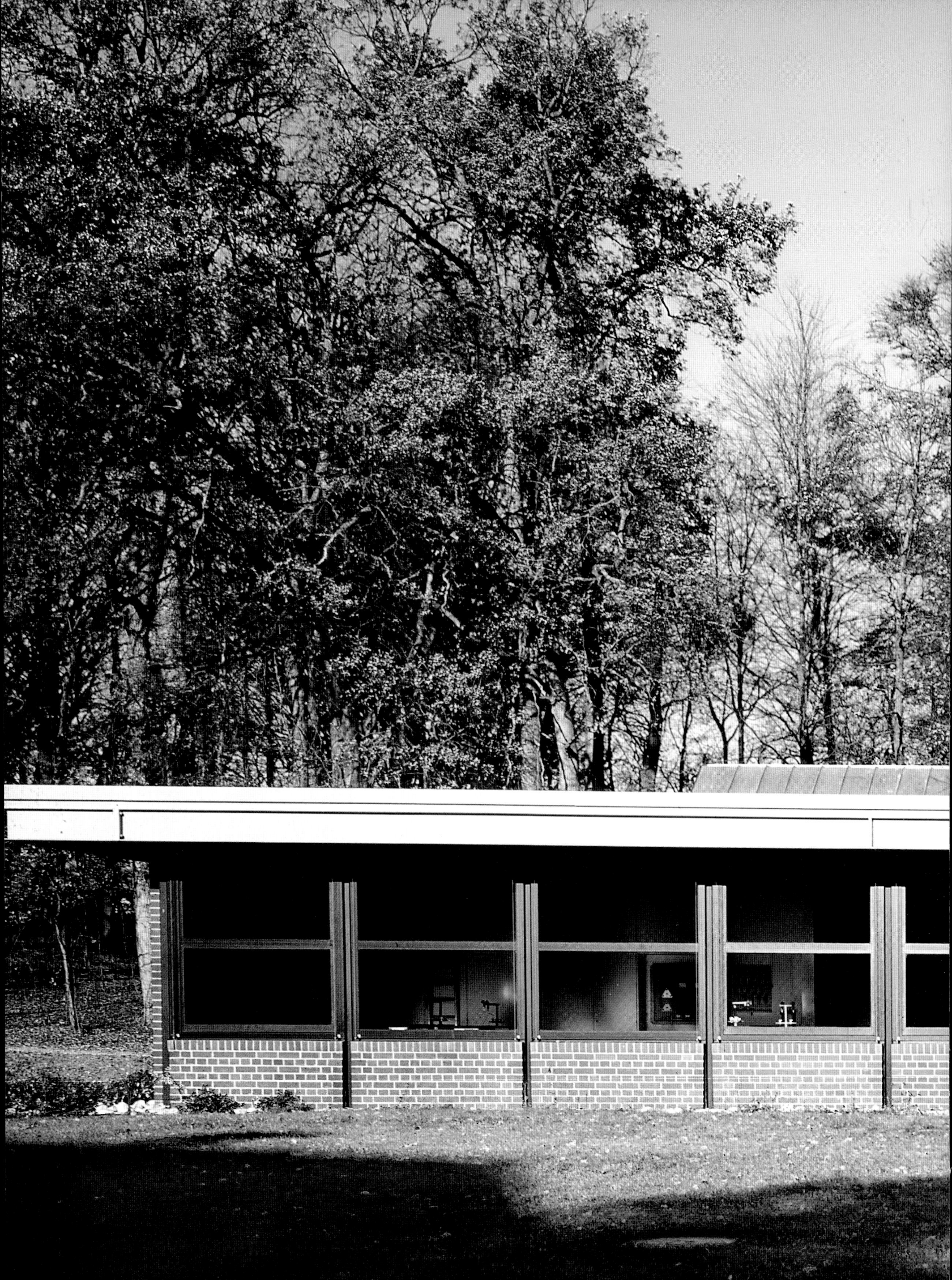

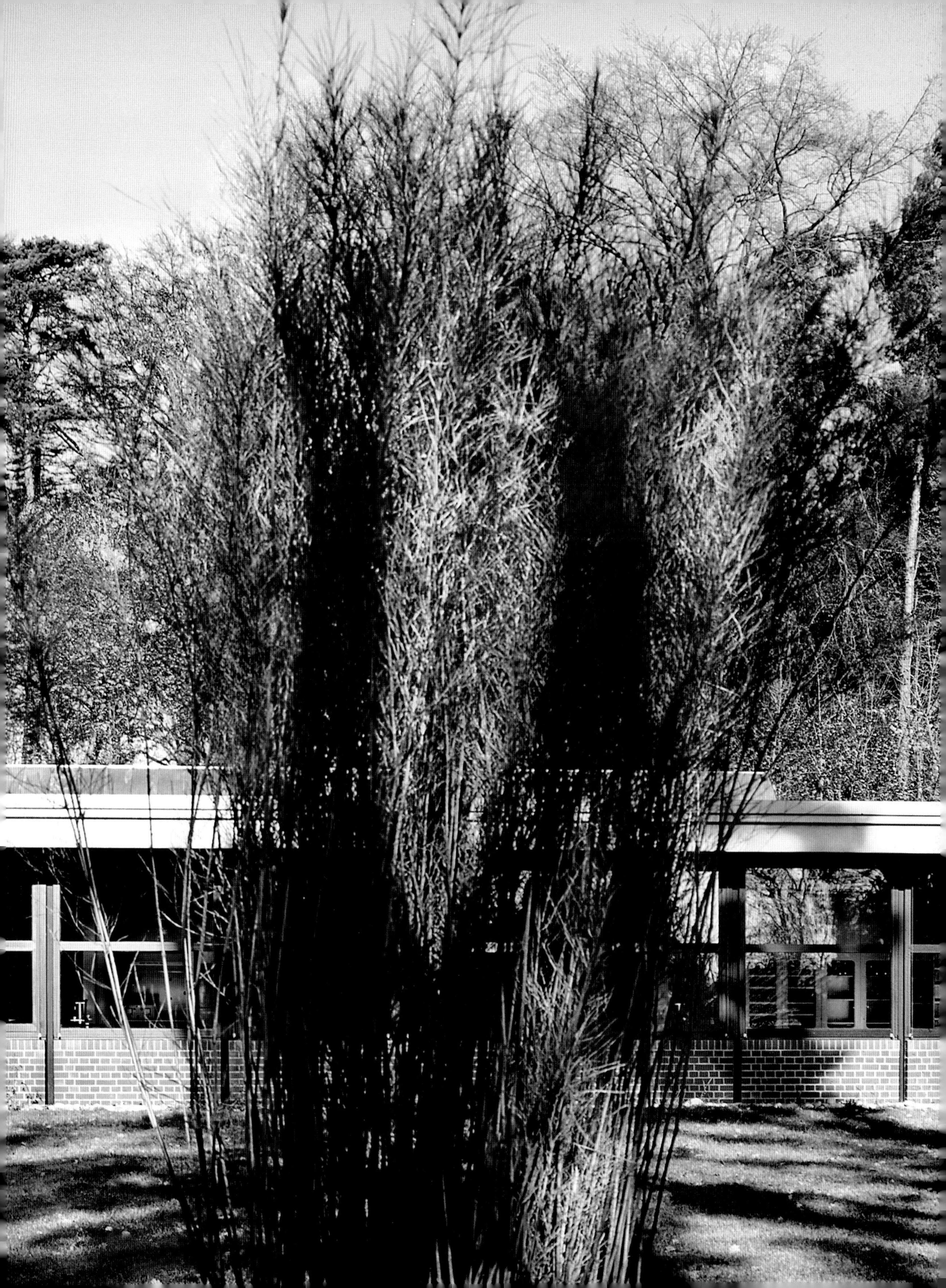

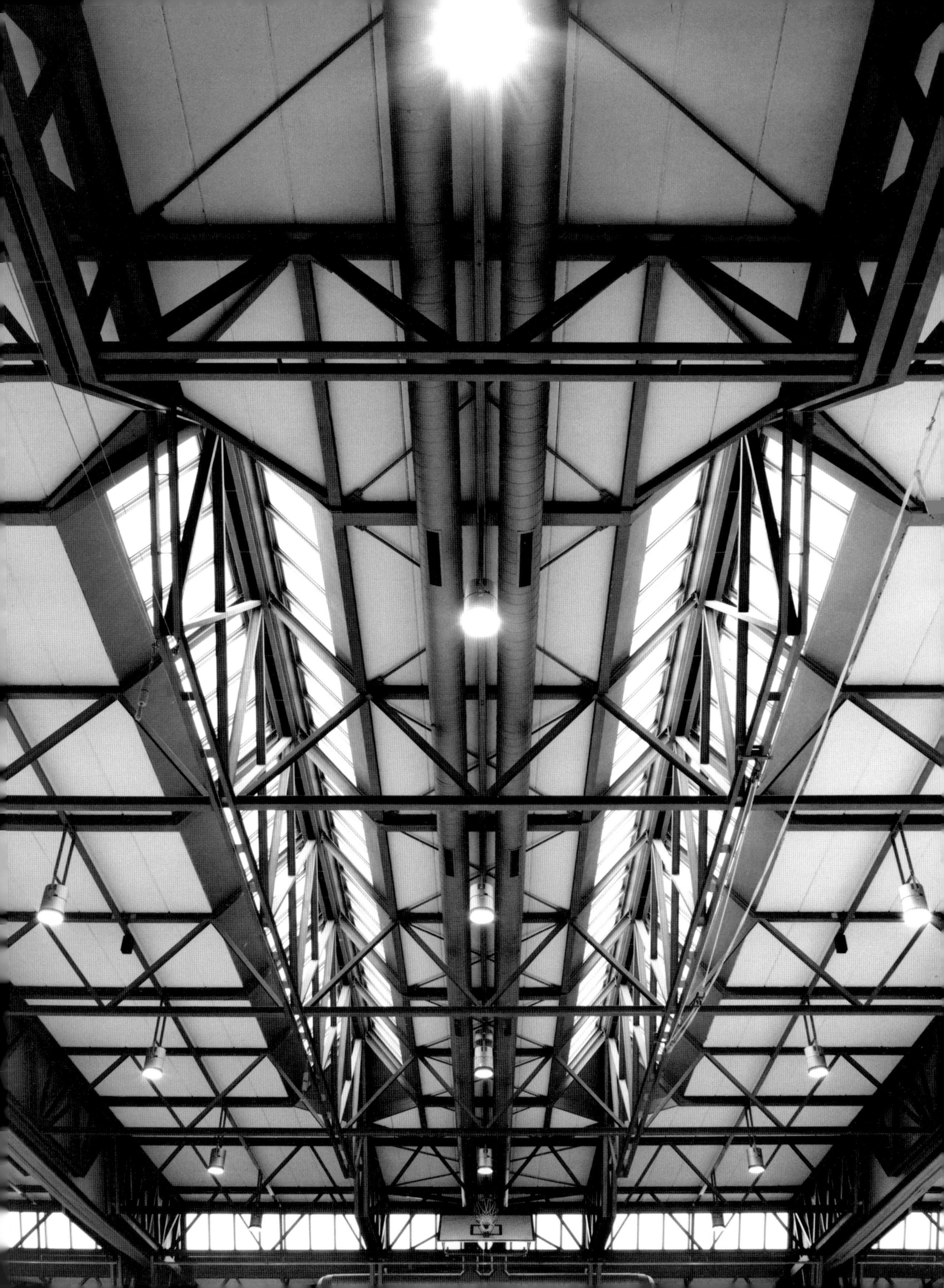

Mehrzweckhalle der Grund- und Hauptschule,
Herrsching am Ammersee, 1977–82

Bauherr: Gemeinde Herrsching

Multi-purpose hall for the primary and secondary school,
Herrsching am Ammersee, 1977–82

Client: Herrsching local authority

Daß eine von Detlef Schreiber erdachte und gebaute Stahlhalle mit weitspannendem Dachtragwerk logisch, erfindungsreich und ästhetisch vorzüglich ausfällt, ist, wenn man sein Schaffen kennt, nicht verwunderlich. Wie er aber eine Dreifachturn- und Festhalle auf einem eigentlich nicht ausreichend großen Grundstück plaziert, das den Rahmen der Umgebung sprengende, ausgedehnte Gebäude mit aller Kunst – durch Versenken um die halbe Höhe, Modellieren der Dachfläche, durch Material, Farbe und maßstäbliche Plastizität – ins Gelände am Hang einfügt und den ganzen Umgriff durch ein Baukunstwerk aufwertet, läßt Bewunderung aufkommen.

Das Urteil mag subjektiv klingen, aber diese so viel über die maßvolle Art und Kreativität des Architekten verratende Halle gehört zu seinen besten Arbeiten. Zudem ist sie eines der hervorragenden Stahlbaubeispiele der Erbauungszeit. Die strenge Funktionalität von Sportbauten wurde mit dieser Architektur zum innen- und außenräumlichen Erlebnis.

Baubeschreibung des Architekten

»Das Schulgrundstück zwischen Martinsweg und Nikolausstraße ließ infolge seiner unregelmäßigen Begrenzung und seiner verhältnismäßig kleinen Fläche nur geringen Spielraum für die Situierung des großen Bauvolumens einer Dreifachturnhalle. Zudem mußte in der Hanglage und mit Rücksicht auf die umgebende Wohnbebauung eine sorgfältige städtebauliche Einfügung gewährleistet sein.

Die beträchtliche Höhe des Bauwerks wurde dadurch optisch verringert, daß die Halle zur Hälfte in die Erde versenkt wurde und die auf dem Niveau des Hallenbodens liegenden Nebenräume (Garderoben, Waschräume, Geräteräume), von oben begrünt, unter Terrain liegen und so in der Grundstücksfläche verschwinden. Das große Hallendach paßt sich in seiner durch die Konstruktion vorgezeichneten, abgestuften Ausformung dem natürlichen Geländeverlauf an und zeigt in der Draufsicht, die vom Hang her eingesehen werden kann, eine stark gegliederte Dachlandschaft, welche sich in die Vielfalt der umgebenden Erscheinungsformen harmonisch einfügt.

Die große Halle von 27 × 45 Metern läßt sich in drei kleinere Halleneinheiten von 27 × 15 Metern unterteilen. Jedem Hallenteil ist eine Geräteraumeinheit eine Garderoben- und Waschraumeinheit mit Stiefelgang und Turnschuhgang zugeordnet. Zwischen der Halle und den Nebenräumen ist eine Teleskoptribüne angeordnet, welche zwi-

If one knows his work, it is not surprising that a steel hall with long-span roof support structure devised and built by Detlef Schreiber should turn out to be excellent in terms of logic, inventiveness and aesthetics. But it is more than admirable that he was able to place a triple gym and assembly hall on a plot that is actually not large enough, fitting the extensive building that bursts out of the framework surrounding it into the sloping site with every possible artifice – by submerging it to half its height, modelling the roof area, through material, colour and plasticity of scale – and in doing this adds value to the whole intervention by creating a work of architectural art.

This judgement may sound subjective, but this hall, which reveals so much about the architect's moderation and creativity, is one of his best pieces of work. All in all it is one of the outstanding steel buildings of its period. This architecture made the austere functionality of buildings intended for sport into an experience both inside and out.

The architect's description of the building

»Because of its irregular boundaries and relatively small area, the school plot between Martinsweg and Nikolausstraße left very little scope for placing the large building volume of a triple gym. And as well as this, it was essential to guarantee careful integration into the urban landscape because of the sloping situation, and because the surrounding housing had to be taken into consideration.

The considerable height of the building was reduced visually by placing half the hall underground. Also, the ancillary rooms at hall floor level (cloakrooms, washrooms, equipment stores) are planted on top and below the surface, and thus disappear within the area of the plot. The large roof of the hall is stepped as a result of the construction, and so fits in with the natural lie of the land. Seen from above, which is possible from the slope, it displays a strongly articulated roof-scape, blending harmoniously with the variety of phenomena around it.

The large hall measures 27 × 45 m, and can be divided into three smaller hall units of 27 × 15 m. Each section of the hall has an equip-

Links: Blick in die Dachkonstruktion

Left page: view of the roof structure

schen dem Niveau des Hallenbodens und jenem der Besuchergalerie im ausgefahrenen Zustand eine direkte Verbindung herstellt. Auf der Galerie sind die Hallenwarträume, eine Theke mit Teeküche, die Garderoben und die Besucher-WCs untergebracht. Der Zugang für Zuschauer erfolgt ebenerdig von der Nikolausstraße, während eine direkte Verbindung zwischen der Pausenhalle der Schule und dem Stiefelgang über eine interne Treppe den kurzen und witterungsunabhängigen Weg sicherstellt. Eine weitere Treppe verbindet den Eingang im Erdgeschoß für die außerschulische Nutzung durch die örtlichen Vereine. Auch von den Freisportanlagen – Allwetterplatz (28 x 44 Meter) mit Hoch- und Weitsprunggruben – sind die Garderoben und Waschräume, der Konditionsraum und der Außengeräteraum über gesonderte Treppen bzw. Rampen direkt zugänglich.

Das Untergeschoß der Halle ist eine Stahlbetonkonstruktion. Die Konstruktion des Erdgeschosses sowie des weitgespannten Daches besteht aus Stahlträgern. Die tragenden Stahlstützen sind in der Stahlbetonkonstruktion des Untergeschosses eingespannt und führen neben der Lastabtragung auch die Windkräfte ab, welche aus den Windverbänden im räumlichen Dachtragwerk eingeleitet werden. Das Dachtragwerk besteht aus sich überkreuzenden Stahlfachwerkbindern, welche ein räumliches Tragwerk bilden, das einerseits auf den druckbeanspruchten Stahlstützen ruht und andererseits von den über Kragträgern abgespannten Zugstäben stabilisiert wird. Die nichttragenden Außenwände sind im geschlossenen Bereich aus Sichtmauerwerk, die geöffneten Bereiche sind als thermisch getrennte Aluminium-Glaswände konstruiert. Die Hallendecke besteht aus modular gegliederten Gasbetonplatten mit unverkleideten Oberflächen.

In der Halle wurden alle geschlossenen Wandteile mit lärchenfurnierten Holzpaneelen (Industriesperrholz) verkleidet. Im Spielbereich sind die Paneele elastisch gelagert und decken überall die eingebrachten Schallschluckplatten ab. Der gerichteten natürlichen Lichtführung aus Seiten- und Oberlicht entspricht auch die künstliche Beleuchtung mittels gleichmäßig verteilter Tiefstrahler.

Der Sporthallenboden ist flächenelastisch aufgebaut (Schwingboden), hat PVC-Belag und integriert in seiner Konstruktionshöhe die Fußboden-Hohlraumheizung. Die Halle und die Nebenräume haben Fußbodenheizung und eine mit Wärmerückgewinnung versehene Lüftungsanlage. In den Nebenräumen und Fluren liegen ebenfalls PVC-Bahnen, die Waschräume sind gefliest, die Besuchergalerie hat einen Keramikbodenbelag. Die abgehängten Decken im Untergeschoß bestehen aus Holzbrettern. Zur Ausstattung der Halle gehören neben den Sportgeräten eine elektromechanisch betriebene Teleskopbühne, eine Spielzeituhr und eine Lautsprecheranlage. Der Hauptregieraum ist mit den beiden Nebenregieräumen durch Leitungen gekoppelt, so daß jede Halleneinheit über eine eigene Regiezentrale verfügt.

Die räumliche Atmosphäre der Halle ist geprägt durch die vielfältige Lichtführung, durch die mit Holzeinbauten gedämpfte Akustik, durch die Farb- und Materialwerte von Boden und Wandverkleidungen, vor allem aber durch die lichtdurchflutete, silbergrau gestrichene Stahlfachwerkkonstruktion des bestimmenden Dachs, die in ihrer Offenheit und filigranen Leichtigkeit einen fließenden Übergang von innen nach außen vermittelt.«

ment store on one side and on the opposite side cloakroom and washing facilities with access for outdoor footwear or gym shoe wearers. Between the hall and the ancillary rooms is a telescopic stand, which when extended creates a direct link between the hall floor level and that of the visitors' gallery. The gallery contains the hall care-taker's rooms, a counter with small kitchen, the cloakrooms and visitors' toilets. Spectator access is at ground level from Nikolausstraße, while a direct link between the school's break hall and the outdoor footwear corridor provides a short route independent of the weather via an internal staircase. Another staircase links the ground floor entrance with both the outdoor footwear corridor and with the gym shoe corridor for non-school use by local clubs. There is also direct access via separate stairs or ramps to the cloakrooms and washrooms, the fitness room and the outside equipment room from the open air sports facilities – all-weather pitch (28 x 44 m) with high- and long-jump pits.

The basement floor of the hall is a reinforced concrete structure. Steel beams form the basis of the ground floor structure, and that of the long-span roof. The load-bearing steel columns are fixed into the reinforced concrete structure of the basement floor, and absorb wind loads from the wind bracing in the stereometric roof structure, as well as structural loads. The roof support structure consists of crossing lattice steel trusses forming a stereometric support structure, resting on the one hand on the pressure-loaded steel columns, and is also stabilized by the tension bars anchored above the cantilever beams. The non-load-bearing exterior walls are in exposed masonry in the closed area, and the open areas are constructed as thermally separated aluminium glass walls. The hall ceiling consists of gas concrete slabs in modular articulation, and their surfaces remain unclad.

In the hall, all the closed wall sections were clad with larch-veneered timber panels (industrial plywood). In the play area the wooden panels are elastically supported and mask the sound-absorbing panels everywhere. The directed natural lighting from side- and skylights also complements the artificial lighting from evenly distributed narrow-angled spots.

The sports hall floor is sprung, has a PVC covering and the floor cavity heating is built into it. The hall and ancillary rooms have under-floor heating and a ventilation plant with heat recovery. The ancillary rooms and corridors also have PVC strip floor coverings, the washrooms are tiled, the visitors' gallery has a ceramic floor covering. The suspended ceilings in the basement consist of timber planks.

The hall's furnishing includes, as well as the sports equipment, an electro-mechanically driven telescope stage, a time clock and a loudspeaker system. The main control room is wired through to the two ancillary control rooms, so that each hall unit has its own control centre.

The spatial atmosphere of the hall is defined by the varied lighting, the acoustics modulated by timber fittings, by the colour and material values of floor and wall claddings, but above all by the light-flooded, silver-grey painted steel framework structure of the dominating roof, whose openness and filigree lightness provides a fluent transition from inside to outside.«

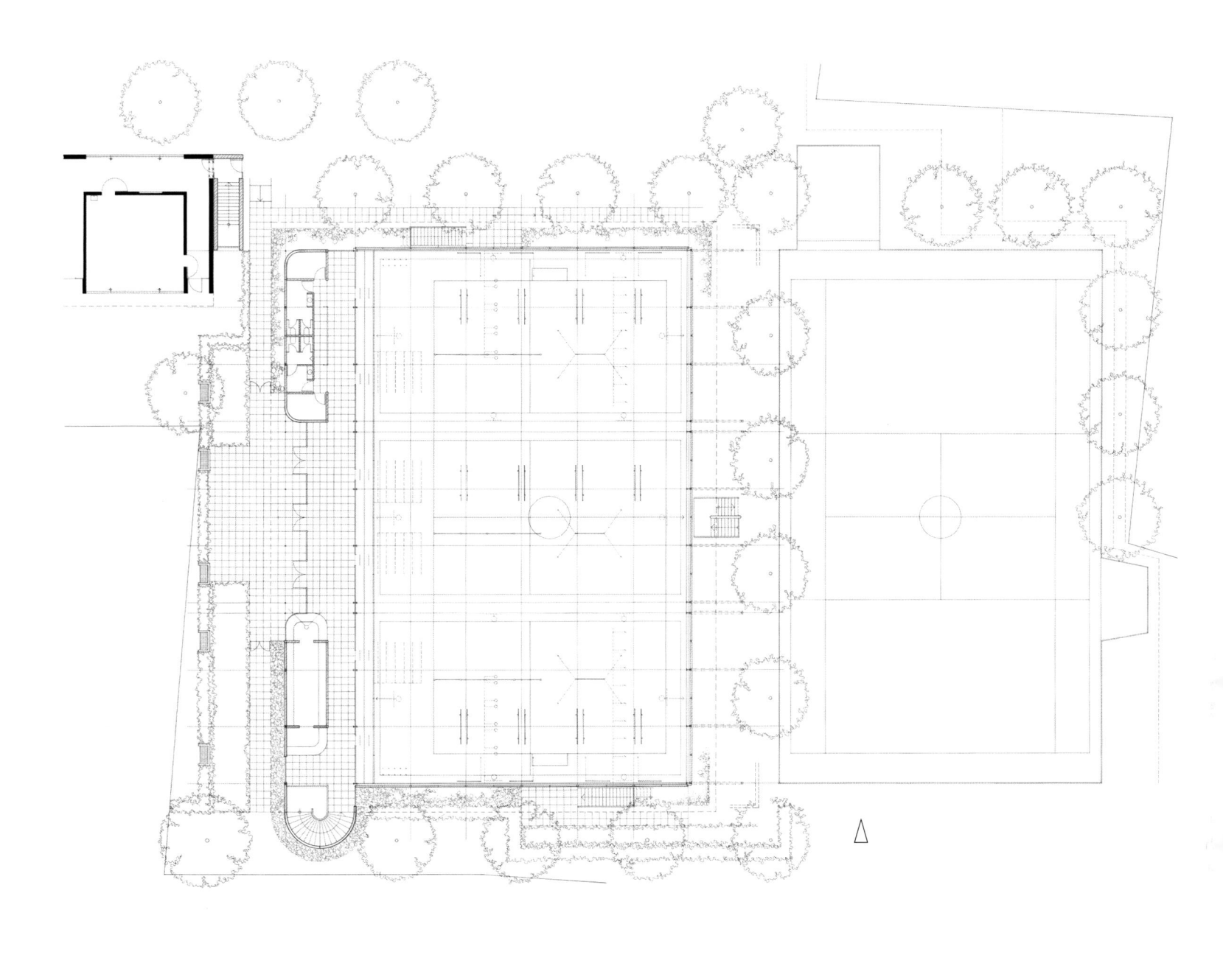

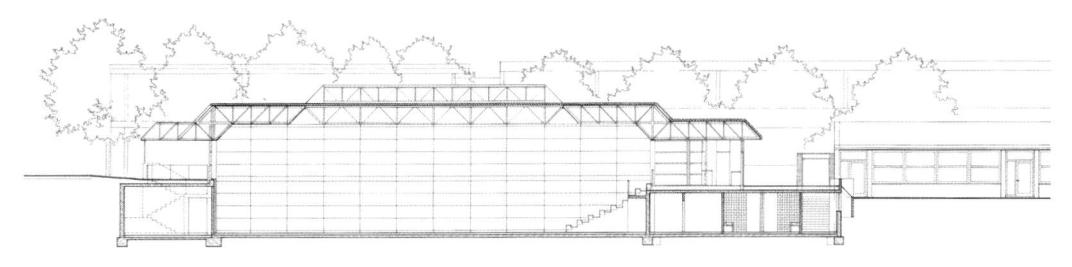

Oben: Grundriß Erdgeschoß
Unten: Schnitt

Top: floor plan, ground floor
Bottom: cross-section

FOLGENDE DOPPELSEITE:
Halleninnenraum mit Zuschauertribüne

NEXT DOUBLE PAGE:
Interior of the hall with spectator terrace

81

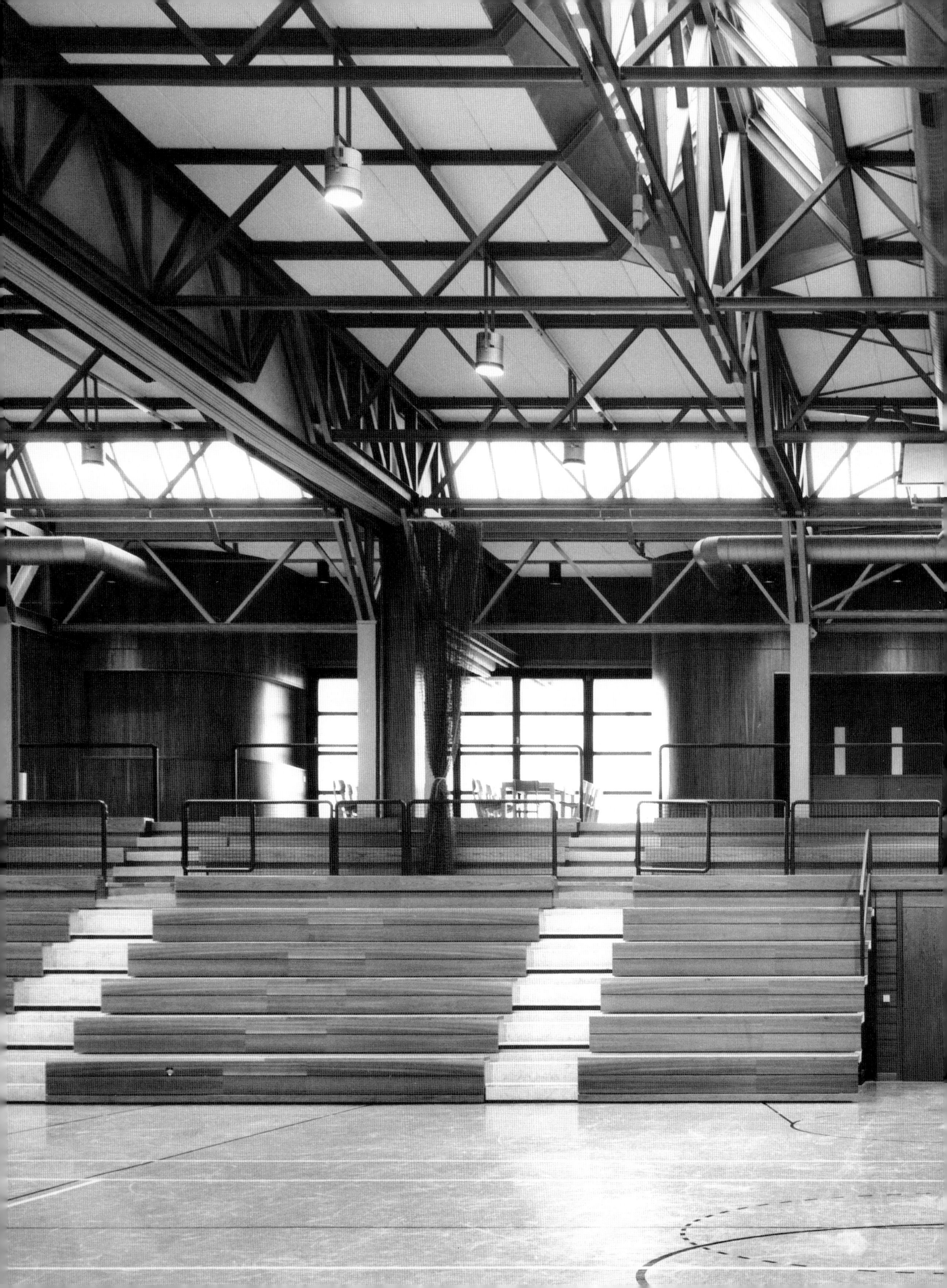

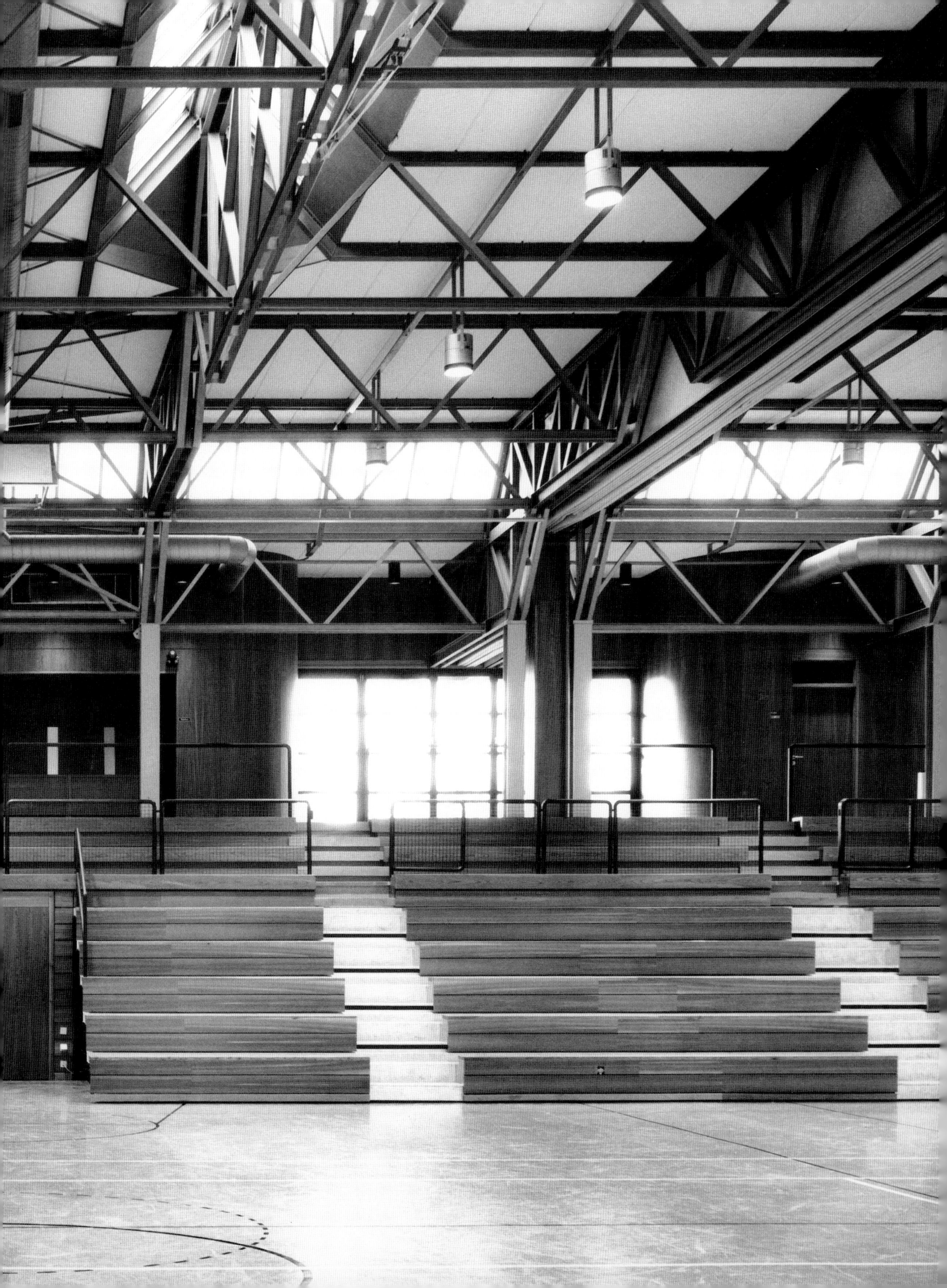

Eingang an der Nikolausstraße

Entrance from Nikolausstrasse

Hallenseite zum Hartplatz mit auskragenden Trägern

Side of the hall facing the hard pitch with projecting girders

FOLGENDE DOPPELSEITE:
Nachtaufnahme, Seite mit auskragenden Trägern

NEXT DOUBLE PAGE:
View at night, side of the hall with projecting girders

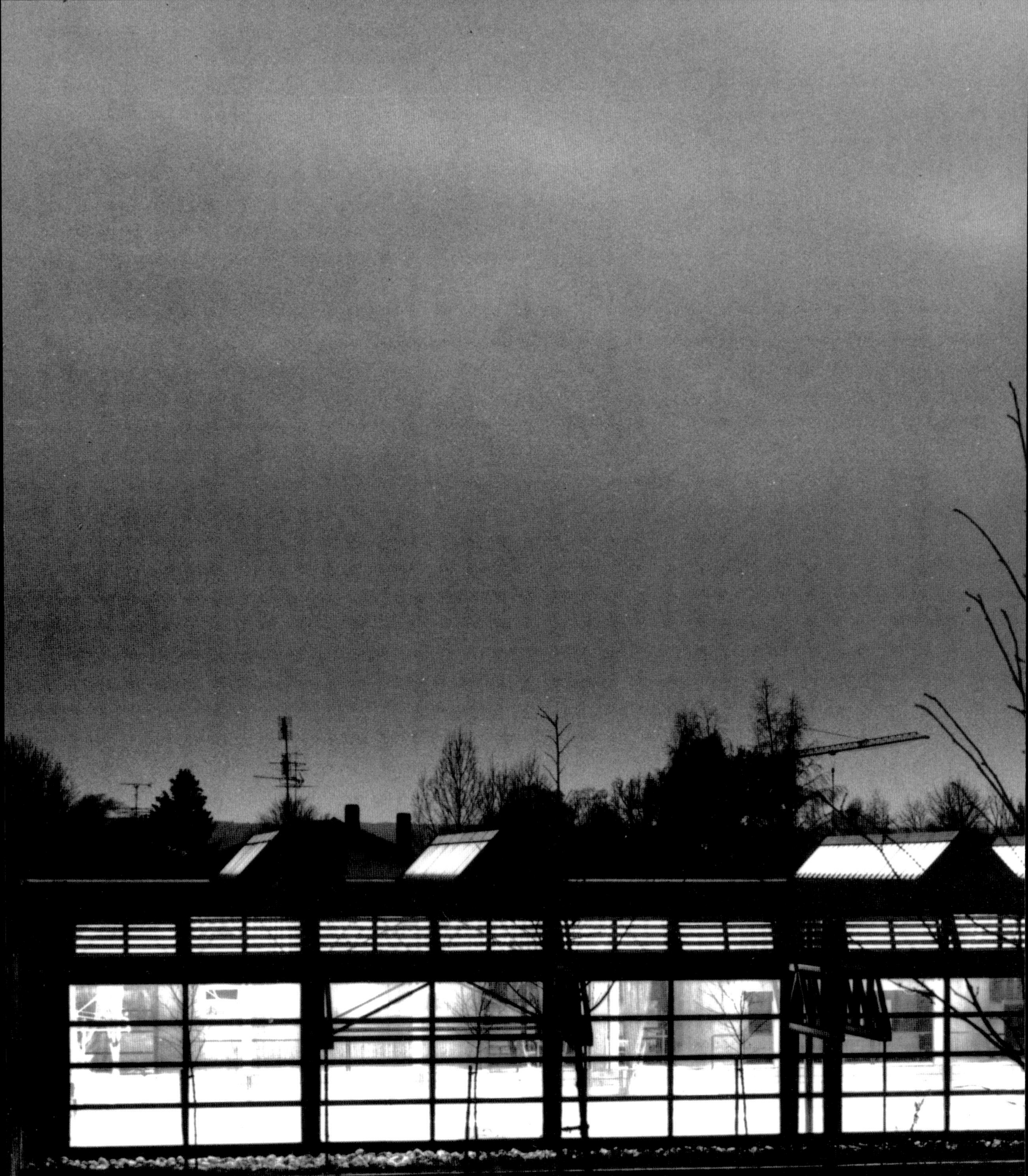

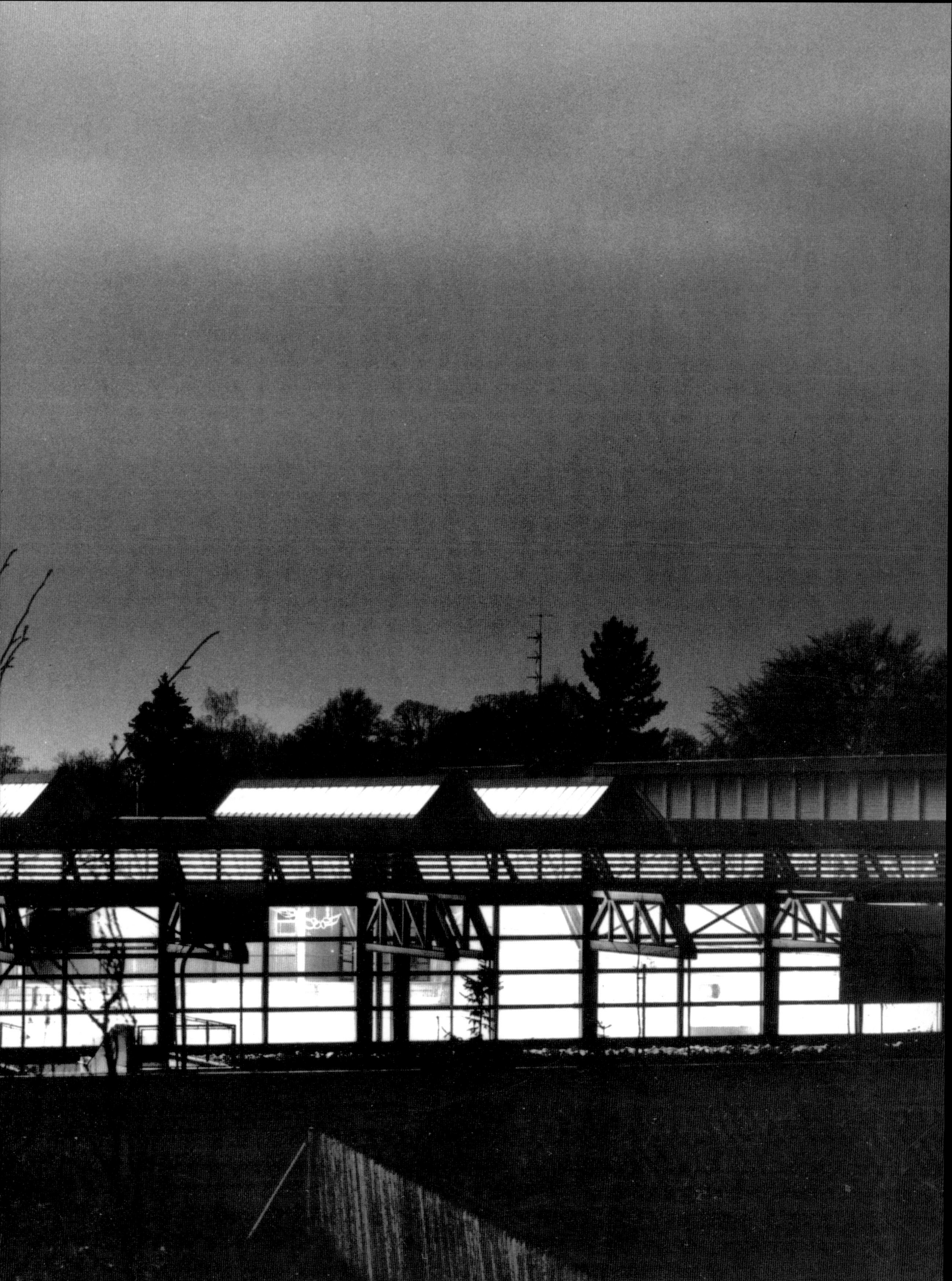

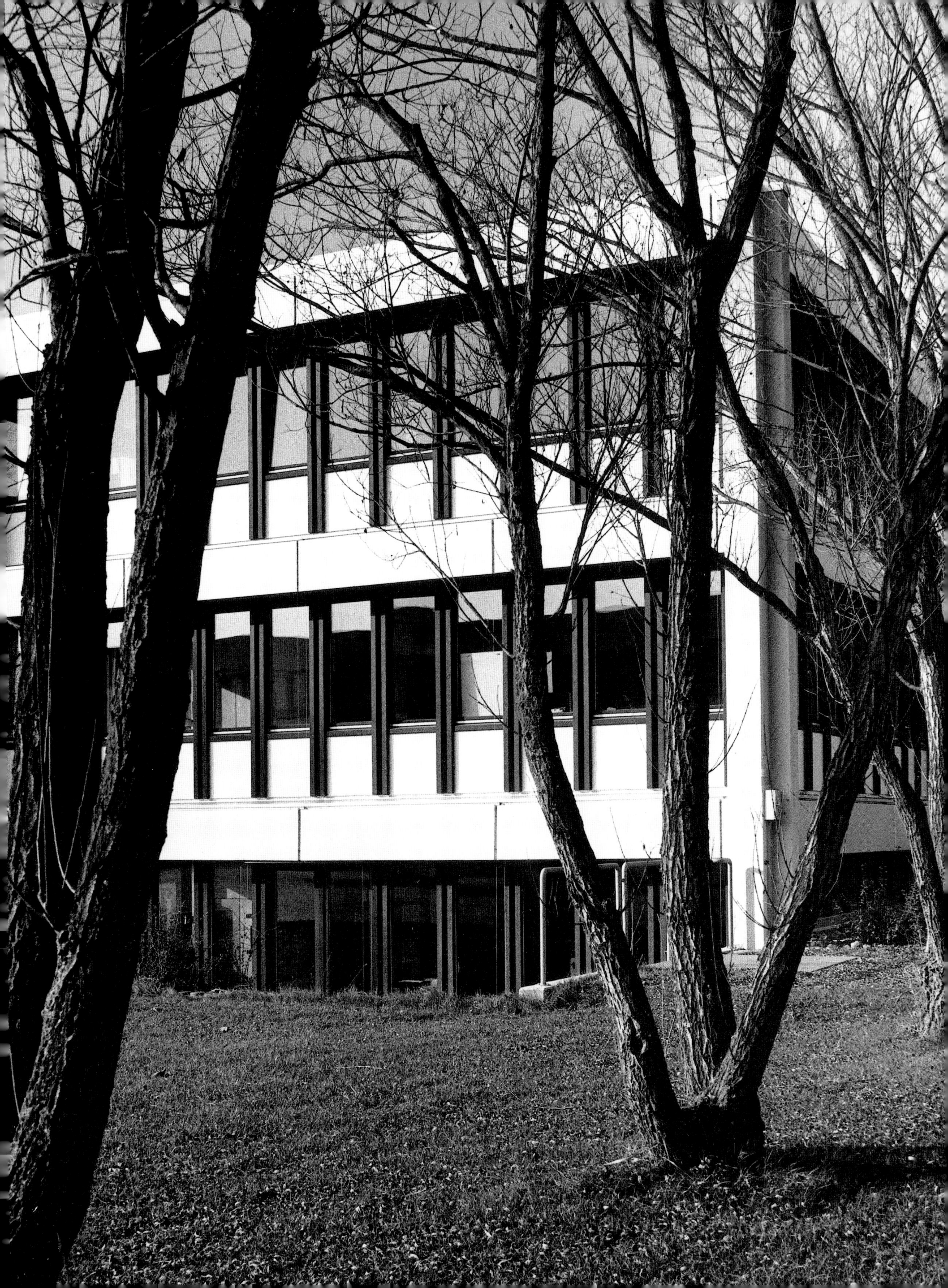

Büro- und Laborgebäude für die Gesellschaft für Anlagen- und Reaktorsicherheit

Bauherr: Gesellschaft für Anlagen- und Reaktorsicherheit mbH

Office and laboratory buildings for the Gesellschaft für Anlagen- und Reaktorsicherheit (Reactor Safety Company)

Client: Gesellschaft für Anlagen- und Reaktorsicherheit mbH

Büro- und Laborgebäude GRS I, Garching bei München, 1978–81

Dieses vor allem durch seine gelungene Konstruktion und die so zutage tretende Ordnung ausgezeichnete, langgestreckte Bürogebäude war das erste Werk einer über Jahrzehnte reichenden, fruchtbaren Zusammenarbeit. Es sollte in seiner formalen und materiellen Aussage Teil einer wirkungsvoll in die Umgebung eingefügten Gebäudegruppierung werden.

In der Logik des Gefüges, in Grund- und Aufriß klingt eine Art Klassik an, welche sich indes zuweilen – diese Erscheinung findet sich schon im Klassizismus – unvermeidlicher Nützlichkeit beugen muß. Bei unserem Beispiel zeigt sich dies an den prägnanten, Wandanschluß gewährleistenden Fensterstützen.

Detlef Schreiber: Situation und Landschaft

»Im Norden von München, auf dem Gebiet der Gemeinde Garching, liegt das Forschungsgelände der Technischen Universität München. Dort sind sowohl universitäre als auch private Forschungs- und Lehrinstitute geplant und gebaut worden. Das Gebäude der GRS ist eine Erweiterung der bereits vorhandenen GRS-Bauten.

Die städtebauliche und landschaftliche Situation wird durch die vorhandene Bebauung einerseits bestimmt und andererseits durch die weite Topographie der Kiesschotterebene mit Isarauen. Ein wesentliches Merkmal im Bereich des Grundstücks war eine markante Reihe von Weiden, die einst wohl einen Entwässerungskanal begleitet haben.

In der ausgeräumten Landschaft erschien diese Baumreihe als bedeutsames Wahrzeichen, das unbedingt zu erhalten war. Das Bauwerk mußte deshalb den Baumbestand berücksichtigen und in Maßstäblichkeit, Flächenausdehnung und Höhenentwicklung Rücksicht darauf nehmen.

Diese Rücksicht ließ einen Baukörper von höchstens 13 Metern Tiefe, eine Höhenentwicklung von zwei Vollgeschossen und ein geringfügig über die Geländeoberkante angehobenes Untergeschoß zu.

GRS I office and laboratory building, Garching near Munich, 1978–1981

This long office building, distinguished above all by its successful structure and the order that this reveals, was the first realized result of a co-operation that had continued for decades. Its formal and material statement was intended to become part of a group of buildings that fitted into its surroundings effectively.

A kind of Cassicism can be discerned in the logic of the structure, the ground plan and elevation, though in the mean time – and this phenomenon appears even at the time of Classicism – it has to defer to inevitable functionality. In our example this can be seen from the minimal window supports, which guarantee elegant wall junctions.

Detlef Schreiber: Situation and landscape

»North of Munich, within the Garching municipality, is the Technische Universität München's research precinct. University and private research institutions have been planned and built there. The GRS building is an extension of the GRS buildings already on site.

The urban and landscape situation is determined by the existing buildings on the one hand and then by the spacious topography of the gravel plain with Isar meadows. A key feature of the site area was a striking row of willows, which once probably ran alongside a drainage canal.

In the cleared landscape, this row of trees appeared as a significant landmark, which definitely had to be retained. For this reason

Links: Fassade Seitenansicht

Left page: side façade elevation

FOLGENDE DOPPELSEITE:
Gesamtplan mit Grundrissen von GRS I, GRS II und GRS III. Die anderen Gebäude wurden nicht gebaut.

NEXT DOUBLE PAGE:
Plan of the whole complex, with floor plans of GRS I, GRS II and GRS III. The other buildings were not built.

GRS I

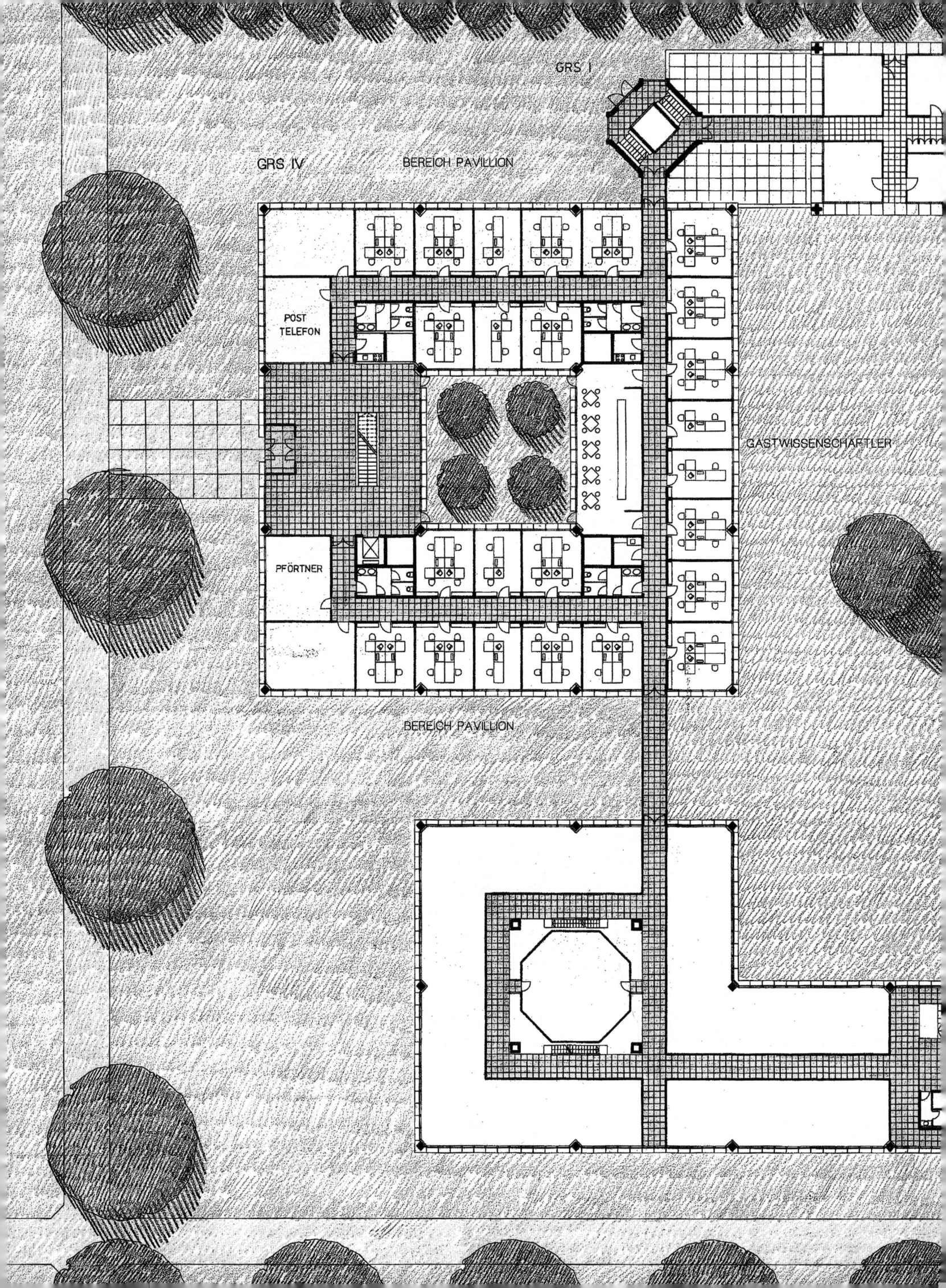

GRS IV   BEREICH PAVILLON

POST TELEFON

GASTWISSENSCHAFTLER

PFÖRTNER

BEREICH PAVILLON

GRS II

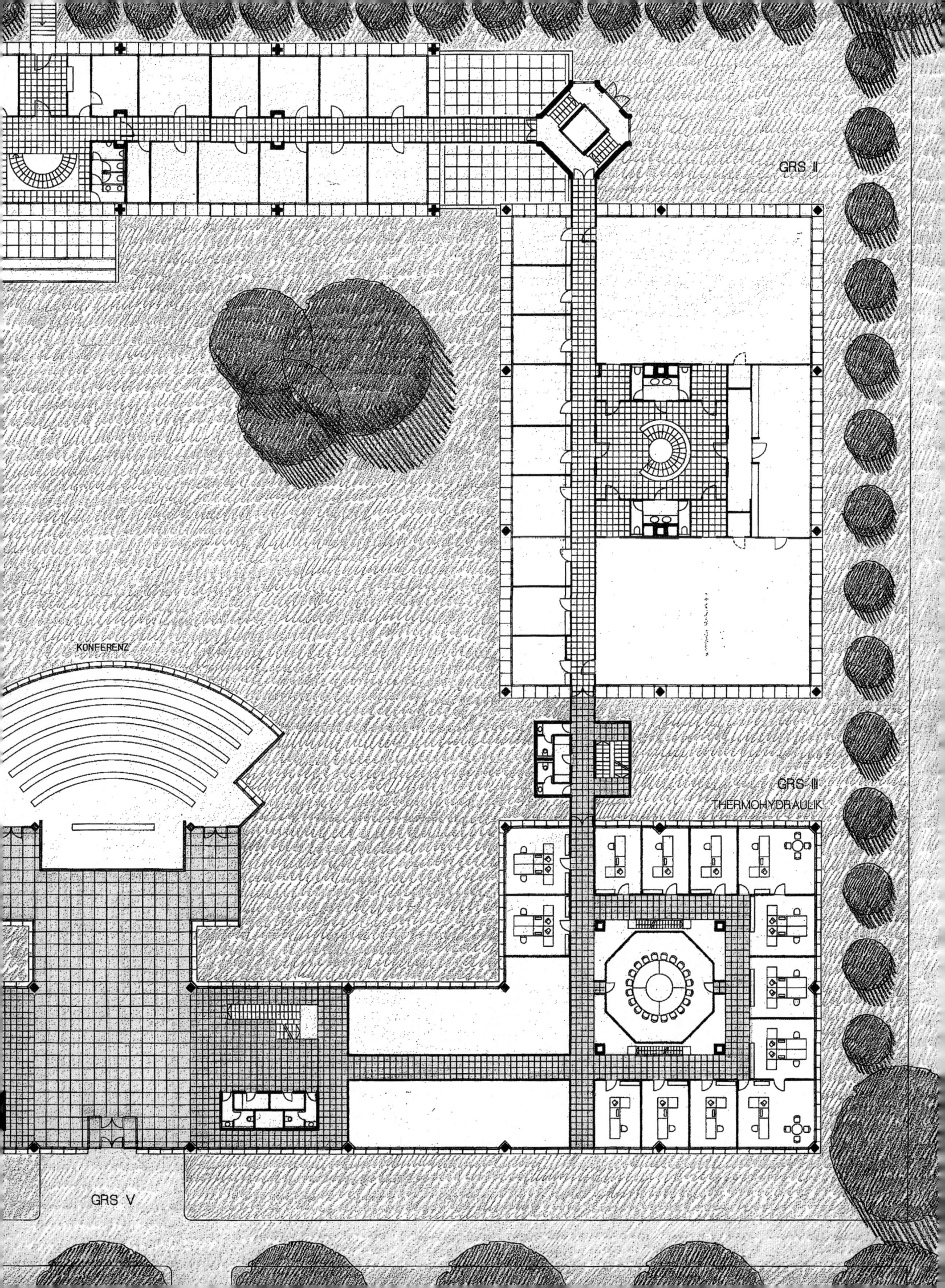

KONFERENZ

GRS III
THERMOHYDRAULIK

GRS V

Funktion und Gebäudekonzept

Das Bauprogramm forderte variabel unterteilbare Flächen (auch für kleinste Raumeinheiten) für Büro und Labornutzungen und damit einen weitgehend stützenfreien Raum mit einer Vielzahl von Wandanschlußmöglichkeiten an Decke und Fassade. Daraus entwickelten sich logisch das im Inneren stützenfreie, tragende Konstruktionssystem mit der modularen Kasettendecke und das in der Sekundärachse versetzte Ausbausystem nichttragender Elemente.

Der gemeinsame Raster beider Systeme hat ein Modulmaß von neunzig Zentimetern, die Systemverschiebung beträgt ein halbes Modul oder 45 Zentimeter.

Konstruktion und Installation

Die Gebäudekonstruktion addiert sich aus vier aneinandergereihten Quadraten. Die zwischen je vier Stützen freigespannten Decken haben eine Größe von 11,70 (= 13 x 0,90 m) x 11,70 m.

Die modular halbversetzten Ausbauelemente (Fassade, Trennwände) ergeben je Stützenquadrat einen frei unterteilbaren Raum von 10,80 x 10,80 Metern (jeweils 12 x 0,90 Meter) und als Zwischenband 10,80 x 0,90 Meter. In diesen Bändern liegen die Dehnfugen und, zur Gebäudemitte zugeordnet, jeweils paarweise die Vertikalschächte für die Installation.

Diese Schächte übernehmen auch die Windkräfte aus den Deckenscheiben und führen die Lasten in die Fundamente ab. Die U-förmigen Vertikalschächte münden in der Deckenzone jeweils im ebenfalls U-förmigen horizontalen Zwischenband, so daß hier eine Verteilung der Versorgungsleitungen in der Ebene zu den Fenster-Ringkanälen im Estrich vorgenommen werden kann.

Die Nachinstallation, vor allem von Elektro- und EDV-Leitungen, ist so gewährleistet.

the building had to consider the existing trees and relate to them in terms of scale, area and height.

These concerns led to a building 13 m deep at the most, a height of two full storeys and a basement that was very slightly raised above the surface of the site.

Function and building concept

The building programme called for areas that could be divided up variably (even for the smallest room units) for office and lab use, and thus a largely column-free space with a large number of wall junction possibilities on the ceilings and façade. The load-bearing construction system, column-free in the interior, developed logically from this, with its modular coffered ceiling and interior finish system made up of non-load-bearing elements shifted on to the secondary axis.

The two systems share a grid with a module dimension of 90 cm, and the system shift is by 1/2 module, or 45 cm.

Construction and installation

The building structure is an accumulation of four squares placed one after the other. The ceilings are hung free between four supports in each case, and are 11.7 (=13 x 0.9 m) x 11.7 m in size.

The finishing elements (façade, dividing walls) produce a space that can be divided as wished of 10.8 x 10.8 m (12 x 0.9 m in each case) in each support square, and 10.8 m x 0.9 m as an intermediate band. These bands contain the expansion joints and, in the central section of the building, the vertical shafts for services, in pairs in each case.

These shafts also absorb the wind forces from the ceiling panels and disperse the loads into the foundations. In the ceiling zone, the

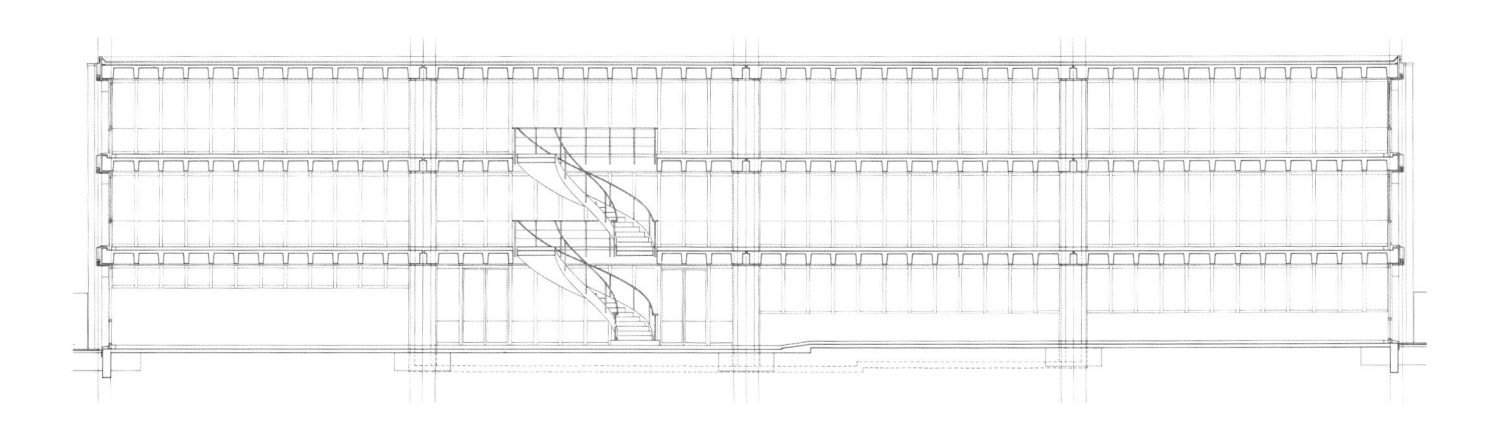

Schnitt

Sectional view

Material und Gestaltung

Die zehn vor die Fassade gestellten Sichtbetonstützen gewinnen ihrer Kreuzform wegen, trotz großer Querschnitte, optische Schlankheit. Diese wirkt im Kontrast zur engen, fast massigen Teilung der Holzfassade. Die Deckenfelder liegen auf Konsolen mit thermischer Trennung durch Neoprene-Lager auf den Kreuzstützen, sind außen mit Wärmedämmung versehen und mit abgekanteten, eloxierten Aluminiumblechen verkleidet.

Bei der äußeren Erscheinung dieses Stahlbetonbaus wird Beton nicht als Verkleidungselement, sondern ausschließlich als Konstruktionselement verwendet und deutlich sichtbar gemacht. Nichttragende und verkleidete Bauelemente treten zugunsten der die großen Spannweiten tragenden Betonstützen zurück. Diese bestimmen zusammen mit den Kassettendecken die formale Charakteristik des Bauwerks.

Haustechnik und Raumtechnik

Das Gebäude wird, mit Ausnahme der EDV-Labors, natürlich (durch Fenster) belüftet und belichtet. Die Fußbodenheizung mit vielfältig unterteilten Regelzonen sorgt für ausgeglichene Wärmeversorgung. Die große Befensterung mit außenliegendem Sonnenschutz liefert hierzu einen Beitrag durch passive Sonnenenergienutzung. Die offen exponierten Betonkassettendecken leisten Erhebliches als Klimaspeicher. Die elastischen Fassaden- und Trennwandelemente, der schwimmende Estrich und der Teppichboden sorgen zusammen mit den größeren Flächenanteilen der Kassettendecke für eine positive Schalldämpfung, so daß die Kassetten als Sichtbetonelemente unverkleidet bleiben konnten und so als konstruktives und architektonisches Element die Innenräume qualitätvoll prägen. In den Kassettenfeldern wurden auch die Beleuchtungen in einfacher Form integriert.

U-shaped vertical shafts end in the horizontal intermediate band, which is also U-shaped, in each case, so that it is possible to distribute the supply ducts on that level to the window guide channels in the screed.

This means that all the electrical and IT supplies can be installed subsequently.

Material and design

The ten exposed concrete columns in front of the façade look slender visually because of their cruciform shape, despite large cross-sections. This contrasts with the tight, almost bulky division of the timber façade. The ceiling fields sit on brackets with thermal separation by neoprene bearings on the cruciform columns. They have external heat insulation and are clad in bevelled, anodized sheet aluminium.

In terms of the outward appearance of the reinforced concrete building, concrete is not used as a cladding element but exclusively structurally, and is left clearly visible. Non-load-bearing and clad structural elements draw back in favour of the concrete columns, which carry large spans. These and the coffered ceilings determine the building's formal characteristics.

Building and room services

With the exception of the IT lab, the building is ventilated and lit naturally (by windows). The under-floor heating has a wide range of regulation zones to provide balanced heating. The large windows with external sunshades contribute to this by using passive energy. The openly exposed coffered ceilings perform a considerable service as air-conditioning stores. The elastic façade and dividing wall elements, the floating screed and carpeting offer positive sound

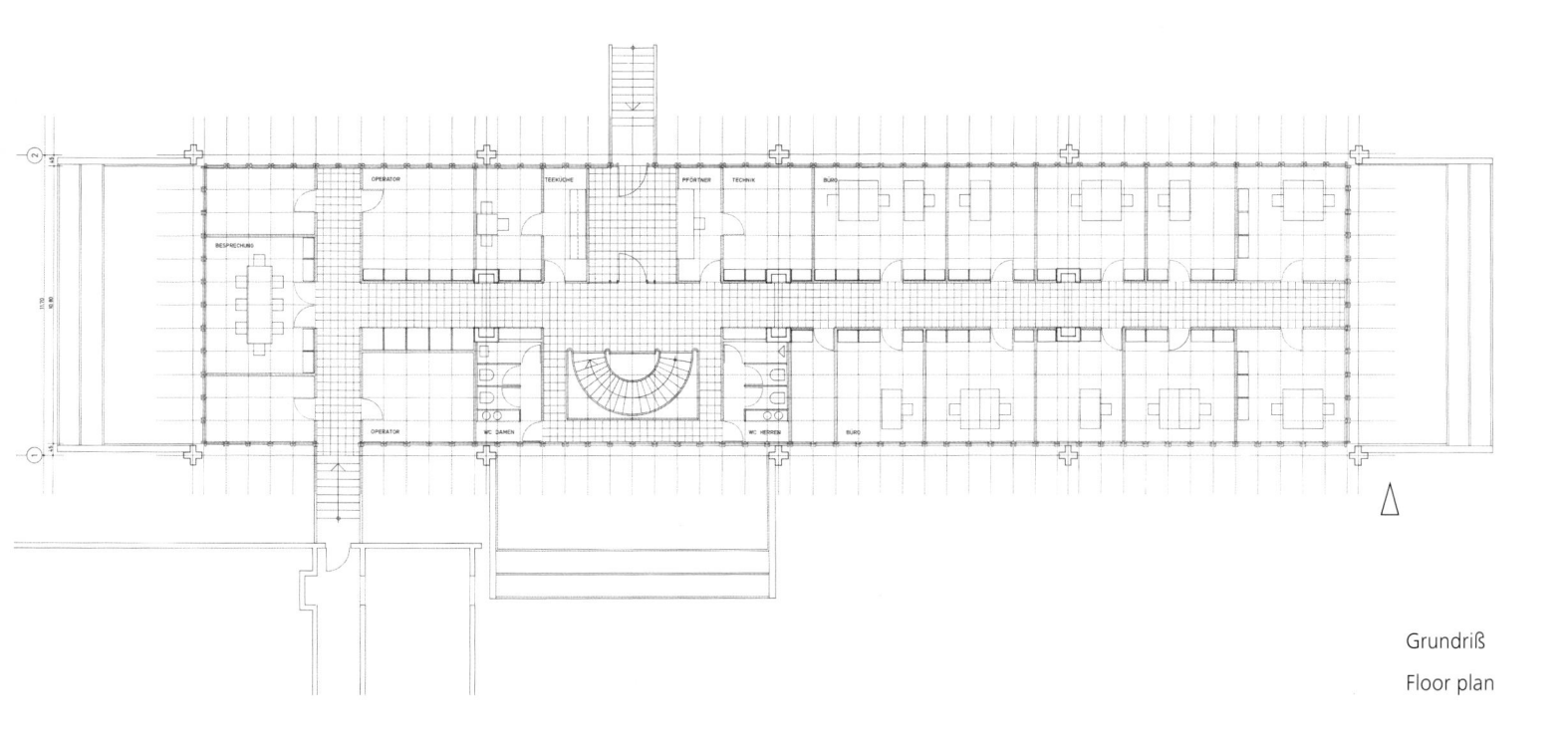

Grundriß
Floor plan

Nutzungsvariabilität und Wirtschaftlichkeit

Die stützenfreien Flächen, das Achsmaß der Deckenkassetten von 90 Zentimetern und der Pfostenabstand der Fassadenelemente von 90 Zentimetern erlauben vielfältige Raumunterteilungen.

Trotz der großen Spannweite erwies sich die Herstellung des Gebäudes als besonders wirtschaftlich. Die Reduzierung der Stützenzahlen wirkte sich in der Masse selbst, aber auch bei den Fundierungen aus. Durch die vier quadratischen Gebäudeelemente ergaben sich vier Bautakte in den drei Höhenebenen, was zu einer höchst rationellen Wiederverwendbarkeit der vorgefertigten Schalungen und zu einer Art serieller Fertigung mit geringem Personalaufwand auf der Baustelle führte.

Ein besonderer Rationalisierungseffekt für die Ausbauelemente konnte auch mit der Verschiebung der beiden modularen Systeme um je eine halbe Achse – Konstruktionsraster, Ausbauraster – erzielt werden. Dadurch konnten Sonder- und Paßelemente vermieden und die Anschlußprobleme auf ein Minimum verringert werden.

Das Material Beton wird bei den wichtigen konstruktiven Elementen (Stützen und Decken) hervorgehoben und sichtbar gemacht und erfährt durch die zum Ausdruck gebrachte hohe Leistungsfähigkeit bei den großen Spannweiten eine besondere architektonische Qualität.«

insulation, along with the coffered ceiling. This meant that the coffers could remain unclad as visual elements and thus make a high-quality impact on the interior as a structural and architectural element. It was also possible to integrate light fittings into the coffers in a simple form.

Variable use and economic viability

The column-free areas, the axis dimensions of the ceiling coffers of 0.9 m and the distance between the posts of the façade elements of 0.9 m make it possible to divide the rooms up in many ways.

Despite the large span, building the structure proved to be very economical. The reduction of the number of columns impacted on the mass itself, but also on the foundations. The use of four square building elements meant four building stages at the three height levels, which led to the fact that the prefabricated shuttering could be used in a highly rational way, and to a kind of serial manufacture with few personnel needed on the building site.

It was also possible to rationalize the finishing elements particularly by shifting each of the two modular systems by half an axis – structure module, finish module. This avoided special and locating elements and reduced connection problems to a minimum.

Concrete is emphasized as a material for the important structural elements (columns and ceilings). It is left visible, and acquires a special architectural quality because of the high performance it expresses in relation to the large spans.«

Treppenhaus

Staircase

FOLGENDE DOPPELSEITE:
Gesamtansicht Bolzmannstraße

NEXT DOUBLE PAGE:
Overall elevation facing Bolzmannstrasse

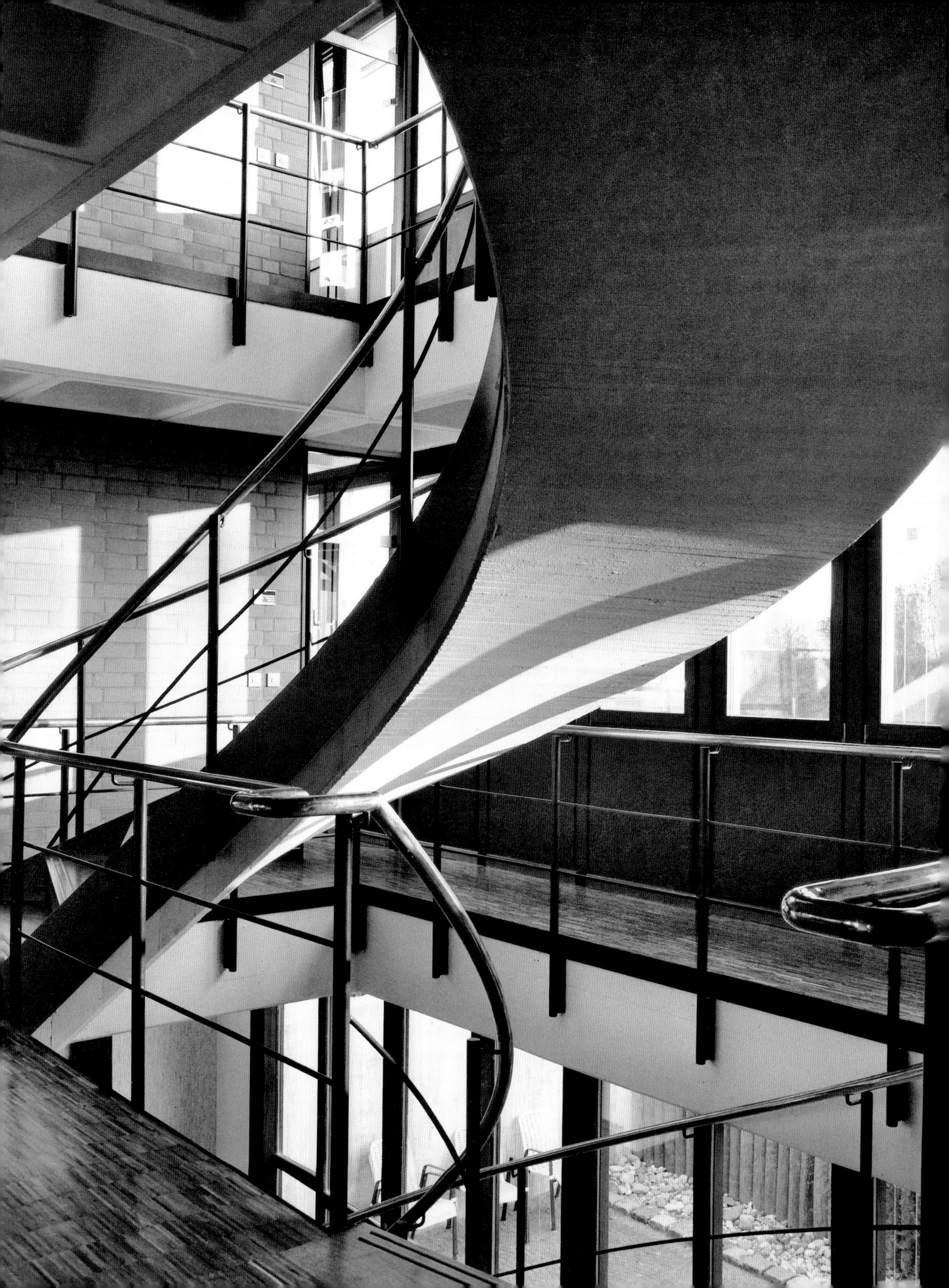

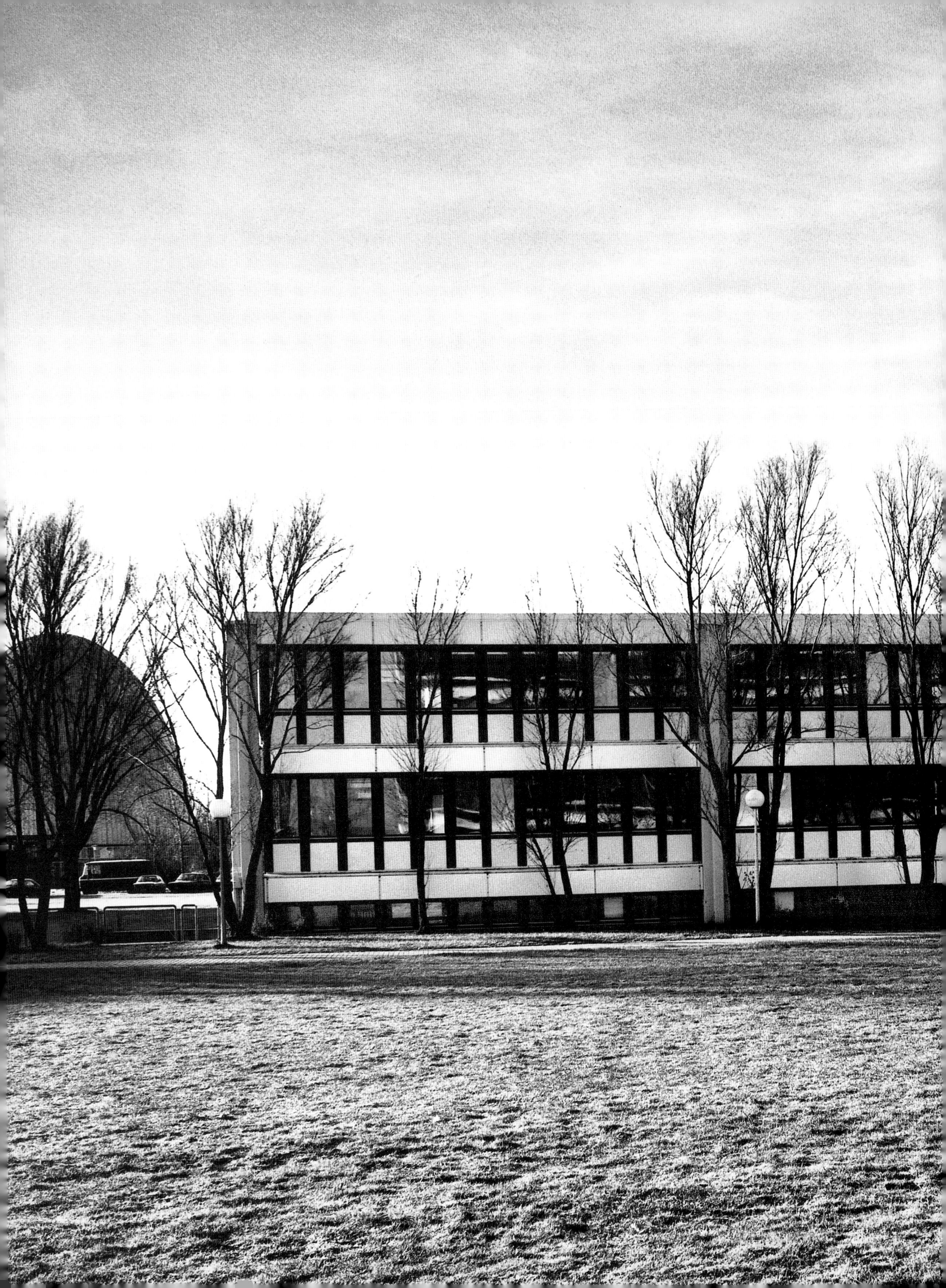

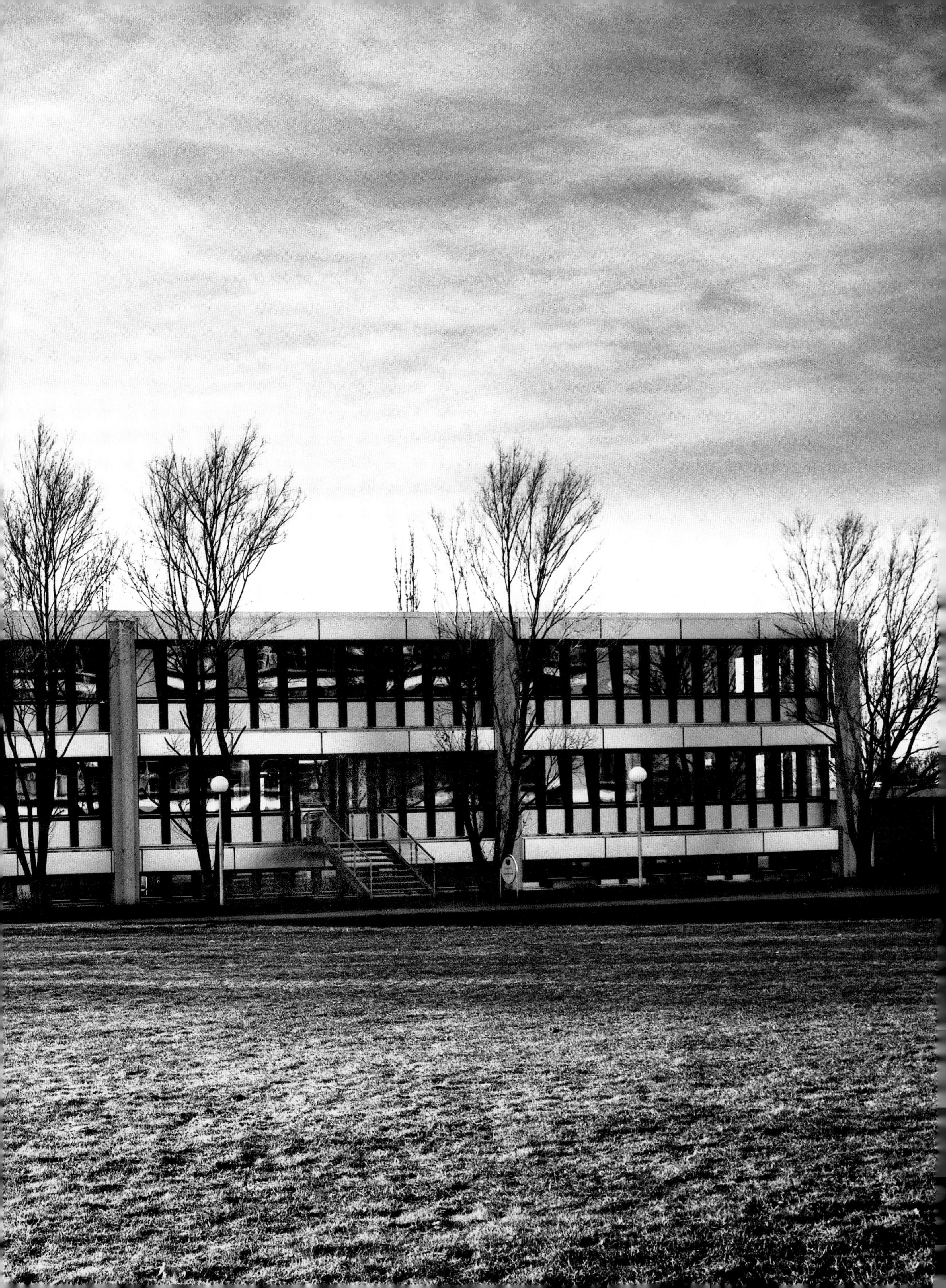

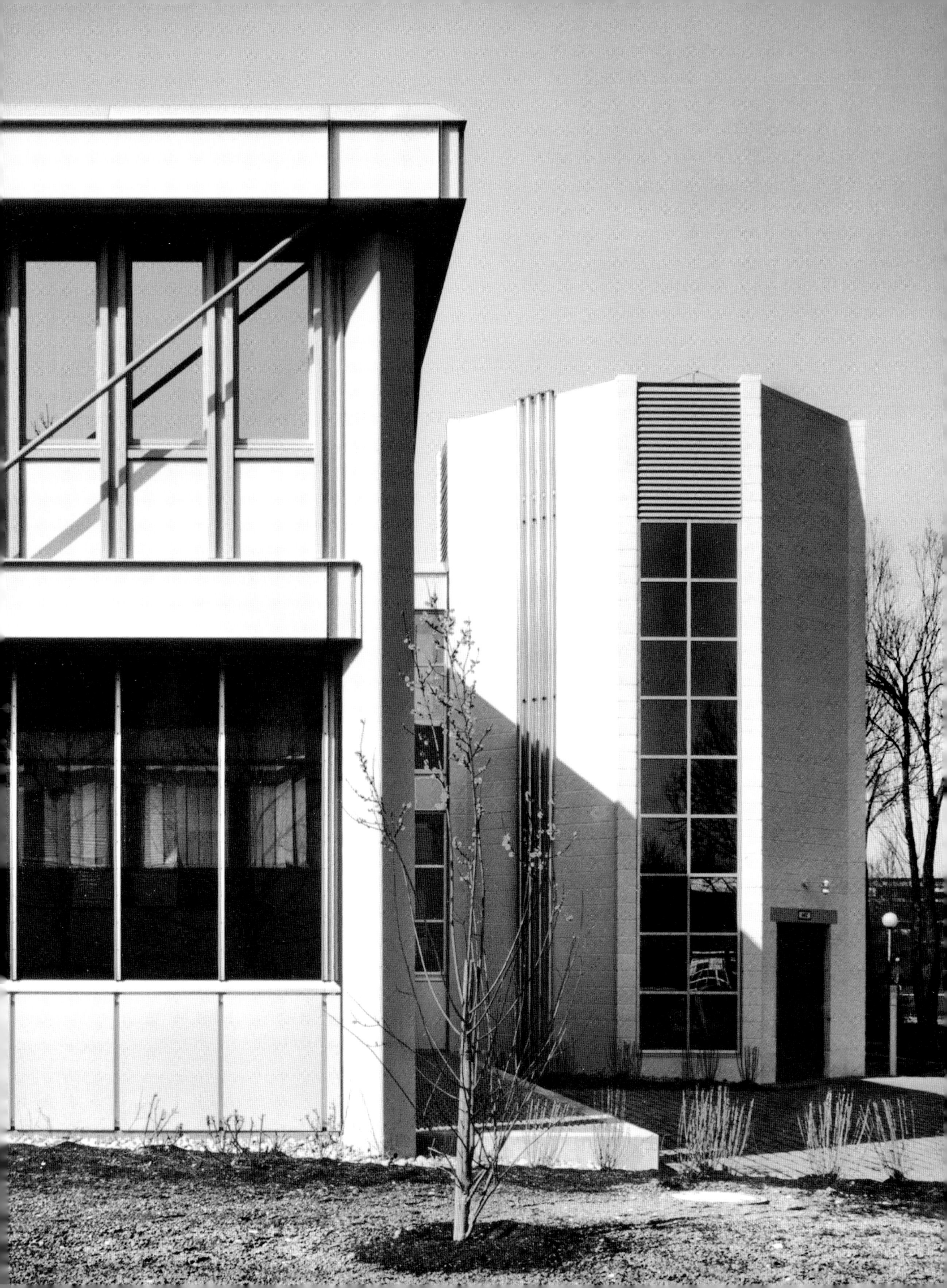

Büro- und Laborgebäude GRS II, Garching bei München, 1986–89

Die steigende Bedeutung der elektronischen Datenverarbeitung wurde unversehens zur neuen Herausforderung und ließ es angeraten erscheinen, sich intensive Gedanken zu machen, wie auf die besonderen Anforderungen notwendiger Klimatisierung und Kabelvernetzung, unter Berücksichtigung höchster Flexibilität und Nachrüstbarkeit, zu antworten sei. Die Ergebnisse solchen Eingehens auf die Bedingungen liegen eigentlich wesentlich näher beim Labor als beim Bürobauen. Das Garchinger Gebäude ist, betrachtet man seine Außenabmessungen, 36 x 34 Meter und drei Geschosse hoch, nicht groß.

Die gefundenen Lösungen indes, Details und architektonische Haltung, können als beispielhafter Beitrag zur Gestaltung der wissenschaftlichen Arbeitswelt gelten. Besonders erwähnenswert ist die hervorragende Einfügung unter städtebaulichen und den Charakter der Landschaft wahrenden Gesichtspunkten.

Bemerkenswert ist, daß Klimatisierung und Entlüftung nur dort eingesetzt wurden, wo die Datenverarbeitungsmaschinen dies erforderten. Die Rückkehr zur natürlichen Belüftung hat seither auch bei großen Einheiten stattgefunden.

Baubeschreibung des Architekten

»Die Gesellschaft für Reaktorsicherheit in Köln war die Bauherrin. Sie ließ auf dem Forschungsgelände Garching, Ecke James-Franck-Straße/Boltzmannstraße ein dreigeschossiges Gebäude mit UG, EG und OG errichten. Die Anbindung an das 1981 errichtete Bürogebäude mit zentraler Pforte erfolgte über eine erdgeschossige Stahlbrücke und einen viergeschossigen Treppenturm mit Aufzug. Dieser Turm wurde konventionell in Stahlbeton und Mauerwerk gebaut.

Das Untergeschoß dient ausschließlich der technischen Gebäudeversorgung und der Aufnahme der zentralen Datenverarbeitung mit Nebenraumzone. Es ist fensterlos, hat eine geschlossen umlaufende Betonaußenwand und stützt sich auf zwei Kernstützen und vier Betonscheiben, die um das zentrale Treppenhaus angeordnet sind. Die durchlaufende Bodenplatte liegt ca. fünfzig Zentimeter unter dem Fertigfußboden. Abgesehen von der Raumluftzentrale erhält das Geschoß einen Doppelboden als Klima- und Installationsboden. Die Decke ist als Flachdecke mit Unterzügen konstruiert.

Das Erdgeschoß nimmt die bedienten Datenverarbeitungsmaschinen und eine Testwarte (Anforderungen ähnlich den EDV-Räumen) mit unmittelbar zugeordneten Büros auf. Die Bodenplatte liegt ca. dreißig Zentimeter unter dem Fertigfußboden. Das ganze Geschoß erhält einen Doppelboden als Klima- und Installationsboden. Die Decke wurde als Betonkassettendecke mit einem Achsmaß von neunzig Zentimetern ausgeführt. Die Decke über dem Erdgeschoß führt die Lasten auf acht freistehende Außenstützen und zwei Kernstützen sowie vier Betonscheiben um das zentrale Teppenhaus ab.

GRS II office and laboratory building, Garching near Munich, 1986–89

The increasing need for computer facilities suddenly became a new challenge and made it seem advisable to think intensively about how to respond to the special demands this raised for air-conditioning and cabling, with an eye to the greatest possible flexibility and upgrading. The results of addressing the conditions in this way are actually considerably more related to lab than office building. The Garching building is not large: its outer dimensions are 36 x 34 m and it is three storeys high.

However, the solutions found, details and an architectural approach, can be seen as an exemplary contribution to designing the scientific working world. It is particularly worth mentioning the outstanding way the building fits in while preserving urban and landscape character.

It should be noted that air-conditioning and venting are used only where the computer equipment required it. Large units have since also returned to natural ventilation.

The architect's description of the building

»The client was the Cologne Gesellschaft für Reaktorsicherheit (Reactor Safety Company). It commissioned a three-storey building with basement, ground floor and first floor in the Garching research precinct at the junction of James-Franck-Straße and Boltzmannstraße. The new building was linked to the office building dating from 1981 with a central entrance by a steel bridge at ground level and a four-storey staircase tower with lift. This tower was built conventionally in reinforced concrete and masonry.

The basement is used only to provide technical services and house the central computer equipment with an ancillary zone. It is windowless, has a closed, continuous concrete outer wall round it and is supported on two core columns and four concrete slabs arranged around the central staircase. The continuous floor slab is about 50 cm below the finished floor. Apart from the internal air control room, the storey has a double floor as an air-conditioning and services floor. The ceiling is constructed as a flat ceiling with binding beams.

The ground floor accommodates the computers served from the basement and a test control centre (requirement similar to IT rooms) with offices directly adjacent. The floor slab is about 30 cm below the finished floor. The whole storey has a double floor as an air-conditioning and services floor. The ceiling is a concrete coffered ceiling with 90 cm axes. The ceiling above the ground floor disperses loads in eight free-standing external supports and two core supports, and also four concrete slabs around the central staircase.

The top floor contains offices on the façade, and also meeting and ancillary zones in the inside area. The inside area, the staircase

Links: Verbindungsturm vom GRS I zum Neubau GRS II
Left page: connecting tower between GRS I and the new building GRS II

Das Obergeschoß enthält Büroräume an der Fassade sowie Besprechungs- und Nebenzonen im Innenbereich. Der Innenbereich, das Treppenhaus und die Flure werden durch Oberlichtpyramiden belichtet. Der Boden erhält einen konventionellen Fußbodenaufbau mit Fußbodenheizung. Die Decke gleicht jener über dem Erdgeschoß.

Das Dach ist als Warmdach mit bituminöser Abdichtung ausgeführt. Die Fassade im Erdgeschoß ist eine Metallfassade in Pfosten-Riegel-Bauweise, die lediglich auf der Westseite Öffnungsflügel aufweist.

Die Fassade im Obergeschoß ist als Holzfassade in Rahmenbauweise ausgeführt. Hier wurde jedes Element mit Öffnungselementen versehen.

Im Innenausbau wird auf größtmögliche Flexibilität Wert gelegt. Als Innenwände wurden grundsätzlich Leichtbauwände (F30/F90) errichtet. Lediglich im Untergeschoß ist die Trafoeinheit mit Beton bzw. Mauerwerk umfaßt. Abgehängte Decken sind nicht vorgesehen. Alle Deckeninstallationen sind Sichtinstallationen. Im Obergeschoß verläuft entlang der Fassade ein Bodenkanal für Installationen.«

and the corridors are lit from skylight pyramids. The floor has a conventional finish with under-floor heating. The ceiling is the same as the one above the ground floor.

The roof is a non-ventilated flat roof insulated with bitumen. The ground floor façade is a post-and-rail metal façade with ventilating units on the west side only.

The top floor façade is a wooden façade with a frame construction. Here every element was ventilated.

The greatest possible flexibility was the key concern for the interior finishing. Light-weight walls (F30/F90) provided the interior walls. Only the transformer plant in the basement was walled in concrete or masonry. No suspended ceilings have been provided for. All the ceiling fittings are visible. A floor duct for services runs along the top storey façade.«

Ansicht GRS I mit Verbindungsturm zu GRS II

View of GRS I with the connecting tower to GRS II

FOLGENDE DOPPELSEITEN:
S. 102: Wendeltreppe von oben nach unten
S. 103: Wendeltreppe Seitenansicht
S. 104–105: Ansicht Ostseite

NEXT DOUBLE PAGES:
P. 102: Spiral staircase looking downwards
P. 103: Spiral staircase seen from the side
P. 104–105: View of the eastern side

101

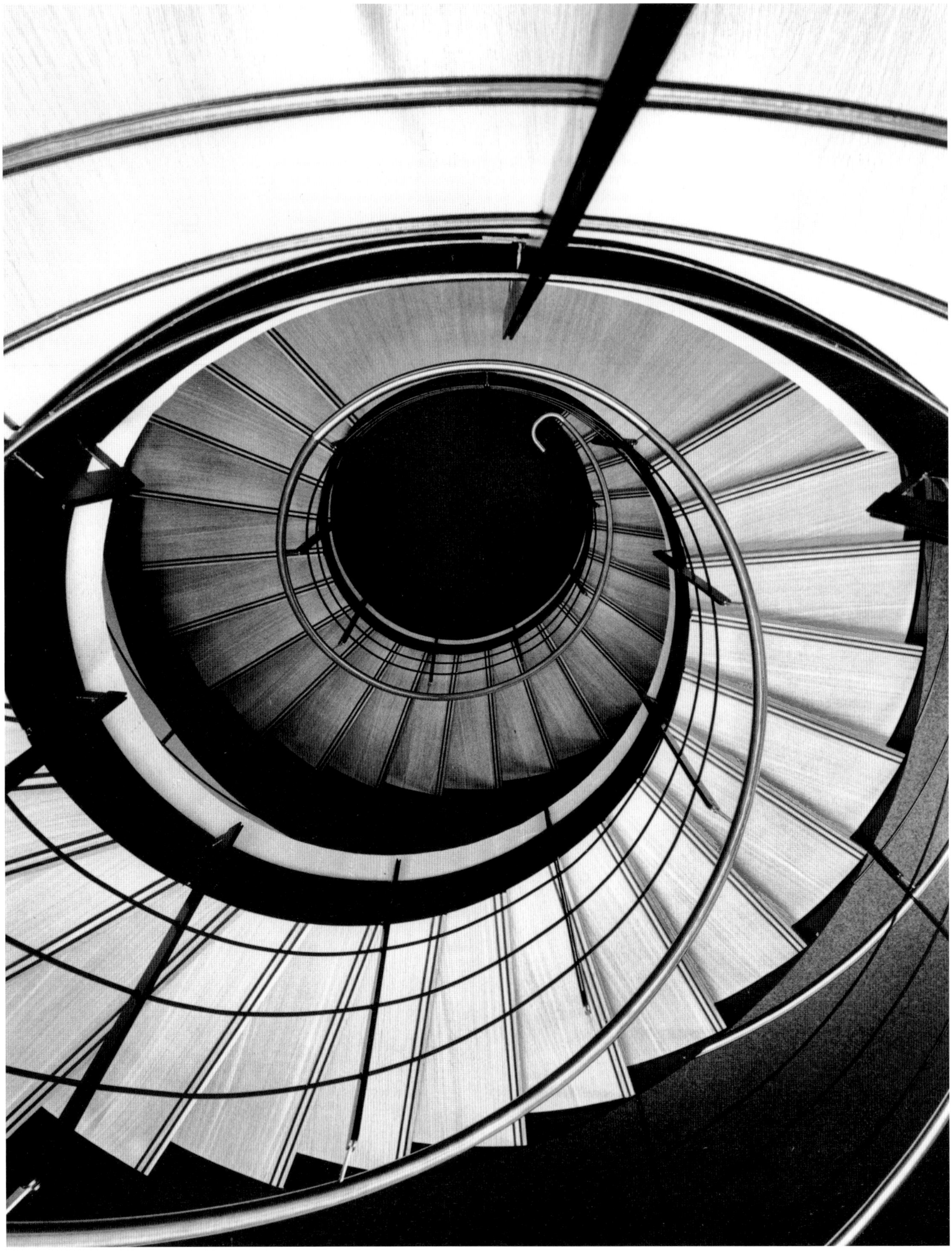

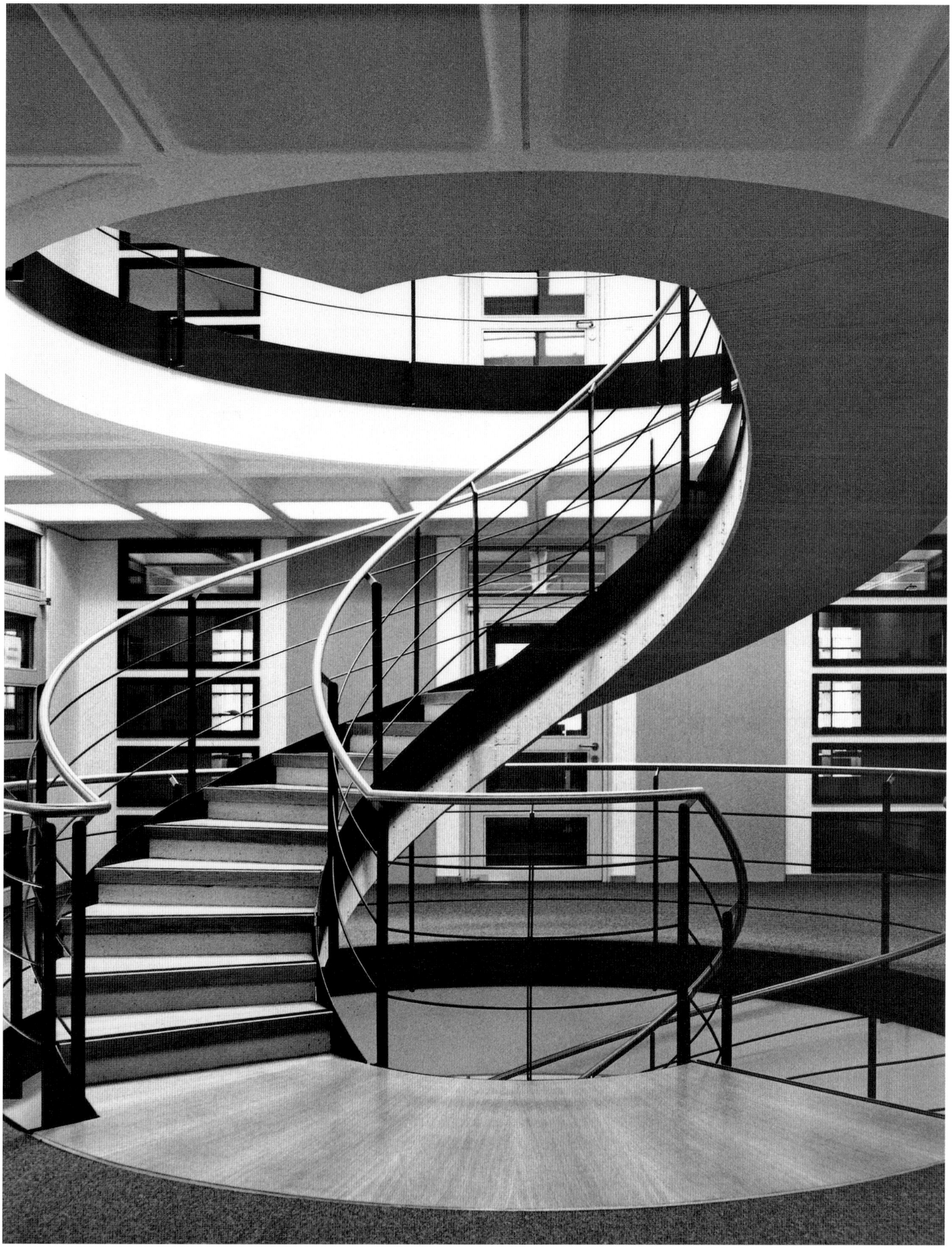

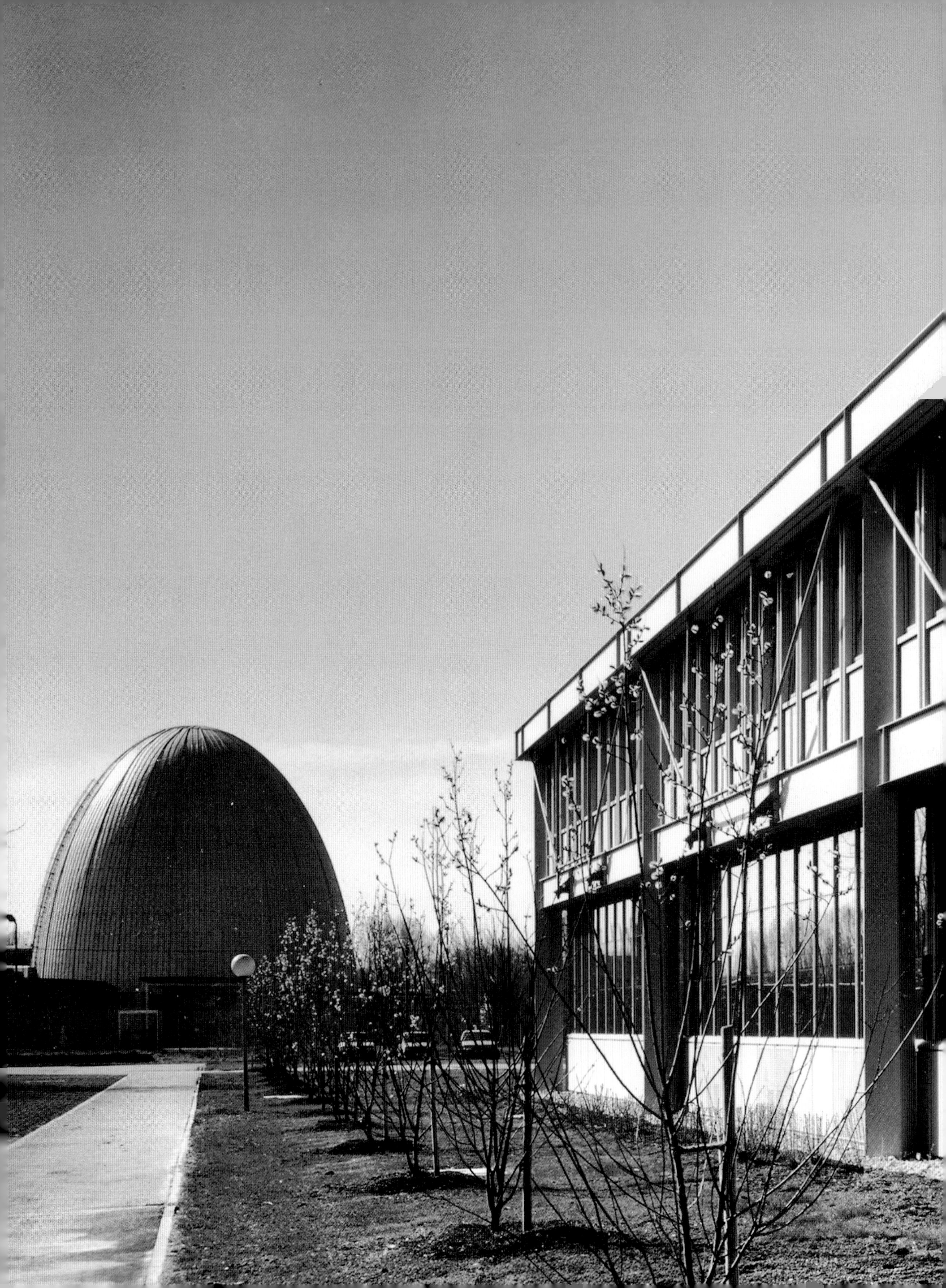

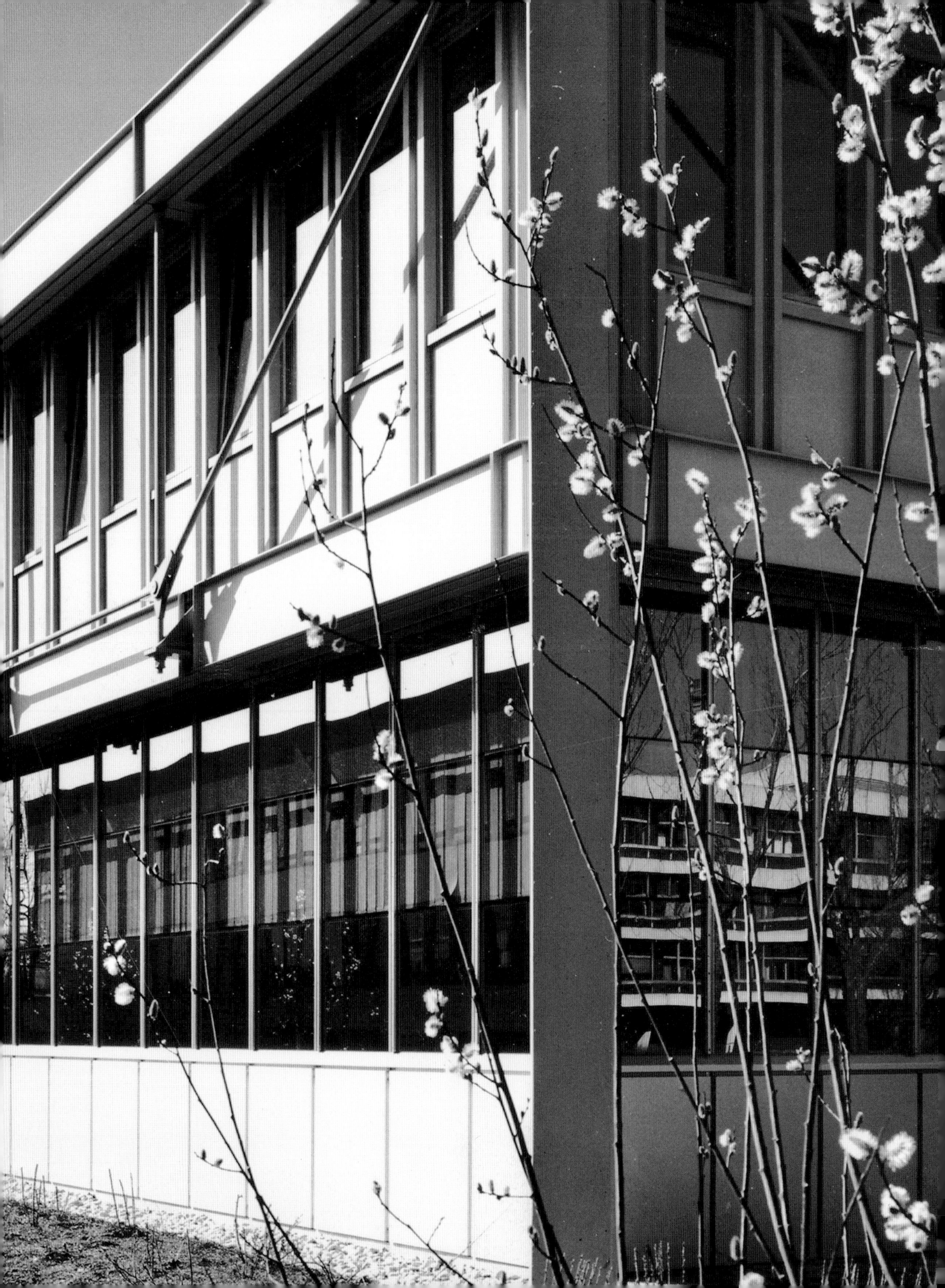

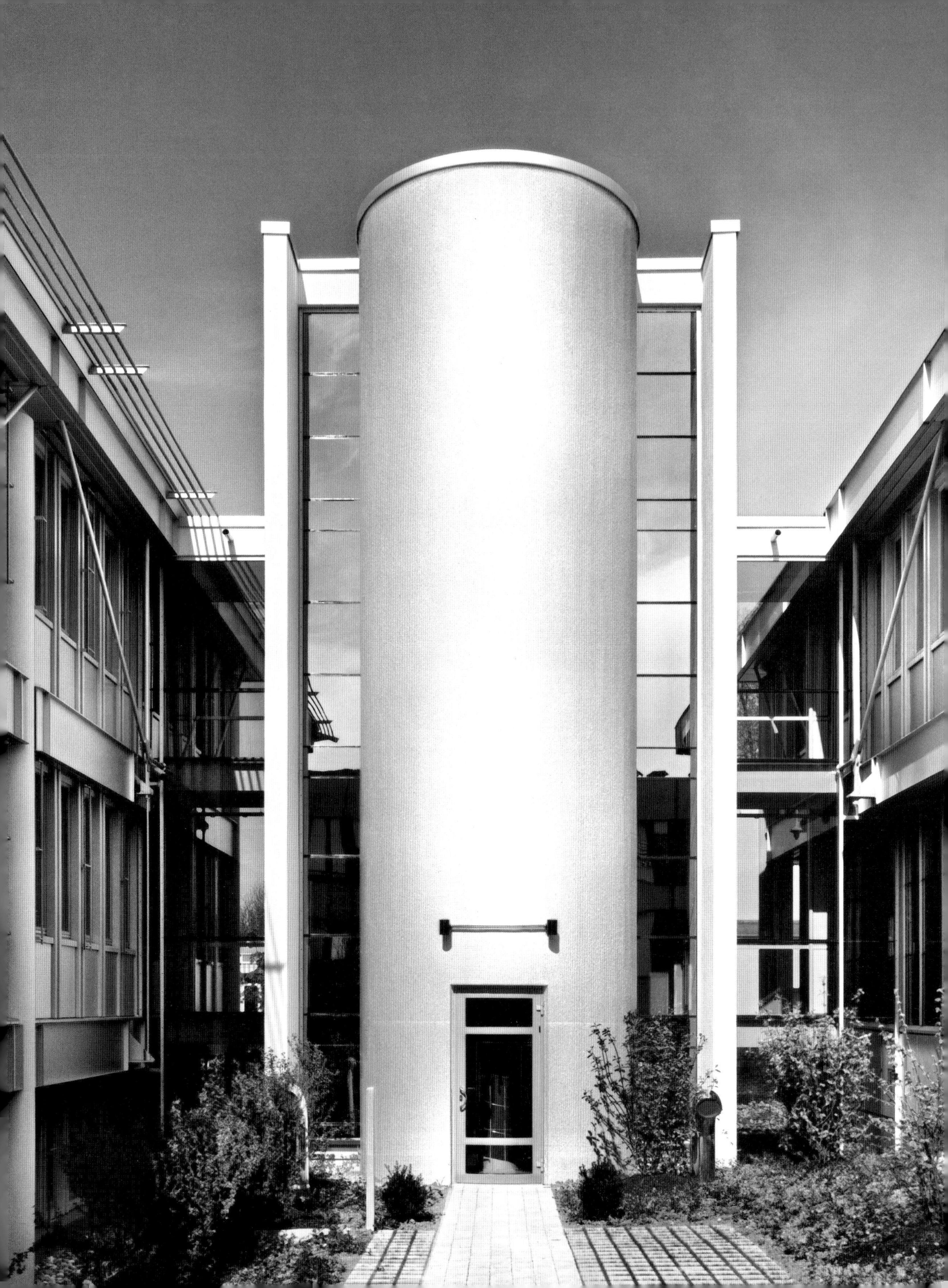

Bürogebäude GRS III, Garching bei München, 1994–96

Dem Datenverarbeitungsgebäude folgte, dieses städtebaulich und gestalthaft aufs beste ergänzend, ein quadratisches Bürogebäude.

Anläßlich der Einweihung hielt Detlef Schreiber eine den Bau ausdeutende, gedankenreiche Ansprache, die nun zu Teilen wiedergegeben werden soll. Man erfährt aus seinen Darlegungen, mit welcher Sorgfalt und Umsicht oder besser: Weltsicht und mit welchem Ernst und Verantwortungsbewußtsein Bauen – das ist ja ein Verändern und Bereichern der Erde, ein Kultivieren – betrieben werden sollte:

»Als Architekt wird man manchmal gefragt, was man sich dabei gedacht habe, dieses Haus gerade so zu bauen. Die Antwort ist zunächst einfach. Das Bauwerk sollte dauerhaft, praktisch und nützlich sein, nicht zu teuer werden und dabei möglichst allen Leuten gefallen. Es wäre sicher unredlich, wenn ich es bei dieser Antwort beließe, auch dann, wenn ich mich dabei der seit Aristoteles gültigen vier Ursachen für das Entstehen eines Werkes bediente:

der *causa materialis*, des Materials,
der *causa efficiens*, der Herstellung,
der *causa finalis*, des Zwecks
und *der causa formalis*, der Form.

Gleich ist zu bemerken, daß sich seit Aristoteles einige wesentliche Gewichtsverlagerungen bei der Bewertung der Grundlagen und Bedingungen für den Bau eines Hauses ergeben haben.

Die Bedeutung der Wirtschaftlichkeit, was Herstellung und Betrieb anlangt, ist in der Aristotelischen Aufzählung nur schwer zu plazieren – genauso wie die Parameter des Umweltschutzes, der Energieeinsparung und der Ökologie. Doch davon später.

Zunächst zur *causa materialis*: Material und Herstellung treten im Inneren und Äußeren des Gebäudes selbsterklärend in Erscheinung. Der Verlauf von Zug- und Druckkräften, von tragenden, schweren Bauteilen und einhüllenden, leichten, nichttragenden bewirken den Ausdruck des inneren und äußeren Erscheinungsbildes.

Flexibilität oder Anpassungsfähigkeit, Transparenz, Offenheit, Dynamik und Beweglichkeit bestimmen heute die Lebens- und Arbeitsweise und nicht Status und hierarchische Strukturen. Diesen Prinzipien kommt unser transparentes, offenes Haus entgegen. Die öffentlichen Bereiche in allen Geschossen werden zu überschaubaren und lichtdurchfluteten Raumfolgen, die privaten Büros bleiben akustisch geschützte Bereiche. Diese Innenwelten haben Bezug zur Außenwelt der Umgebung und zu den Übergangsbereichen der Kommunikationszonen.

Das Tageslicht ist ja nicht nur eine elektromagnetische Strahlung, die eine bestimmte Menge Helligkeit ergibt. Zum eigentlichen Tageslicht wird es erst, wenn die Strahlungswellen den Menschen darüber informieren, ob es schneit oder regnet oder ob es Tag oder Nacht ist, ob die Sonne scheint oder nicht. Neben der Vermittlung solcher Eindrücke spielt aber auch die Mindestbeleuchtungsstärke für die biolo-

GRS III office and laboratory building, Garching near Munich, 1994–96

A square office building followed the IT building, complementing it ideally in terms of urban quality and design.

At the opening, Detlef Schreiber gave a thoughtful address interpreting the building; only parts of the speech will be reproduced here. His descriptions how carefully building has to be approached, and with what circumspection, or better, with what a full view of the world, how seriously, and with what awareness of one's responsibilities. Building here in all the implications of enriching the earth, cultivating it, that the German word »bauen« carries:

»One is sometimes asked as an architect what one had in mind when constructing a building in a particular way. The answer is usually quite simple. The building should be durable, practical and useful, should not become too expensive, and should please everyone if possible. It would certainly be dishonest to leave it at that even though I was using the four causes for the emergence of a work that have applied since Aristotle:

the *causa materialis*, the material,
the *causa efficiens*, the manufacture,
the *causa finalis*, the purpose,
and the *causa formalis*, the form.

It should be pointed out immediately that since the time of Aristotle there has been a considerable shift of weight when evaluating the principles and conditions involved in building a house.

The significance of economic viability as far as manufacture and running are concerned is difficult to place in the Aristotelian list – just like the parameters of environmental protection, energy saving and ecology. But more of that later.

First of all, the *causa materialis*: Material and manufacture are visible in a self-explanatory fashion in the interior and exterior of a building. The flow of tensile and pressure forces, of load-bearing, heavy sections of the building and light, covering, non-load-bearing ones, create the expressive quality of its interior and exterior appearance.

Today, life and the way people work are determined by flexibility or adaptability, transparency, openness, dynamics and mobility, not by status and hierarchical structures. Our transparent, open building conforms with these principles. The public areas on all floors become manageable, light-flooded sequences of space, the private offices remain sound-proofed areas. These interior worlds relate to the exterior world of the surroundings and the transitional areas of the communication zones.

Of course daylight is not just electro-magnetic radiation that provides a certain quantity of brightness. It only becomes actual daylight

Links: Verbindungsturm von GRS II (rechts) zu GRS III (links)
Left page: tower connecting GRS II (right) to GRS III (left)

gischen Funktionen des Menschen eine wichtige Rolle. Das alles setzt voraus, daß die Raumtiefen der Büros nicht zu groß sind, d. h. bei ca. fünf Metern m liegen sollen und daß die verbleibenden Innenzonen auch Tageslicht erhalten. Das trifft bei unserem Bau zu und führt darüber hinaus zu beachtlichen Energieeinsparungen. [...]

Als Architekt weiß ich, daß der CO_2-Ausstoß und der anderer Schadstoffe beim Häuserbau einen beträchtlichen Anteil ausmacht und daß es gilt, diesen durch alternative Energieträger, vor allem aber durch intelligente Baukonstruktionen zu verringern. Wir haben uns für die zweite, preisgünstigere Lösung entschieden und auf aktive Wind- und Sonnenenergie sowie auf mechanische Wärmepumpen verzichtet. All das war teurer als das durch ›gewußt wie‹-Erreichte.
Die Qualitäten unseres Bauwerks:
– kompakte Bauform mit günstigen Werten für Volumen und Hüllfläche (A/V = 0.365),
– vernünftige Anteile und günstige Verteilung von Befensterungen, geschlossenen Wandflächen und Dachflächen (40 % / 60 %),
– hohe Wärmedämmwerte der Außenwandteile (K = 0,5) und Verbesserung des Dämmwerts durch das Gründach,
– große innere Speichermassen durch die unverkleideten Betonkassetten der Decken, die mit ihrem hohen Oberflächenanteil einen günstigen Regulierungsfaktor bei Wärme- und Kältespeicherung haben,
– schwere Bauart durch Decke und Estrich (Speichermasse/Außenwandfläche 1256 kg/m^2 > 600 kg/m^2), (5 % bei der Heizenergie).
Durch die Wahl dieser baulichen Mittel konnte der Jahresheizenergiebedarf von 172.892 kW/h/a auf 79.539 kW/h/a gesenkt werden. Das sind 108 %. Und damit gelangen wir um 27 % unter den geforderten Wert der Wärmeschutzverordnung 1995 und erfüllen auch die Kriterien eines Niedrigenergiehauses.

Als weitere Energieeinsparungen, die in der obigen Berechnung nicht berücksichtigt wurden, können zur Reduzierung der theoretischen Kühllast genannt werden:
– außenliegender Sonnenschutz mit Tageslichttechnik um 50 %,
– Nachtabkühlung der Speichermassen mit differenzierten Fensterlüftungsmöglichkeiten.
Einsparungen bei der Elektroenergie, die ebenfalls nicht in der Energiebilanz enthalten sind:
– Kunstlichteinsparung durch die Oberlichtpyramiden 5000 kW/h/a,
– Tageslichttechnik des Sonnenschutzes 4000 kW/h/a,
– tageslichtabhängige Steuerung der Beleuchtung 4000 kW/h/a.
Eigentlich haben wir sogar ein Nullenergiehaus, denn wir nutzen die Abwärme des Rechenzentrums und können damit die Heizenergie für das ganze Jahr einsparen. Dies zwingt uns leider zu der makabren Feststellung, daß Rechnerabwärme eine Wärmequelle ist.

Dem Aspekt der Ökologie wurde bei der Planung besondere Aufmerksamkeit gewidmet, nachdem nunmehr auch neben Wasser und Luft der natürliche Boden unter besonderen Schutz gestellt werden soll. Genauso wie bei der Energieeinsparung wollte die GRS auch hier vorbildlich sein, und unser Landschaftsarchitekt und wir fühlten uns selbstverständlich verpflichtet, diesen Anspruch soweit irgend möglich nachzukommen. [...]

when the radiation waves inform people whether it is snowing or raining, and whether it is day or night, whether the sun is shining or not. But as well as conveying such impressions, the minimum lighting level has an important influence on man's biological functions. This all requires that office rooms are not too deep, not more than 5 m, and that the remaining interior areas also receive daylight. This also applies to our building, and also leads to considerable energy savings. [...]

As an architect, I am aware that emissions of CO_2 and other dangerous substances are a significant factor in building, and that it is necessary to reduce them by using alternative energy sources, but above all by intelligent construction design. We opted for the second, more reasonably priced solution, and chose not to use wind and solar power or mechanical heat pumps. All that was dearer than what was achieved by »knowing how«.
The qualities of our building:
– compact shape with favourable volume and covering area values (A/V = 0.365),
– reasonable ratio and favourable distribution of windows, closed wall areas and roof areas (40 % / 60 %)
– high heat insulation values for the exterior wall sections (K = 0.5) and improvement of insulation values by the planted roof,
– large internal storage masses because of the unclad concrete coffers in the ceilings, which have a favourable regulation factor for storing heat and cold through their high surface ratio,
– heavy building mode through ceiling and screed (storage mass / exterior wall area 1256 kg/sq m > 600 kg/sq m), (5 % for heating energy).
Choosing these construction resources made it possible to reduce the annual heat energy requirements from 172,892 kW/h/a to 79.539 kW/h/a. That is 108 %. And that takes us 27 % below the required value laid down in the 1995 heat insulation regulations, and also meets the criteria for a low-energy building.

Further energy savings not accounted for in the above calculation can be named for reduction of the theoretical cooling load:
– external sunshading with daylight technology by 50 %.
– night cooling of the storage masses by using sophisticated window ventilation possibilities.
Electricity savings, also not contained in the energy balance:
– artificial light saved by skylight pyramids 5000 kW/h/a,
– sunshading daylight technology 4000 kW/h/a,
– daylight dependent lighting control 4000 kW/h/a.
Actually we even have a zero energy building, as we use the waste heat from the computer centre, thus saving heating energy all the year round. This unfortunately faces us with the macabre realization that waste computer heat is a heat source.

Particular attention was paid to the ecology aspect in the planning phase, now that the natural ground was to be particularly protected as well as water and air. GRS wanted to behave in an exemplary fashion here, just as they did in energy saving, and so did our landscape architect. We therefore felt it our duty to do as much as we could in respect of this aspect. [...]

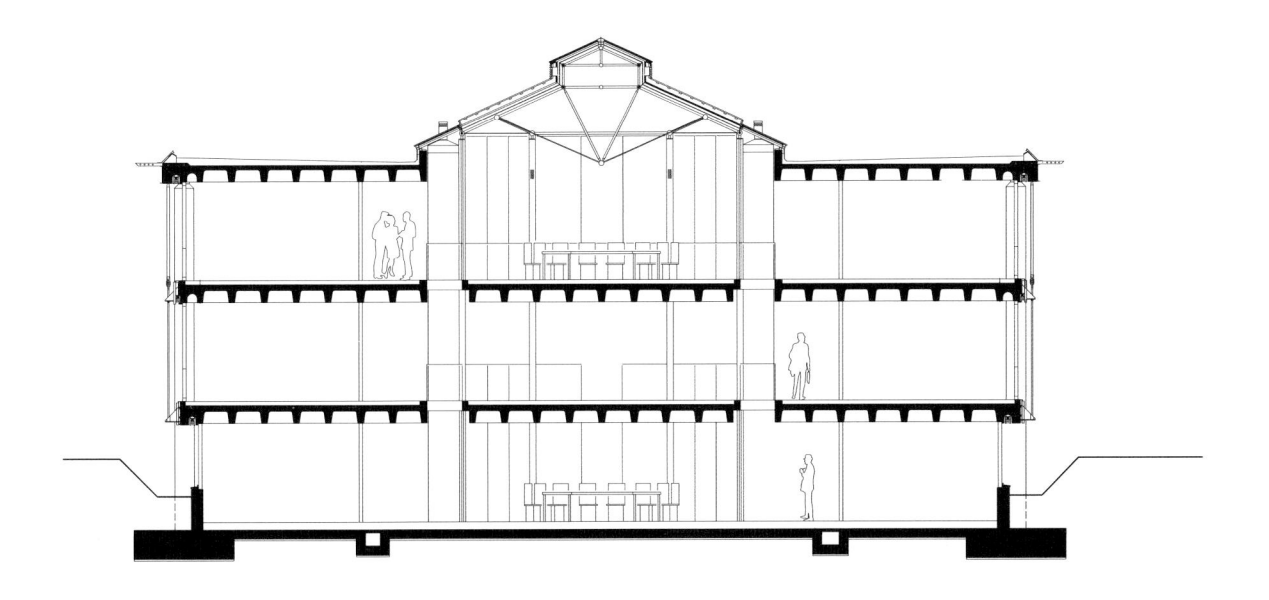

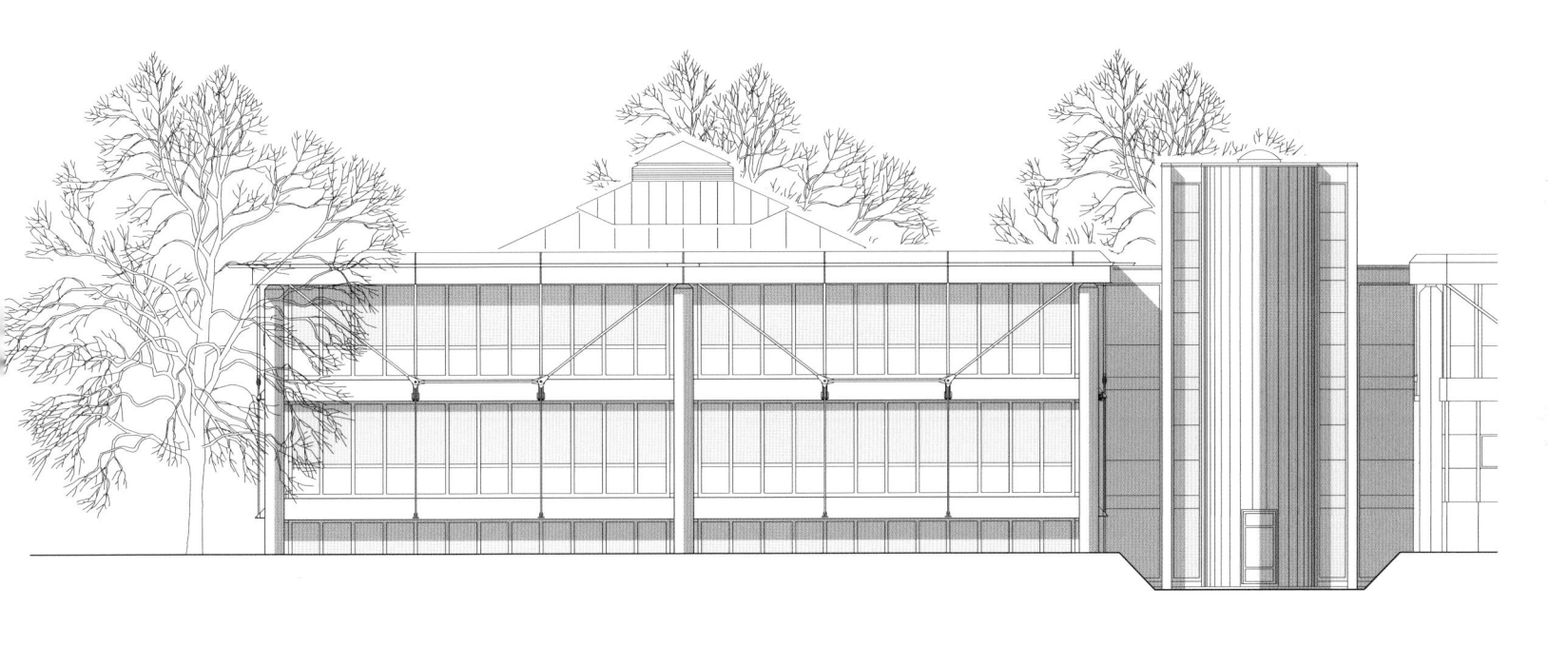

Oben: Schnitt
Unten: Ansicht Osten

Top: cross-section
Bottom: view from the east

109

110

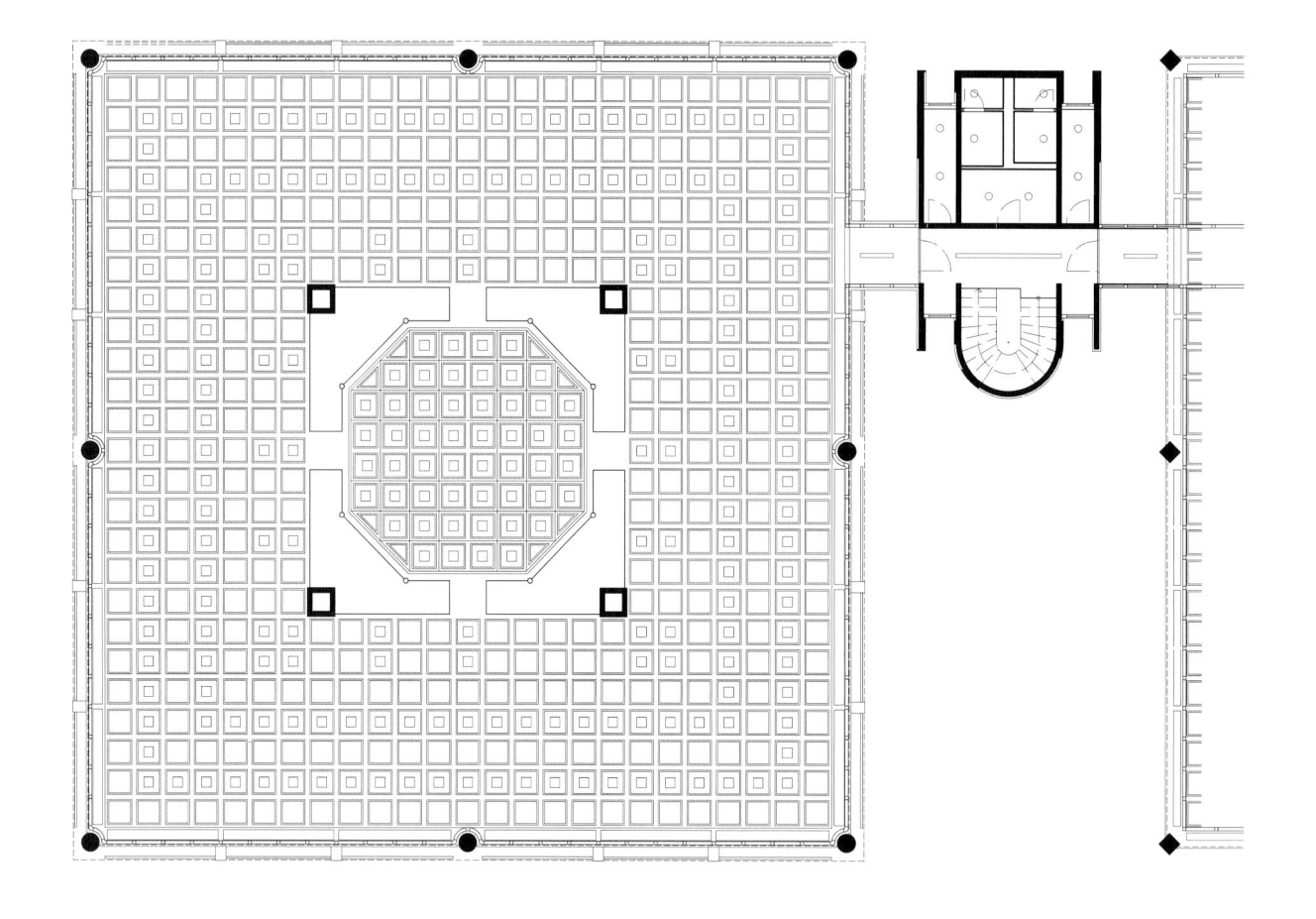

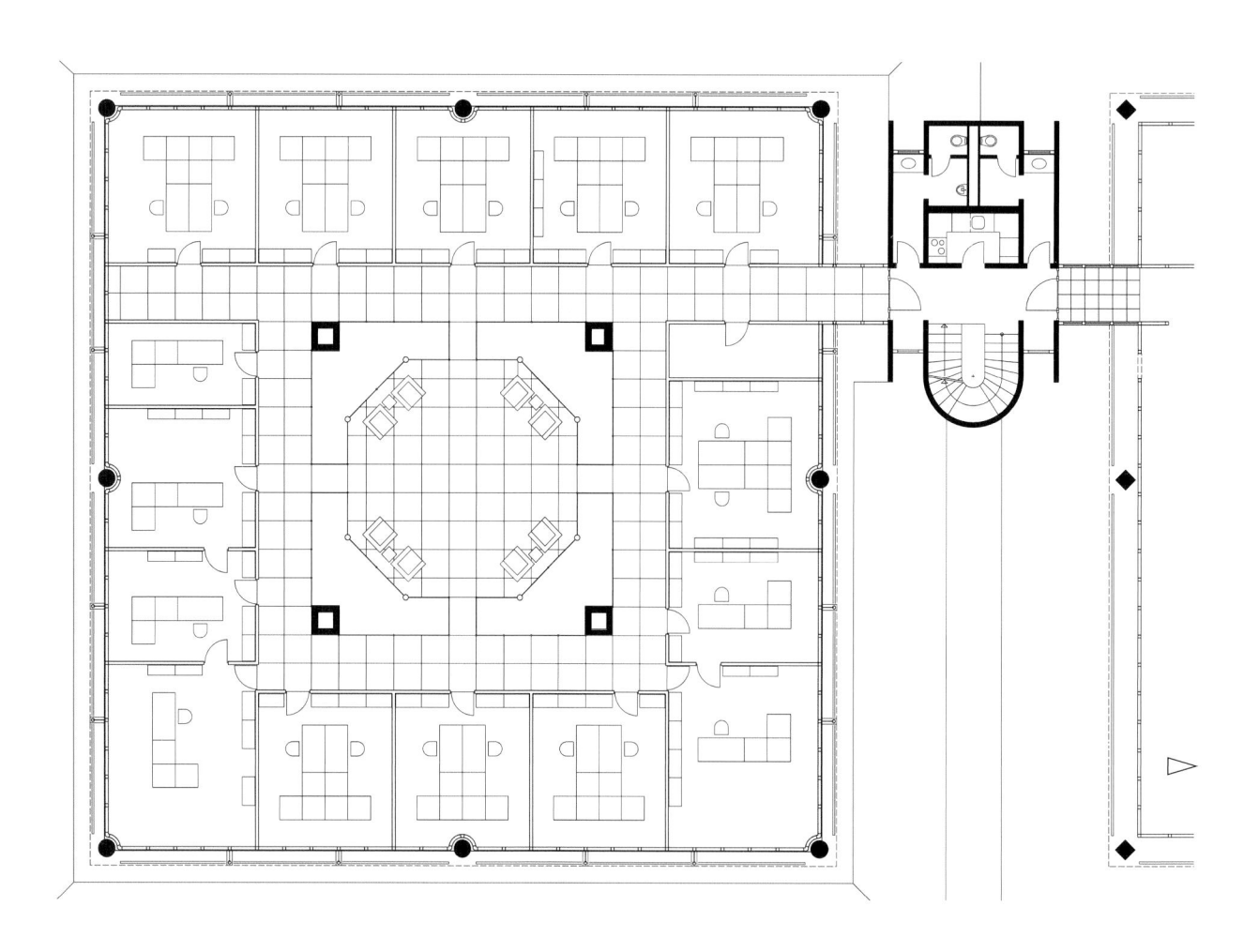

Selbst das Dach haben wir begrünt und einen Gewinn von 104 Quadratmetern erzielt und die Gehwege und Parkplätze mit Rasenpflaster und offenen Fugen ausgebildet, was einen weiteren Gewinn brachte. [...]

Zuletzt zur *causa formalis:* Ein Bauwerk schöpft die Qualitäten für seine Erscheinungsform aus dem Wert der Baumaterialien, der Lichtführung, der plastischen und farblichen Gliederung und vor allem aus den Proportionen der Körper, der Räume und der Flächen. Diese Einzelmerkmale müssen in ihrer Vielfalt zu einer harmonischen Einheit führen, die vom Betrachter auch ganzheitlich erfaßt werden kann. Von dieser muß eine bestimmte Anmutung ausgehen. Für mich ist der Gestaltungsprozeß, der zu solchen Ergebnissen führen soll, keine Beschäftigung mit Einzelmerkmalen, sondern eine mit der ganzheitlichen Struktur und dem ganzen Organismus. [...]

Baubeschreibung

Es handelt sich um einen dreigeschossigen Bau mit Unter-, Erd- und Obergeschoß. Die Anbindung an den 2. Bauabschnitt erfolgt über einen Treppenturm, in dem auch Sanitärräume zusammengefaßt sind. Im gesamten Gebäude ist eine reine Büronutzung vorgesehen. Das Untergeschoß ist gegenüber dem Gelände angehoben. Durch entsprechende Abböschungen kann es bei normaler Fensterbrüstungshöhe mit Tageslicht versorgt werden.

Die Grundrißform des Bürogebäudes ist ein Quadrat mit den Achsmaßen 23,40 x 23,40 m.

Die äußeren quadratischen, über Eck gestellten Betonstützen tragen, zusammen mit den vier innenliegenden Schachtstützen, die Stahlbetonkassettendecken im Achsmaß von neunzig Zentimetern. Alle Betonstützen wurden als dreigeschossige Fertigteile aufgestellt.

Die drei Decken haben im zentralen Bereich eine quadratische Aussparung mit der Abmessung 9,70 x 9,70 m, so daß sich ein über die drei Geschosse durchgehender Luftraum ergibt. In diesem Luftraum ist in jedem Geschoß ein achteckiger Raum eingestellt, dessen Decke von acht Stahlrohrstützen getragen wird. Diese Decke wird ebenfalls als Kassettendecke ausgeführt.

Über dem Erdgeschoß bildet eine verglaste Stahlkonstruktion den oberen Raumabschluß. Sie ruht auf den vier Schacht- und den acht Stahlrohrstützen.

Alle Decken und Stützen sind in Sichtbeton ausgeführt. Nur die Naßräume im Treppenturm wurden für Fliesenbeläge verputzt.

Die Dachkonstruktion ist als Warmdach mit Gefällebeton ausgeführt. Die Fassade ist eine Holzfassade in Rahmenbauweise. Alle Elemente haben Lüftungsflügel. Die Heizung erfolgt über eine Fußbodenheizung im gesamten Gebäude. Als Bodenbeläge wurden Teppiche in den Büro- und Flurzonen sowie Fliesen in den Sanitärräumen auf schwimmenden Heizestrichen verlegt.«

Oben: Deckenuntersicht
Unten: Grundriß Erdgeschoß

Top: ceiling
Bottom: floor plan, ground floor

We even planted the roof, gaining 104 sq m, and based the paths and parking spaces with turf and open joints, which represented a further gain. [...]

And last of all to the *causa formalis:* a building draws the qualities for its appearance from the value of the building materials, the treatment of light, the articulation of sculptural features and colour and above all from the proportions of the sections of the building, of the rooms and open areas. The diversity of these individual characteristics must lead to a harmonious unity, which can be grasped as a whole by the viewer. This harmony must exude a certain elegance. For me a design process that can lead to results of this kind is not about addressing individual features, but about addressing the structure as a whole and the entire organism. [...]

Building description

This is a three-storey building with basement, ground and first floor. It is linked to phase 2 by a staircase tower that also contains the sanitary facilities. The entire building is intended for office use only. The basement is higher that the terrain. Appropriate bank sloping means that it can be lit naturally by windows of normal sill height.

The building has a square ground plan with axis dimensions of 23.4 x 23.4 m.

The external square, diagonally placed concrete columns, together with the four internal shaft columns, carry the reinforced concrete coffers with an axis dimension of 90 cm. All the concrete columns were made as three-storey prefabricated sections.

The three ceilings have a square gap in the central area measuring 9.7 x 9.7 m, creating an air-space rising through all three storeys. Within this air-space, an octagonal space is inserted in each storey, with its ceiling carried by eight tubular steel columns. This ceiling is also coffered.

On the ground floor a glazed steel structure concluded the space at the top. It is supported by the four shaft columns and the eight tubular steel columns.

All the ceilings and columns are in exposed concrete. Only the wet rooms in the staircase tower were rendered for tiling.

The roof is constructed as a non-ventilated flat roof with sloping concrete. The façade is in timber and built on a frame system. All the elements have air vents. Dividing walls were built using the dry construction system. Heating is by under-floor heating throughout the building. Carpets were laid as floor coverings in the office and corridor zones, with tiles in the sanitary rooms on floating heat screed.«

Oben: Aufenthaltsraum im Oktagon
Rechts: Konferenzraum im Oktagon

Above: common room in the octagon
Right page: conference rooms in the octagon

FOLGENDE DOPPELSEITE
Gesamtansicht von Osten

NEXT DOUBLE PAGE
View from the east

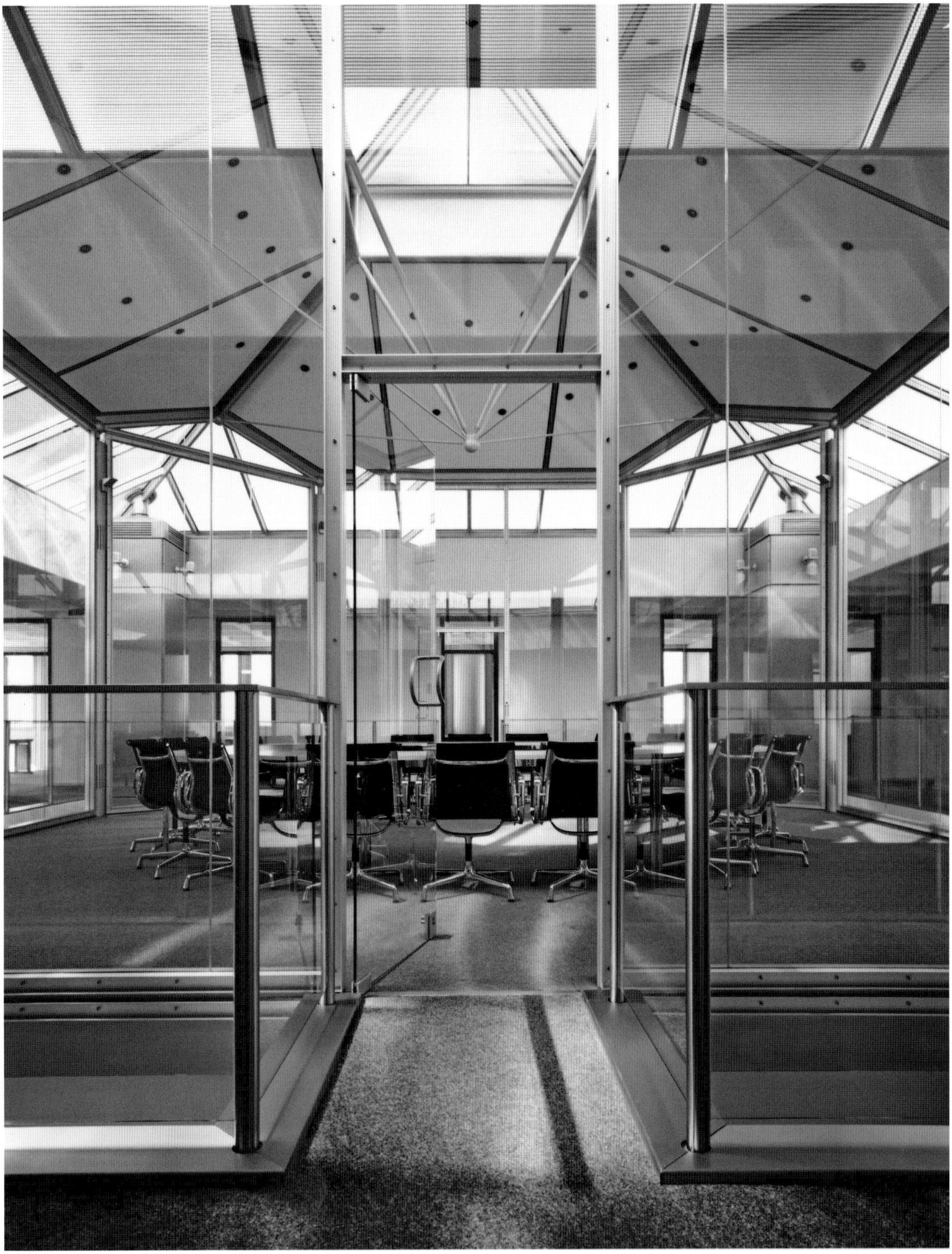

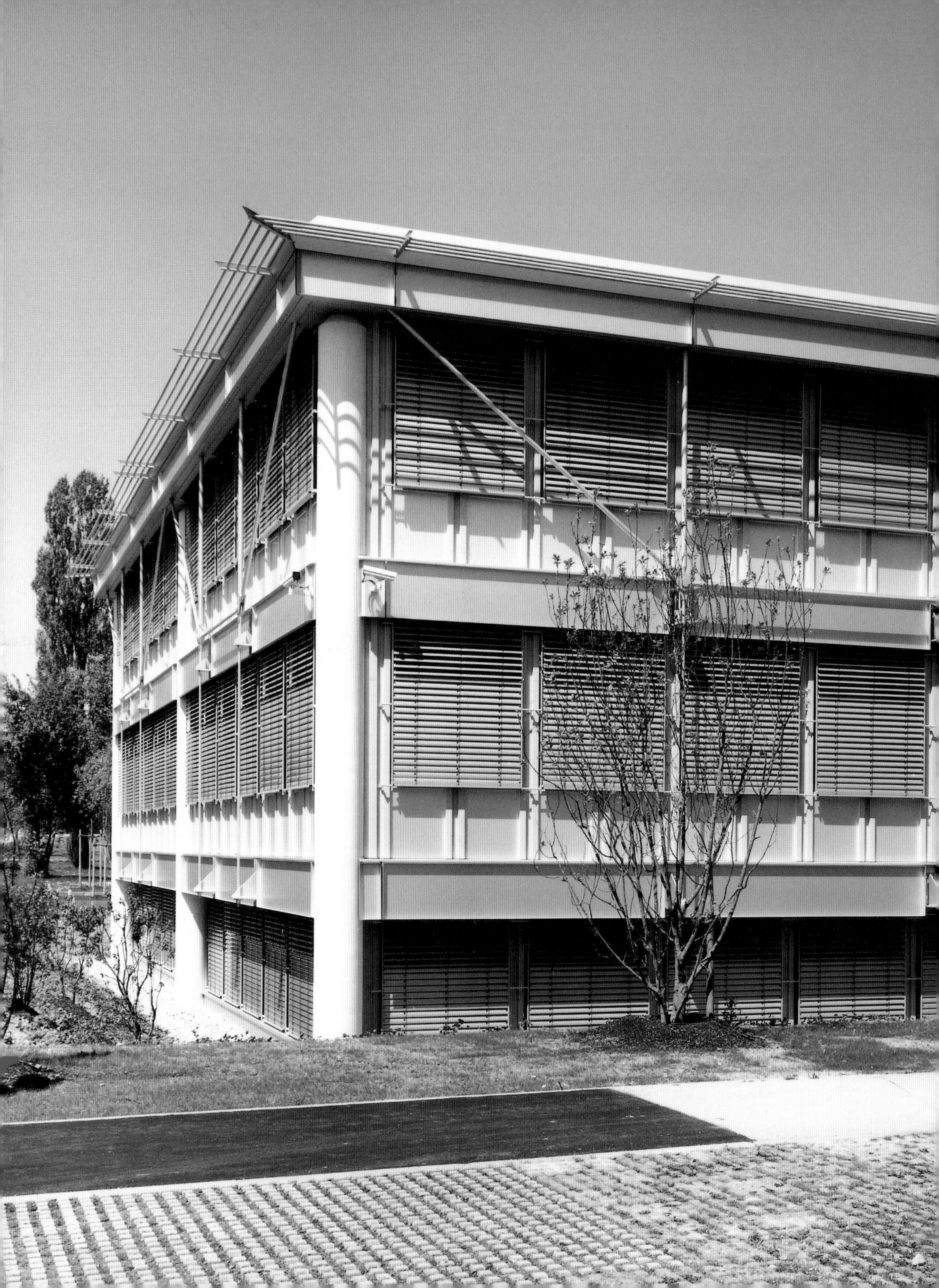

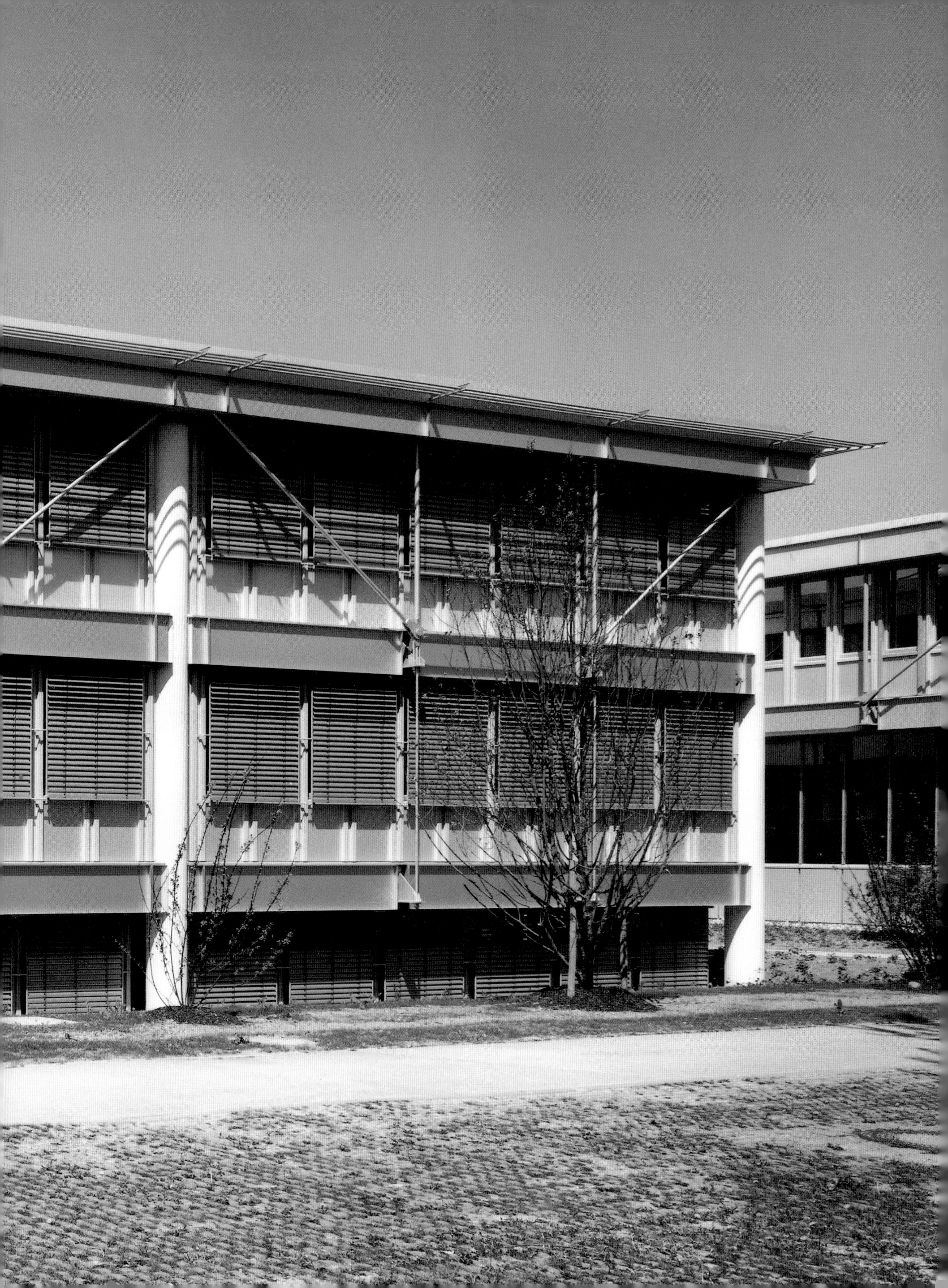

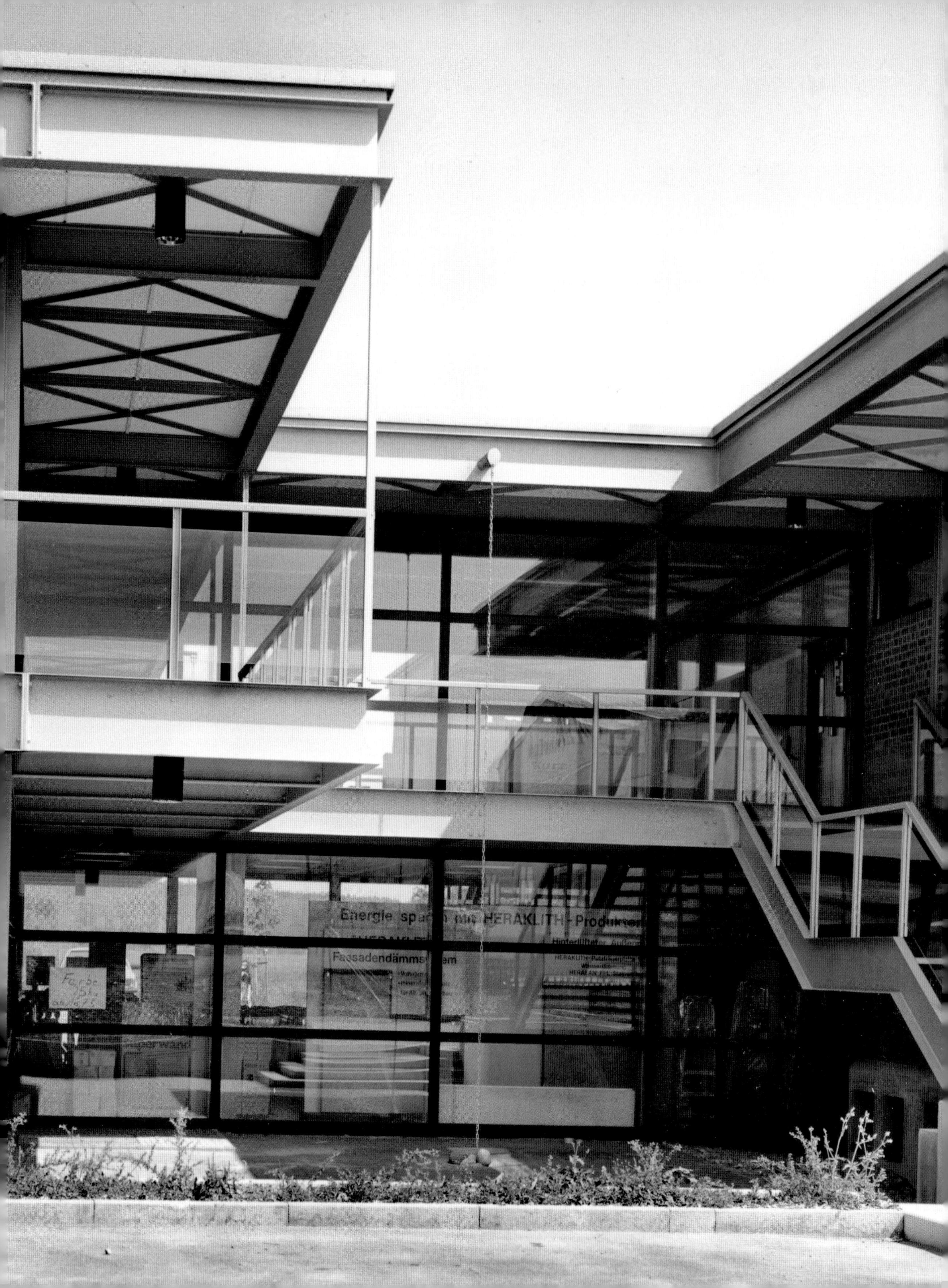

Ausstellungs- und Lagerhalle in Herrsching am Ammersee, 1979–81
Bauherr: Bauwaren Haas

Showroom and warehouse in Herrsching am Ammersee, 1979–81
Client: Bauwaren Haas

Wer sich in Gewerbegebieten mit deren normalerweise acht- und einfallslosen Bauten umgesehen hat, wird dem gelungenen Versuch einer Bauherrschaft und ihres Architekten, auch das Alltägliche wertvoll und bewußt zu gestalten, seine Hochachtung nicht versagen können.

In exemplarischer Weise hat Detlef Schreiber aus einer Alltäglichkeit, was Gebäudezweck und Nutzen betrifft, ein Werk rationaler Architektur gestaltet. Konstruktive und ökonomische Gesichtspunkte führen durch eine streng sachgerechte und disziplinierte Verwendung des stabförmigen Baustoffs Stahl zu hoher ästhetischer Qualität. Unter weit ausladenden Dächern wurde das vorgegebene Programm in Vielfalt vereint. Die Genauigkeit, der Anstand und die Unaufgeregtheit des Details machen diesen an sich bescheidenen Bau zu einer Aussage von hohem Rang.

Baubeschreibung des Architekten

»Das Baugrundstück liegt am Rand des Gewerbegebiets der Gemeinde Herrsching, am Übergang zur freien Landschaft. Diese Lage und das geneigte Gelände verlangten eine bedachtsame Einfügung der großen Baumasse und eine ihr angemessene Gestaltung der Baukörper. Der Bebauungsplan ließ nur eine beschränkte Höhenentwicklung zu, die für die Lagerhalle ausreichend war, nicht aber für den zweigeschossigen Ausstellungsteil. Die Hofflächen wurden dem natürlichen Geländeverlauf angepaßt, der unmittelbare Umgriff um den Ausstellungsteil aber leicht abgesenkt, um zwei Geschosse zu ermöglichen und einen Ausstellungshof zu schaffen. Das Raumprogramm verlangte eine LKW-befahrbare Lagerhalle von tausend Quadratmetern und Ausstellungsflächen von insgesamt ebenfalls tausend Quadratmetern. Eine möglichst große Schaufensterfläche war Bedingung.

Für die Lagerhalle bot sich eine quadratische Grundrißfläche – unterteilt in neun Quadrate mit jeweils 9,60 x 9,60 Metern Achsmaß – an. Für den Ausstellungsbau wurde ein kreuzförmiger Grundriß, bestehend aus fünf Quadraten, ebenfalls mit jeweils 9,60 x 9,60 Metern Achsmaß, gewählt.

So konnte die Außenwandfläche der Lagerhalle minimiert und bei der zweigeschossigen Ausstellungshalle durch die große Abwicklungslänge optimiert werden. Im Ausstellungsgebäude erschließt ein umlaufender 2,40 Meter breiter Balkon mit zwei gegenüberliegenden Treppen das 1. Obergeschoß. Im Inneren verbinden eine Treppe und

Anyone who has looked round industrial estates, with their structures that are normally built without attention or inspiration, will not fail to appreciate a successful attempt by clients and their architect to design even something ordinary thoughtfully and with a sense of its value.

Detlef Schreiber has created a work of rational architecture in an exemplary fashion from an entirely ordinary situation in terms of the purpose and use of the building. His structural and economic view leads to high aesthetic quality through a strictly appropriate and disciplined use of steel in bar form. The prescribed programme was brought together in diversity under widely protruding roofs. The precision, the decency and the lack of excitement in the details make this essentially modest building into a statement of the first order.

The architect's description of the building

»The plot is on the outskirts of the industrial estate in Herrsching, at the point where the open countryside begins. This situation and the sloping site meant that the substantial building mass had to be fitted in carefully, with an appropriate design for the individual buildings. The development plan permitted only limited height development, which was adequate for the warehouse but not for the two-storey showroom section. The yard spaces conformed with the natural lie of the terrain, but the area immediately adjacent to the showroom section was sunk slightly to make it possible to build two storeys and create a show yard. The spatial programme required a 1000 sq m warehouse into which lorries could drive, and another 1000 sq m of showroom space. One of the conditions was the largest possible area of display windows.

A square ground plan suggested itself for the warehouse – divided into nine squares, each with axial dimensions of 9.6 x 9.6 m. A cruciform ground plan was chosen for the showroom building, consisting of five squares each with axial dimensions of 9.6 x 9.6 m.

In this way it was possible to minimize the exterior wall area of the warehouse, while it was optimized for the two-storey showroom hall because of the great development length. Access to the 1st floor of

Links: Verbindung von Ausstellungs- zur Lagerhalle

Left page: connection from the exhibition hall to the storage hall

ein Lastenaufzug alle Ebenen, sowohl die der beiden Ausstellungsgeschosse als auch die der Lagerhalle. Ein Teil des Gebäudes ist unterkellert. Dort befinden sich die Personalräume und die Technikzentrale mit einem Ölheizkessel und einer zuschaltbaren Grundwasserwärmepumpe. Der Ausstellungsteil wird über den Fußboden beheizt, die Lagerhalle über Warmluftgeräte an der Decke. Durch die Oberlichtpyramiden und die großen Glaswände, welche durch weit auskragende Vordächer gegen Überhitzung geschützt sind, wird passiv Solarenergie gewonnen. Dies wirkt sich auf die Energiebilanz äußerst positiv aus. Dem Gebäude liegt ein einheitlicher Konstruktionsraster von 9,60 x 9,60 Metern zugrunde und ein Außenraster von 2,40 Metern. Die Fundamente und der Keller sind in Beton ausgeführt. Die Lagerhalle und der zweigeschossige Ausstellungsteil bestehen aus einer Profilstahlkonstruktion für Stützen, Binder und Träger, mit Ziegelwandausfachungen bzw. einer vorgesetzten, thermisch getrennten Aluminium-Glaswandkonstruktion. Die Stahlkonstruktion bot sich sowohl unter konstruktiv gestalterischen als auch funktional wirtschaftlichen Gesichtspunkten an. Der empfindliche Baugrund verlangte eine leichte, setzungsunempfindliche Konstruktion. Die großen Spannweiten und die vom Baurecht vorgegebene Limitierung der Höhenentwicklung führten eindeutig zur Wahl des Baustoffs Stahl. Ins Gewicht fielen auch die Vorteile einer Vorfertigung im Werk samt Präzision und einer beachtlichen Beschleunigung des Bauvorgangs. Die Montagestöße wurden mittels Kopfplatten und Schrauben bewerkstelligt – das Schweißen an der Baustelle wurde weitestgehend vermieden und blieb der Ausnahmefall.

Die tragende Konstruktion besteht aus Normprofilen, zusammengesetzten kreuzförmigen Stützen im Quadratraster 9,60 x 9,60 Meter, die in Köcherfundamente eingespannt sind. Sie nehmen die Windkräfte aus allen Richtungen aus dem umlaufenden Windverbandträger im auskragenden Vordach auf. Zwischen den Stützen überspannen als Hauptträger Fachwerkbinder die Spannweite von jeweils 9,60 Metern. In dieses Quadrat der Hauptbinder wurden die Nebenträger aus Normprofilen in den Viertelspunkten so versetzt eingefügt, dass die Dachlast gleichmäßig auf alle vier Hauptbinder und auf die Stützen abgetragen wird. Das sich in Feldmitte ergebende Feld von 4,80 x 4,80 Metern wurde als Zargenträger ausgebildet, auf dem die Leichtkonstruktionen für die kittlos verglasten Pyramiden aufgesetzt werden konnten. Auf den Nebenträgern liegen in wechselnden Spannrichtungen vorgefertigte Gasbetondachplattenelemente, die zusammen mit den aufgelegten PU-Hartschaumplatten die Wärmedämmung übernehmen. Die Dachhaut besteht aus PVC-Folie, welche mit einer Kiesauflage beschwert ist.

Das auskragende Vordach und bei der zweigeschossigen Ausstellungshalle der Balkon sind als horizontale Windverbandsträger mit Aussteifungsdiagonalen ausgebildet. Über die Kragträger in den Hauptachsen werden die Kräfte in die eingespannten Stützen geleitet.

Bei der Lagerhalle bestehen die Wandausfachungen aus zweiseitigem Sichtmauerwerk; die Tore sind als verglaste Stahlfalttore ausgebildet. Das Ausstellungsgebäude umschließt eine thermisch getrennte Aluminium-Glaswandkonstruktion aus Pfosten und Riegeln mit Neoprene-Druckverglasung.«

the showroom building is via a continuous balcony 2.4 m wide with two flights of steps opposite each other. Inside, stairs and a goods lift link all levels, both the two showroom floors and also in the warehouse. Part of the building has a basement. These contain the staffrooms and the services control room with a central heating boiler and a selectable ground-water heat pump. The showroom section has under-floor heating, the warehouse has warm air devices on the ceiling. The toplight pyramids and the large glass walls, protected against overheating by the widely protruding canopies, absorb passive solar energy. This has an extremely positive effect on the energy balance. The building is based on a uniform structural grid of 9.6 x 9.6 m, and an exterior grid of 2.4 m. The foundations and the basement are in concrete. The warehouse and the two-storey showroom building consist of a sectional steel structure for columns, trusses and beams, with brick infill or a thermally separated aluminium glass wall structure placed in front. The steel structure suggested itself for reasons of both structural design and financial viability. The sensitive subsoil required a light structure that was not susceptible to subsidence. The large spans and the high limitations laid down by the building regulations made steel the only possible choice as a building material. Other factors were the advantages of factory prefabrication and a considerably faster building programme. The assembly joints were created with the head-plates and screws – on-site welding was avoided as much as possible, and remained an exception.

The load-bearing structure consists of standard sections, composite cruciform columns on a square grid of 9.6 x 9.6 m, fixed into bucket foundations. They absorb the wind loads from all directions from the continuous wind bracing beams in the projecting roof. Between the columns, the main beams are trussed girders each spanning 9.6 m. The subsidiary beams are fitted into this square of main beams, and staggered so that the roof load is distributed evenly over all four main beams and the columns. The 4.8 x 4.8 m field produced in the middle was formed as a frame beam able to support the lightweight structures for the pyramids, which are glazed without putty. The subsidiary beams support prefabricated gas concrete roof slab elements in alternating stress directions; these and the PU rigid foam sheets on top of them provide heat insulation. The roof is covered in PVC sheeting weighted with a layer of gravel.

The projecting roof and the balcony in the case of the two-storey showroom section are structured as horizontal wind brace beams with reinforcing diagonals. The cantilever girders in the main axes distribute the forces into the fixed columns.

For the warehouse, the wall infill is in two-sided exposed masonry; the doors are in the form of glazed steel folding doors.

The showroom building is enclosed in a thermally separated aluminium-glass post-and-rail wall structure with neoprene pressure glazing.«

Oben: Grundriß Erdgeschoß
Unten: Schnitt

Top: floor plan, ground floor
Bottom: cross-section

119

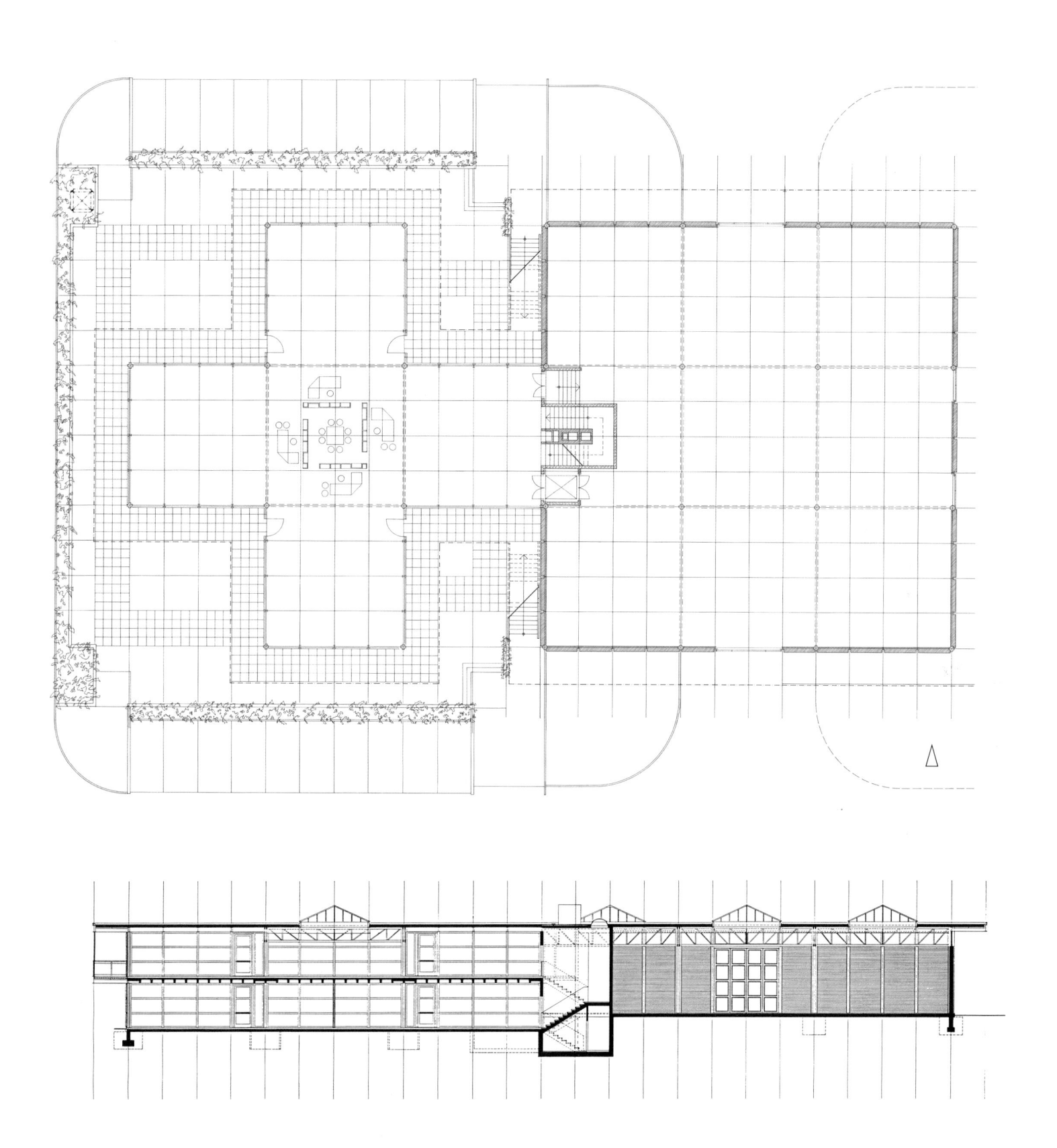

Erdgeschoß, Ausstellungsräume
Ground floor, exhibition rooms

Obergeschoß, Ausstellungsräume

Upper floor, exhibition rooms

FOLGENDE DOPPELSEITE:
Gesamtansicht an der Gewerbestraße

NEXT DOUBLE PAGE:
Elevation facing Gewerbestrasse

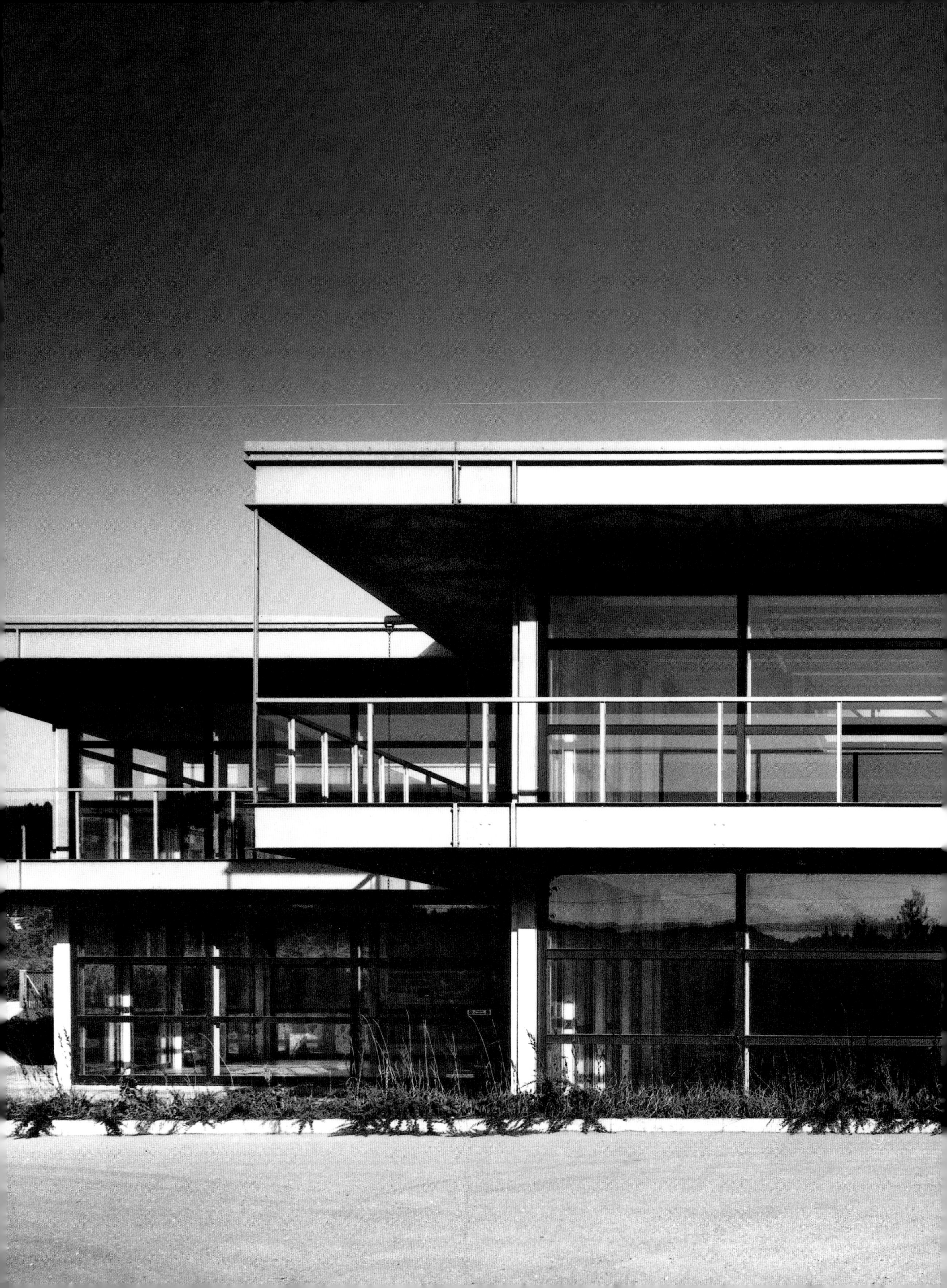

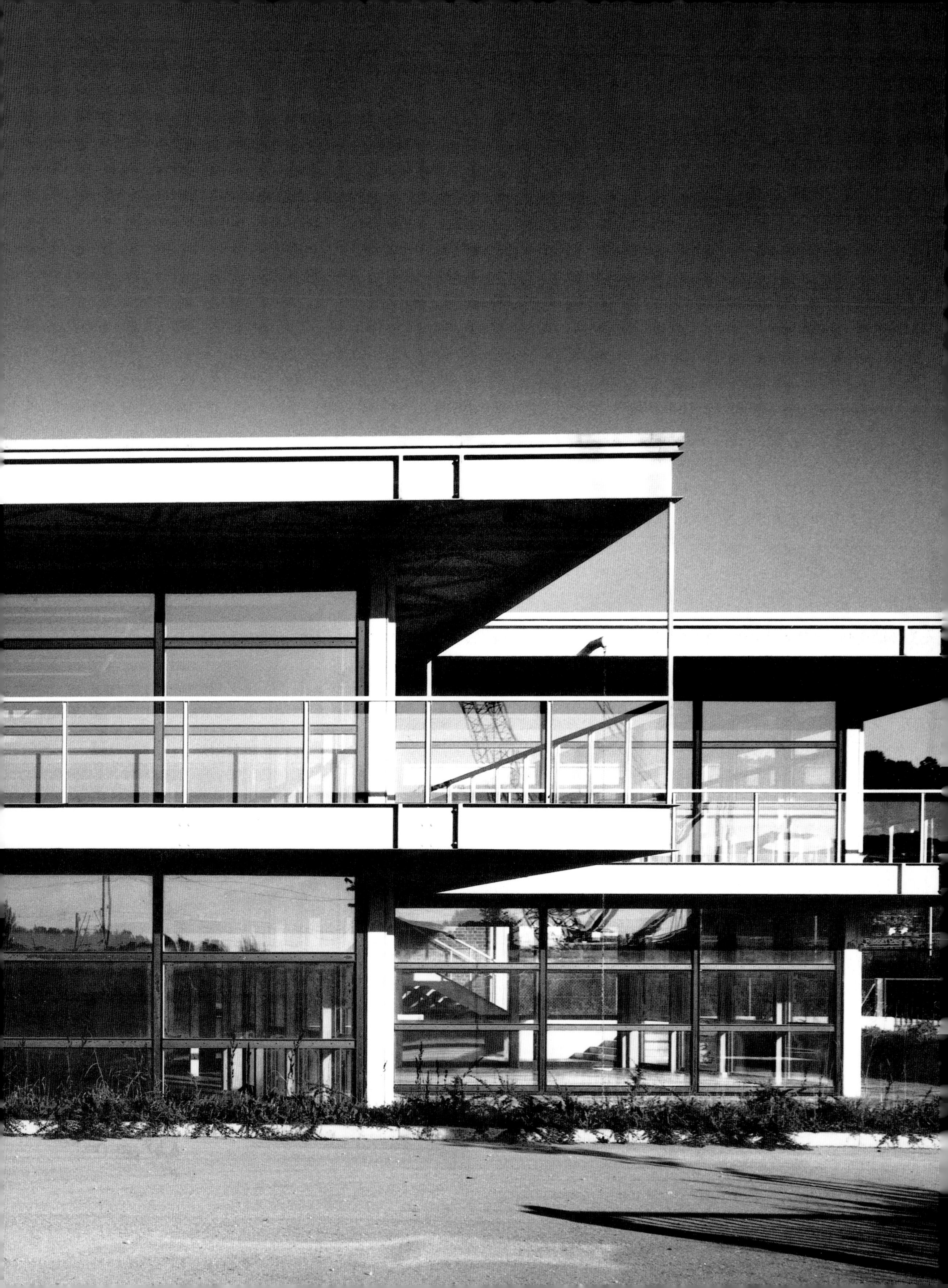

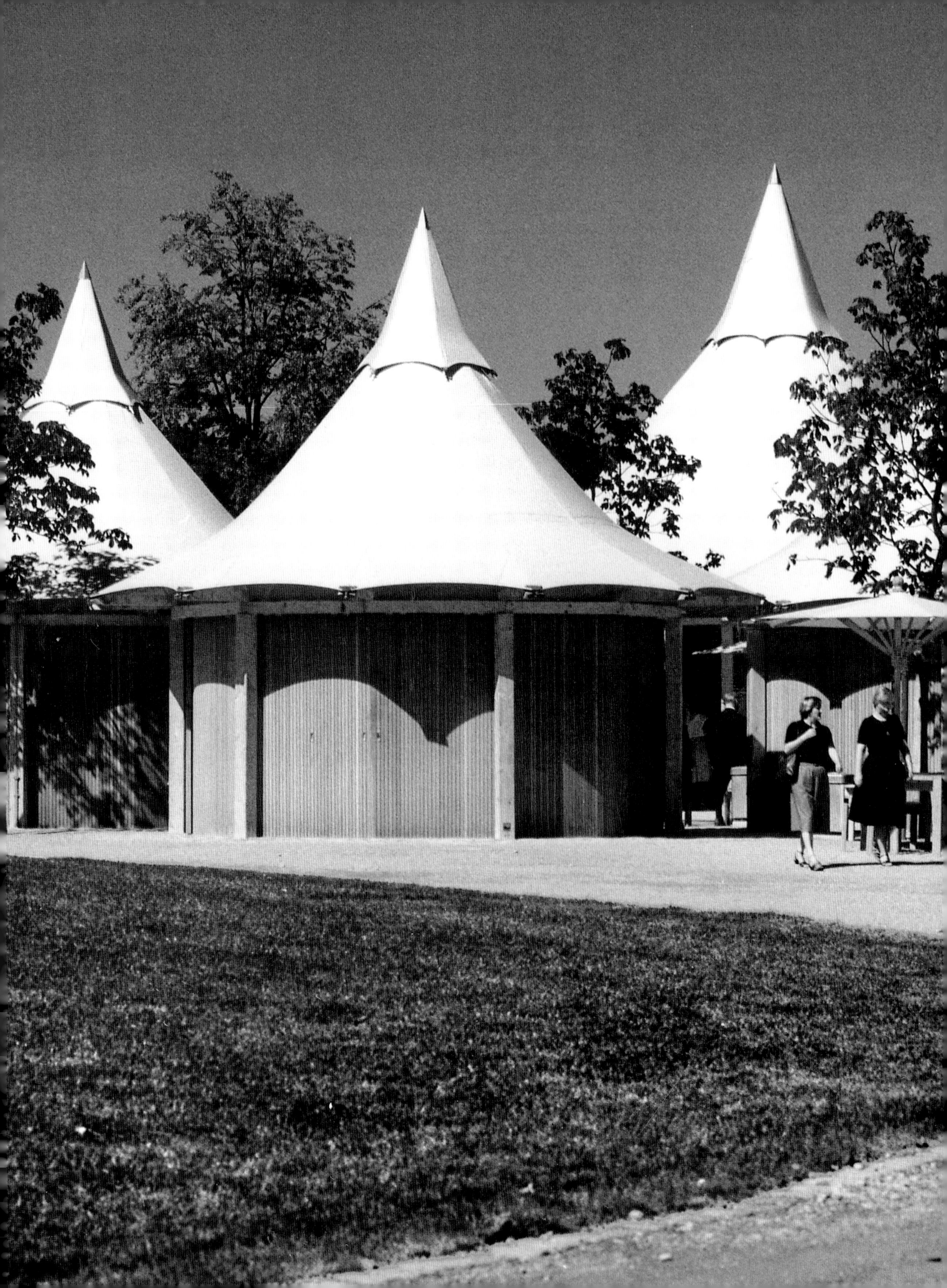

Spielhäuser am Jackl, Westpark, München, 1982 – 83
Bauherr: Stadt München

Am Jackl play houses, Westpark, Munich, 1982 – 83
Client: City of Munich

Für Detlef Schreiber waren diese aus Holz gefügten, fast schirmartig wirkenden, mit transluzenten Textilmembranen bespannten Rundbauten tatsächlich Spiel, Anlaß zur spielerischen, bis ins letzte durchgehaltenen Erfindung. Etwas scheinbar Einfaches hochkomplex zur Perfektion zu bringen war ihm Vergnügen und Freude. So gesehen, erweisen sich die Spielhäuser als eine Art Schlüssel zu Schreibers architektonischem Empfinden und Denken.

Entwurfskonzept

»Zunächst wurden die Häuser – es wurden vier – als kleines Dorf um einen baumbestandenen Anger zwischen künstlichen Hügeln derart gruppiert, daß deren zu öffnende Innenräume einen gemeinsamen Außenraum umschlossen. Die Häuser wurden nämlich mit zwei Paar gegeneinander verschiebbaren Rundtoren ausgestattet, um größte Variabilität und Öffnungsmöglichkeiten in alle Richtungen zu erreichen. Die Dächer sind transluzent. Es ist also trotz der Holzwände hell in den Häusern. Lüftung erfolgt über sogenannte Lüftungshüte; es entsteht Zug und somit rascher Luftwechsel.

Die strenge Forderung nach äußerster Wirtschaftlichkeit führte zur Erarbeitung von Alternativen, deren preiswerteste zur Ausführung kam.

Aus einer Grundüberlegung wurden unterschiedliche Vieleckkonstruktionen entwickelt. Die eine basiert auf einem Sechseck mit sechs Stützen, sechs Hauptträgern und sechs zusätzlich eingehängten Trägern. Das ergibt im Grundriß ein Zwölfeck.

Die Variante basiert auf einem Achteck mit acht Stützen, acht Haupt- und acht Einhängeträgern, also einem Sechzehneck.

Die aus Holz gefertigten, im Grundriß einem Kreissegment entsprechenden Schiebetore passen sich in Laufschienen der jeweiligen Außenform an.

Die Dachkonstruktion

Das Dachtragwerk besteht aus einem räumlich verbundenen System von leichten, unterspannten Holzfachwerkträgern, die im Firstpunkt biegesteif verbunden sind. Sie liegen auf den vorhin beschriebenen äußeren Holzstützen, dort gegen Verschieben gesichert, auf. Neben den Trägern zwischen First und Traufe wurden auch umlaufende Ringträger angeordnet, welche das System konzentrisch stabilisieren.

For Detlef Schreiber these round, jointed-timber structures, looking almost like umbrellas covered with translucent textile membranes, really were a game, stimulating him to feats of playful invention that persisted to the last. Perfecting something apparently simple in a highly complex fashion was a source of joy and pleasure to him. Seen in this way, the play houses prove to furnish a sort of key to Schreiber's architectural sensibilities and thinking.

Design concept

»First the houses – four of them were built – were grouped like a small village around a meadow with trees between artificial mounds in such a way that their interiors, which could be opened up, surrounded a common exterior. The houses were in fact equipped with two pairs of round doors that could slide counter to each other in order to achieve the greatest possible variability and openness in all directions. The roofs are translucent, so it is light in the houses despite the wooden walls. Ventilation is via so-called ventilation hats; they create a draught, and thus a rapid change of air.

A strict requirement for extreme economy led to the devising of alternatives, the cheapest of which was executed.

Various polygonal structures were developed for basic reasons. One is based on a hexagon with six columns, six main beams and six additional suspended beams. This produces a dodecagonal cross-section.

The variant is based on an octagon with eight columns, eight main and eight suspended beams, in other words a hexadecagon.

The wooden sliding doors, corresponding to a segment of a circle in ground plan, fit into runners following the appropriate external shape.

The roof structure

The roof is supported by a three-dimensionally linked system of light, wooden truss beams connected rigidly at the ridge point. They are supported on the previously described outer wooden columns, and

Links: Blick auf drei Spielhäuser
Left page: three play houses

Dadurch können die hohen Zugkräfte des in zwei Richtungen gespannten Membrandachs ohne weiteres aufgenommen werden. Die Membran ist außerdem durch ein umlaufendes Zugband im deutlich von außen sichtbaren Knickpunkt nach unten verspannt, da durch die Offenheit der Dachkonstruktion bei offenen Toren auch von unten her starke, abhebende Windkräfte auftreten können.

Die Gestaltung

Die Erscheinungsform der vier Häuser bringt zunächst die konstruktive Idee zum Ausdruck, verselbständigt sich aber unversehens zu einem Zeichen. Dieses steht nach Form und Farbe in harmonischem Kontrast zu seiner Umgebung.

Zwischen den Bauten mit ihren spitzen prismatischen Dächern und den umgebenden rundlichen Hügeln entsteht Harmonie. Das Blattwerk und die Äste der Bäume zeigen sich als Schattenmuster auf der Innenseite der Membran; umgekehrt bildet sich die filigrane Konstruktion als Schattenriß bei künstlicher Beleuchtung nach außen hin ab.«

secured against sliding at that point. Continuous ring beams were also put in place, as well as the beams between ridge and eaves, and these stabilize the system concentrically. This means that the high tensile forces in the membrane roof, which is stretched in two directions, can be absorbed without difficulty. The membrane is also braced by a continuous tension band at the nick-point, which is clearly visible from the outside, as considerable lifting wind forces can come from below when the doors are open because of the openness of the roof structure.

The design

The appearance of the four houses expresses the structural idea first and foremost, but also suddenly becomes a sign in its own right. This contrasts harmoniously with its surroundings in shape and colour.

Harmony emerges between the buildings with their pointed prismatic roofs and rounded mounds between them. The foliage and branches of the trees show as a shadow pattern on the inside of the membrane; conversely, the filigree structure stands out as a silhouette under artificial lighting at night.«

Oben: Ansicht Schnitt
Unten: Grundriß

Top: elevation, sectional view
Bottom: ground layout

FOLGENDE DOPPELSEITEN:
S. 128–129: Blick in die Zeltkonstruktion
S. 130–131: Gesamtansicht der Anlage

NEXT DOUBLE PAGES:
P. 128–129: View of the tent-like structure
P. 130–131: Overall view of the complex

127

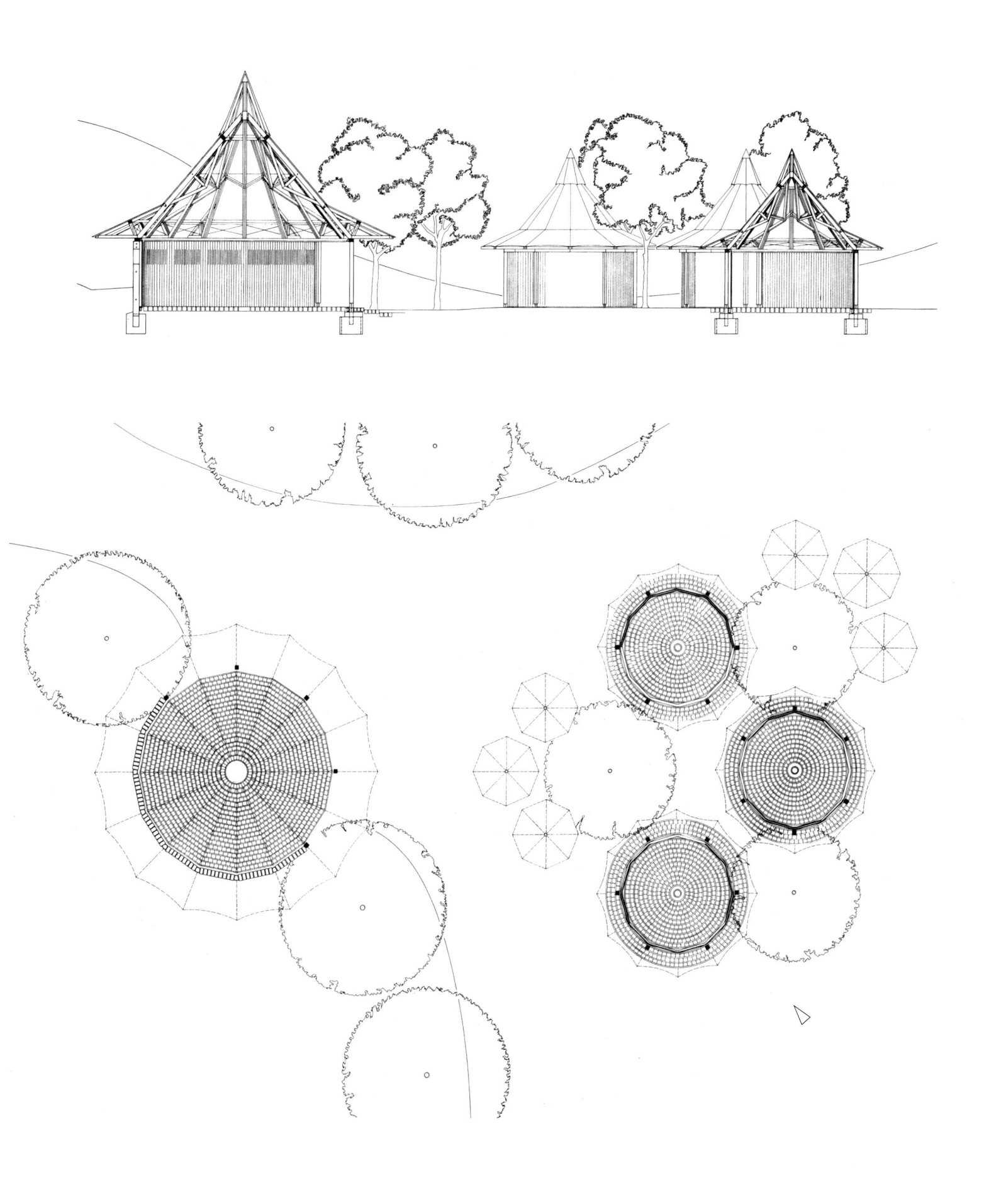

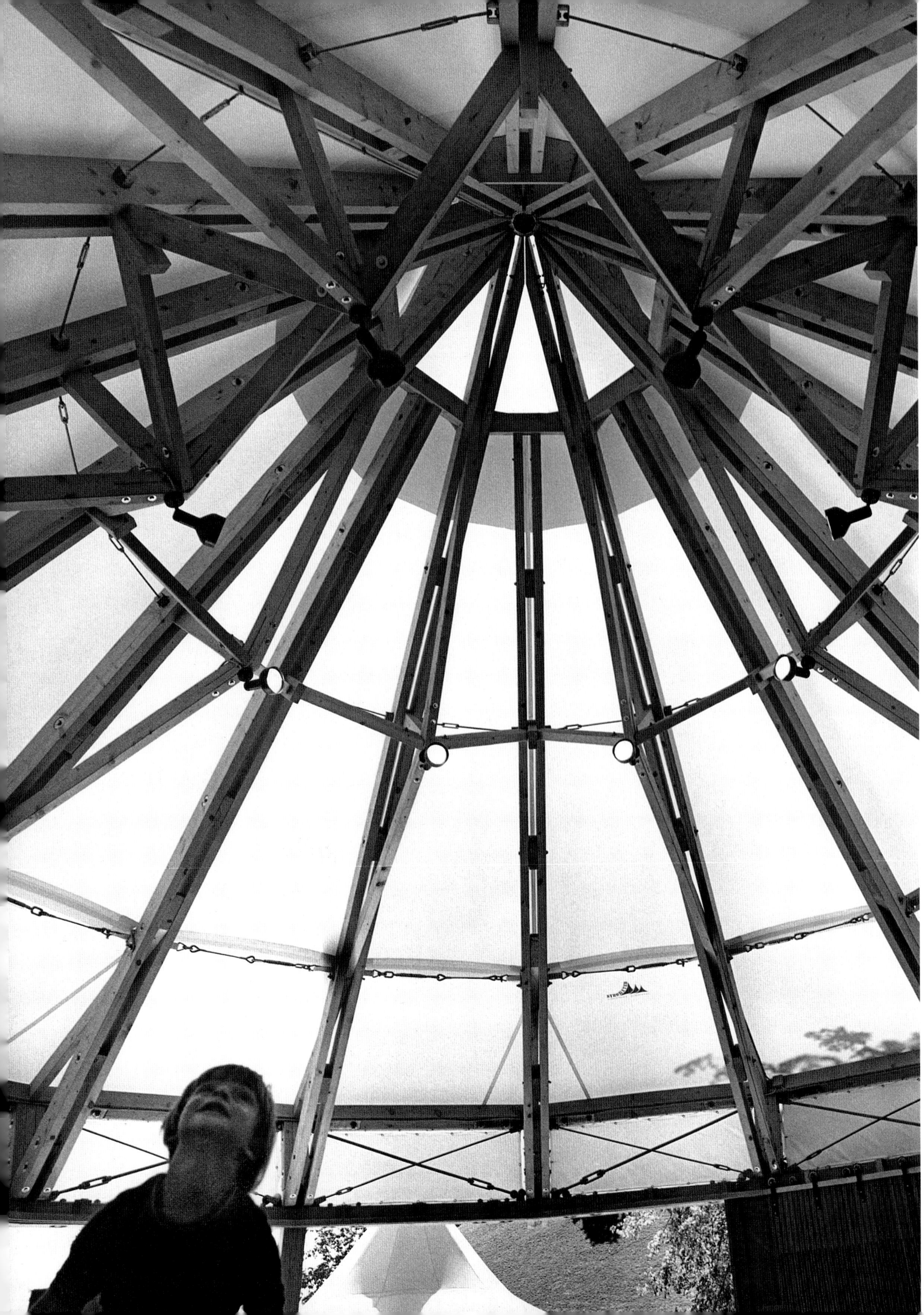

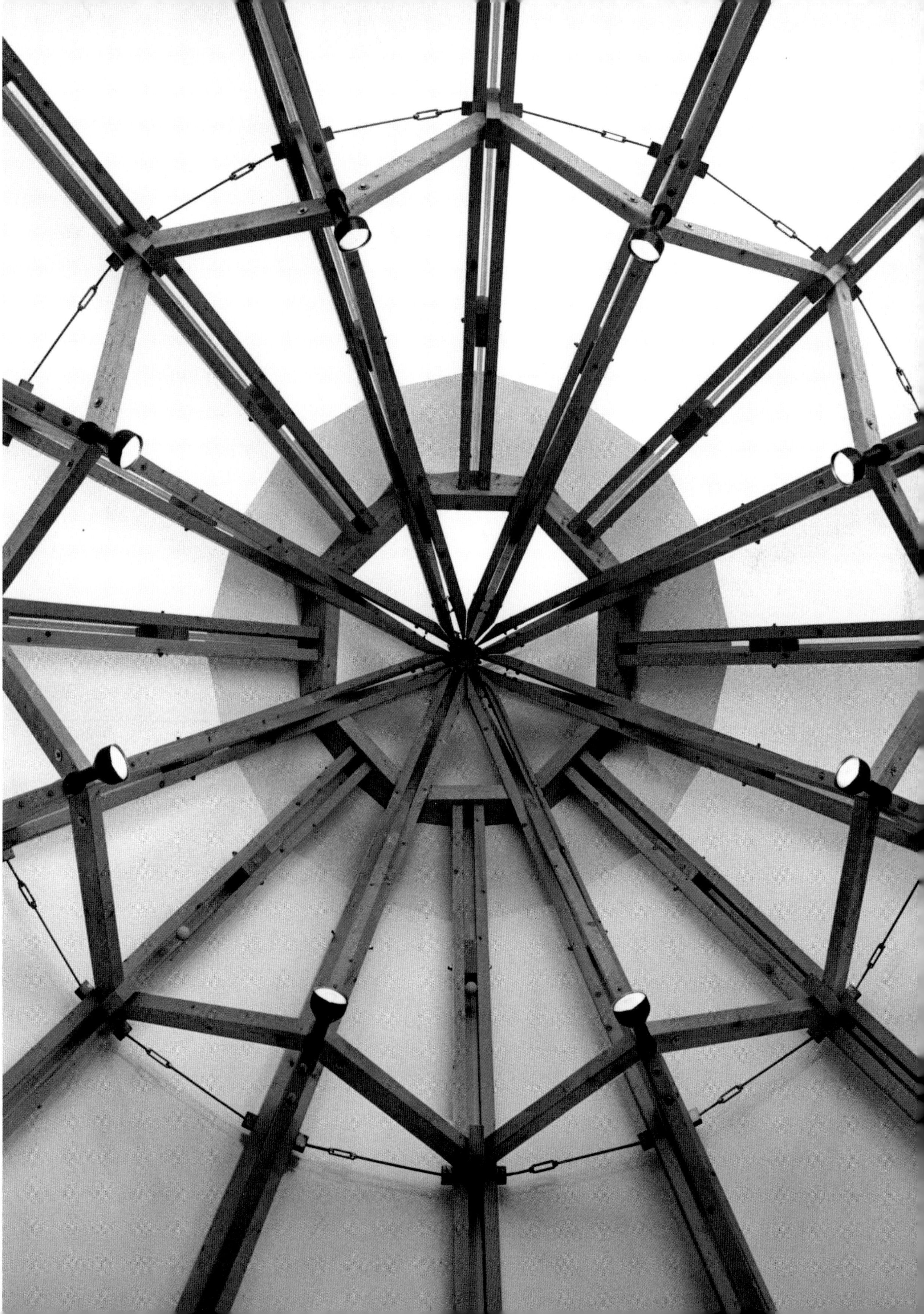

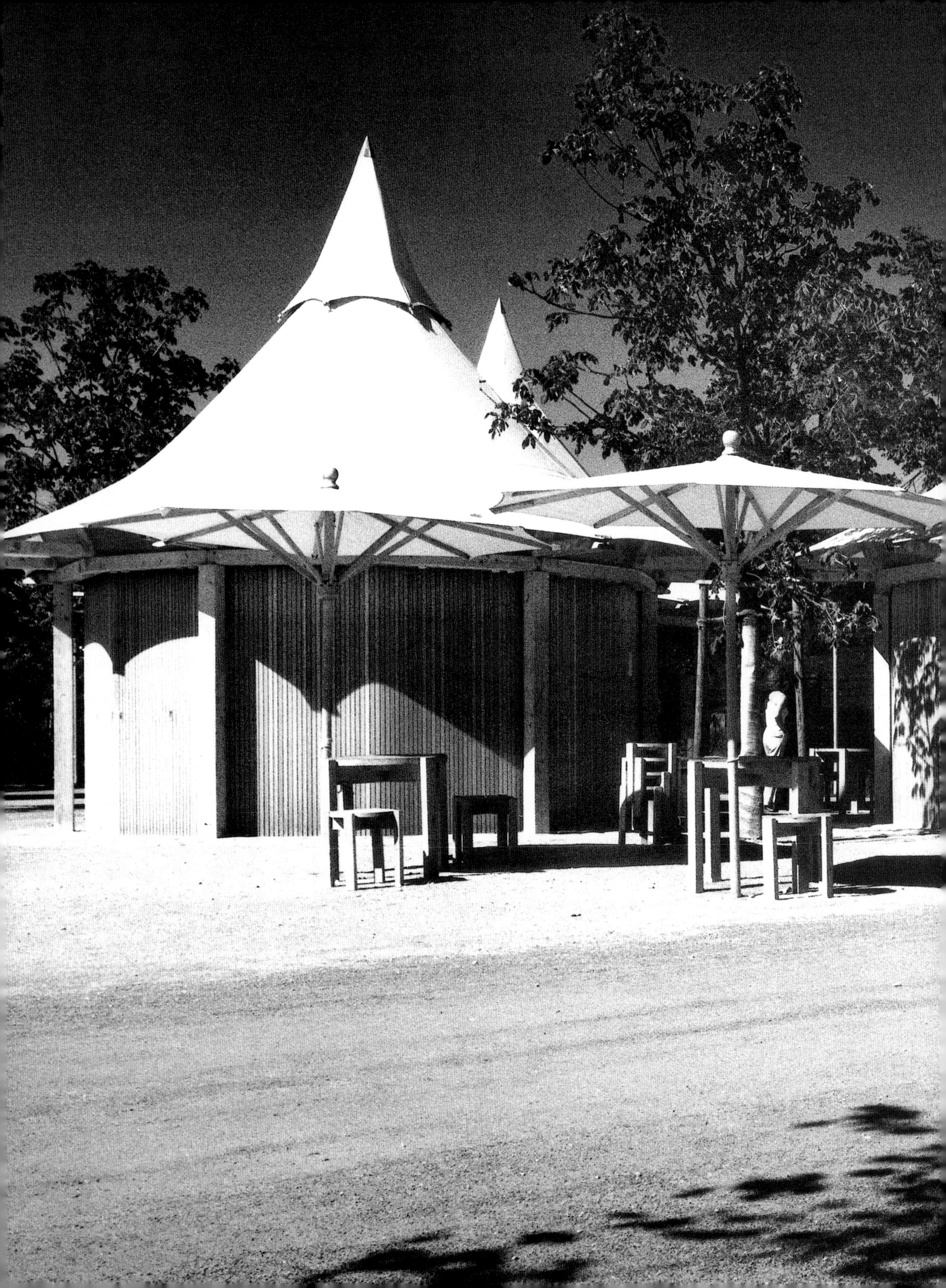

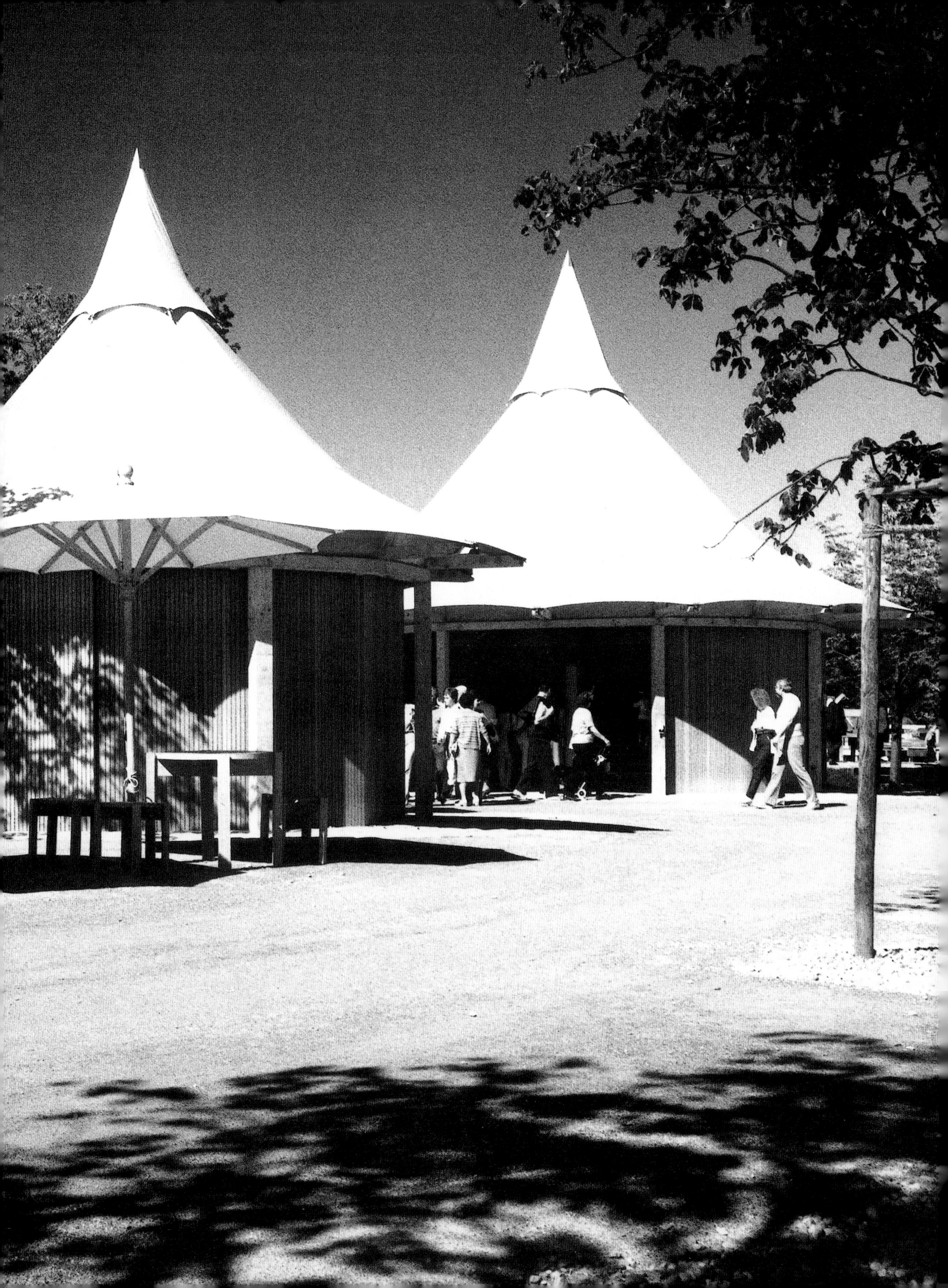

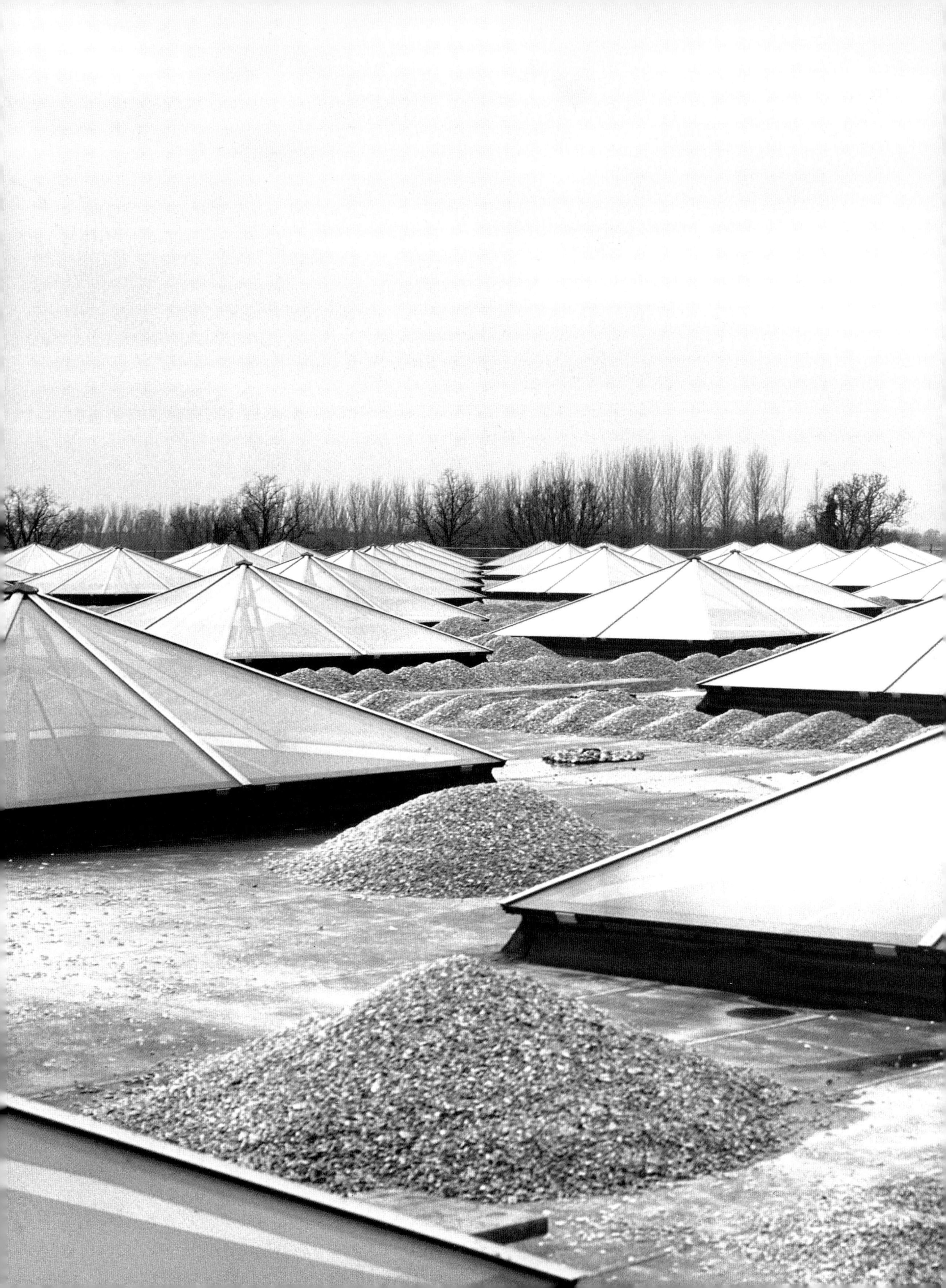

Ein Bausystem für Stahlhallen und zwei Anwendungen – Lagerhalle in Gundelfingen, 1984 – 87, und Montagehalle in Stonehouse bei Bristol, 1986 – 89
Bauherr: Josef Gartner GmbH

Two applications of a hall construction system – warehouse in Gundelfingen, 1984 – 87, and factory shop in Stonehouse near Bristol, 1986 – 89
Client: Josef Gartner GmbH

Kennzeichnend für Stahlhallen ist zumeist deren Dachkonstruktion. Diese weitgespannten Hallendächer haben sich im Verlauf der besonderen Geschichte des Bauens in Eisen und Stahl wesentlich verändert. Gab es im 19. Jahrhundert wahre filigrane Wunder an Fachwerken, unterspannten Sparren- und Pfettenkonstruktionen bis hin zu modular zusammensetzbaren Eisenguß-Tragwerken, so bevorzugte die klassische Moderne parallele Vollwandträger oder Vollwandgitterroste, so Mies van der Rohe bei der Crown Hall oder für die Nationalgalerie in Berlin. Die Geschlossenheit der baulichen Konfiguration und vor allem die Erreichung der die Gebäude oben abschließenden Horizontale war Ziel der konstruktiv lapidaren Bestrebungen.

Wenig später änderte sich die Architekturauffassung. Das Baumaterial Stahl sollte, ähnlich wie schon im Ingenieurbau des 19. Jahrhunderts, seine Leistungsfähigkeit, Leichtigkeit und die große Zahl der Möglichkeiten unter Beweis stellen. Im Sinne eines nicht nur ästhetisch verstandenen, ethisch vorgetragenen Minimalismus, sondern einer tatsächlich bis an den Rand des Artistischen gehenden Minimierung galt es, mit den einwirkenden Kräften fertigzuwerden. So entstand eine neue, ungewöhnliche Freiheit. Nicht von ungefähr waren es junge Engländer, welche das Sainsbury Centre, die abgespannten Hallen des Renault-Montagewerks (Norman Foster) und die Inmos-Fabrik (Richard Rogers) erfanden. Nahezu nichts blieb unversucht um der fast lapidaren, klassisch verschulten Stahlverwendung der Zeit davor zu entrinnen. Jetzt wurde komplex konstruiert, filigran gedacht und der Stahl nach seinen immanenten Gesetzen und den neuen Möglichkeiten des rechnergestützten Konstruierens ins Spiel gebracht.

Mag auch die Schreibersche Art des Konstruierens zunächst verhaltener erscheinen, so ist sie doch, was Rationalität und intelligente Bewältigung anbelangt, den englischen Beispielen nahe, obwohl sie zu anderen konstruktiv-formalen Lösungen gelangte.

Neue Gemeinsamkeit war, daß das Gewicht einer Konstruktion, ihre intelligente Unterteilung, serielle Vorfertigung und leichte, schnelle Montierbarkeit große Bedeutung errangen. Das klassische System der Säulen und Architrave wurde erneut Historie.

Daß die neuen Konstruktionen auch im Sinn des Wortes schön, elegant, ja voller Witz waren, lag wohl daran, daß sie von Architekten gemeinsam mit Ingenieuren gestaltet wurden.

The roof structure is usually a characteristic feature of steel halls. These wide-span hall roofs have changed considerably in the course of the long history of iron and steel construction. The 19th century saw real filigree miracles of lattice work, trussed rafter and purlin constructions down to modular cast-iron load-bearing systems to be assembled, while classical Modernism preferred parallel solid-web girders or solid-web grids, as in the case of Mies van der Rohe for the Crown Hall in Chicago or the Nationalgalerie in Berlin.

The aim of these structurally succinct efforts was to close the structural configuration and above all to achieve the horizontal concluding of the building at the top.

The architectural approach changed shortly afterwards. Steel as a material, similarly to its role in 19th century structural engineering, was to prove its abilities, lightness and then large number of possibilities it offered. The aim was to deal with the forces in the structure in the spirit of a minimalism that was not just perceived aesthetically and presented ethically, but a minimization that really did go to the ultimate artistic limits. This led to a new and unusual freedom. It was no coincidence that it was young British architects who devised the Sainsbury Centre, the braced halls of the Renault assembly plant (Norman Foster) and the Inmos factory (Richard Rogers). Almost nothing remained untried in order to escape from the almost terse, classically schooled use of steel of the previous period. Now buildings were structured in a complex fashion, conceived as filigree and steel was brought into play in accordance with its inherent laws and the new possibilities of computer-aided construction.

Even though Schreiber's construction approach seems more reticent at first, as far as rationality and intelligent handling are concerned it is close to the British examples, even though it arrived at different structural and formal solutions.

Another new common feature was that the weight of a structure, its intelligent subdivision, serial prefabrication, ease and speed of assembly acquired great significance. The classical system of columns and architrave was history again.

Links: Dachaufsicht; Montagehalle Stonehouse
Left page: looking down on the roof; Stonehouse assembly building

Zeichen dieser Entwicklung war auch, daß die Ingenieurkollegen, die im 19. Jahrhundert so Großartiges geleistet hatten, in die neue Konkurrenz eintraten und die Entwicklung brillant immer weiter vorantrieben.

Baubeschreibung des Architekten

»Die Firma Josef Gartner stellte 1986 die Aufgabe, für ihr Werksgelände in Gundelfingen eine hohen Ansprüchen genügende Hallenkonstruktion zu entwerfen. Als dort 1987 mit dem Bau begonnen wurde, folgte als weiterer Auftrag, das Konzept für das englische Zweigwerk der Firma Gartner fortzuentwickeln.

Da sich die Konstruktion der Lagerhalle in Gundelfingen als äußerst vorteilhaft herausstellte und der Bauherr die vielseitige Anwendbarkeit des Systems erkannte, lag es nahe, dieses auch für die Montagehalle in Stonehouse und gegebenenfalls für weitere Bauten zu verwenden. Verwirklicht wurden, obwohl es Projekte für Herrsching, Schöneberg und eine weitere Halle in Stonehouse gab, nur die Halle in Gundelfingen und jene in Stonehouse. Alle Hallen bauen auf dem gleichen quadratischen Konstruktionsprinzip einer Stahlleichtkonstruktion mit konstruktiv integrierten Lichtkuppeln und der im Dachhauptträger angelegten Kranbahn auf. Die Höhen verändern sich mit zunehmenden Stützabständen. Das modulare Ordnungssystem bleibt aber konstant, und die Bauelemente – Metallpaneele, Fenster, Türen, Faltschiebetore und Oberlichtpyramiden – gleichen sich. So ergibt sich für alle Hallen eine von Material, Konstruktion, Detail und System geprägte Erscheinungsform, die trotzdem individuelle Züge trägt.

Nutzung

Für die industrielle Fertigung von Bauteilen werden lange Produktionsstrecken benötigt, die sich aber bei differenzierten Arbeitsabläufen nicht nur linear in einer Richtung entwickeln, sondern auch verknüpfende Querverbindungen brauchen. Deshalb wurde ein richtungsneutrales Hallensystem konzipiert, in welchem flächenhafte Kranbestreichung in Längs- und Querrichtung erfolgen konnte.

Der Wunsch, möglichst große, nicht durch Stützen gestörte Arbeitsbereiche mit Ausdehnungsmöglichkeit zu schaffen und dabei flexibel zu bleiben, führt zwangsläufig zu großen Spannweiten in Längs- und Querrichtung und somit zum quadratischen Konstruktionsraster. Bei diesem System ergeben sich Moduleinheiten von 117 bis 804 Quadratmetern. Die großen Hallenflächen bedürfen auch natürlicher Belichtung und ausreichender Sichtbeziehung nach außen, um für die dort Beschäftigten gute Arbeitsbedingungen zu schaffen. Die gleichmäßig verteilten Lichtpyramiden, die Oberlicht- und Fensterbänder lassen, wenn sie klar verglast sind, solche Aussicht zu, andererseits kann auch gerichtetes Licht aus allen vier Himmelsrichtungen verwirklicht werden. Ein derartiges Belichtungskonzept schafft Tageslichtatmosphäre und unterstützt die Empfindung von Leichtigkeit der Dachkonstruktion. Die wenigen in großen Abständen stehenden Stützen behindern die Freizügigkeit der Nutzung nirgends und verstärken den erwünschten Raumeindruck von Weite.

The fact that the new structures were also literally beautiful, elegant, indeed witty, was probably because they were designed by architects working with engineers.

Other signs of this development were also that the engineering colleagues who had achieved such wonderful things in the 19th century joined in with the new competition and constantly drove development forward brilliantly.

The architect's description of the building

»In 1986, Josef Gartner commissioned a design for a hall structure to meet the requirements of their Gundelfingen factory site. When building started there in 1987, a second commission followed to develop the concept further for Gartner's branch in England.

As the structure for the Gundelfingen warehouse turned out to be extremely advantageous, and the client acknowledged the many ways in which the system could be used, it seemed obvious to apply it to the assembly hall in Stonehouse and if necessary for other buildings. Although there were projects for Herrsching, Schöneberg and another hall in Stonehouse, only the hall in Gundelfingen and the first one in Stonehouse were realized.

All the halls are built on the same square construction principle of a light-weight steel structure with integrated light domes and the crane track built into the main roof girder. Heights change as the distances between the columns increase. But the modular ordering system remains constant and the construction elements – metal panels, windows, doors, folding sliding doors and toplight pyramids – are the same. So all the halls have individual features, but their appearance is determined by the same material, structure detail and system.

Use

The industrial manufacture of construction parts requires long production runs, but these do not just develop in one direction in a linear fashion for differentiated working sequences, they also need linking lateral connections. Hence a hall system was conceived that was neutral in terms of direction, in which crane runs over the surface can be either longitudinal or lateral.

The desire for working areas that are column-free to as large an extent as possible with the possibility of extension while remaining flexible at the same time inevitably lead to long longitudinal and lateral spans and thus to a square construction grid. This system produces modular units of 117 to 804 sq m. The large hall areas also need natural lighting and adequate views of the outside world in order to create good working conditions for the people working there. The evenly distributed light pyramids, the skylights and continuous windows provide such views with clear glazing, and directed light from all four points of the compass can also be provided. A lighting concept of this kind creates a daylight atmosphere and enhances the sense of a light roof structure. The few columns set a great distance apart at no point restrict freedom of use, and reinforce the desired broad spatial impression.

Konstruktion

Die aus den Nutzungsansprüchen resultierenden Forderungen – flexible Arbeitsbereiche, große Spannweiten, flächenhafter Kraneinsatz ohne einengende Portalkranstützen – führten logisch zu einem Stahltragwerk von hoher Leistungsfähigkeit. Ein wichtiges Ziel war auch, dessen Gewicht aus montagetechnischen und ökonomischen, nicht zuletzt aber auch aus ethischen und ästhetischen Gründen zu minimieren.

Das Dachtragwerk ist als gelenkig aufgelegter Trägerrost konstruiert, dessen beide Richtungen als Durchlaufträger wirken. Die Horizontalkräfte (Wind, Kran) werden von einem das Tragwerk umrahmenden Horizontalträger aus Vordach und Diagonalen aufgenommen und über die Hauptträger auf die eingespannten Innenstützen übertragen. Der Windverband verbindet mit seinen Diagonalen auch die um ein halbes Achsmaß versetzten Pendelstützen der Außenwand mit dem Tragsystem.

Das horizontale Achsmaß beträgt 2,10 Meter. Die Teilungen in der Höhe folgen dem Raster von 65 Zentimetern.

Wirtschaftlichkeit

Ein derartiges Bausystem wird, auch bei hohen qualitativen Ansprüchen, dann besonders wirtschaftlich, wenn die Vorteile der Mehrfachanwendung genutzt werden. Wenige Bauelemente in großer Stückzahl – tiefgezogene Metallpaneele, Fenster, Türen, Faltschiebetore, Lichtpyramiden und deren Verbindungsdetails – werden durch die Serie preiswert. Diese Art des Bauens führt zur konsequenten Vorfertigung möglichst vieler Teile im Werk. Auch die Produktion der konstruktiven Bauteile kann in die Fabrik verlegt werden.

Sowohl in Gundelfingen als auch in Stonehouse wurden die Stahltragwerke im Werk vorgefertigt und nach Zusammenfügung auf der Baustelle als komplexe Bauelemente montiert. Dies führte zu sehr kurzen Bauzeiten.

Eine Besonderheit

Beim Zusammenschluß des 1. und 2. Bauabschnitts in Stonehouse konnte Bauabschnitt 1 völlig ungestört funktionieren, der 2. Teil wurde im Abstand von 6,30 Metern daneben gebaut. Nach Fertigstellung mußten an den Hauptstützen der Bauabschnitte nur die Auflagerpunkte für die Dreiecksquerträger an den 6 Hauptstützen freigelegt werden. Das verbindende, längslaufende Glasprisma ist in Längeneinheiten von 19,5 Metern darüber gelegt und verbindet die Räume. Im so entstandenen Zwischenbau wurden die notwendigen Sozialräume und Konstruktionsbüros untergebracht.

Gestaltung

Logische, gut durchdachte und klare Konstruktionen und präzise, einfache Details entsprechen voll den Gestaltungsabsichten. Alles konzentriert sich auf wenige architektonische Grundprinzipien und sachgerechten Materialeinsatz. […]«

Structure

The demands resulting from the required uses – flexible working areas, wide spans, crane use over a large area without being hampered by restrictive gantry crane supports – logically led to a high-performance steel load-bearing system. Another important aim was to minimize its weight for reasons of assembly technology and finance, but not least also for ethical and aesthetic reasons.

The roof is structured as a hinge-mounted steel grid, working in both directions as a continuous girder. The horizontal forces (wind, crane) are absorbed from the canopy and diagonals by a horizontal girder framing the supporting structure. The wind-bracing diagonals also connect the hinged columns of the outer wall, offset by half an axis unit, with the supporting system.

The horizontal axis unit is 2.1 m. The height divisions follow a 0.65 m module.

Economic viability

A structural system of this kind, even when the demands on quality are very high, is particularly economical if the advantages of multiple use are applied. A small number of building elements in large quantities – deep-drawn metal panels, windows, doors, sliding folding doors, light pyramids and the detailed items needed to connect them – become reasonably priced in this sort of series. The production of the structural components can also be shifted into the factory.

The steel support systems were prefabricated in the factory in both Gundelfingen and Stonehouse and assembled as complex structural elements after being fitted together on the building site. This meant that the buildings went up very quickly.

A special feature

When the 1st and 2nd building phases in Stonehouse were ready to join up, building phase 1 was able to function quite undisturbed, the 2nd phase was built 6.3 m away alongside it. After completion, only the bearing points for the triangular lateral girders had to be exposed on the 6 main columns in each section. The linking, longitudinal glass prism was then laid on top in length units of 19.5 m to connect the spaces. The intermediate structure that this created housed the necessary social facilities and the construction offices.

Design

Logical, well considered and lucid structures and precise, simple details correspond completely with the design intentions. Everything is concentrated on a few basic architectural principles and appropriate use of materials. […]«

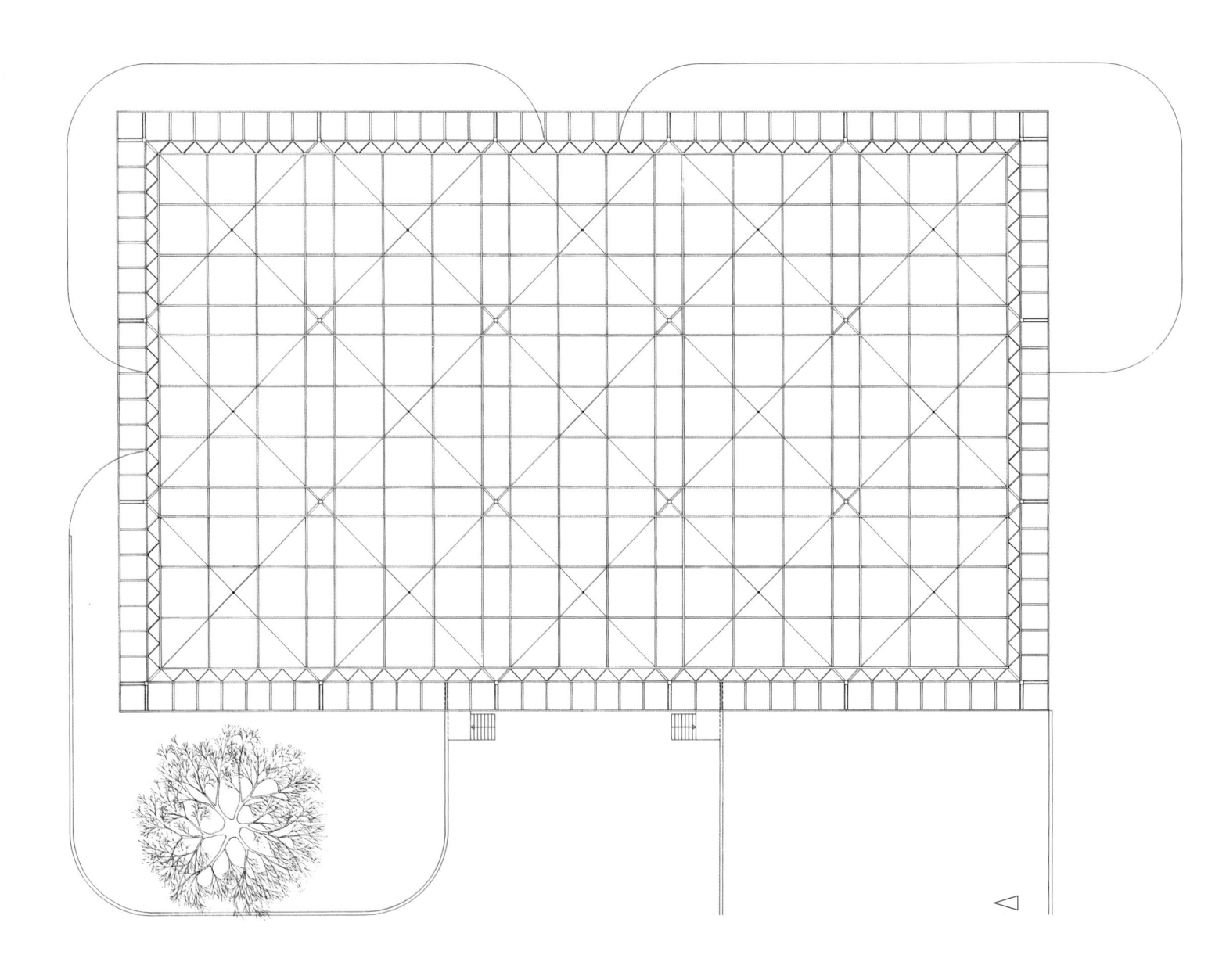

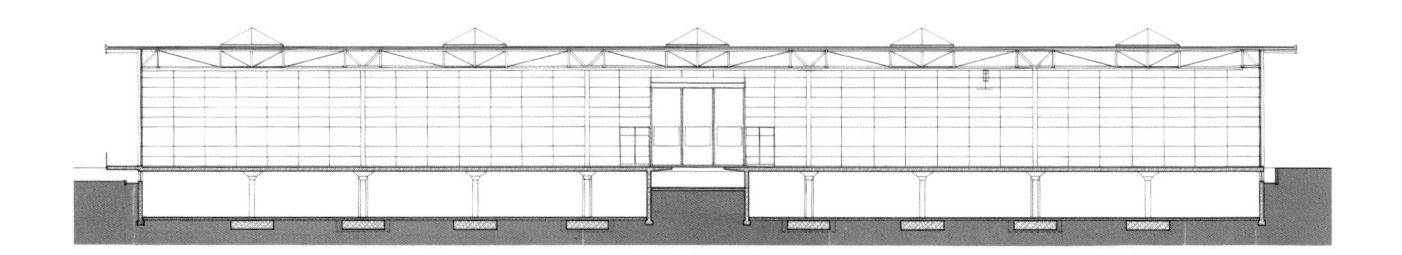

Oben: Halle Gundelfingen, Trägerlage
Unten: Halle Gundelfingen, Schnitt, Trägerlage

Top: Gundelfingen hall, load-bearing system
Bottom: Gundelfingen hall, sectional view, load-bearing system

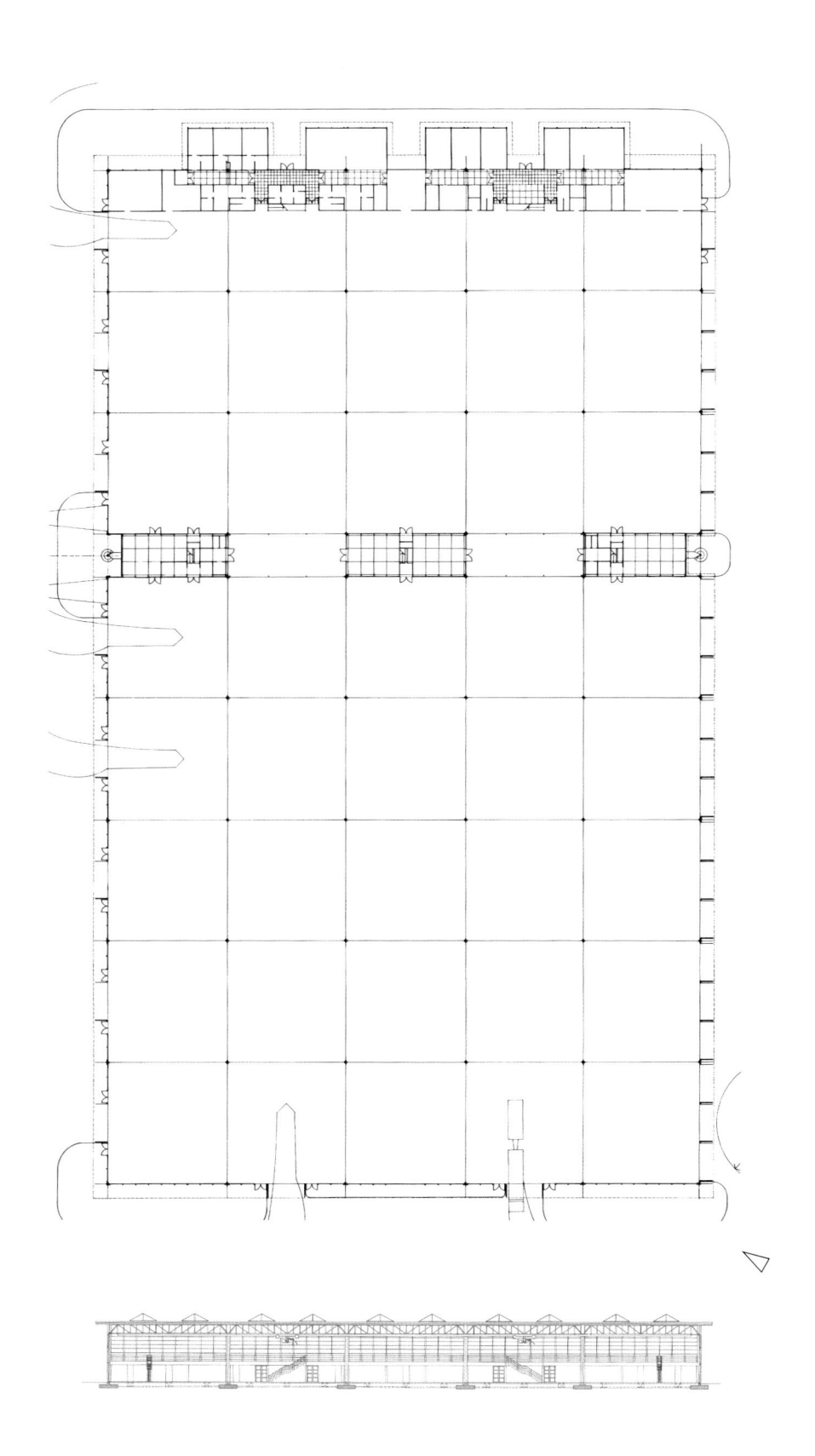

Oben: Grundriß Halle Stonehouse
Unten: Schnitt Trägerachse Halle Stonehouse

Top: floor plan, Stonehouse hall
Bottom: sectional view of load-bearing axis, Stonehouse hall

FOLGENDE DOPPELSEITEN:
S. 138–139: Halle Gundelfingen Ansicht Nordwest-Ecke
S. 140–141: Halle Stonehouse

NEXT DOUBLE PAGES:
P. 138–139: Gundelfingen hall, view of the north-west corner
P. 140–141: Stonehouse hall

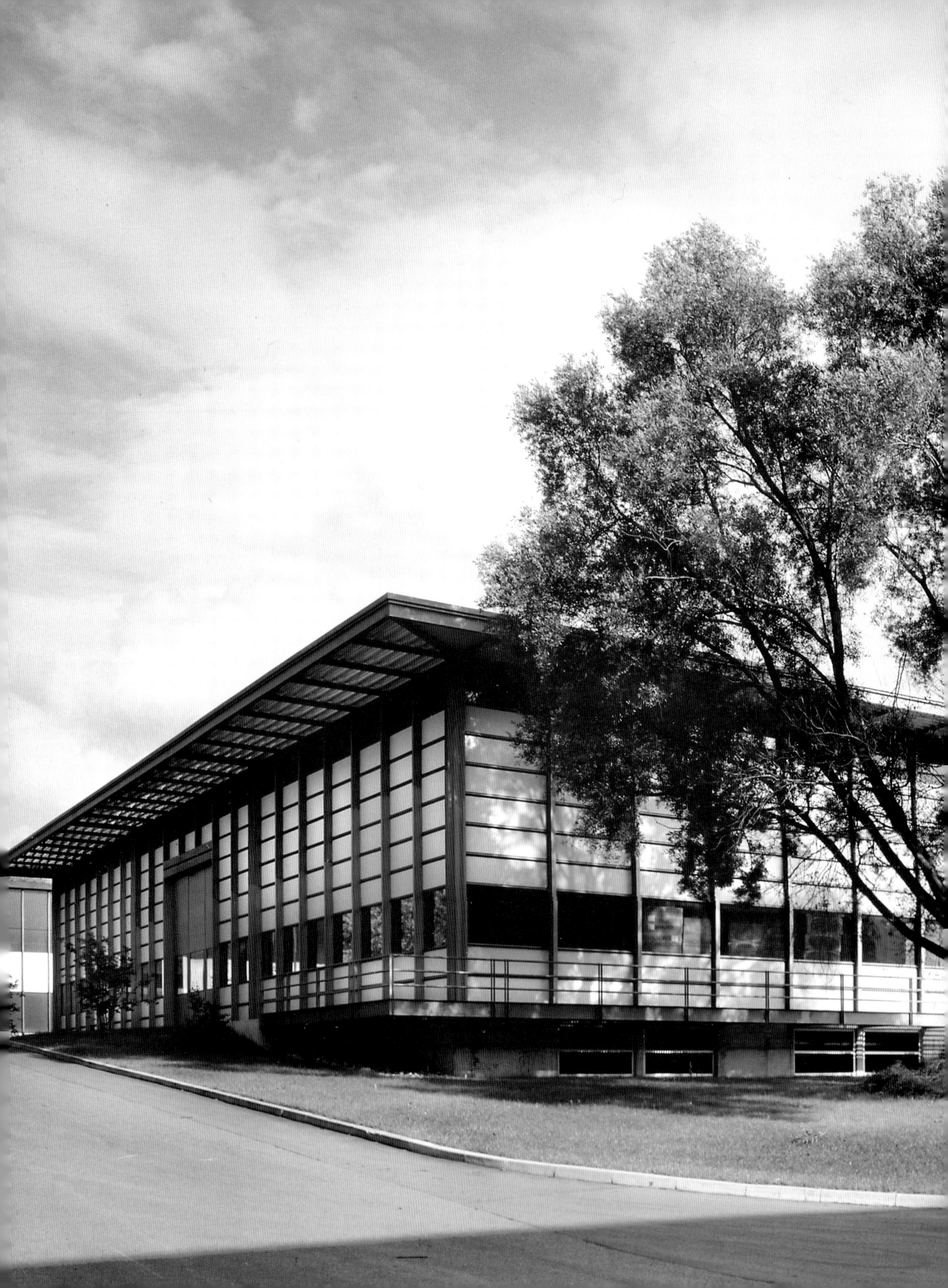

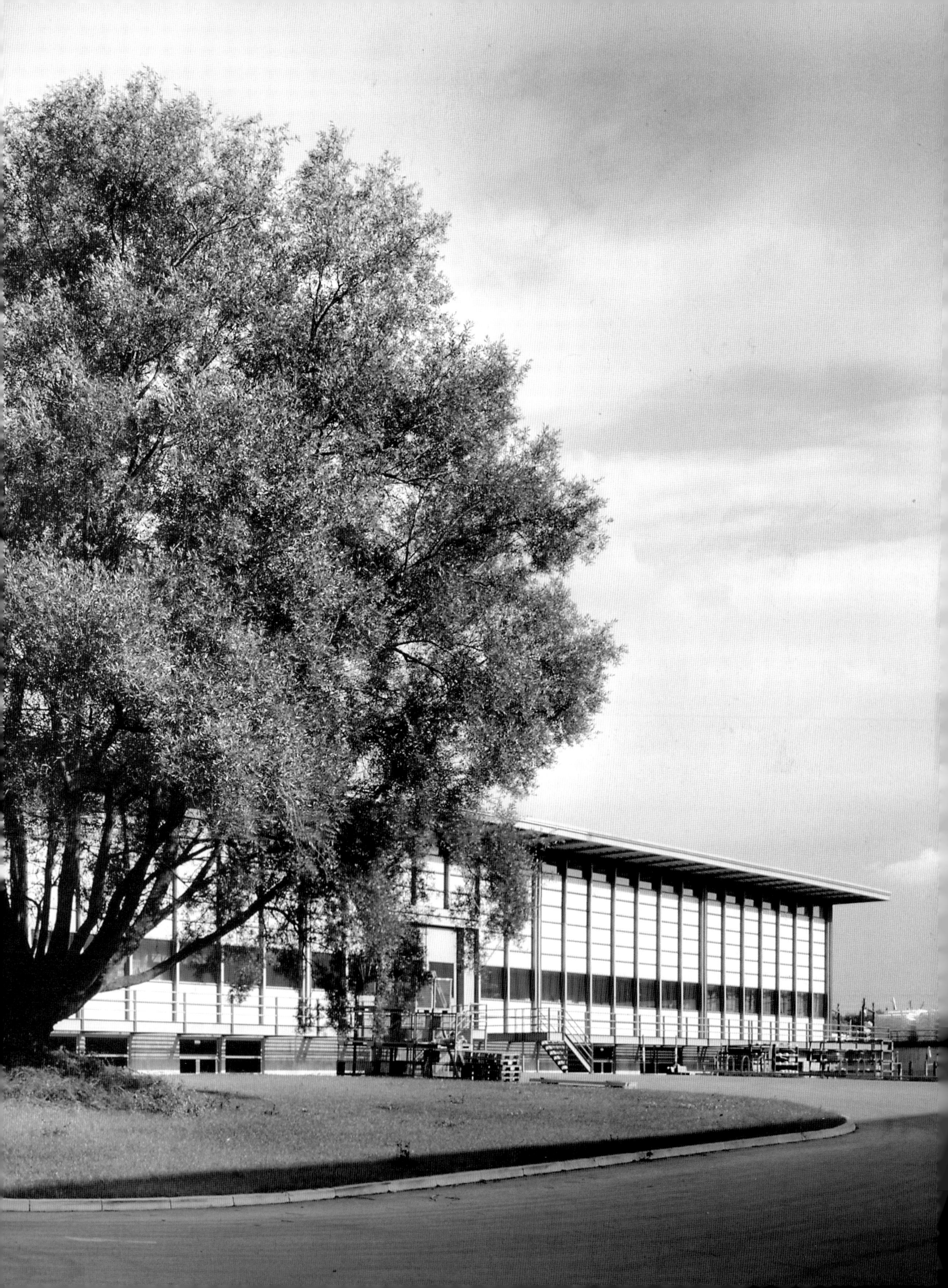

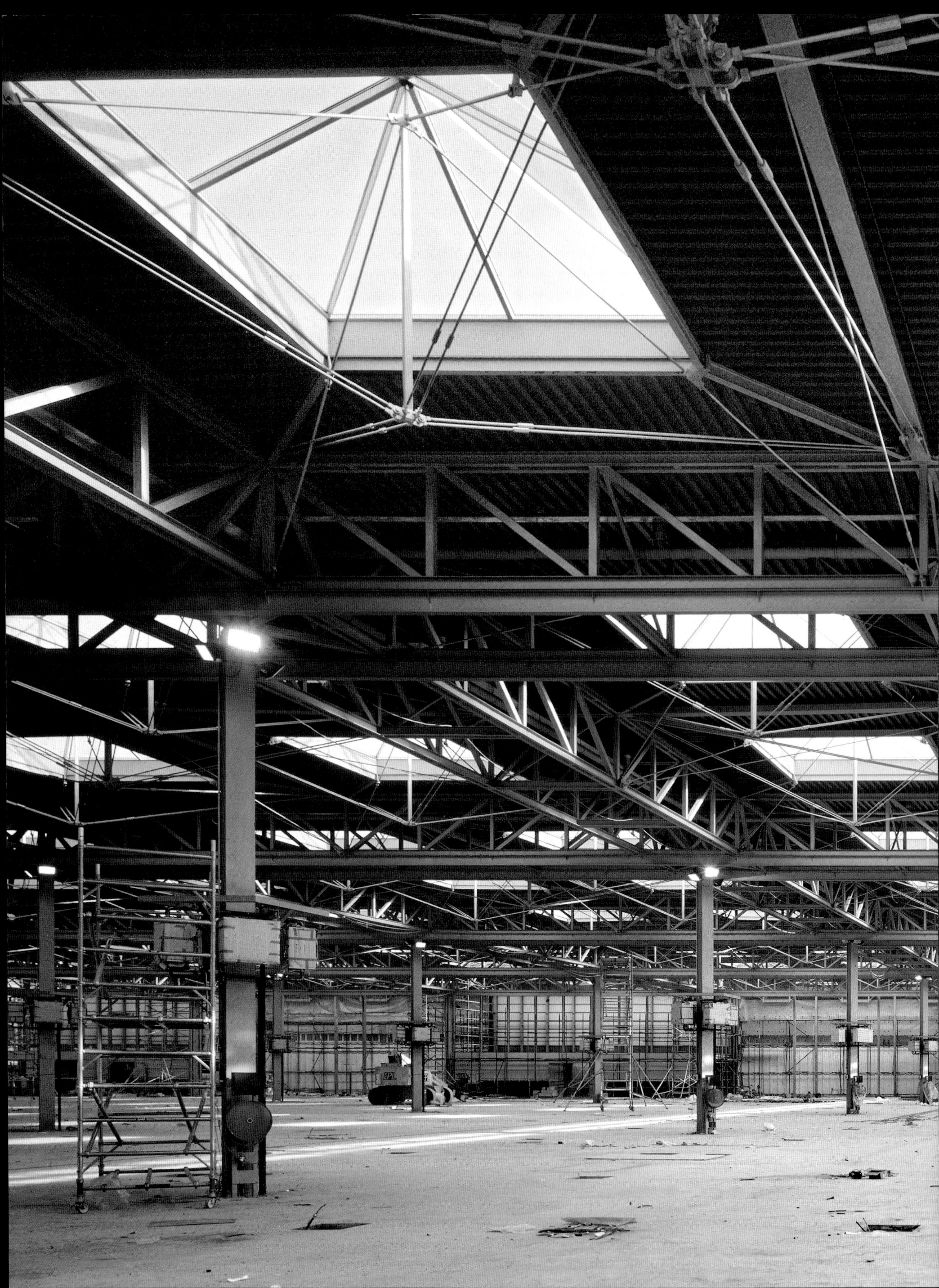

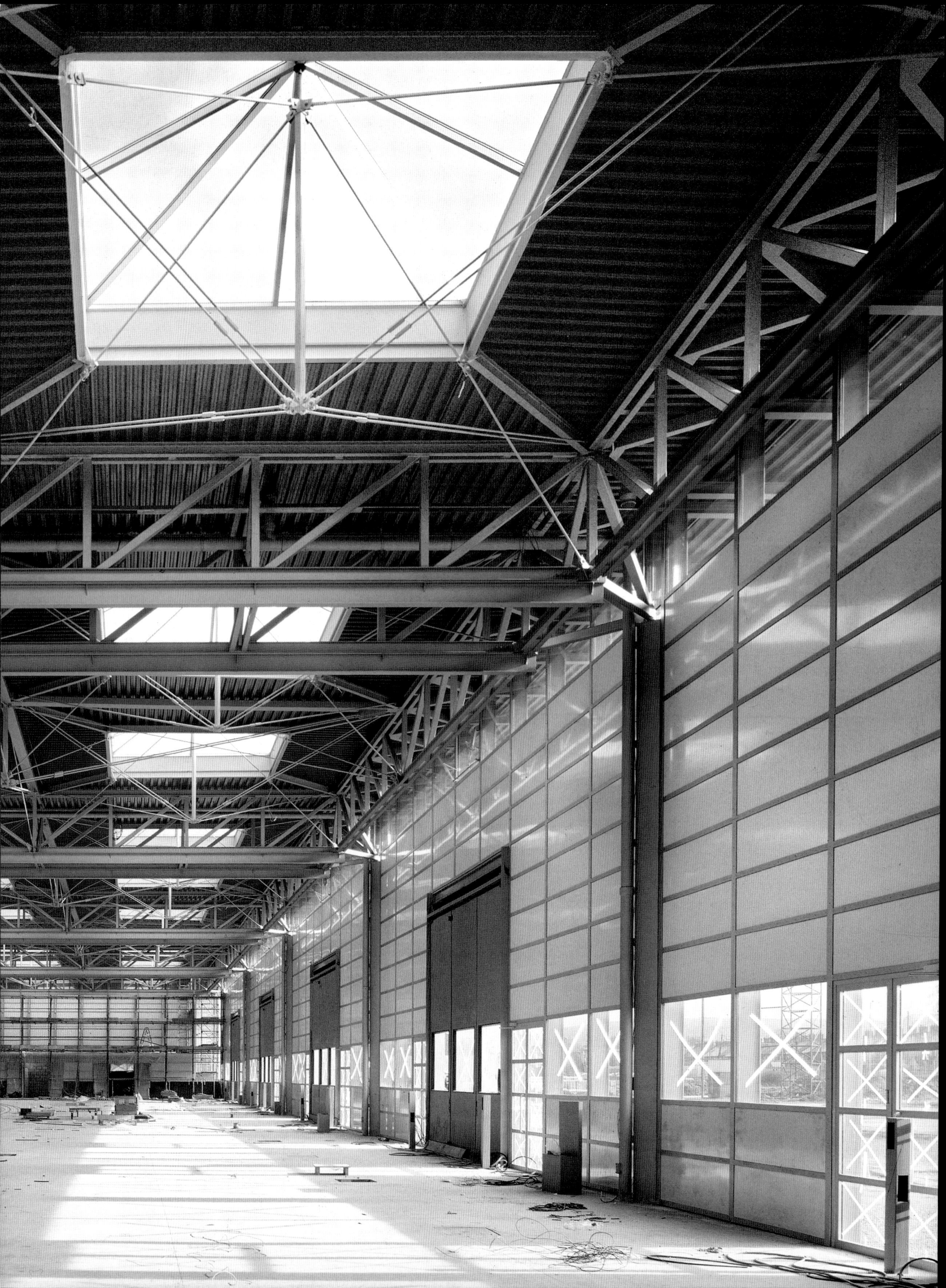

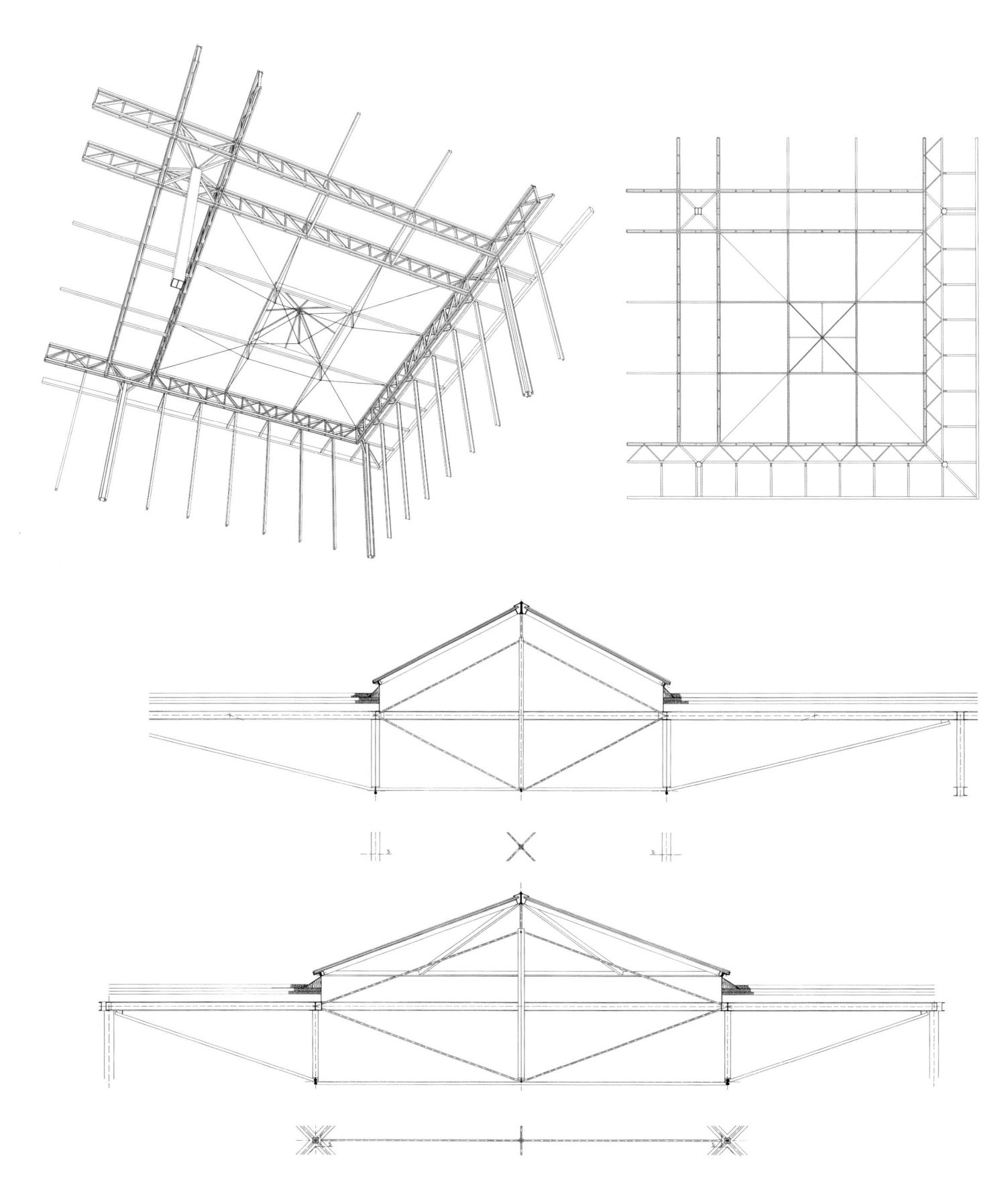

Halle Gundelfingen
Oben: Untersichtsperspektive der Hallenecke
und daneben Systemzeichnung der Hallenecke
Unten: Unterspannung Lichtkuppel

Gundelfingen hall
Top: hall ceiling seen from below, next to it a
drawing of the system in the corner of the hall
Bottom: support system for the skylight

Rechts: Normalstütze, die die Fachwerkträger
mit Kranbahn trägt

Right page: normal support bearing the girder
framework with the crane runway

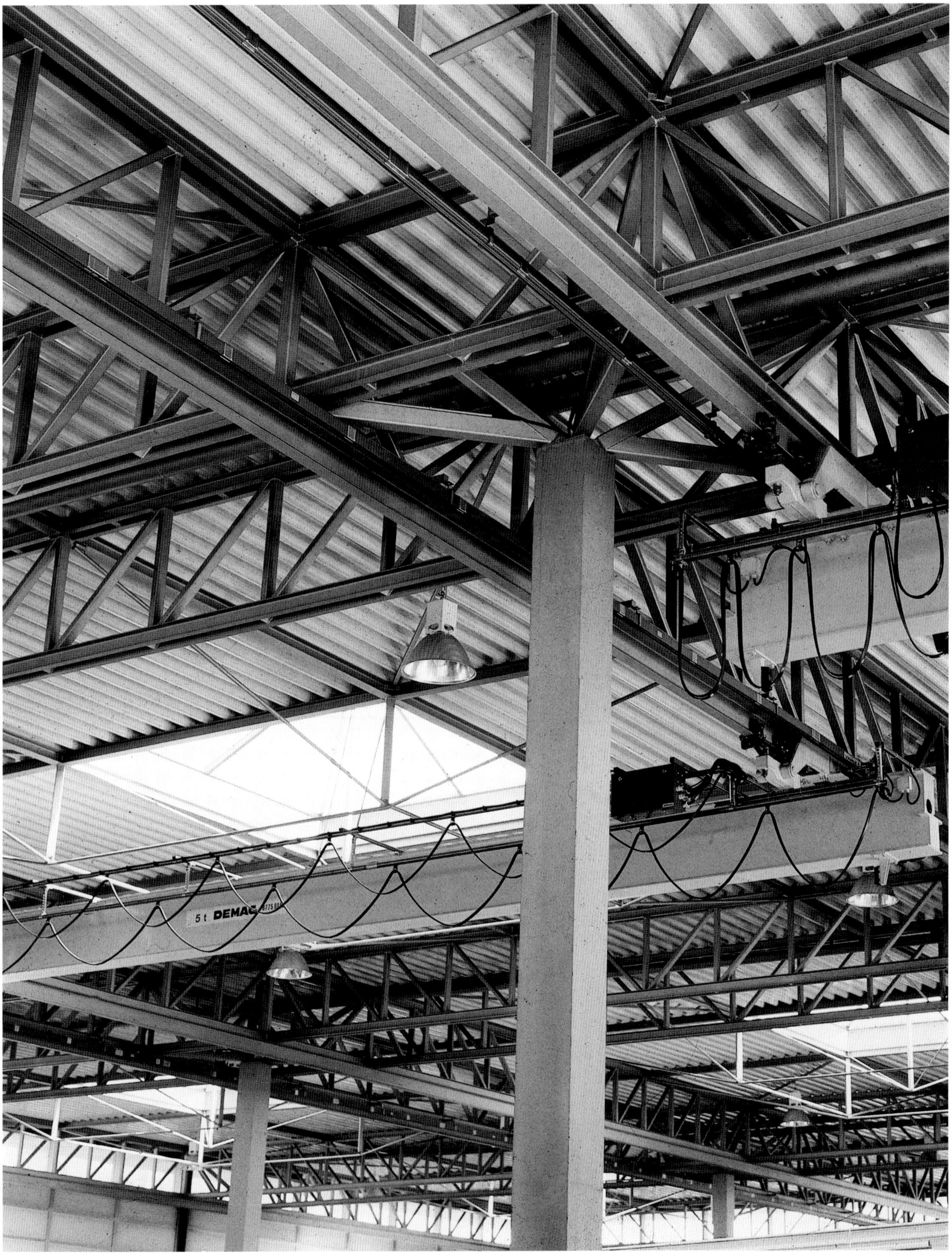
5 t DEMAG

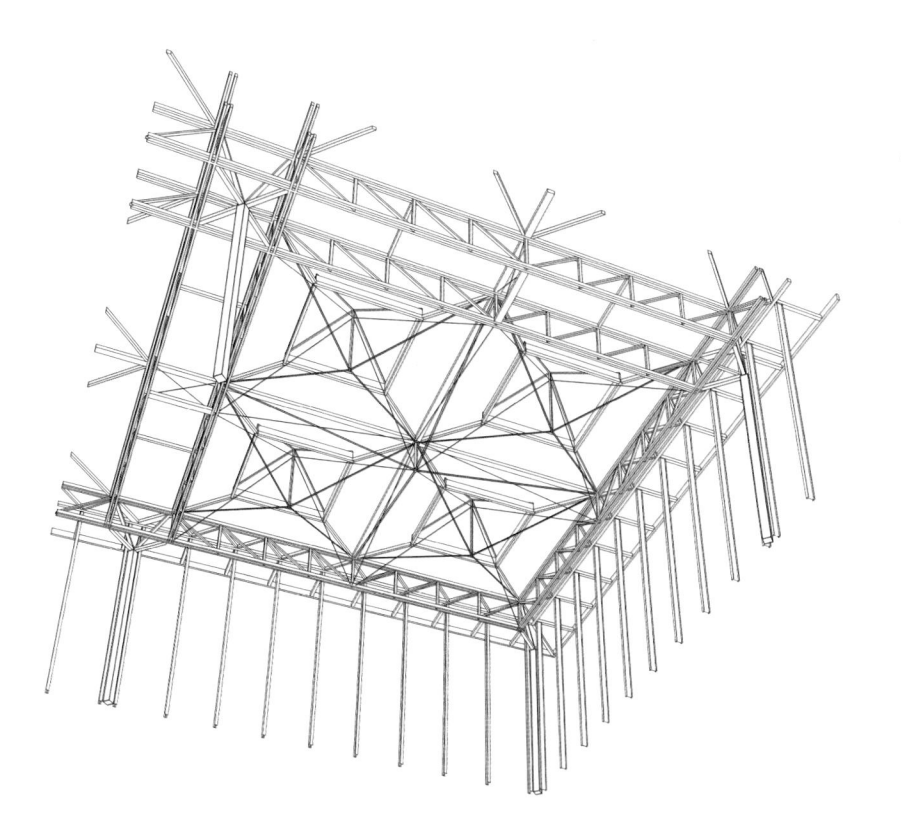

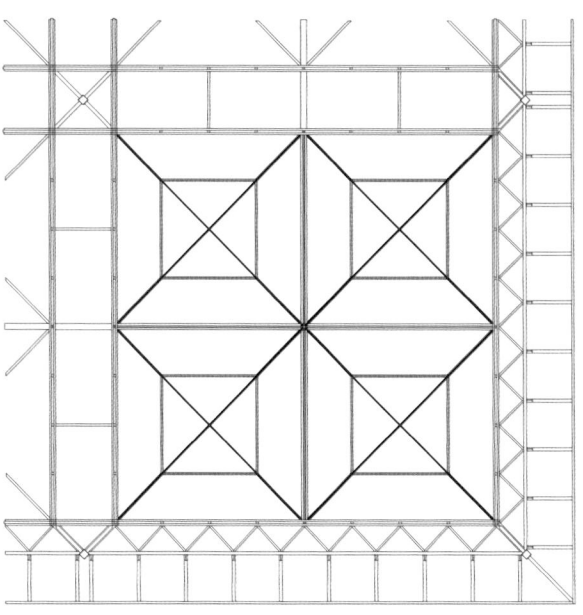

Halle Stonehouse
Oben: Untersichtsperspektive der Hallenecke und daneben Systemzeichnung der Hallenecke

Rechts: Filigrane Abspannung der Lichtkuppeln

Stonehouse hall
Above: hall ceiling seen from below, next to it a drawing of the system in the corner of the hall

Right page: filigree bracing for the skylights

FOLGENDE DOPPELSEITEN:
S. 146: Halle Stonehouse
Glaspyramide des Verbindungselements

S. 147: Halle Gundelfingen
Blick in die Lichtkuppel

S. 148–149: Halle Stonehouse
Gesamtansicht von Süden mit *Mockupstand*, an diesem Gerüst werden Fassadenelemente den Sturmkräften eines Hurrikans ausgesetzt.

NEXT DOUBLE PAGES:
P. 146: Stonehouse hall
Glass pyramid of the connecting element

P. 147: Gundelfingen hall
View into the skylight

P. 148–149: Stonehouse hall
Overall view from the south with the *mock-up stand*, a frame which will be used to attach façade elements which will then be exposed to the force of a hurricane.

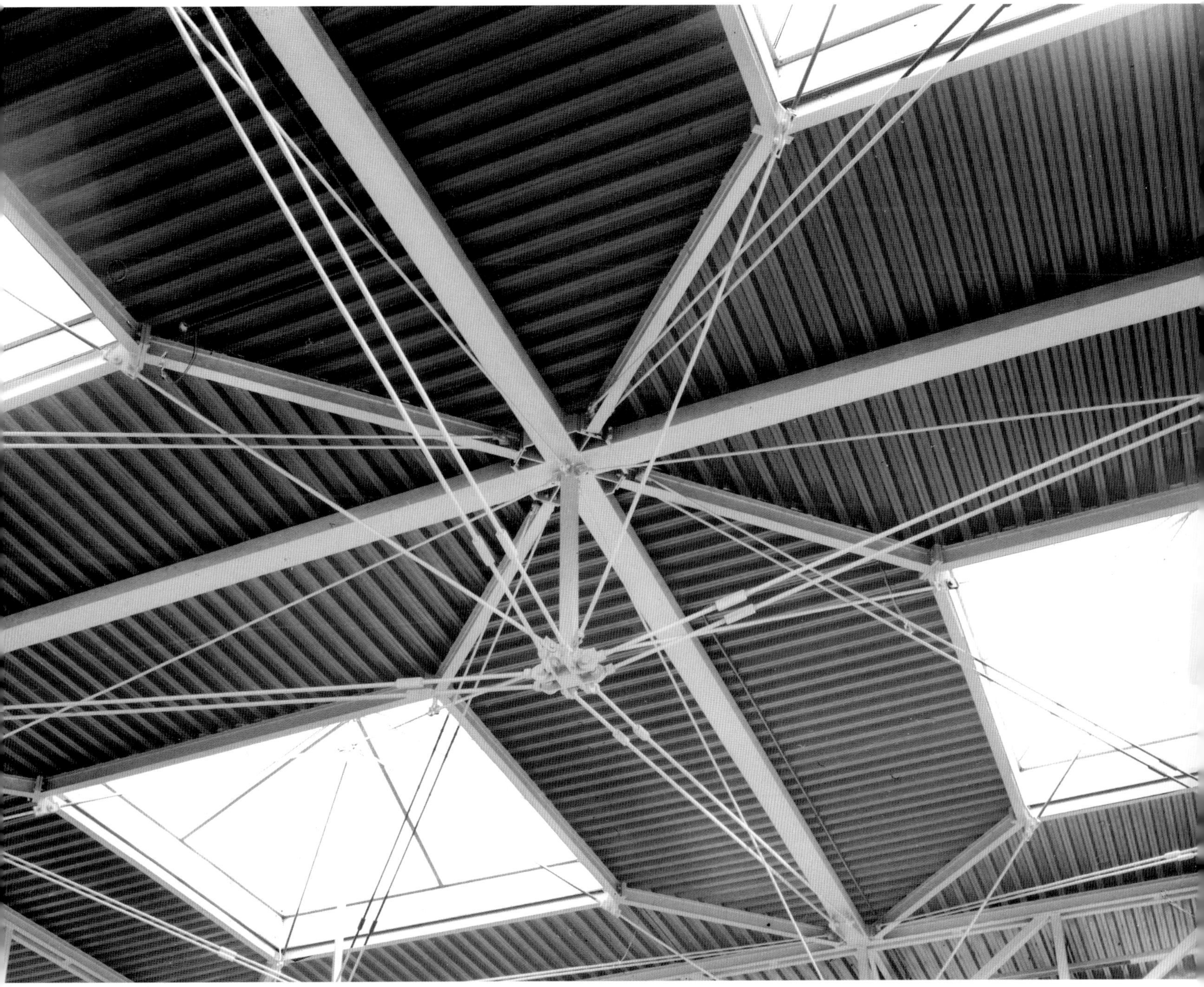

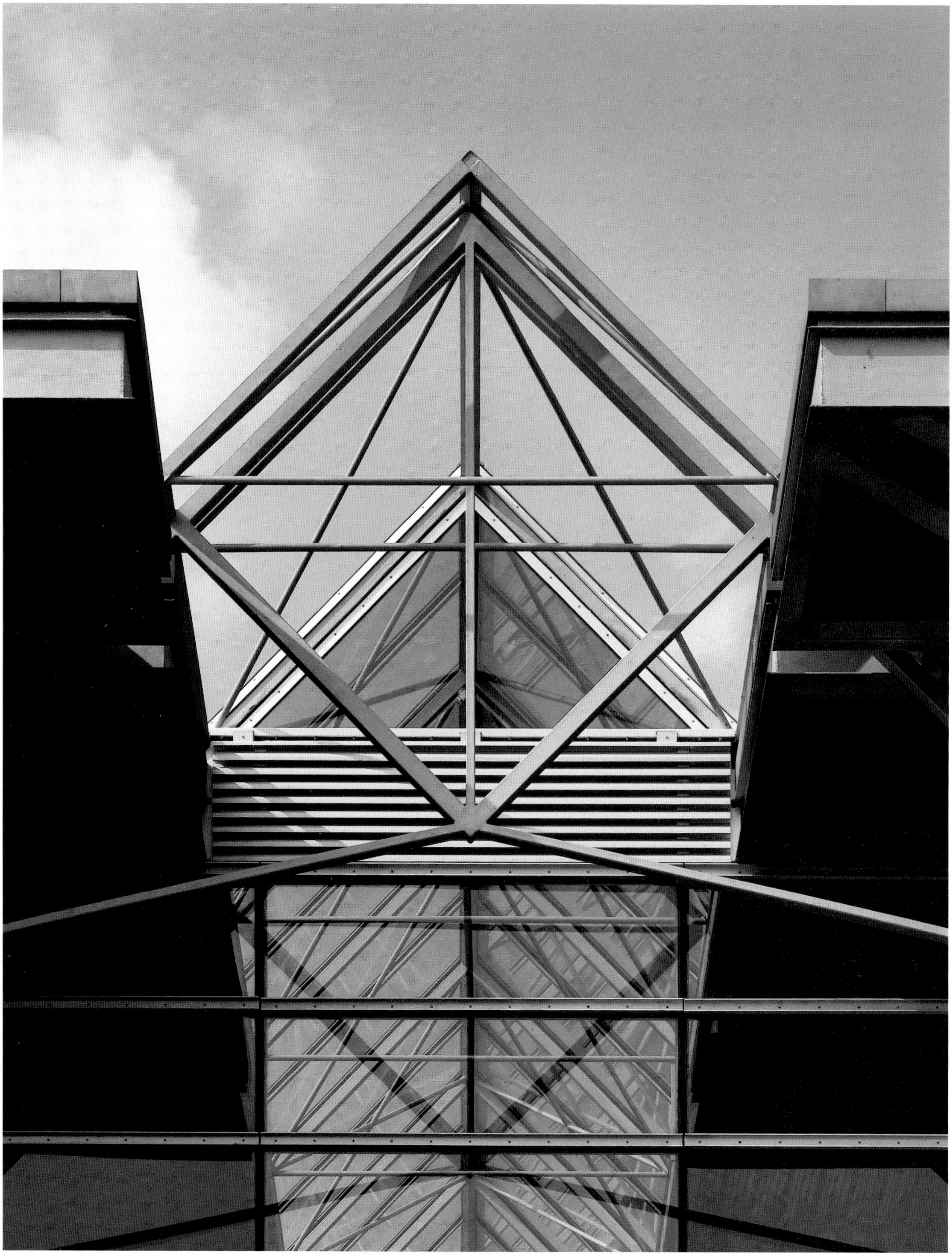

147

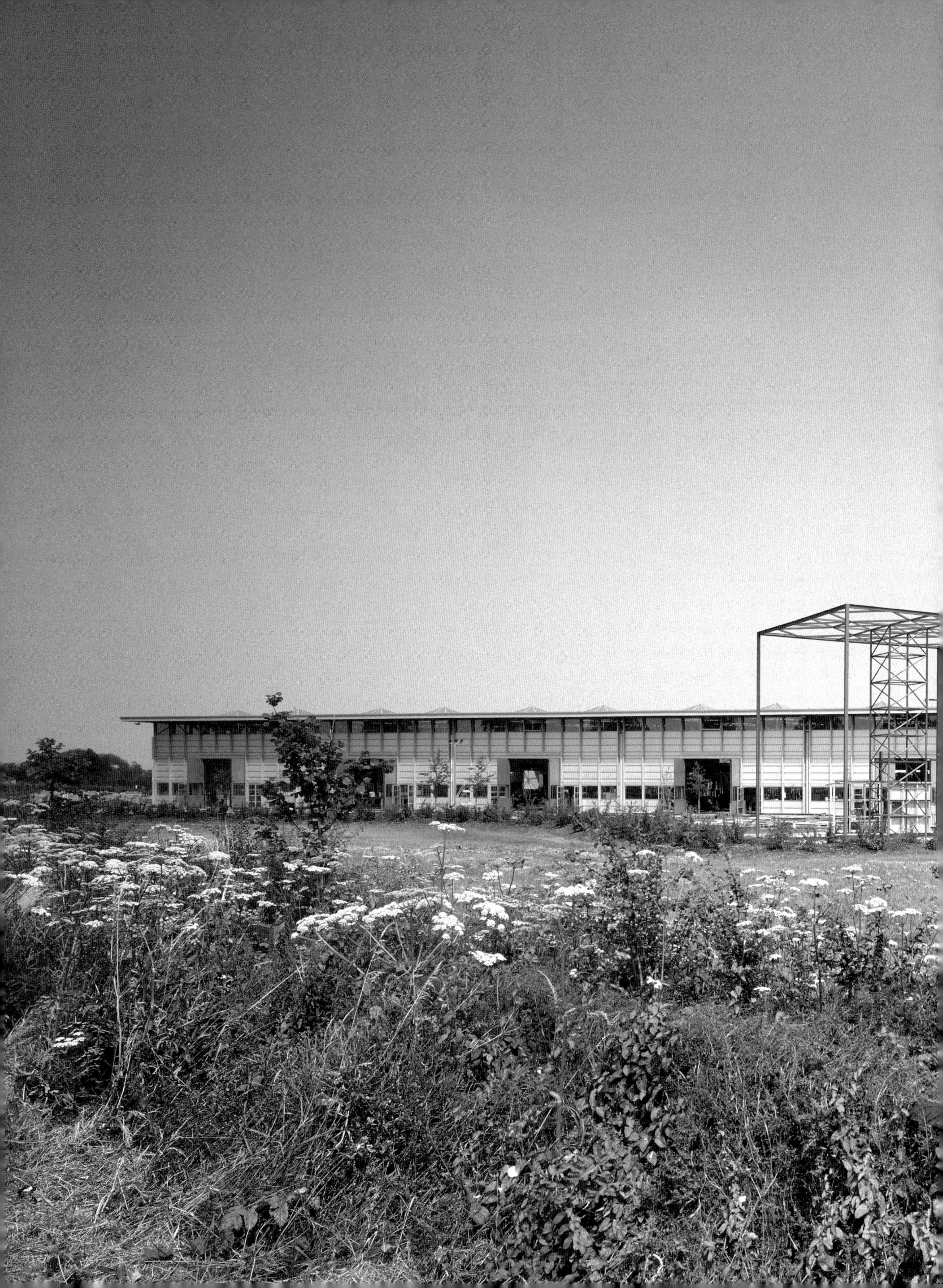

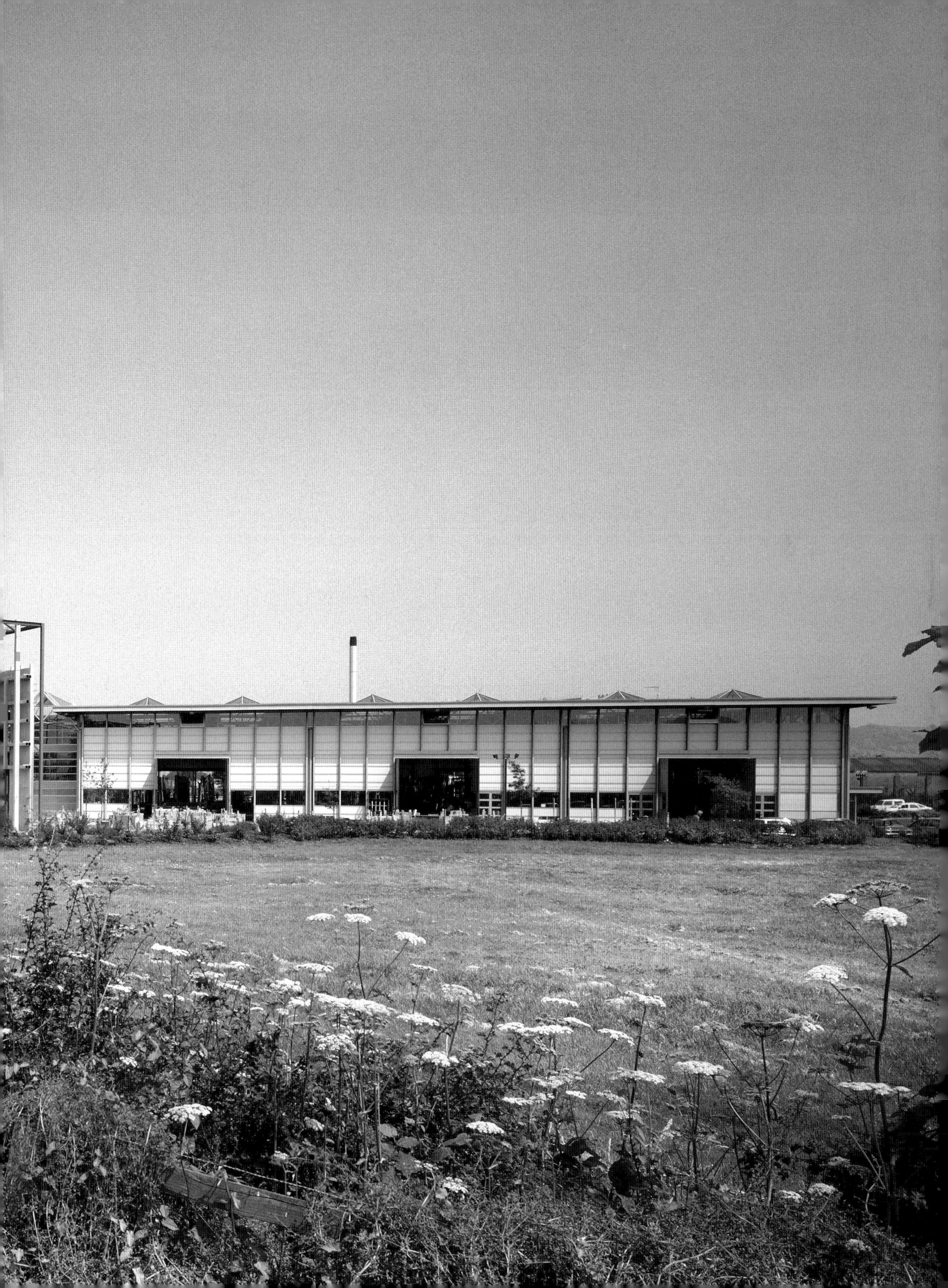

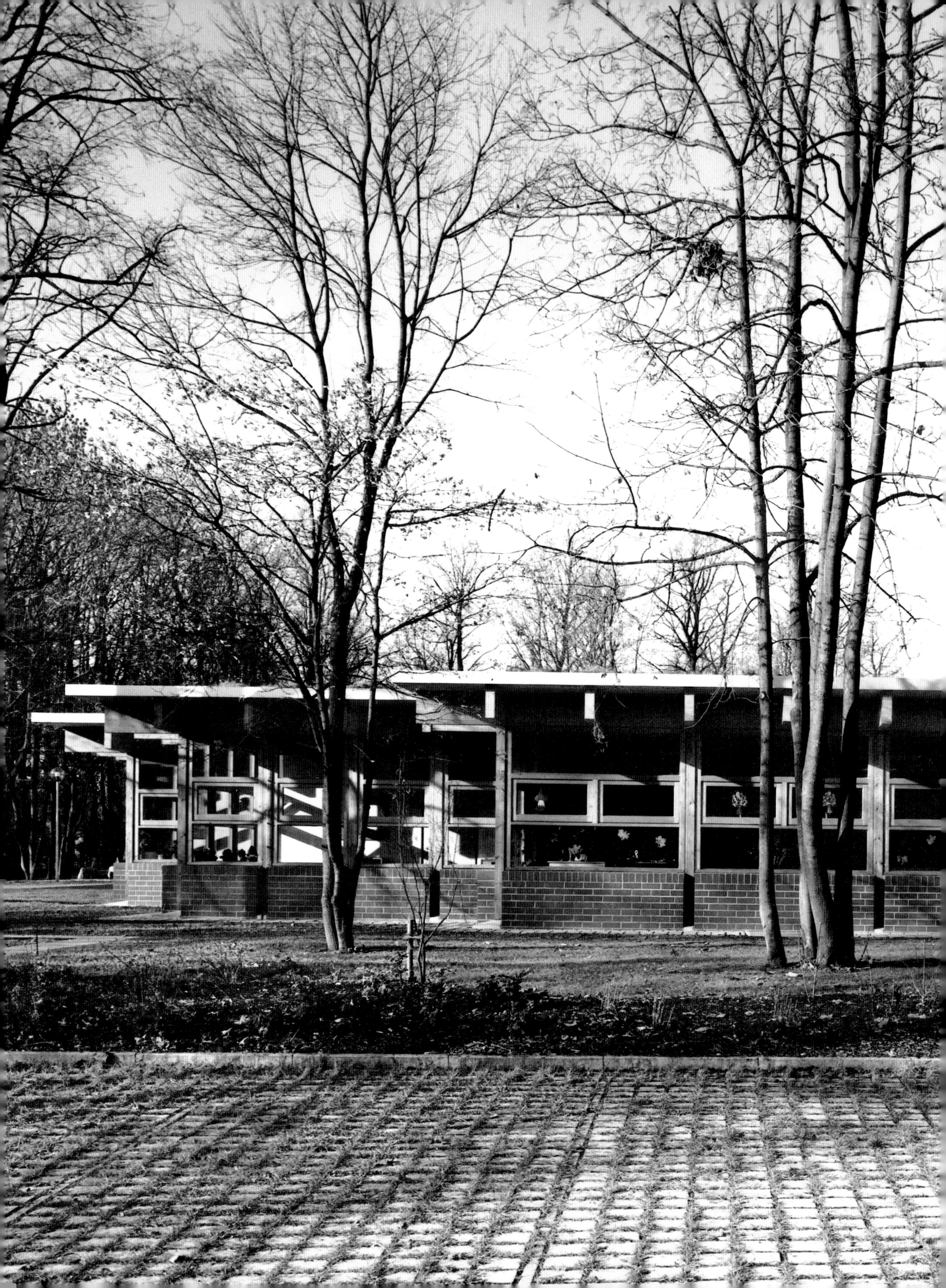

Kindergarten in der Angererstraße, München, 1988 – 90
Bauherr: Stadt München

Kindergarten in Angererstraße, Munich, 1988 – 90
Client: City of Munich

Der ebenerdige Kindergarten erstreckt sich längs der Südseite der stark befahrenen Karl-Theodor-Straße an einem der Ränder des Luitpoldparks. Das baumbestandene Grundstück geht im Süden und Westen in den anschließenden, mit alten Bäumen bestandenen öffentlichen Grünraum über.

Diese besondere Situation legte den Entwurf eines langgestreckten, symmetrischen Gebäudes nahe, welches sich nach Norden, zur lärmreichen Straße hin geschlossen zeigt, während es sich nach Süden, Osten und Westen, zum Garten und zum umgebenden Park hin öffnet. Die den Bau umschließenden Gartenmauern schirmen die im Osten, im Westen und besonders im Süden liegenden Freispielflächen wirkungsvoll vom Straßenlärm ab.

Prägende Elemente sind die tragenden und raumabschließenden Ziegelwandscheiben, die Fassadenstützen aus Holz und der Rost aus verleimten Holzbalken, welcher als Flächentragwerk des Daches die Raumfolgen überspannt und das auf Holzbohlen angelegte begrünte Dach trägt.

Das Raumprogramm

Die Raumabfolgen des für vier Gruppen dimensionierten, hundert Kindern Platz bietenden Kindergartens wiederholen sich symmetrisch rechts und links einer Mittelachse. Je zwei Gruppen bilden eine eigene Einheit mit eigenen Nebenräumen und eigenem Hauszugang. Die zwei Hauseinheiten, die eine östlich, die andere westlich gelegen, sind durch die Spange gemeinsam zu nutzender Räume, die Verwaltung, Räume der Erzieherinnen, Küche und Mehrzweckraum verbunden.

Jede der zwei Doppelgruppen hat ihre eigene Spielterrasse. Mit dieser Zuordnung und Aufteilung sollte familiäre Abgeschlossenheit der einzelnen Gruppen ermöglicht werden.

Der künstlerisch gestaltete, mit einer begehbaren Sonnenuhr im Haupteingangsbereich ausgestattete Hof ist Treffpunkt und gemeinsamer Spielbereich für alle.

Die klare Konstruktion mit ihrem modularen System stellt ein Ordnungsprinzip dar und verdeutlicht die Übereinstimmung der Teile und des Ganzen. Die Beschränkung auf wenige, altbewährte Materialien, Holz im Naturton, roter, sichtbarer Backstein, Holz- und Ziegelböden, bringt warme Farbigkeit, die gut mit der natürlichen Umgebung harmoniert und großzügige Klarheit bewirkt.

This single-storey kindergarten extends along the south side of busy Karl-Theodor-Straße on one side of the Luitpoldpark. The site with its trees adjoins the adjacent public green space with old trees to the south and west.

This special situation suggested designing a long, symmetrical building closed on the north side by the noisy street, but opening up to the south, east and west, to the garden and the surrounding park. The garden walls around the building screen the open-air playing areas effectively from the road noise on the east, west and particularly south sides.

The appearance of the building is determined by the load-bearing brick walls enclosing the space, the wooden façade columns and the grid of glued timber beam spanning the sequence of spaces as a framework to support the roof, and the planted roof placed on planks of timber.

The spatial programme

The spatial sequences in this kindergarten, intended for a hundred children in four groups, repeat themselves symmetrically to the right and left of a central axis. Two groups in each case occupy their own unit with its own ancillary rooms and entrance to the building. The two building units, one on the east and one on the west side, are linked by the run of rooms for joint use, the offices, staff rooms, kitchen and multi-purpose room.

Each of the two double groups has its own play terrace. This allocation and division is intended to make each of the two groups into a secluded family.

The artistically designed yard, decorated with a sundial that can be walked on in the main entrance area, is a meeting point and common play area for all.

The clear structure with its modular system represents an ordering principle and illustrates the harmony of the parts and the whole. Restricting the materials to a few tried-and-tested ones like natural wood, exposed red brick, wooden and brick floors creates a sense of warm colour that harmonizes well with the natural surroundings and creates generous clarity.

Links: Seitenansicht
Left page: side view

Oben: Gymnastikraum
Above: gymnastics room

Rechts oben: Schnitt
Mitte: Ansicht
Unten: Grundriß

Right page, top: sectional view
Middle: general view
Bottom: ground layout

153

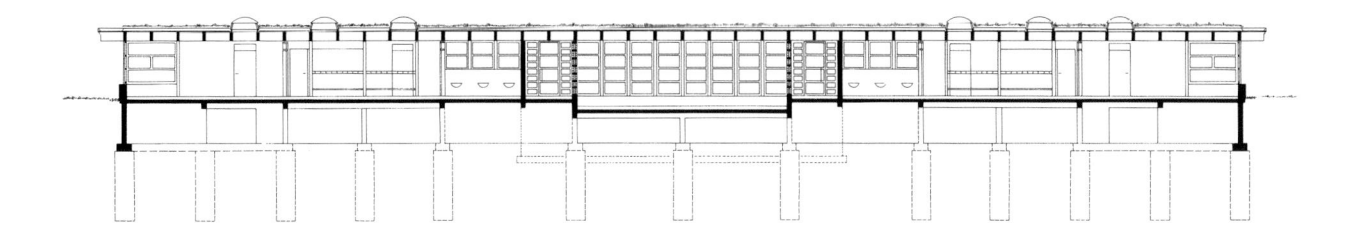

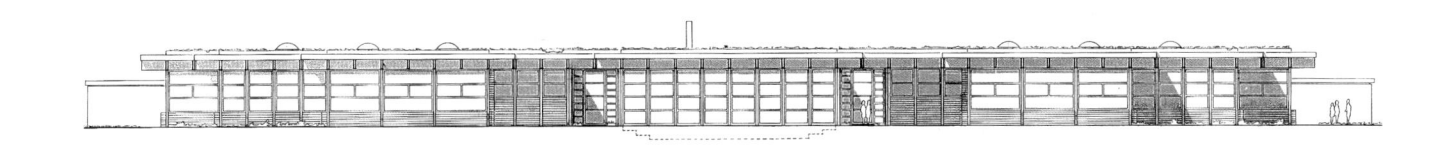

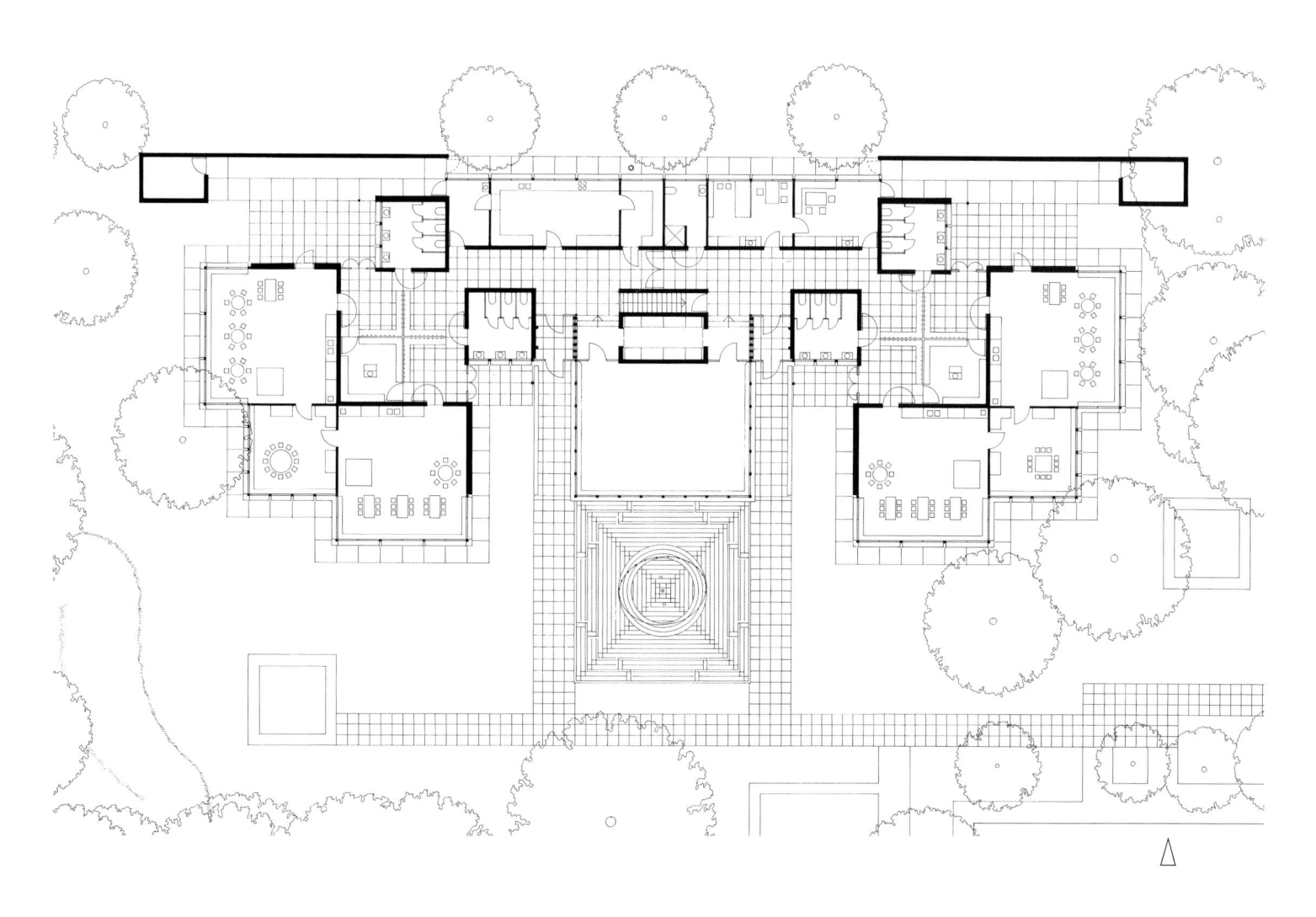

Gruppenraum

Group room

Garderoben

Cloakroom

FOLGENDE DOPPELSEITE:
Innenhof mit Sonnenuhr und Pflaster von Blasius Gerg

NEXT DOUBLE PAGE:
Inner courtyard with sundial and paving tiles by Blasius Gerg

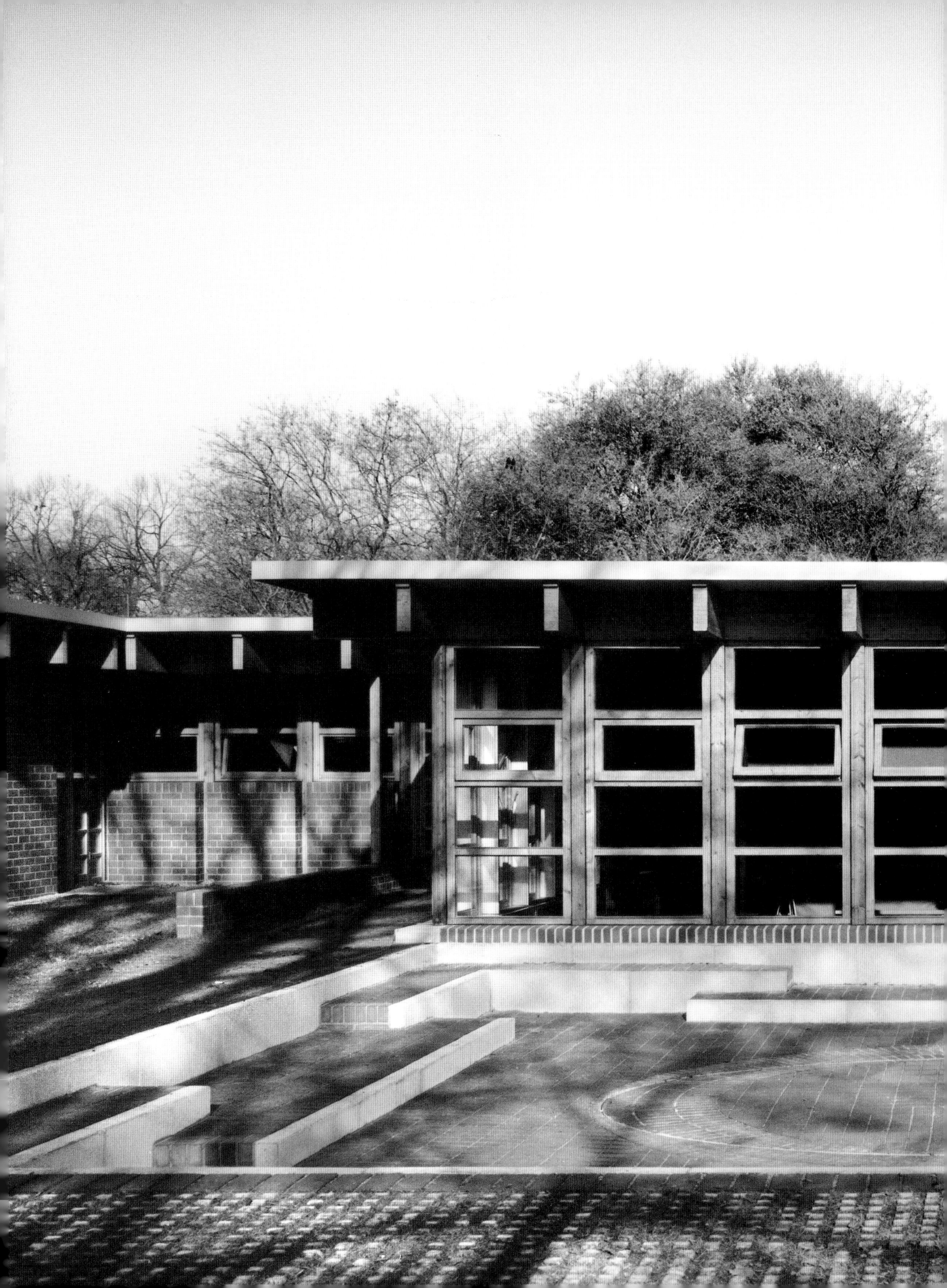

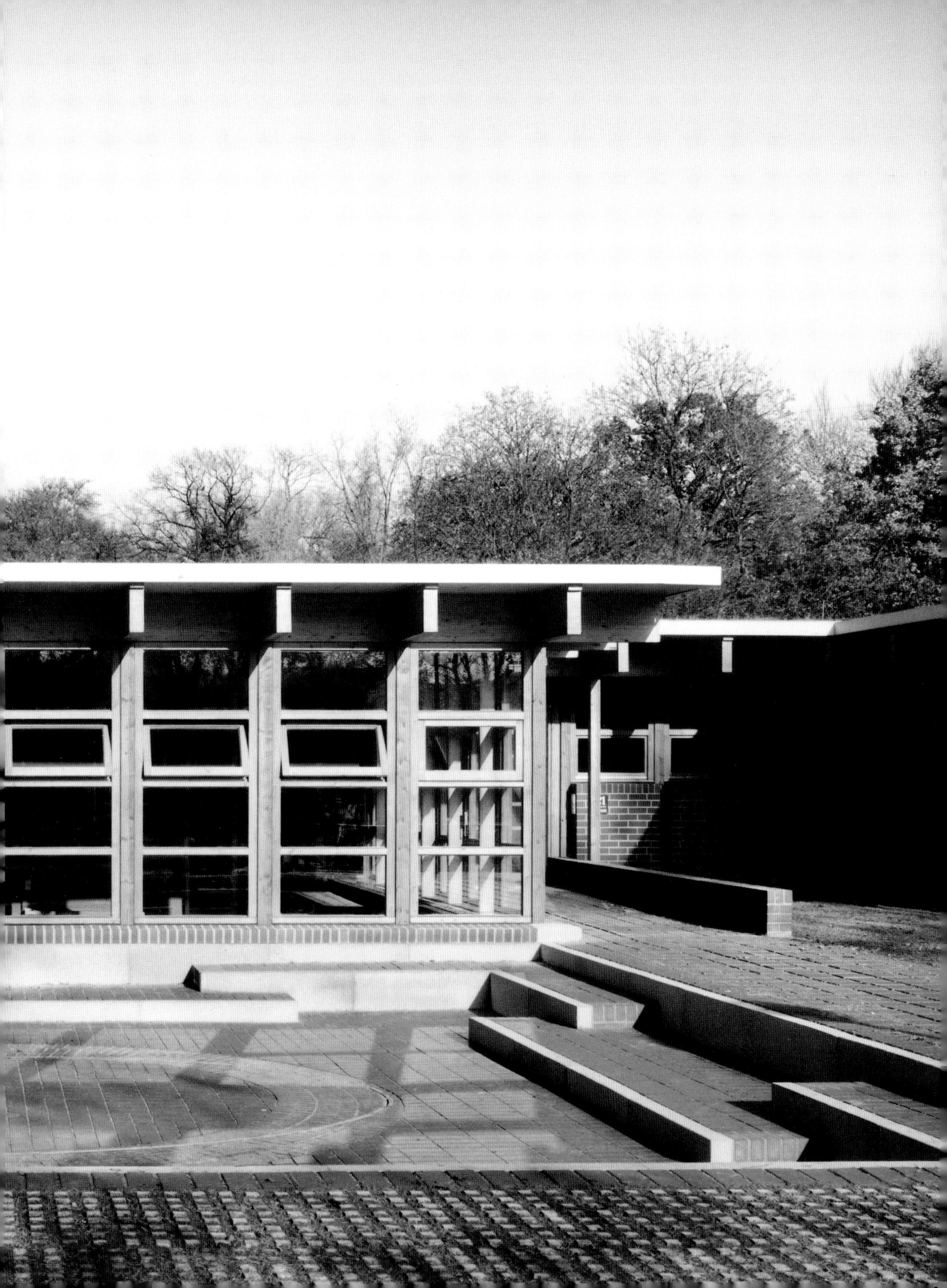

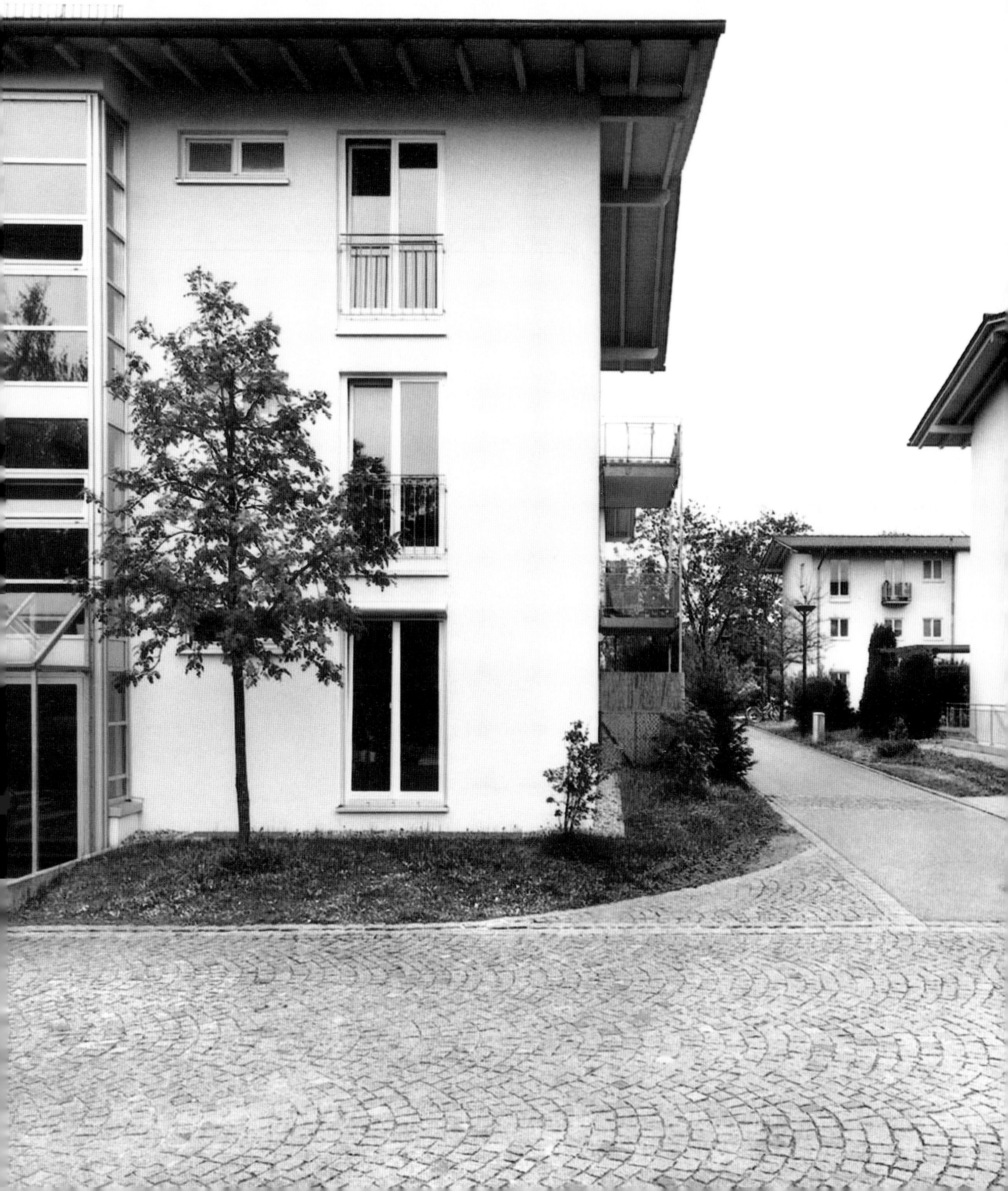

Wohnanlage in der Lenbachallee, Ottobrunn bei München, 1996 – 2002
Bauherr: Wohnanlage Ottobrunn GmbH

Housing complex in Lenbachallee, Ottobrunn near Munich, 1996 – 2002
Client: Wohnanlage Ottobrunn GmbH

Im Großraum München besteht noch immer nennenswerter Bedarf an gut erreichbaren, sozial vernünftigen Wohnungen. Um einer weiteren Ausdehnung der Peripherie mit all den inzwischen bekannten Problemen zu entgehen, wurde auch in und um München herum erfolgreich versucht, zur Vermeidung weiterer infrastruktureller Belastungen im Bestand nachzuverdichten.

Der Schonungsgedanke stand leider, nicht nur in München, so im Vordergrund, daß die längst zwingend gewordene gleichzeitige Modernisierung, die breite Ermöglichung barrierefreien Wohnens für die rasch alternde Bevölkerung, kaum Beachtung fand. Noch immer stehen Energiesparkonzepte, alternative Energiegewinnung und Verkehrsreduktion beherrschend im Vordergrund. Seit den Zeiten der ersten Ölkrise mußte nahezu jedem im politischen, sozialen, baulichen und logistischen Bereich Informierten klar werden, daß uns das demographische Problem in kaum zu bewältigendem Ausmaß zunächst unmerklich, dafür aber in absehbarer Zeit in Schwierigkeiten bringen würde.

Milliarden von Euro flossen jedes Jahr über Wohnbauzuschüsse in die abgeschmackteste, dazu den überregelten Arbeitsmarkt unterlaufende Eigenheimerzeugung. Die Bürger bauten auf Vorrat irgendwo, nicht nur fern von den Zentren der Arbeit und des Verdienstes, sondern – das ist ebenso bedrückend – ohne Rücksicht auf den steigenden Altenanteil und ihr eigenes Altern. In Kürze wird die Allgemeinheit erneut gezwungen werden, zur Herstellung vernünftiger Wohnzustände Milliarden in die soeben erst fertiggestellten Gedankenlosigkeiten zu pumpen, um diese dem Bedarf anzupassen. Dieses Memento richtet sich nicht gegen die gelungene Verdichtung, welche Detlef Schreiber in Ottobrunn gestalterisch und städtebaulich mit Sorgfalt und hohem Aufwand geleistet hat, sondern gegen die undurchdachten Bedingungen, unter denen Architekten arbeiten müssen, wenn die überlegen ordnende Einsicht in die Probleme fehlt.

Baubeschreibung des Architekten

»Das etwa 20 Hektar große Areal der Parkwohnanlage liegt im Nordosten von Ottobrunn, einer Stadtrandgemeinde im Großraum München. Die Siedlung wurde Anfang der 1960er Jahre von den Münchner Architekten Georg A. Roemmich und Hans Rach geplant. So entstand die angenehm lockere Gruppierung einzelner Punkthäuser in

Greater Munich still has a significant need for accessible, socially acceptable housing. To avoid the outskirts extending even further, with all the problems that have now come to light, successful attempts were also made in and around Munich to avoid further infrastructural strains on the existing housing stock by increasing density.

Unfortunately, and this does not just apply to Munich, the idea of protection was so much to the fore that little attention was paid to simultaneous modernization, which had long since become essential, making it possible for large numbers of the rapidly ageing population to enjoy barrier-free living. Energy saving concepts, alternative energy sources and reducing traffic are still dominant in the foreground. Since the time of the first oil crisis almost every informed person in the political, social, architectural and logistical spheres must have realized, or will realize, that the demographic problems would quietly, but in the not too distant future, cause difficulties on a scarcely manageable scale.

Billions of euros flowed into the poorest quality housing, at the same time failing to address the over-regulated employment market. Citizens built where they could, anywhere, not only far from centres of work and earning but – and this is equally depressing – without considering the increasing proportion of old people and the fact that they were ageing as well. In order to create reasonable living conditions, the general public will shortly be compelled once more to pump billions into the nonsense that has just been completed, to meet this need. This memo is not directed at the successful increase in density that Detlef Schreiber achieved in terms of design and urban quality in Ottobrunn, working with care and a lot of effort. But it does say a lot about the ill-considered conditions under which architects have to work when there is no ordering insight of a superior nature into the problems involved.

The architect's description of the building

»The site for the park housing complex, about 20 ha in area, is northeast of Ottobrunn, a municipality on the outskirts of Greater Munich. The estate was planned in the early 1960s by the Munich architects Georg A. Roemmich and Hans Rach. This produced a pleasantly loose

Links: Blick in die Wohnanlage, Riemenschneider Straße 1–3
Left page: view of the residential complex, Riemenschneider Strasse 1–3

einer überwiegend zwei- bis dreigeschossigen Zeilenbebauung mit Geschoßwohnungen und Reihenhäusern in einem parkartigen Gelände. [...] Diese besondere Qualität sollte bei der Erneuerung und Verdichtung des Gebiets von 500 auf knapp 800 Wohneinheiten erhalten bleiben. Daher schlug der nach einem Wettbewerb mit diesen Maßnahmen betraute Architekt vor, nur wenige neue Baukörper in die Zwischenräume einzufügen, teilweise an bestehende Gebäude anzubauen, vorrangig aber dort aufzustocken, wo dies die Abstandsflächen erlaubten. Die Wohnanlage kam tatsächlich, anders als dies beim Münchner Pilotprojekt am Hasenbergl geschah, ohne auffällig als Kontrast zum Bestand wirkende neue Gebäude aus. So bilden die vorsichtig eingefügten An- und Neubauten sowie Aufstockungen eine Einheit mit dem renovierten Bestand, wobei die neuen, leichten, auskragenden Dächer die starken Vor- und Rücksprünge der Fassaden des Bestandes zusammenfassen. Die Modernisierung erhält den Charakter des Ensembles und schafft gleichzeitig eine gestalterische Weiterentwicklung mit heutigen Formelementen, welche die Attraktivität der Gebäude erheblich steigert. Dazu wurde durch private, von Hecken und Pergolen geschützte Gartenanteile vor den Eigentumswohnungen ein fließender Übergang von den Sockelzonen der Gebäude zur natürlichen Umgebung der Parkanlage geschaffen.

Die erforderlichen Stellplätze, einer pro Wohneinheit, wurden großenteils in einem Parkdeck und in Tiefgaragen untergebracht. Trotz der um nahezu 60 % erhöhten Anzahl der Wohnungen stieg der ursprüngliche Grad der Versiegelung nicht wesentlich an. Der Nadelholzbestand am Ostrand der Wohnanlage wird in einen Laubmischwald mit integrierten Spiel- und Erholungsflächen für jung und alt umgewandelt.

Durch die unterschiedlichen Baumaßnahmen konnte ein breitgefächertes Wohnungsangebot erreicht werden, das Zwei- bis Fünfzimmerwohnungen, Maisonettes und Reihenhäuser umfaßt. Nur ein Viertel der bestehenden Wohnungen blieb unverändert, aber alle Fassaden wurden erneuert, wobei sie Vollwärmeschutz und Wärmeschutzfenster erhielten. Die Aufstockungen wurden teils aufgemauert, teils in Holzständerkonstruktion ausgeführt, um ihnen sowohl physische als auch gestalterische Leichtigkeit zu verleihen.

Bei den zusätzlichen Wohnungen wurde besonderer Wert auf Vielfalt gelegt. Ein Neubau mit übereinander gestapelten Maisonettes ergänzt das bisherige Angebot an Eigenheimen. Die zwei zwischengeschalteten Treppenhäuser ergänzend, erschließt ein Aufzug den Laubengang im dritten Obergeschoß mit der Eingangs- und Wohnebene der oberen Maisonettes. Die jeweiligen Schlafebenen wurden im 1. und 2. Obergeschoß übereinandergelegt, um gegenseitige Störungen gering zu halten. Dazu kamen zwei in der Größe dem Bestand angepaßte, sparsam konzipierte Reihenhaustypen, die entweder als zusätzliche Reihe zwischen den Bestand gebaut oder daran angeschlossen wurden. Auch bei den Aufstockungen über den oft kleingliedrigen Grundrissen entstanden unterschiedlich organisierte Wohnungen, teilweise mit durchgehenden Wohnbereichen. Dabei wurden interessante Lösungen für die Zuordnung von Wohnraum, Küche und Eßplatz entwickelt. Die Bäder sind überwiegend natürlich belichtet. Trotz der wesentlich höheren Zahl an Wohneinheiten blieb der Heizwärmebedarf insgesamt gleich.«

grouping of individual appartment blocks in largely two- to three-storey terraced housing developments with flats and terraced houses on a park-like site. [...] This particular quality is to be retained when renewing and increasing the density of the area from 500 to almost 800 residential units. For this reason, the architect entrusted with these measures after a competition proposed that only a few new buildings should be placed in the gaps, some added to existing buildings, but mainly to raise building heights where the distances in between permitted. This housing complex managed, unlike the Munich pilot project Hasenbergl, without any new buildings creating a marked contrast with the old stock. So the carefully added extensions and new buildings, and the ones with increased height, form a unity with the renovated stock, with the new, light, protruding roofs pulling together the powerful forward and backward thrusts of the façades in the existing stock. The modernization programme keeps the unity of the ensemble and at the same time represents a further design development using current formal elements that make the buildings considerably more attractive. As well as this, private gardens in front of the owner-occupied dwellings, protected by hedges and pergolas, create a fluent transition from the base zones of the buildings to the natural surroundings of the park.

The necessary parking spaces, one per dwelling, were largely accommodated on a parking deck and in underground car-parks. Despite the fact that the number of dwellings has been increased by almost 60 %, the original degree of sealing has not risen significantly. The conifer plantation on the eastern edge of the complex is being turned into a mixed deciduous wood with play and recreation areas for young and old.

These different building measures made it possible to achieve a wide range of housing including one- to four-bedroom flats, maisonettes and terraced houses. Only a quarter of the existing homes remained unchanged, but all the façades were renewed, with full heat-protection and heat-protection windows. Some of the raised storeys were built in masonry, some using wooden post-and-beam structures, so that they looked light physically as well as in terms of design.

For the additional dwellings, considerable emphasis was placed on variety. A new building with maisonettes built one on top of the other completes the previous range of owner-occupied homes. Complementing the two staircases that have been placed in between, a lift gives access to the open corridor on the third floor with the entrance and living area for the upper maisonettes. The sleeping quarters were placed above each other on the 1st and 2nd floors, to keep mutual disturbances down as much as possible. Then there were two economically conceived terraced house types, matching the existing ones in terms of size, built either as an additional row between the existing stock or attached to it. Differently organized dwellings were also created in the raised storeys, which were often above small ground-plans, some with through living areas. Here interesting solutions were developed for the arrangement of living room, kitchen and dining area. Most of the bathrooms have natural lighting. Despite the considerably increased number of residential units, the heating requirements remained the same overall.«

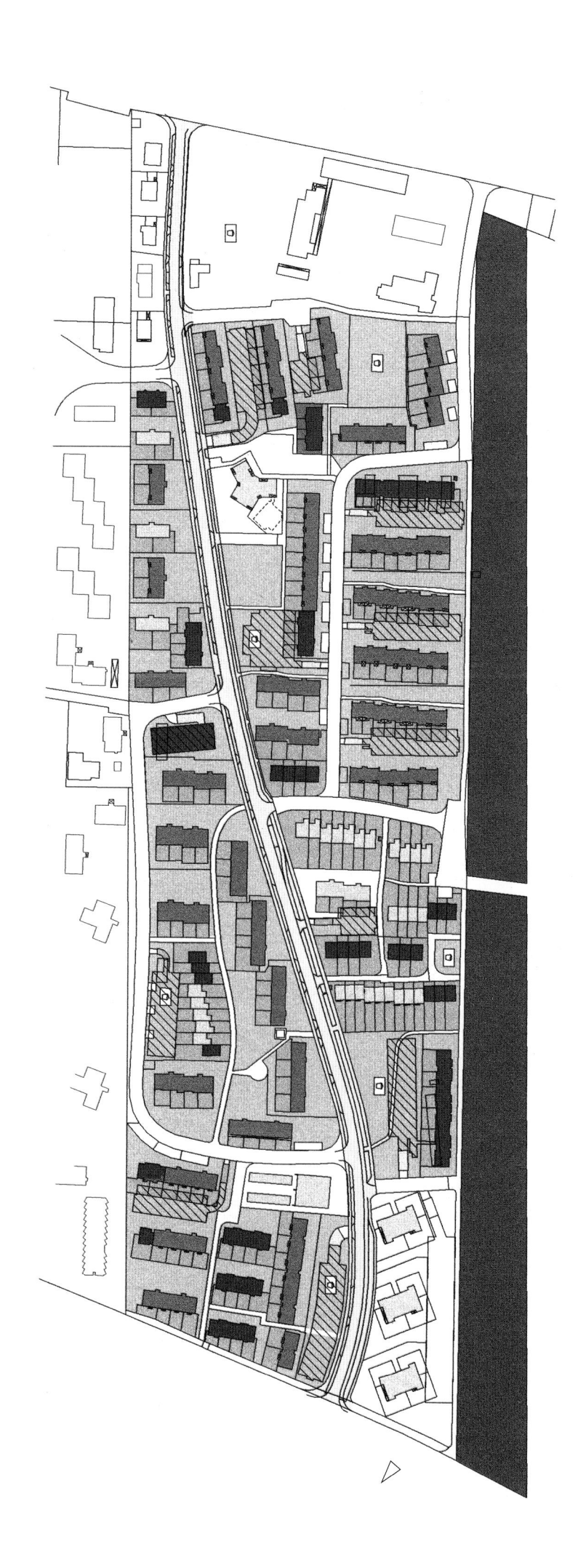

Lageplan der Wohnanlage
Verdichtungskonzept
hellgrau = Gebäude ohne Veränderung
grau = Gebäudeaufstockung
dunkelgrau = Neubau

Site plan of the residential estate,
concept to increase the urban density
light grey = unchanged buildings
grey = vertically extended buildings
dark grey = new buildings

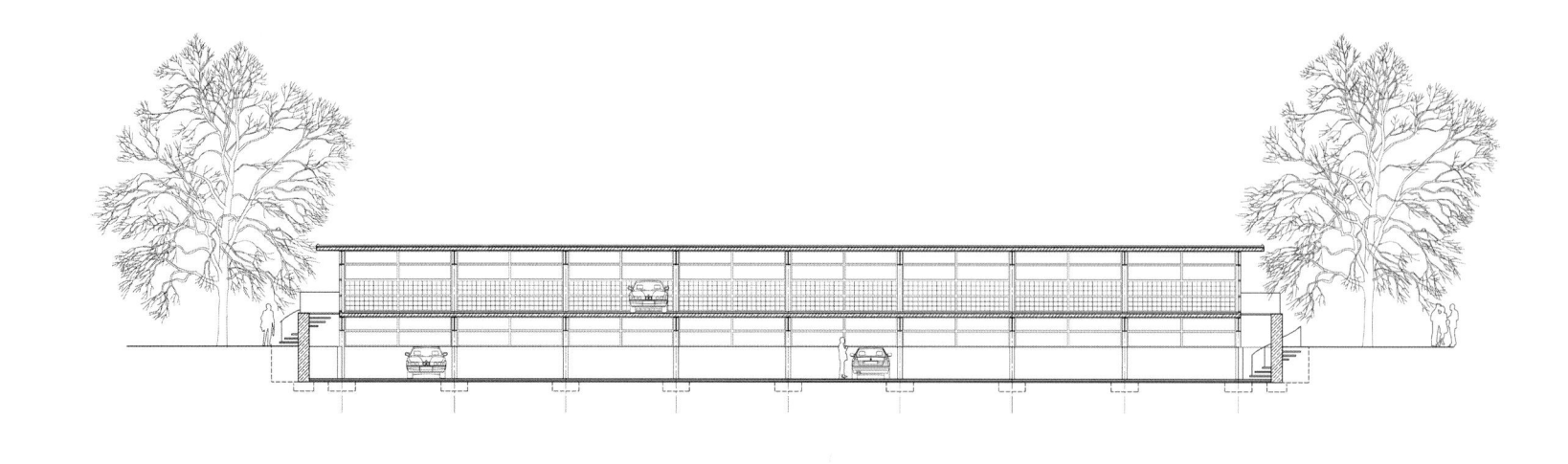

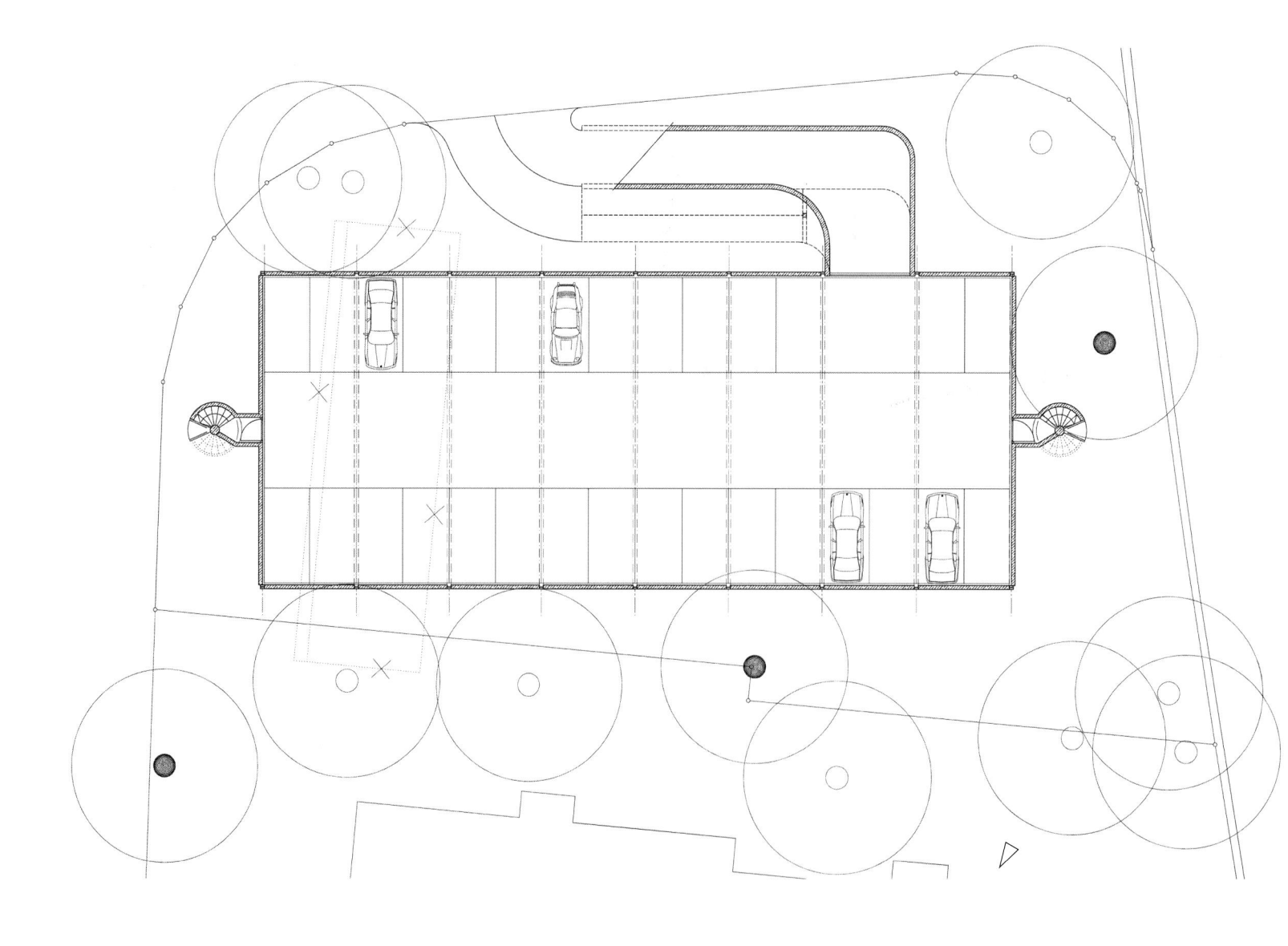

Oben: Schnitt
Unten: Grundriß Parkdeck

Top: cross-section
Bottom: layout of parking deck

Parkdeck Kleisstraße

Parking deck, Kleisstrasse

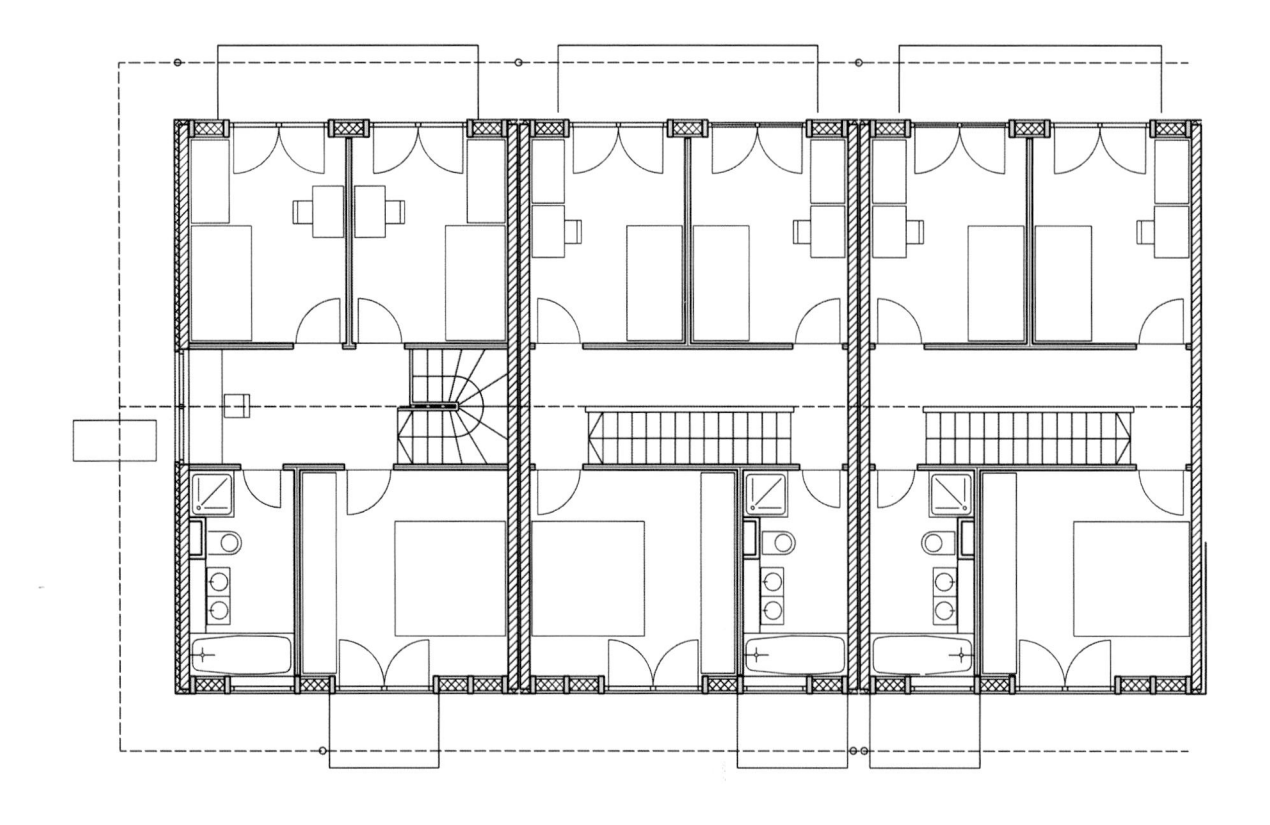

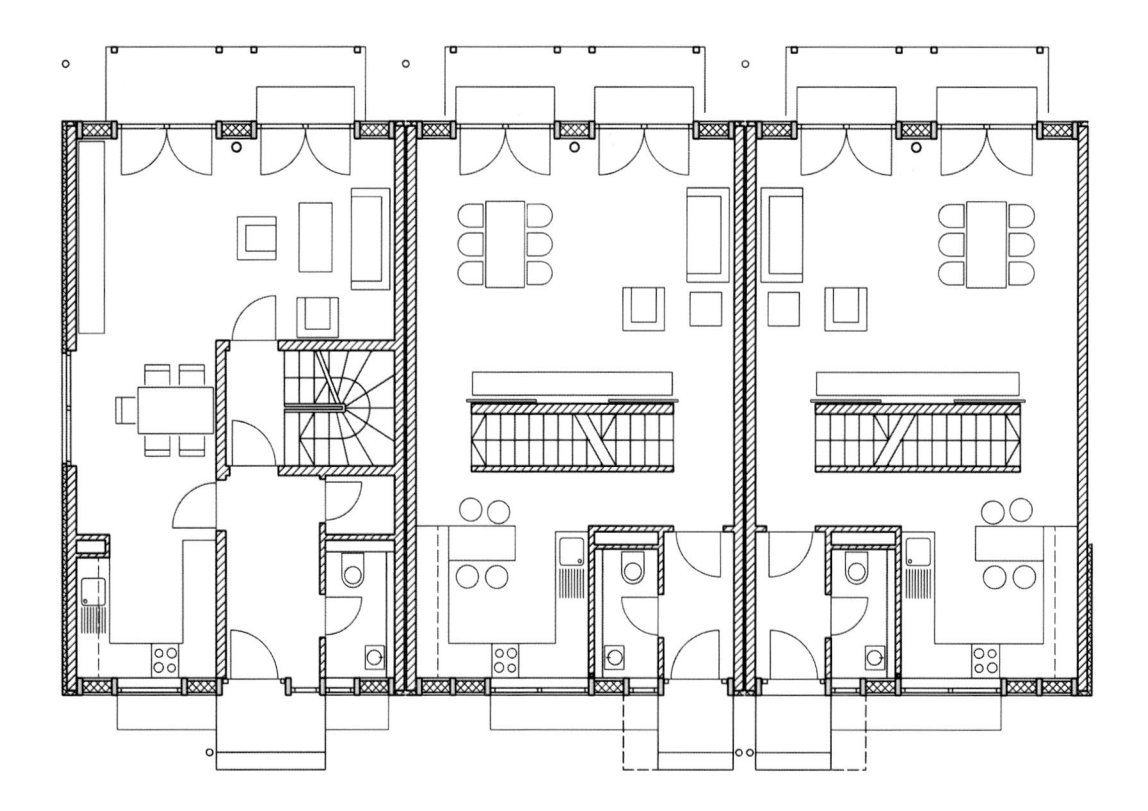

Oben: Grundriß Obergeschoß Reihenhäuser
Unten: Grundriß Erdgeschoß Reihenhäuser

Top: upper floor in terraced houses
Bottom: ground floor in terraced houses

Neubau Reihenhäuser
Hans-Sachs-Straße 21

New terraced houses,
Hans-Sachs-Strasse 21

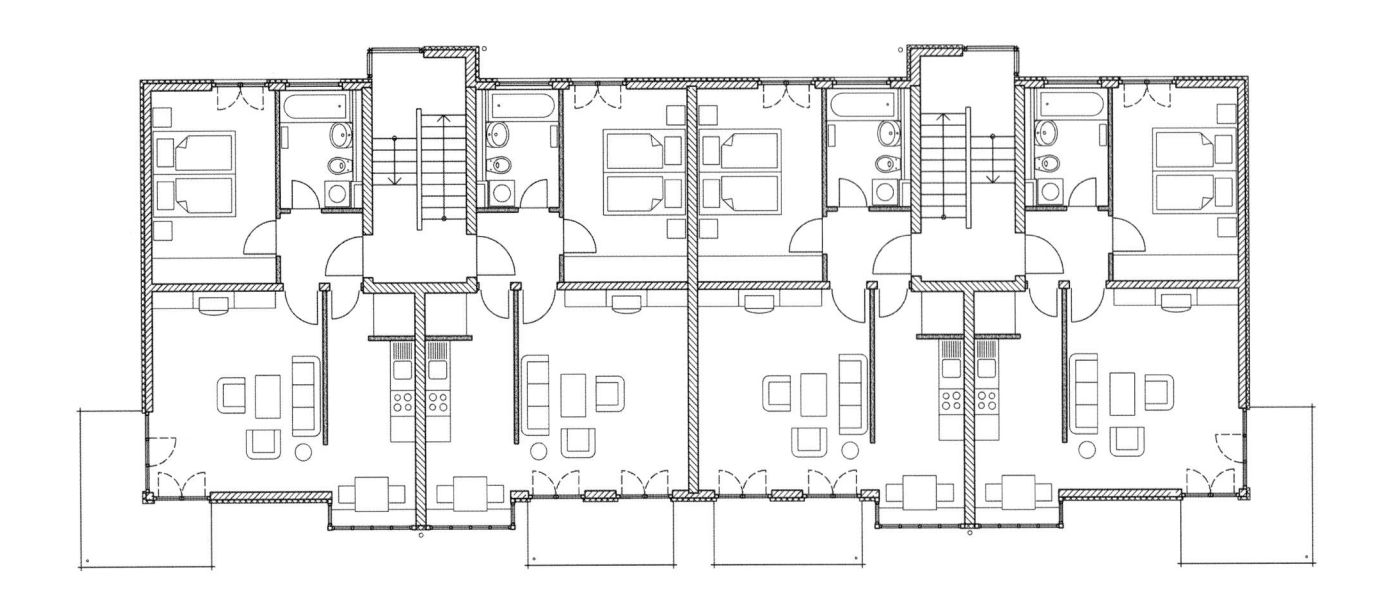

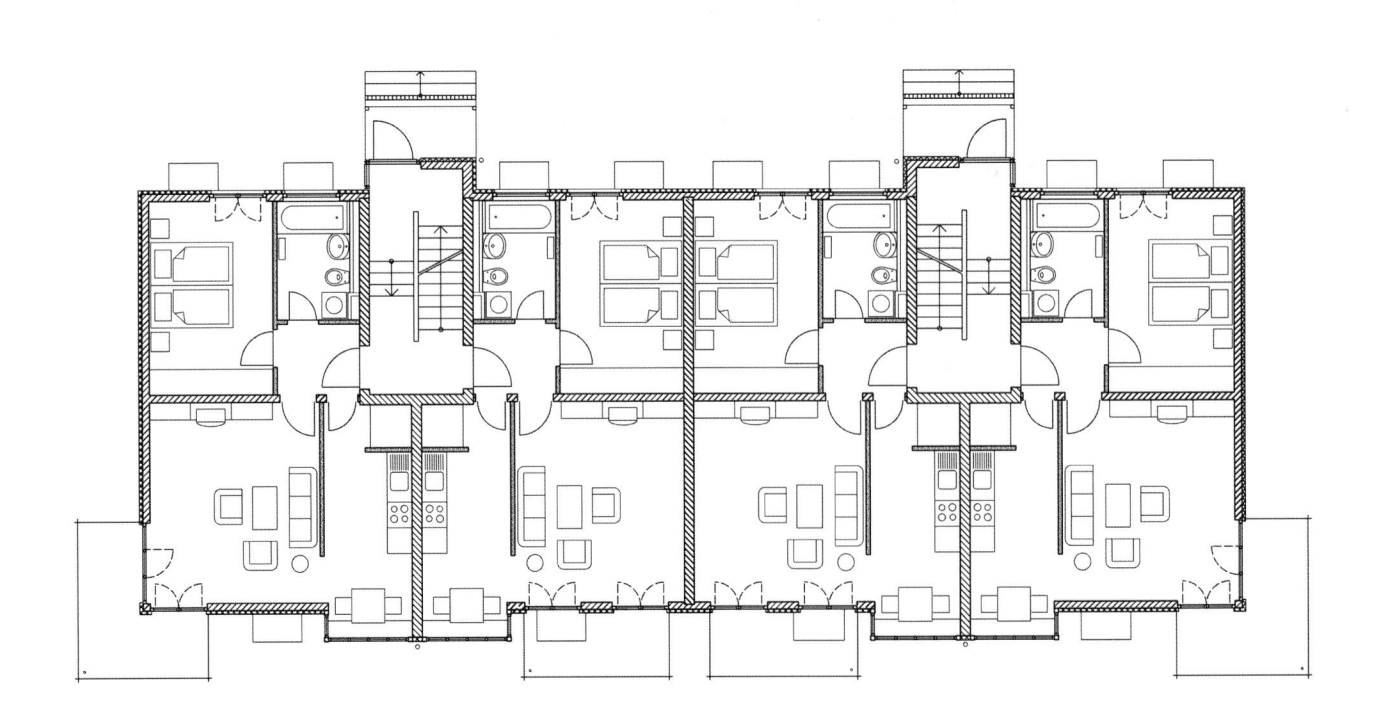

Oben: Grundriß Obergeschoß
Unten: Grundriß Erdgeschoß

Top: floor plan, upper floor
Bottom: floor plan, ground floor

Dreistöckiger Neubau
Rubensstraße 4a und 4b

New three-story building,
Rubensstrasse 4a and 4b

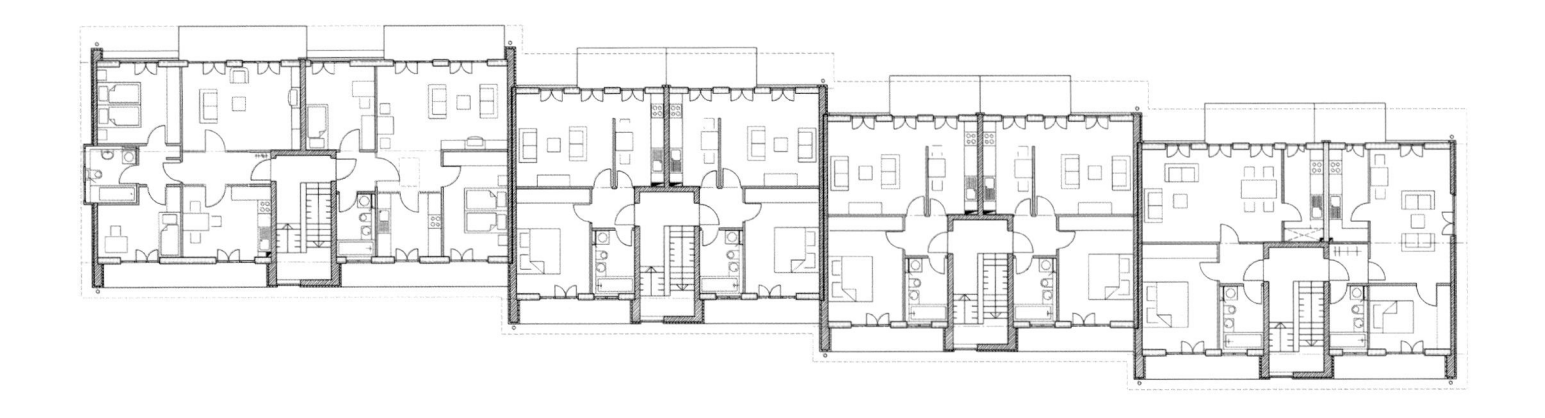

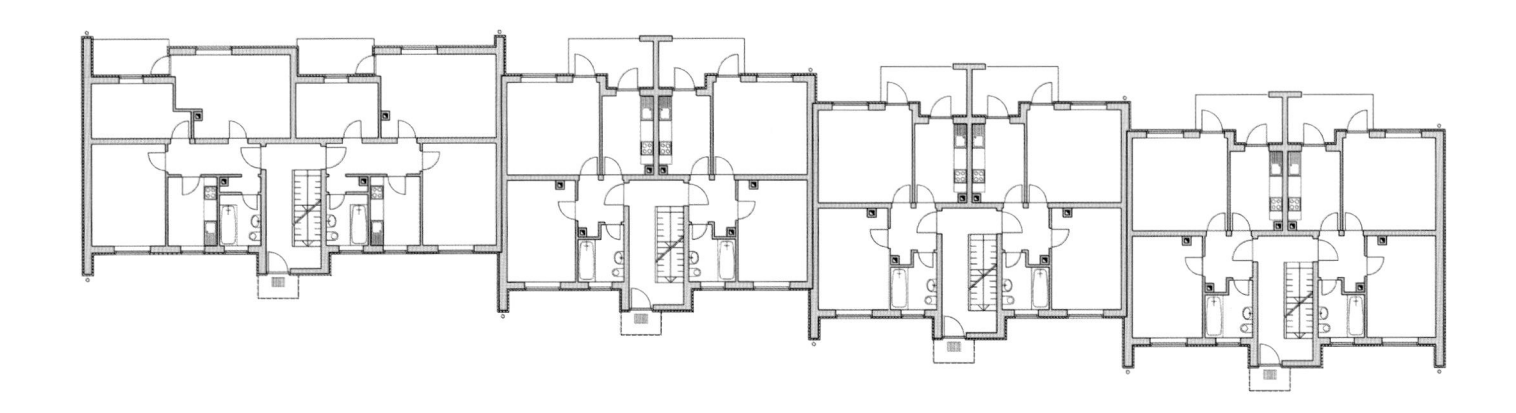

Oben: Grundriß 4. Obergeschoß Aufstockung
Unten: Grundriß Erdgeschoß Bestand

Top: floor plan of 4th floor, vertical extension
Bottom: floor plan of existing ground floor

Aufstockung um ein Geschoß
Rubensstraße 23–29

Vertical extension by one storey
Rubensstrasse 23–29

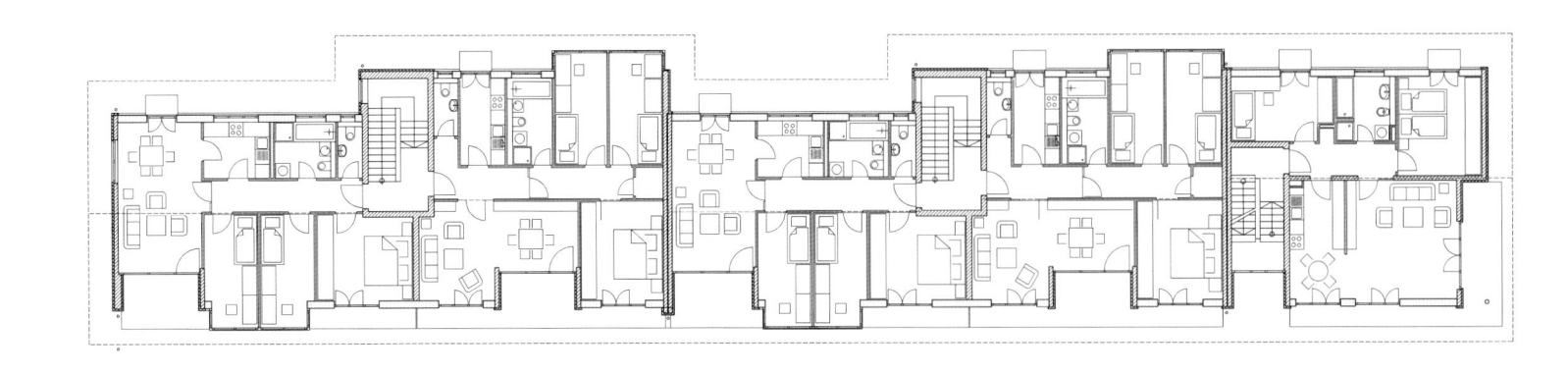

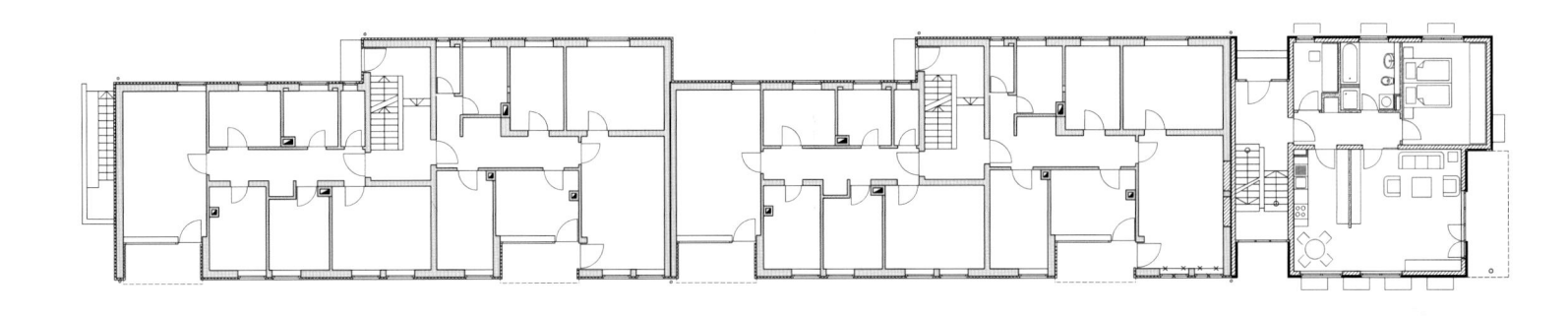

Oben: Grundriß 4. Obergeschoß Aufstockung mit Neubau
Unten: Grundriß Bestand mit Neubau

Top: floor plan, 4th floor, vertical extension with new building
Bottom: floor plan, existing building with new building

Aufstockung um ein Geschoß mit Neubau
Gustav-Freytag-Straße 6–8a

Vertical extension by one storey with new
building, Gustav-Freytag-Strasse 6–8a

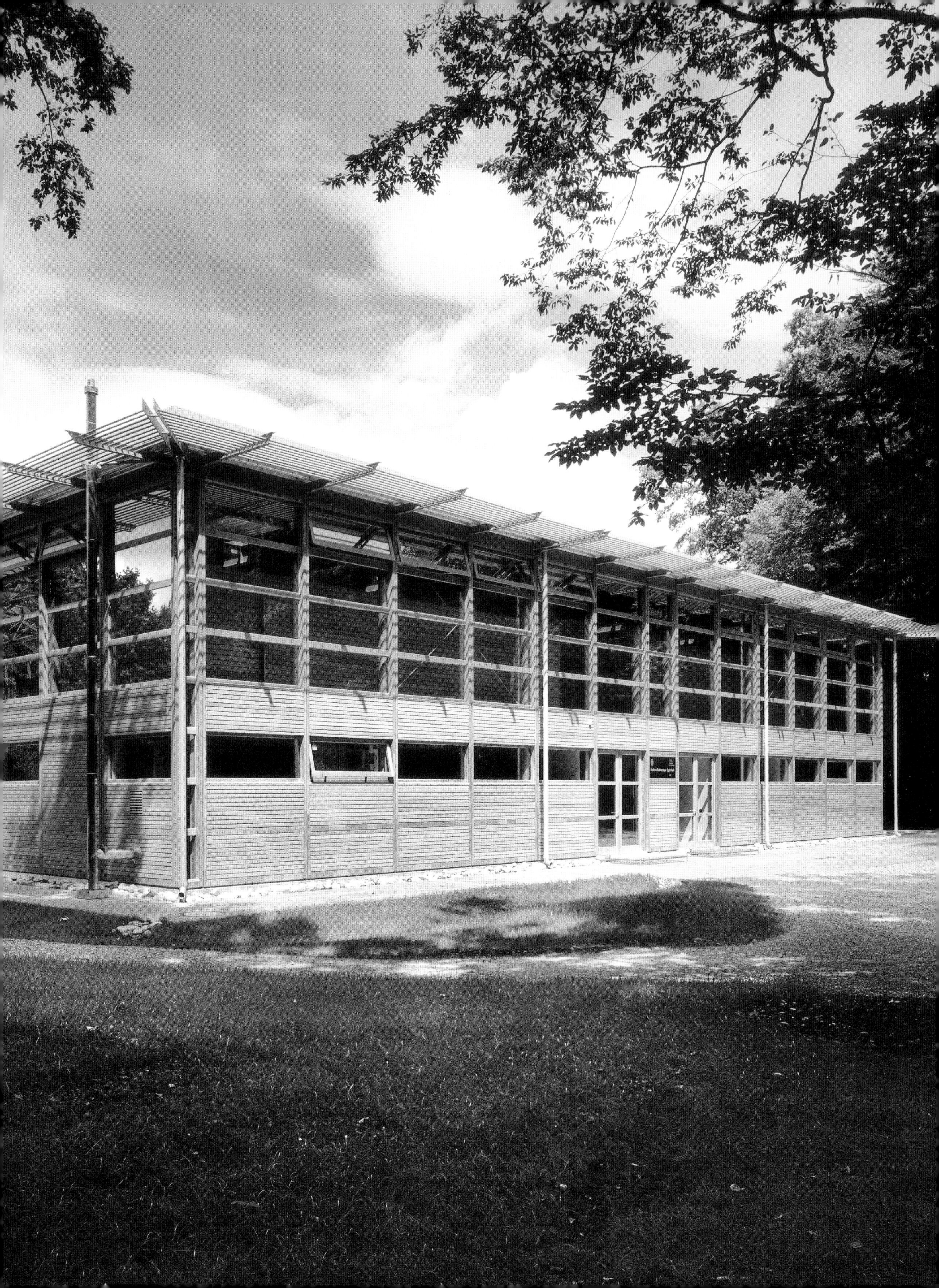

Zweifachsporthalle des Landheims Schondorf, Schondorf am Ammersee, 1998–2001
Bauherr: Stiftung Landheim Schondorf

Dual sports hall for the Schondorf boarding school, Schondorf am Ammersee, 1998–2001
Client: Landheim Schondorf Foundation

Der zwischen 1977 und 1982 für die Gemeinde Herrsching errichteten, so hervorragend in eine schwierige Situation eingefügten Sporthalle entspricht jene in Schondorf vom Raumprogramm her weitgehend. Sportbauten haben ja ihre festen Funktionen und Maße, trotzdem ist die 17 Jahre später gebaute Halle, sowohl was ihre Konstruktion anbelangt als auch von der Erscheinung her, gänzlich anders und eigenständig.

Der hohe Grundwasserstand machte es kaum sinnvoll, die Hallenhöhe durch Tieflage der Spielebene zu reduzieren. Dies wäre auch, anders als in Herrsching, ästhetisch nicht begründet gewesen, steht doch der 27 x 30 Meter messende, sieben Meter hohe Baukörper vor einer Kulisse mächtiger Bäume gut eingebunden im Park des Landschulheims. Dieser Umgebung entspricht auch die ins Auge fallende Materialwahl der flächigen Füllungen des Stahlskelettbaus, welche aus großformatigen, horizontal beplankten Lärchenholzpaneelen bestehen.

Die Doppelsporthalle zeigt sich wohlproportioniert; sie ist von selbstverständlicher Eleganz und Leichtigkeit und eine weitere schöne Architektur nach dem in Schondorf 1974–77 errichteten Laborbau für den naturwissenschaftlichen Unterricht dieser Internatsschule. Sie tritt eigenständig und ohne im geringsten zu stören neben den wertvollen alten Baubestand des Landschulheims.

Baubeschreibung des Architekten

»Die mittig teilbare Doppelhalle dient dem Internatsgymnasium als multifunktionale Sporthalle sowohl für den schulischen Sportunterricht als auch für die vielfältigen gemeinschaftlichen Sportaktivitäten von Schülern und Lehrern. Neben dem klassischen Turnsport werden in der Halle Handball, Volleyball, Basketball, Badminton, Tennis und vor allem Hockey, der Traditionssport des Landheims, gespielt. Zum gemeinsamen Sporterlebnis trägt auch die erhöhte Zuschauertribüne im zweigeschossigen Teil der großen Halle bei.

Die Halle ist im Eingangsbereich zweigeschossig. Auf gleichem Niveau mit der Sporthalle liegen in zwei Gruppen Geräteräume für Innen- und Außensport, Sportlehrerräume, Technikräume und der Konditionsraum mit direktem Zugang zum Freisportgelände. Von der Eingangshalle erreicht man über eine leichte Stahltreppe die Zuschauergalerie, die gleichzeitig Stiefelgang mit Zugang zu den zwei Umkleide- und Waschraumgruppen ist.

The sports hall in Schondorf is the same in many respects in its spatial programme as the one built between 1977 and 1982 for the Herrsching municipality, which fitted into a difficult situation so outstandingly. Sports buildings have fixed functions and dimensions, but nevertheless the hall built 17 years later is completely different and independent in terms of construction and appearance.

The high ground water level meant it scarcely made sense to reduce the hall height by lowering the playing level. And this would not have been aesthetically justifiable as it was in Herrsching, as the building, which measures 27 x 30 m and is 7 m high, is set against a backdrop of towering trees, and thus an integral part of the boarding school park. The striking choice of material for the flat panels for the steel skeleton building also fits in with these surroundings. They consist of large-format larch panels made up of horizontal planks.

The double sports hall is well proportioned; it is naturally elegant and light, and another attractive piece of architecture following the laboratory building created in 1974–77 for science teaching at this boarding school. It looks independent and creates not the slightest sense of disturbance alongside the valuable set of old buildings on the school site.

The architect's description of the building

»The double hall, which can be divided in the middle, is used by the boarding school as a multifunctional sports hall, both for school PE teaching and also for the wide range of community sports activities for pupils and teachers. As well as standard gymnastics, handball, volleyball, basketball, badminton, tennis and above all hockey, the school's traditional sport, are played in the hall. The raised stand for spectators in the two-storey part of the large hall also contributes to the common experience of sport.

The entrance area of the hall is two storeys high. On the same level as the sports hall are two groups of equipment stores for indoor and outdoor sports, sports teachers' rooms, service rooms and the

Links: Eingangsansicht Sporthalle
Left page: sports hall, view of the entrance

Die Halle ist nach allen Seiten hin offen für Ausblicke in die Landschaft und für den Lichteinfall. Auch die Decke ist großzügig verglast. Dies ergibt hervorragende Lichtverhältnisse im Innern. In die Decken-Dachkonstruktion sind der Trennvorhang, die Beleuchtungsbänder und die Heizkörper für die Deckenstrahlungsheizung integriert. Die Sicken der Trapezblechdecken und die Deckenheizplatten sind perforiert und mit Dämmaterial hinterlegt. Zusammen mit den Wandverkleidungen aus sibirischer Lärche und dem Schwingboden aus Eichenholz bewirken sie eine wirksame Schalldämpfung.

Konstruktion

Die Nutzung des Gebäudes erforderte eine weitgespannte, nahezu quadratische Konstruktion. Deshalb bot sich ein räumliches Dachtragwerk mit Lastabtragung nach allen vier Seiten für die Halle an und für den zweigeschossigen Nebenraum- und Tribünenteil ein Flächentragwerk mit geringeren Konstruktionshöhen. Nach Abwägung aller Gegebenheiten und Forderungen entschied man sich für die elementierte Stahlbauweise. Das Dachtragwerk wurde im Werk präzis vorgefertigt, in großen Teilen angeliefert und in kurzer Zeit montiert.

Die filigranen Pendelstützen werden im Hallenteil mit Verbänden ausgesteift, und im zweigeschossigen Nebenraumbereich übernimmt die Betonplatte der Zwischendecke diese Aufgabe. Die nichttragenden Hüllwände der Garderobeneinbauten stehen frei mit großem Abstand zur Decke. Alle elastischen Prallwände und Wandverkleidungen mit Türen bestehen einheitlich aus sibirischer Lärche in Massivholz. Das gleiche gilt für die Außenwandkonstruktion, die Fenster und Türen.

Wirtschaftlichkeit

Dank der konstruktiven Überlegungen zur Modularität konnte das Gebäude in weniger als einem Jahr verwirklicht werden. Die Kürze der Bauzeit, die parallel laufenden Vorfertigungen sowie die Wahl einfacher Konstruktionen und Baumaterialien machten die Halle sehr kostengünstig. Besonders wichtig für die Wirtschaftlichkeit sind die Unterhaltskosten. Sämtliche Bauteile sind mit Ausnahme der Dach- und Fassadenflächen wartungsfrei. Ebenso bedeutsam sind die Energiekosten. Deren Minimierung erreichte man durch:
– kompakte Bauform mit günstigen Verhältnissen von Hüllfläche und Volumen,
– günstige Verteilung von geschlossenen und befensterten Anteilen in Wand und Dach,
– hohe Wärmedämmwerte der Wand- und Dachflächen, keine Kälte-/Wärmebrücken,
– innere Speichermassen zur Pufferung von Wärme und Kälte (Nachtauskühlung),
– passive und aktive Gewinnung von Solarenergie (Sonnenkollektoren auf dem Dach) und Außenverschalungen,
– umweltfreundliches, abgasarmes Heizsystem mit Brennwerttechnik und Strahlungsheizung,

fitness room with direct access to the open air sports area. A light steel staircase leads from the entrance hall to the spectators' gallery, and also provides access in outdoor footwear to the two groups of changing rooms and washrooms.

The hall is open on all sides for views out into the landscape and to provide incident light. The ceiling is also generously glazed. This produced outstanding interior lighting conditions. The separating curtain, the lighting strips and the heaters for the radiant ceiling heating are built into the ceiling/roof structure. The beading in the trapezoidal sheet metal ceilings and the ceiling heating panels are perforated and have insulating material behind it. This, the wall cladding in Siberian larch and the oak sprung floor create effective sound insulation.

Construction

The use of the building required a long-span, almost square structure. For this reason, a stereometric roof support system with load dispersal on all four sides suggested itself for the hall, and a two-dimensional frame structure with lower structural height for the two-storey side-room and stand section. The unit steel construction system was chosen after weighing up the complete situation and the requirements. The roof support structure was precisely prefabricated in the factory, delivered in large sections and assembled in a short time.

The filigree hinged supports are reinforced with bracing in the hall section and in the two-storey ancillary area this role is played by the concrete slab for the intermediate ceiling. The non-load-bearing cladding walls for the built-in cloakrooms are free-standing with a large gap before the ceiling. All the elastic baffle walls and wall cladding with doors are made of uniform solid Siberian larch. The same applies to the exterior wall structure, the windows and the doors.

Economic viability

Thanks to structural ideas leading to modular construction, it proved possible to realize the building in less than a year. The short building period, the prefabrication, which ran in parallel, and the choice of simple structures and building material made the price of the hall very reasonable. Maintenance costs are very important in terms of economic viability. No part of the building, with the exception of the roof and façade areas, requires maintenance.
Energy costs are equally significant. These can be minimized by:
– compact building form with favourable volume and covering area ratios,
– favourable distribution of closed areas and areas with windows in roof and walls,
– high heat insulation values for roofs and walls, no thermal bridges,
– internal storage masses as thermal buffers (night cooling),
– passive and active solar energy gain (solar collectors on the roof) and external lagging,
– environment-friendly heating system with low exhaust emissions with condensation technology and radiant heating,

– Einsparung von elektrischer Energie durch natürliche Belichtung und Belüftung aller Räume,
– umweltfreundliche Entsorgung des Oberflächenwassers über Versickerungsteiche.

Gestaltung

Die Gestaltung des Bauwerks findet ihren Ausdruck in der logischen Selbstverständlichkeit der unverhüllt dargestellten Konstruktion und den in diese integrierten Elementen der Haustechnik. Neben der klaren Ordnung der Bauelemente tragen die Baustoffe zur Erscheinung bei. Das Zusammenwirken aller Teile und ein ablesbares Proportionssystem ergeben eine Einheitlichkeit, die dem Zweck des Bauwerks dient und dies als sinnvoll erscheinen läßt.«

– electricity saved by natural lighting and ventilation for all rooms,
– environment-friendly disposal of surface water via seepage pools.

Design

The design of the building is expressed in the logical naturalness of the openly presented structure and the service elements built into this. The building materials contribute to its appearance as well as the lucid order of the building elements. The way all the parts work together and an intelligible proportion system produce a sense of uniformity that serves the purpose of the building and makes it look meaningful.«

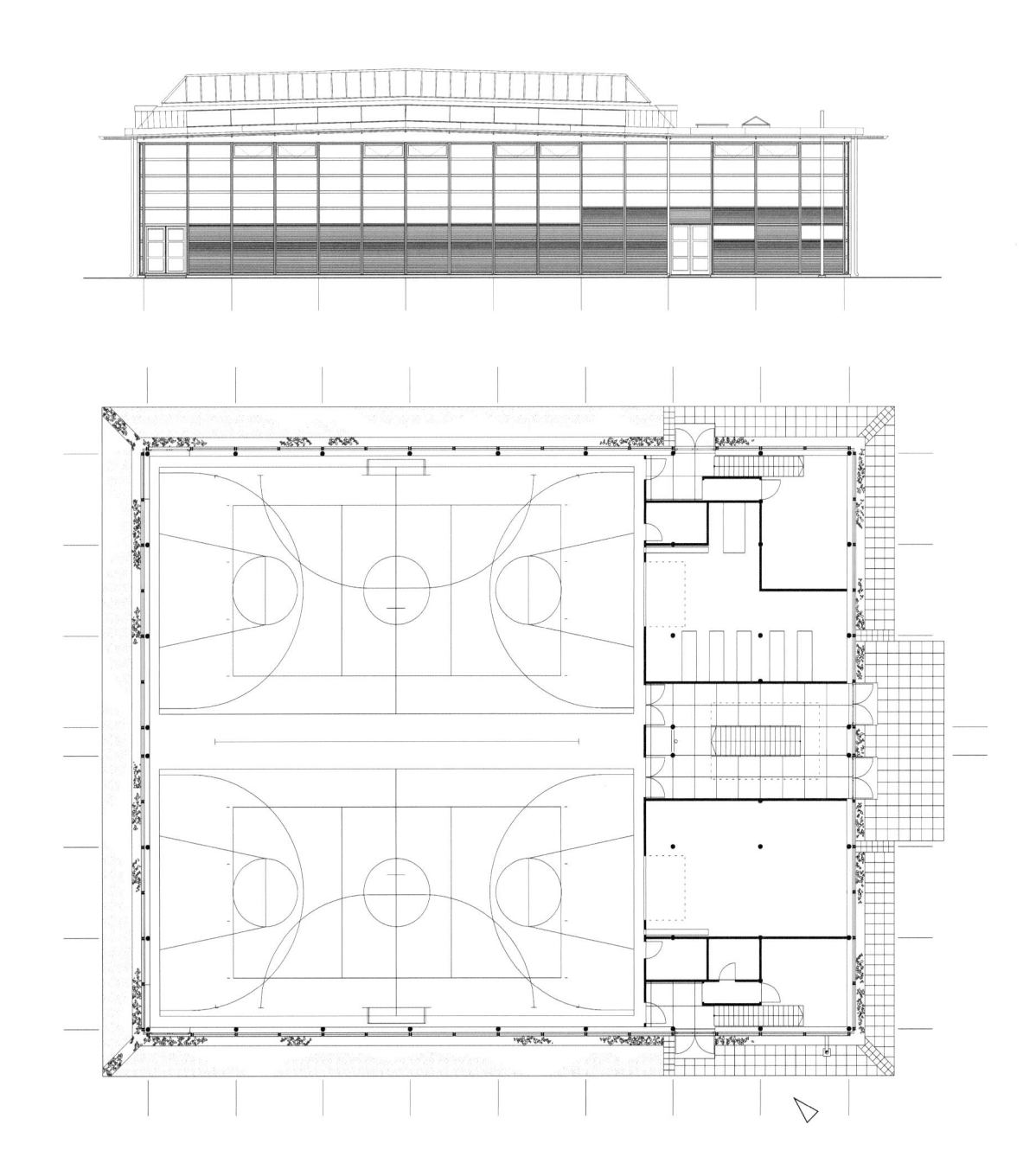

Oben: Ansicht
Unten: Grundriß Erdgeschoß

Top: general view
Bottom: floor plan, ground floor

FOLGENDE DOPPELSEITEN:
S. 176: Treppe zur Tribüne mit Blick in die Halle
S. 177: Turnschuhgang auf der Tribüne
S. 178–179: Blick von der Tribüne in die Halle

NEXT DOUBLE PAGES:
P. 176: stairs to the viewing gallery looking into the hall
P. 177: sports shoes corridor on the gallery
P. 178–179: view of the hall from the gallery

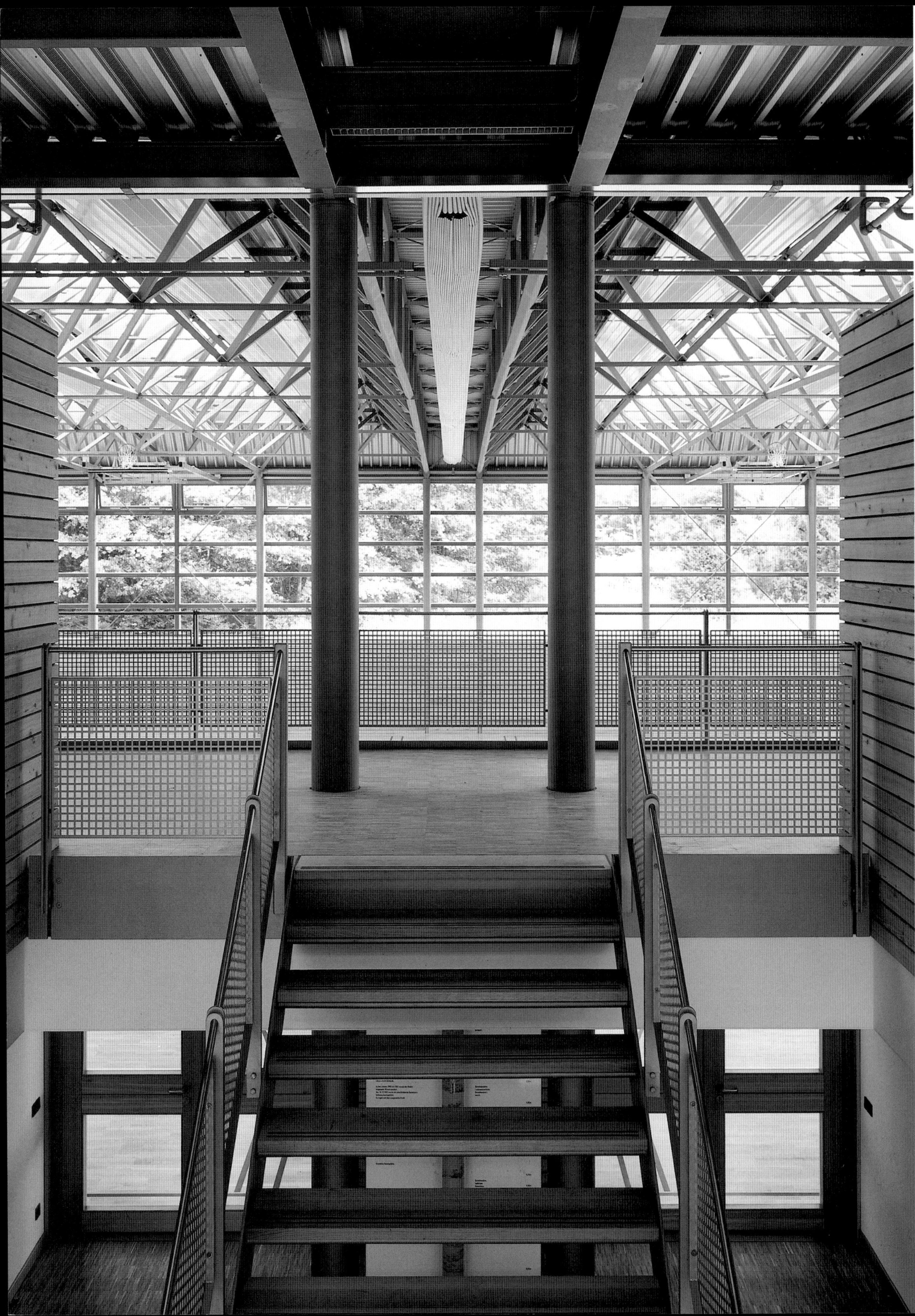

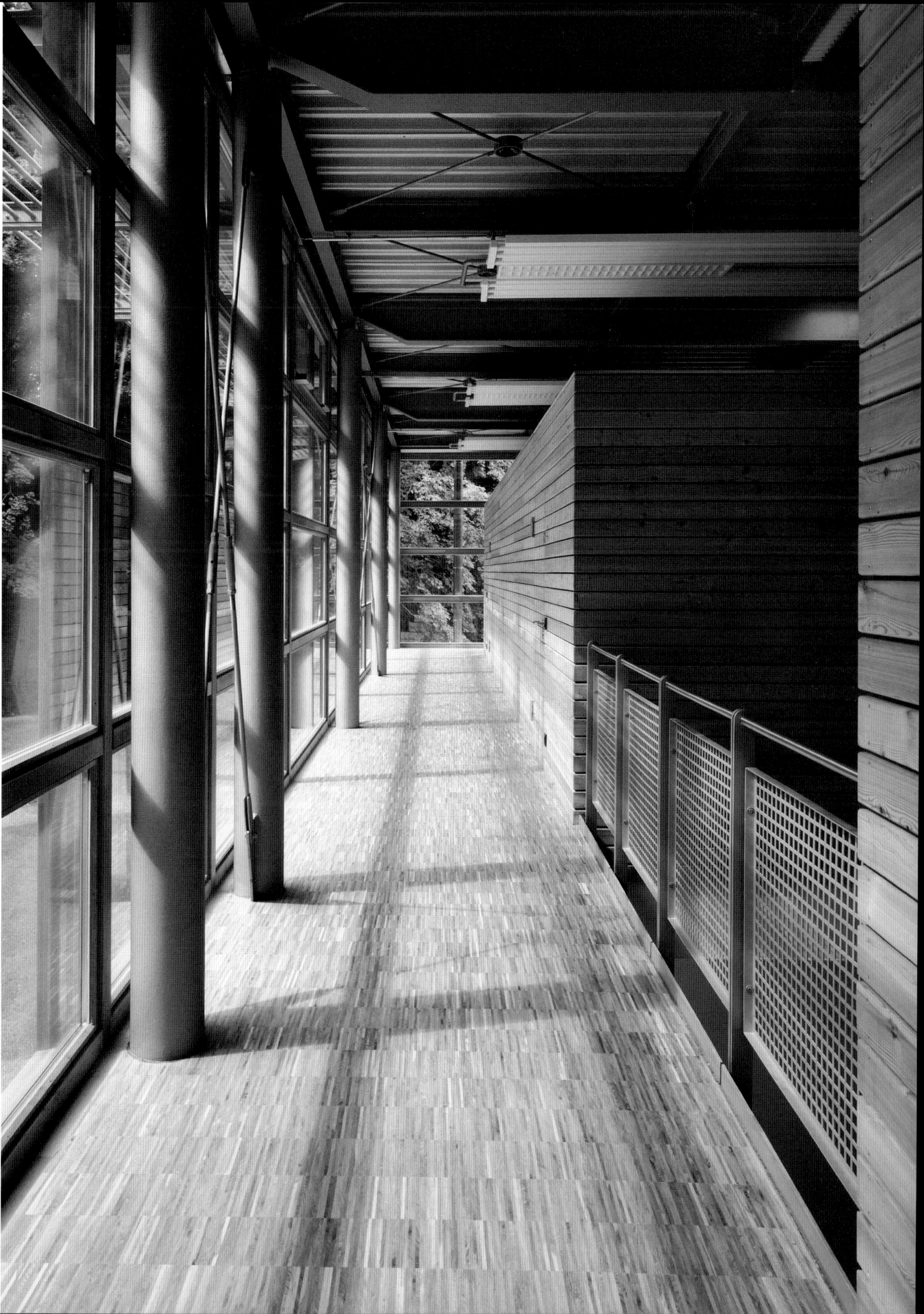

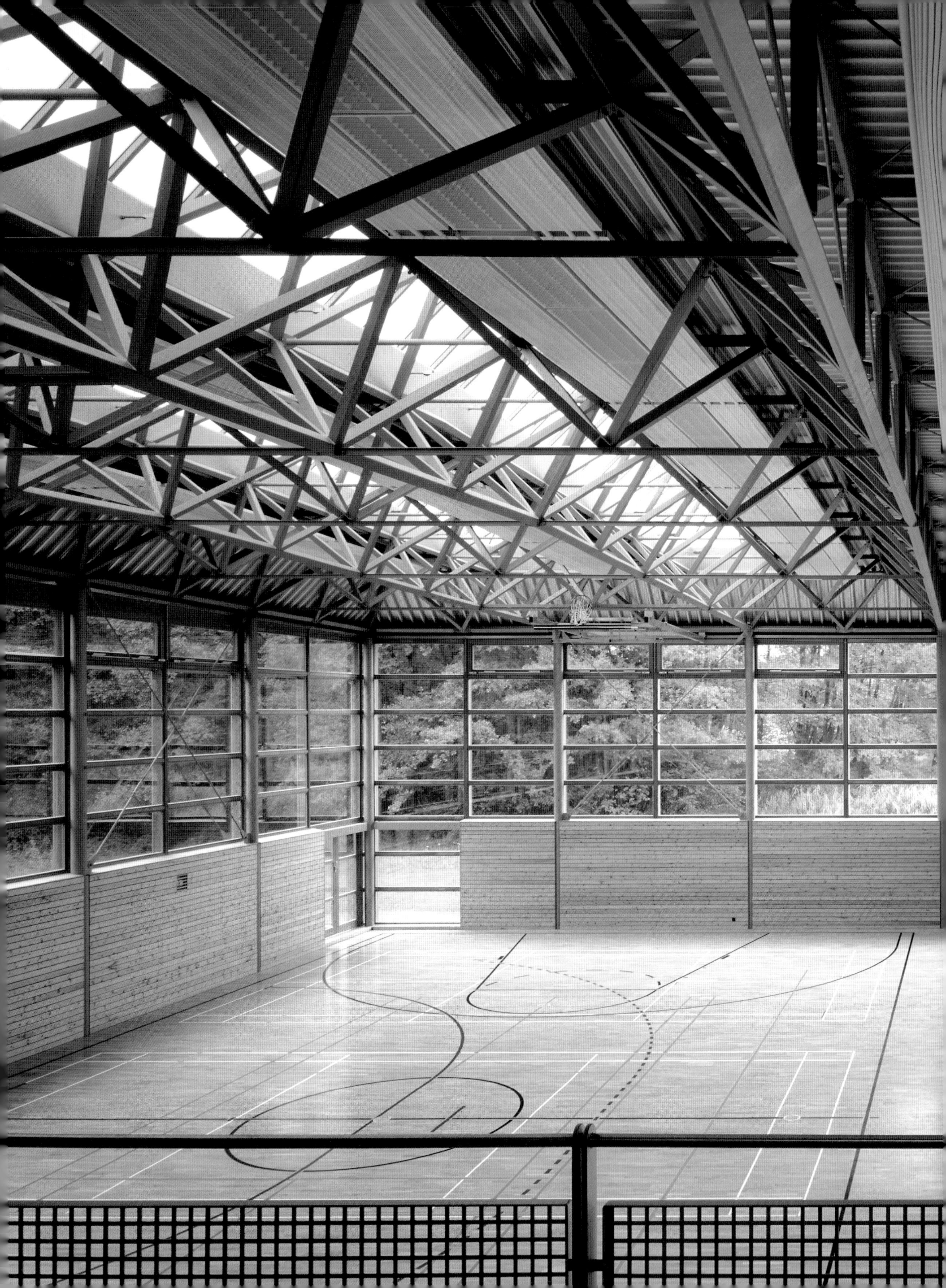

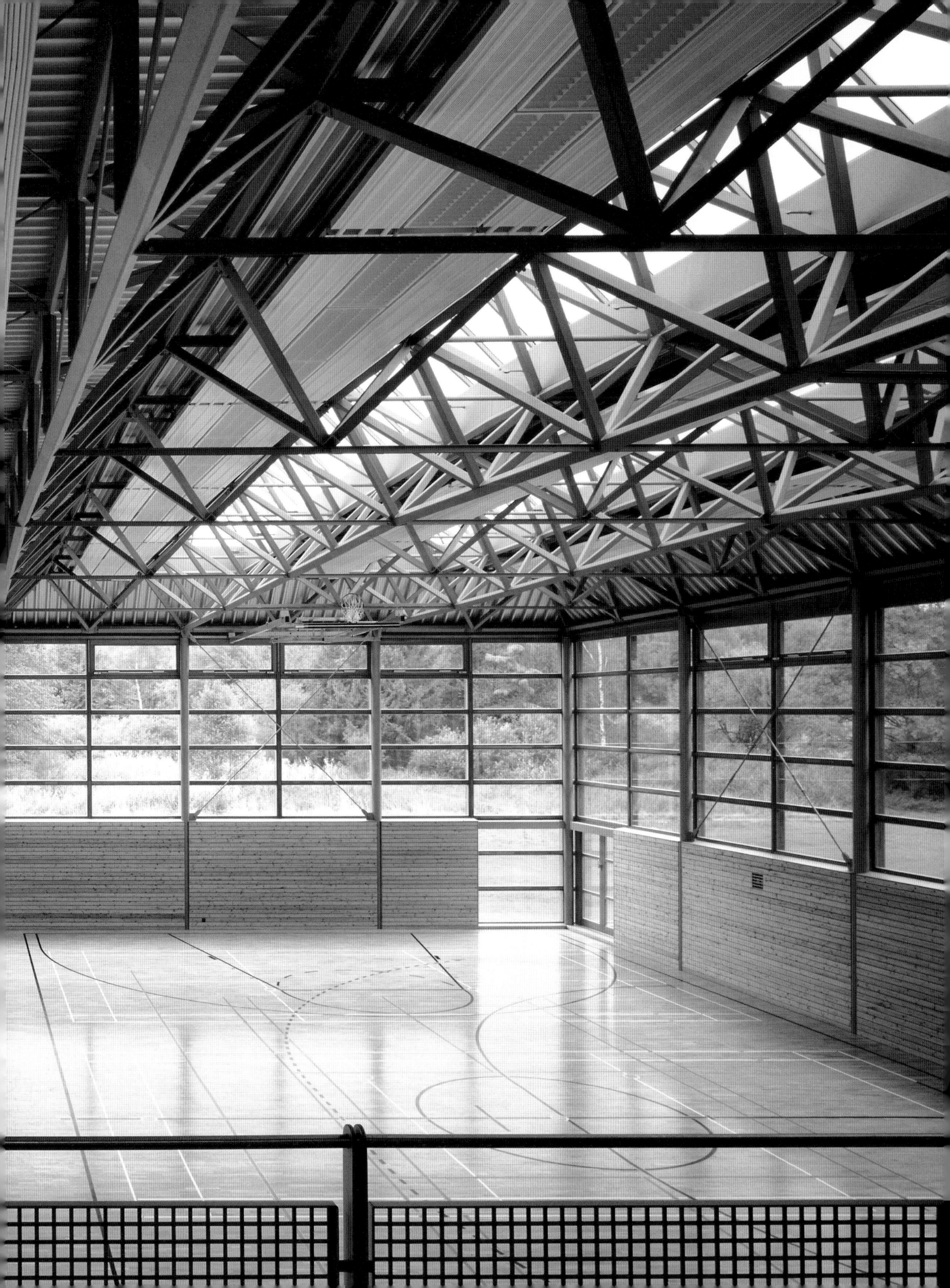

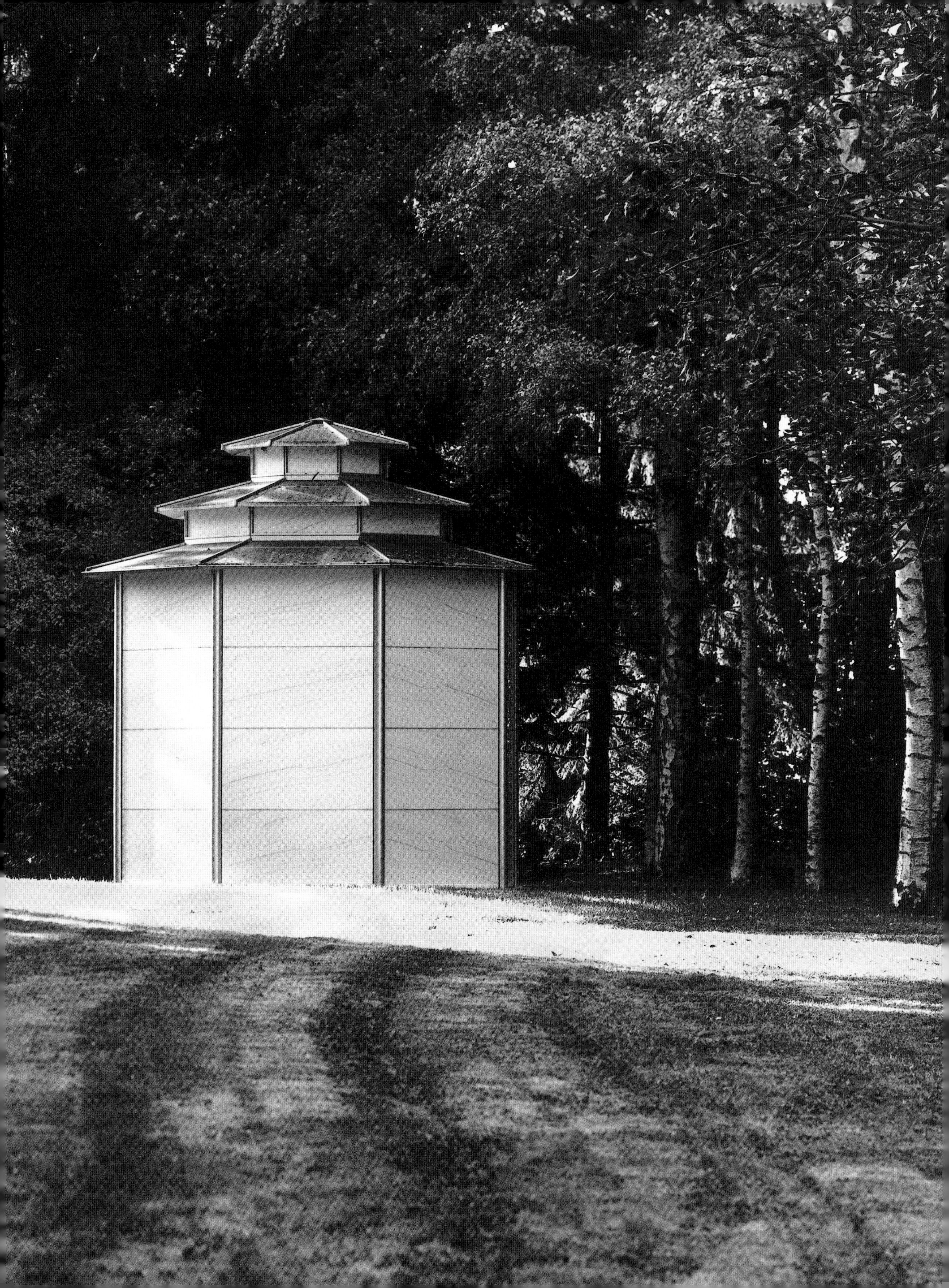

Marienkapelle, Am Vorderen Berg 1, Gundelfingen, 2001/02
Bauherren: Fritz und Heidi Gartner

St. Mary's Chapel, Am Vorderen Berg 1, Gundelfingen, 2001/02
Clients: Fritz and Heidi Gartner

Ein spätes Werk Detlef Schreibers ist dieser oktogonale Ort der Stille und Meditation. Sein Freund Fritz Gartner hatte nach einschneidenden Lebenserfahrungen ein tiefes Bedürfnis nach Zurückgezogenheit, nach Geschlossenheit und danach, sich selbst zu finden und nachzudenken. Makellos sollte dieses Haus werden, Symbol der Unendlichkeit im Kleinen.

Dort wollte Fritz Gartner verweilen und Einkehr bei sich halten, im stummen Dialog mit der von Blasius Gerg geschaffenen Statue der Mutter mit dem Gottessohn.

Seinen Wunsch erfüllte Detlef Schreiber ebenso sensibel wie präzise in Zusammenarbeit mit den weltweit geschätzten Gartnerschen Fachleuten.

Stützen und Tragwerk des mit einem dreistufigen Pagodendach bekrönten oktogonalen Schreins bilden eigens entwickelte Aluminiumprofile. Die Wände bestehen, an römische Achatfenster erinnernd, aus transluzentem Lasa-Marmor und erweisen Detlef Schreibers besonderes Verhältnis zur Macht des Lichtes, ohne das die Körper der Architektur stumm wären, wie schon die Meister der Antike wußten und Le Corbusier unvergeßlich lehrte.

Die drei oktogonalen Dachschirme sind lichtundurchlässig und sorgfältig gedämmt. Sie gleichen so die physikalisch unterschiedlichen Bedingungen der transluzenten Wände aus. Der nachts wie ein Opal schimmernde Schrein weist als ein Höchstmaß an Gartnerscher Kunstfertigkeit der Fassadenkonstruktion auf.

Unwillkürlich stellt sich die Frage nach der Dimension dieses Baus, die sich nur von innen her erfahren läßt. Der dem Oktogon einbeschriebene Kreis hat einen Durchmesser von 3,6 Metern, genauso wie jener imaginäre Kreis, der den Boden, die Marmorwände und die Bedachung tangiert.

Eine verzaubernde Winzigkeit also bewirkt diese Wunscherfüllung, ein Kosmos indes für den diesen Ort mit seiner Besinnlichkeit erfüllenden Menschen.

Wäre noch anzumerken, daß dieses Prisma, dieser Kristall, ohne Beziehungen aufzunehmen, in einem weiten, mit schönen Bäumen bestandenen Park seinen Platz hat, soeben gelandet und ohne Verlegenheit um Ort und Zeit.

Der überraschte Betrachter erfährt zunächst durchaus ratlos, daß Wesentliches nicht immer groß sein muß und daß sich das Ungewöhnliche oft erst auf den zweiten Blick und dann nur dem zum Staunen Bereiten offenbart.

This octagonal place of calm and meditation is a late work by Detlef Schreiber. Following star-reaching experiences, his friend Fritz Gartner had a profound need for seclusion, for unity, and then to find himself and reflect. The building was to be immaculate, a miniature symbol of infinity.

Fritz Gartner wanted to linger there and search his soul, in silent conversation with Blasius Gerg's statue of the Mother with the Son of God.

Detlef Schreiber met his wishes sensitively and precisely, working with Gartner's experts, who are highly esteemed world-wide.

Custom-developed aluminium sections make up the columns and load-bearing system for this octagonal shrine with three-step pagoda roof. The walls, reminiscent of Roman agate windows, are in translucent Lasa marble and show Detlef Schreiber's special relationship with the power of light, without the body of the architecture sitting silent, as the masters of antiquity were already aware, and Le Corbusier unforgettably taught us.

The three octagonal roof umbrellas are opaque and carefully insulated. In this way they balance out the physically varying conditions of the translucent walls. The shrine shimmers like an opal at night, and can be considered to demonstrate Gartner's façade construction skills at their very best.

The question about the dimensions of this building arises spontaneously, as it is only possible to experience them from the inside. The circle inscribed within the octagon is 3.6 m in diameter, just the same as the imaginary circle that touches the floor, the marble walls and the roof.

And so an enchanting miniature fulfils the wish, yet it is a cosmos for the human being filling this place with contemplation.

It should also be noted that this prism, this crystal, stands in a beautiful park with trees, without relating to anything, as though it has just landed and is unembarrassed by place and time.

The surprised viewer discovers at first, entirely at a loss, that the essential does not have to be large, and that the unusual is often revealed only at second glance, and then only to those ready to be amazed.

Links: Außenansicht Kapelle im Park
Left page: exterior view of the chapel in the park

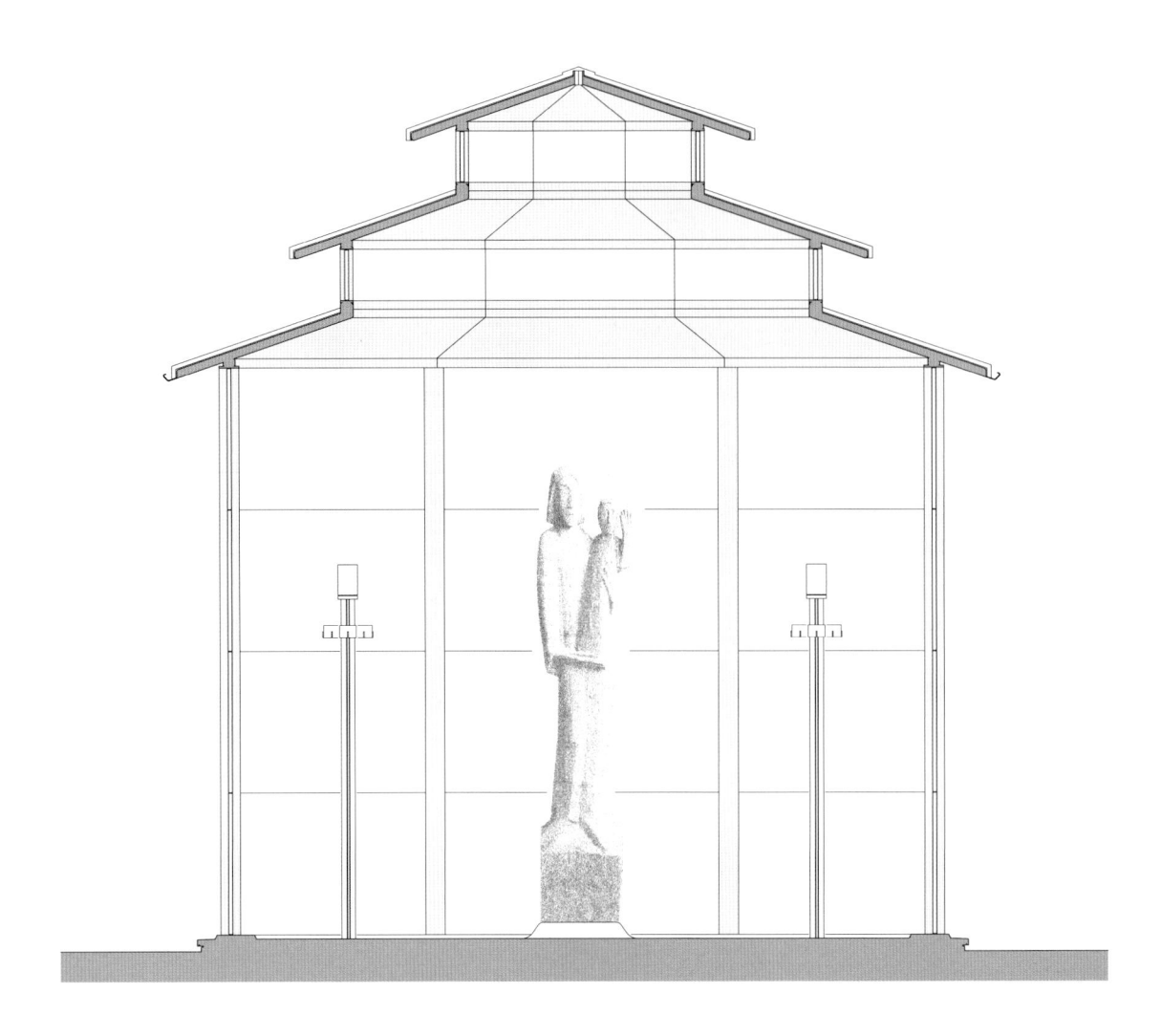

Oben: Schnitt

Rechts: Innenraum, Wände
aus transluzentem Marmor
Madonna: Blasius Gerg

Above: sectional view

Right page: interior, walls
of translucent marble
Madonna: Blasius Gerg

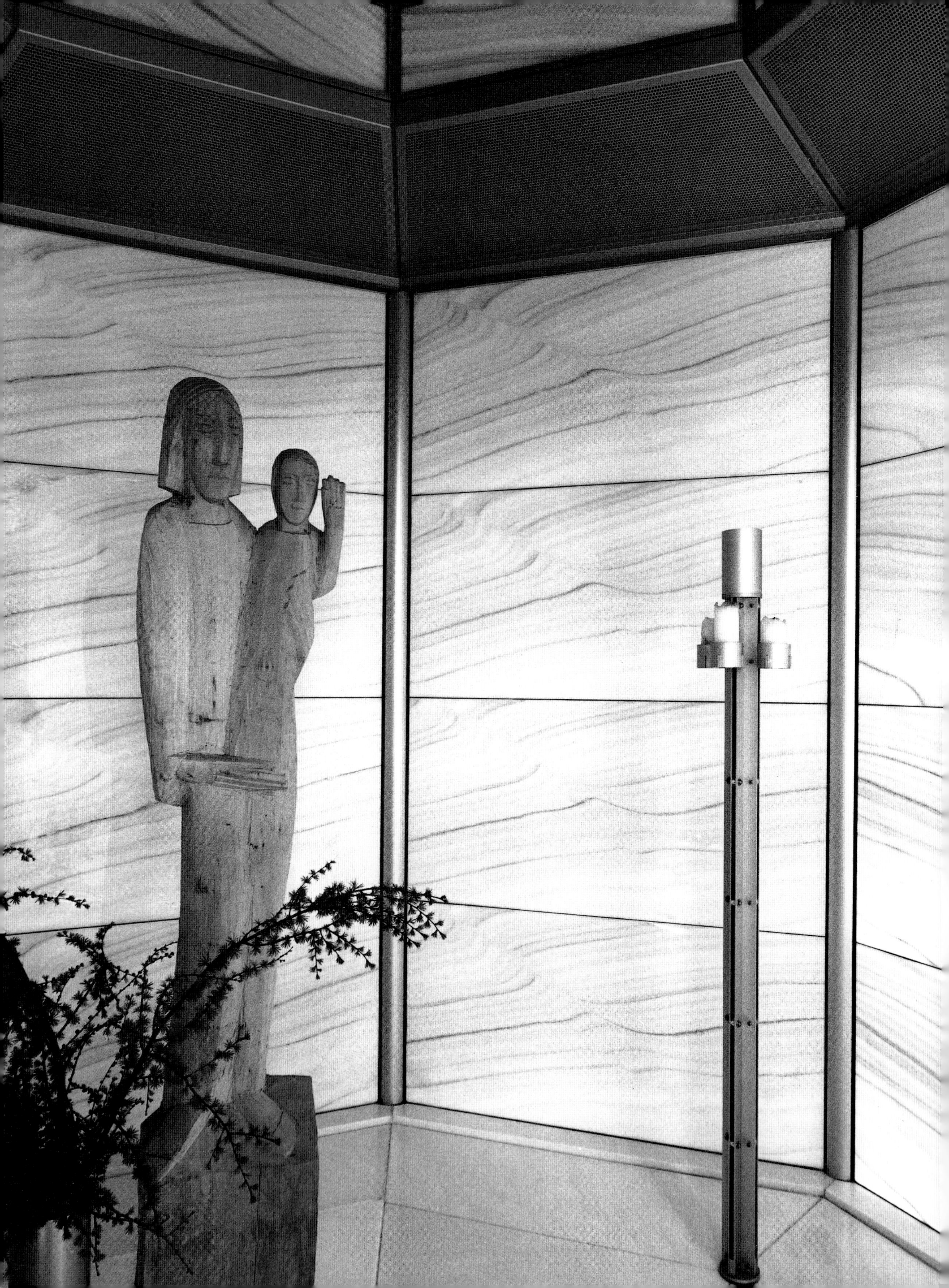

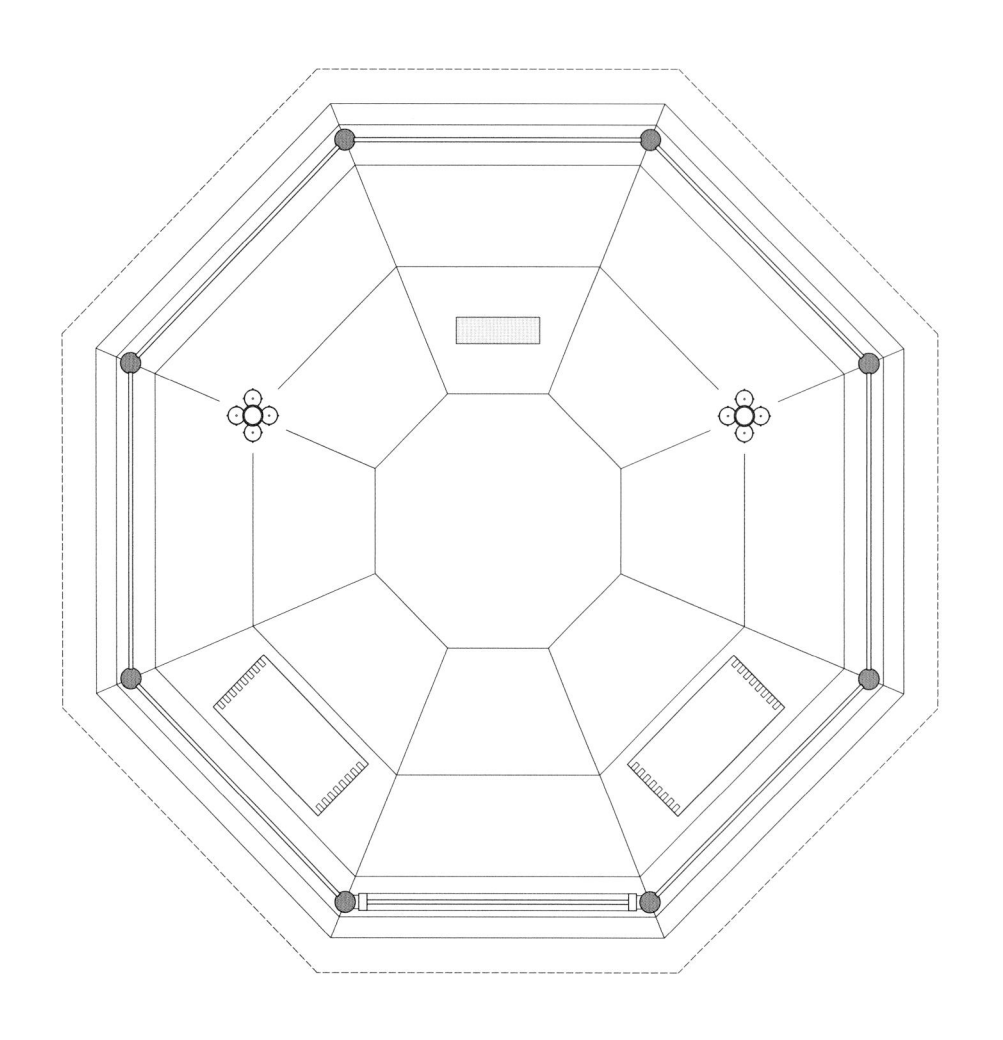

Oben: Grundriß

Rechts: Blick aus der Kapelle in die Landschaft

Above: floor plan

Right page: view of the landscape from the chapel

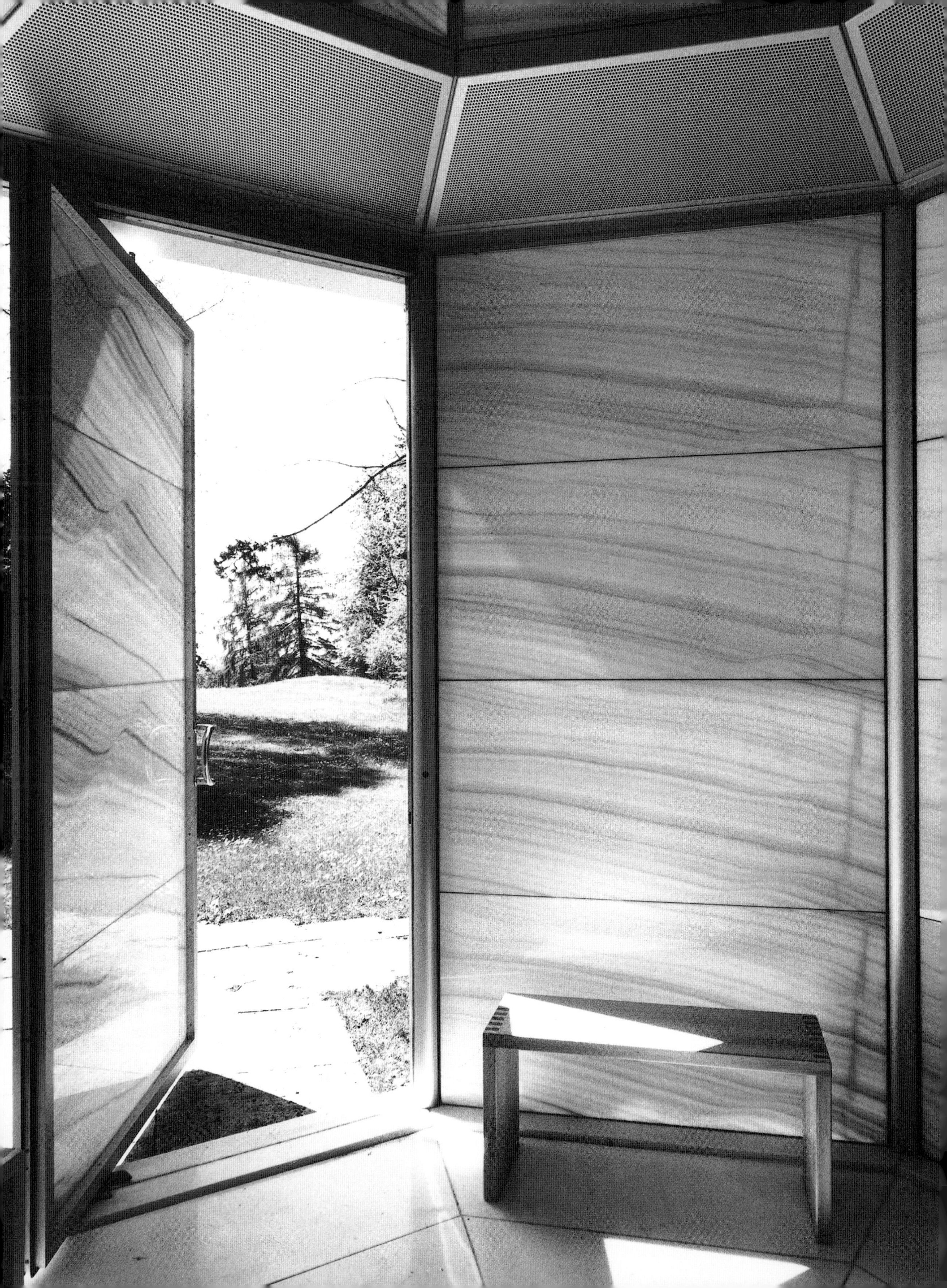

Städtebauliche Planungen
Urban-development planning

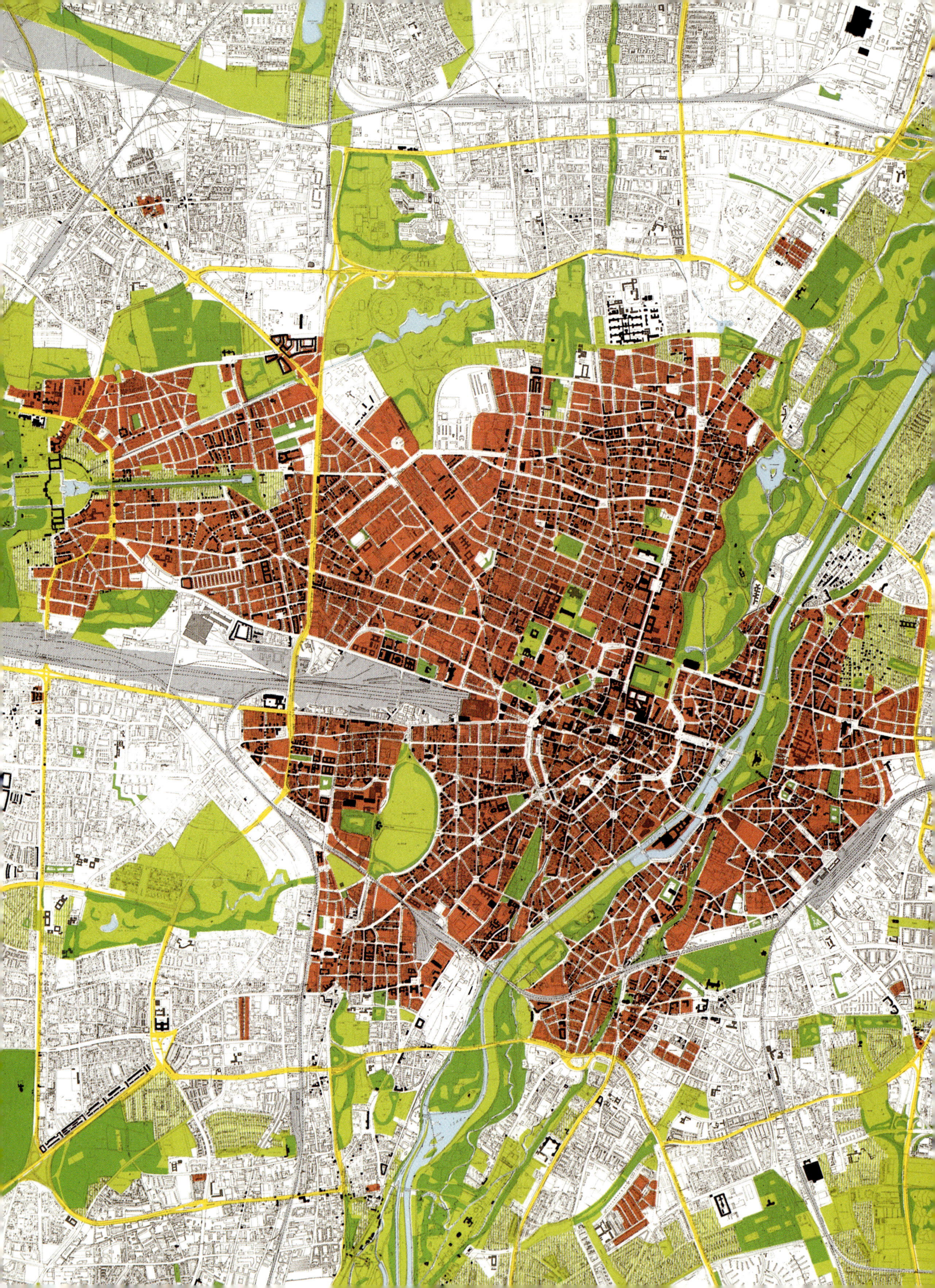

Städtebauliche Planungen, regional-, landschafts- und strukturplanerische Arbeiten
Urban-development planning, work on regional, landscape and structural planning

Als sich eine Anzahl bekannter oder im Aufstieg befindlicher Münchner Architekten 1966 zur »Plan Gesellschaft für Regional-Architektur- und Ingenieurplanungs mbH München« zusammenschlossen, lag dies zwar im Trend der in Kollektive vernarrten Jahre, sollte aber später doch scheitern. Die Zeit war noch nicht reif für derartige Dienstleister. Die Auftraggeberseite, an gänzlich anders strukturierte Partner gewöhnt, kam mit der Rechtsform der »Plan GmbH« nicht zurecht. Die eigentlich notwendige kontinuierliche Akquisition konnte gemäß der Standesordnung nicht marktkonform nach Angebot und Nachfrage betrieben werden.

Die »Plan« war außerdem alles andere als ein Kollektiv. Sie war völlig inhomogen. Es gab Stars; die Einzelbüros bestanden fort und mimten Gesellschafter. Naturgemäß hatten sich hervorragende Akquisiteure eingefunden, die fürs Eigene arbeiteten, Animateure, dazu die üblichen Diskutanten, aufs Wesentliche reduziert: »Chefs und malochende Arbeiter«. Kurz gesagt, die GmbH reüssierte nicht und scheiterte zuletzt, nachdem sich Querköpfe und vorsichtige Partner rechtzeitig ins Trockene begeben hatten, verlustreich an den Baumängeln eines Großauftrags.

Es geht indes nicht darum, jene damals viel Aufsehen erregende »Gründung« in Erinnerung zu rufen. Vielmehr gilt es, Detlef Schreibers arbeitsreichen Anteil an den Exkursen der »Plan« in Richtung Regionalplanung anzusprechen.

Von 1967 bis 1971 betreute er sorgsam und federführend die Gebietsentwicklungsplanung für die Stadt und den Landkreis Ingolstadt. Zusätzlich arbeitete er an der Strukturplanung für die Altstadt der in die Zukunft strebenden ehemaligen Festungs- und Garnisonsstadt, die sich rasch zu einem bedeutenden Industriestandort entwickelte. Diese Planungen trieb er mit aller Umsicht voran und schuf mit Akribie ein planerisches Kompendium, das bis heute zielführend ist.

In einem Vortrag, den Detlef Schreiber im Januar 2003 an der Technischen Universität München hielt, vermerkte er:

»Schon in meiner Studienzeit wuchs die Überzeugung, daß Städtebau und Architektur eine sich gegenseitig bedingende Einheit und keine parallel verlaufenden Einzelwege sind, die sich nur manchmal berühren.
Der einseitig orientierte Hochbauarchitekt sieht nur Bauplätze, während der Städtebauarchitekt sich umfassender orientiert und in jeder Situation den Ort in einem Raumgefüge sucht. Der Platzraum, der Stadt-

When a number of well-known or up-and-coming Munich architects joined together in 1966 to form »Plan Company for Regional Architectural and Engineering Planning Munich Ltd«, this was indeed part of the trend in these years that were so madly in love with collectives, but it was to fail later. The time was not yet ripe for services of this kind. The clients' side, used to quite differently structured partners, was not able to cope with »Plan Ltd« as a legal entity at all. The continuous acquisition that was actually needed could not be pursued in conformity with the market laws of supply and demand in accordance with professional order.

And besides, »Plan« was anything but a collective. It was not at all homogeneous. There were stars; the individual practices continued to exist and played at partners. People who were outstanding at drumming up business were in place as a matter of course, working for themselves, entertainment officers, also the usual people ready to argue, to sum up: »bosses and grafting workers«. In short, the limited company did not succeed. It finally failed after the awkward customers and carefully partners had taken shelter, having made heavy losses on the structural defects of a major commission.

But the point is not to recall that »foundation« that caused such a stir at the time. The intention is to address Detlef Schreiber's labour-intensive share in statements from »Plan« on regional planning.

From 1967 to 1971 he was responsible for the regional development planning for the city and surrounding area of Ingolstadt, devoting great care to it. He also worked on structural planning for the old town in this former fortress and garrison town that was looking to the future; it rapidly developed into an important industrial location.

He pushed this planning process forward with circumspection, meticulously compiling a planning compendium that is still used to define goals.

Here is an extract from a lecture that Detlef Schreiber delivered at the Technische Universität in Munich in January 2003:

Fortschreibung der Hochhausstudie 1995, Kartenausschnitt aus der Karte »Schutzwürdige Grünräume und schutzwürdige Bauräume«

Continuation of the high-rise building study of 1995, extract from the map of green areas deserving protection and built areas deserving protection

raum und seine Silhouette sind ihm wichtiger als das individuell gestaltete Einzelgebäude, dessen Tugenden mit zunehmender Integrationsfähigkeit deutlich an Bedeutung gewinnen. Auf ähnliche Weise kann man über den Stadtraum, seine Platzräume und Straßenräume argumentieren. Durch die vorrangige Funktionalisierung der Stadträume für den motorisierten Verkehr, der mit seinen Qualitäten der Schnelligkeit und der Bequemlichkeit aber auch beträchtliche Potentiale für die Gefährdung der Sicherheit, für Lärm und Erschütterungen sowie Luftverschmutzung besitzt, wurde der Sinn der Straßen- und Platzräume im städtebaulichen Zusammenhang als unentbehrliche öffentliche Kommunikationsräume für die Menschen ad absurdum geführt.

Diese nachteilige Entwicklung, daß Platz- und Straßenräume zu Fahrrinnen verkommen und den zu Fuß gehenden Menschen auf das sehr schmale, unsichere Trottoir verdrängen, passierte nicht nur in Verdichtungsbereichen, sondern auch in den weniger dicht, eher offen bebauten Siedlungsfeldern, in denen der motorisierte Individualverkehr unersetzbar ist. Dagegen ermöglicht die städtische Konzentration den öffentlichen Personenverkehr, der zur Verkehrsberuhigung beitragen kann, der aber den motorisierten Individualverkehr nicht ganz ersetzen wird.

Können wir uns Hoffnungen auf Verkehrsverminderung durch die neuen Kommunikationsmittel wie Funk, Mobiltelefon, Telebild und Internet machen? Ich bin sicher, daß neben der Nutzung dieser virtuellen Kommunikation der Wunsch der Menschen, mit anderen Menschen zusammenzutreffen, ein nicht zu ersetzendes Grundbedürfnis ist: bei der Arbeit, in der Freizeit, beim Einkaufen, beim festlichen Vergnügen, auf Märkten usw.

Deshalb glaube ich an die Notwendigkeit statisch räumlicher Gestaltung im Städtebau und harmonischer Integration der Dynamik der verkehrlichen Erschließung.

Ingolstadt war für mich das erste eindrucksvolle Schlüsselerlebnis bei der Planung zur Verkehrsberuhigung sowohl in der Stadt als auch im Umland, insbesondere in der Altstadt. Wir haben mit dem Projekt in den 1960er Jahren begonnen und es Anfang der 1970er Jahre zum Abschluß gebracht. [...]

Wir waren im Gegensatz zum Verkehrsplaner aber der Meinung, daß wir nicht die Straßenräume nach den Verkehrsprognosen entwickeln sollten, sondern die Planungsmethoden auf den Kopf stellen müßten, um die Forderung zu erheben, die Stadtstruktur zu erhalten und nicht dem Bedarf des Autoverkehrs anzupassen. Vielmehr sollte die umgekehrte Priorität gelten, nämlich die, daß sich der Verkehr der Stadtstruktur anzupassen habe. [...]

Deshalb unterblieben sämtliche diskutierten Straßenaufweitungen und Straßendurchbrüche. Die historische Stadtstruktur blieb ungestört erhalten, und der Straßenverkehr wurde auf das Maß reduziert, welches die Stadträume noch verkraften konnten. Diese Konzeption gilt bis heute. Nach über vierzig Jahren ist die Altstadt von Ingolstadt das Paradebeispiel einer flächenhaft beruhigten großen Innenstadt.«

Das Büro Schreiber hat sich mit seinen Analysen für Ingolstadt großes Ansehen in Fachkreisen erworben und galt als kompetent in Sachen Stadt- und Strukturplanung. Über dreißig Jahre lang erhielt

»Even in my student days I started to be convinced that urban development and architecture form a mutually dependent unit, and are not individual branches running in parallel, only seldom impinging on each other.

A one-sided building architect sees nothing but building sites, while urban development architects address matters more comprehensively and look for a place within a spatial structure in every situation. A square, a townscape and its silhouette are more important to him than the individually designed single building, whose virtues clearly gain in significance the more it is capable of integration. By making a major virtue of adapting urban space to motorized transport, whose speed and comfort also pose a considerable threat to safety, also causing noise, vibration and atmospheric pollution, the meaning of streets and squares in the urban context as essential public communication spaces for human beings has been reduced to nonsense.

This damaging development, whereby streets and squares have become transport lanes, forcing pedestrians on to narrow, insecure pavements, happened not only in high-density areas, but also in less densely populated, essentially open, settlement areas, in which motorized personal transport is essential. Unlike this, urban concentration makes public transport possible. This can contribute to traffic calming, but will never quite replace motorized personal transport.

Can we place any hope in reducing traffic through new communication methods like radio, mobile phones, telepictures and the internet? I am sure that alongside using these virtual communication methods people's desire to meet other people is a basic need that cannot be replaced: at work, at leisure, when shopping, at celebrations, in markets etc.

For this reason I believe in the necessity of statically spacious design in urban development and harmonious integration of the dynamics of transport access.

For me, Ingolstadt was a first impressive key experience in traffic calming planning in the inner city and also in the surrounding area, especially in the old town. We launched the project in the 1960s and concluded it in the early 1970s. […]

But unlike the traffic planners, we felt that we should not develop street spaces according to traffic forecasts, but would have to stand planning methods on their heads to place greater emphasis on the demand that the urban structure should be retained, and not adapted to the needs of the motor-car. On the contrary, the opposite priority should be followed, namely that traffic must adapt to the urban structure. […]

So all the plans for road widening and new roads breaking through old street patterns were not carried out. The historical urban structure survived untouched, and road traffic was reduced to the level that the urban spaces could still sustain. This concept remains until today. After over 40 years the old town in Ingolstadt is still the classic example of town centre that has been calmed over a large area.«

The Schreiber practice made a considerable impact in specialist circles with its analysis for Ingolstadt, and was considered compe-

es Aufträge, Klein- und Mittelstädte unterschiedlich tiefgreifend planerisch zu bearbeiten.

Es wurden Flächennutzungs-, Struktur- und Landschaftspläne, also Leitpläne für die Zukunft aufgestellt, und als 1982 auch Altstadtsanierungen bis hin zu detaillierten Ausführungsplänen für Straßenräume als Aufträge vergeben wurden, war das Büro Schreiber eine wichtige Adresse.

Das Städtebauförderungsgesetz von 1971/76 hatte damals im Verein mit der sogenannten Dorferneuerung reichliche Mittelzuweisungen für rührige Kommunen, welche die erforderlichen Grundlagen- und Strukturplanungen zur Prüfung durch die Oberbehörden vorlegen konnten, vorgesehen. Allenthalben entstanden Ortsbilder von sinnfälliger, überlieferter Geschlossenheit, die bei eingehenderer Betrachtung manchmal posthistorisch wirkten, weil sie nie zuvor solch gleichzeitige Dichte und Schönheit erreicht hatten. Die Schreiberschen Arbeiten suchten dieser oft oberflächlichen Gefälligkeit durch tiefgreifende Erforschung, Erarbeitung und Sicherung historischer Wertigkeiten und Spuren Echtes und Ortstypisches entgegenzusetzen.

Solche Bemühungen, die sich aus vielfältigen kleinen Schritten und richtigen Entscheidungen zusammensetzen, haben indes, will man über sie berichten, einen gewichtigen Nachteil. Sie lassen sich, anders als Architekturen, nur durch umfängliche Dokumentationen flüssig, leserlich und bildhaft darstellen. Die Methode, überarbeitetes, sinnvoll Gestaltetes durch Gegenüberstellung des »Vorher-Nachher« zu schildern, hat ihre Grenzen. Die Eingriffe in ein Ortsbild sind meist, selbst wenn dokumentarisches Material zum vorherigen Zustand vorliegt, nur unzulänglich aufzuzeigen. Man muß im Kontext zu solcher Darstellung stets herausarbeiten, daß fast allerorts ein gänzlicher Funktions- und Bedeutungswandel eingetreten ist und daß die einstige Vielschichtigkeit, das Widersprüchliche des Lebens und der historischen Abläufe heute meist zur mehr oder minder aussagekräftigen Momentaufnahme gerinnt.

Die Beispiele

Aus der beachtlichen Zahl von Planungen und Konzepten sollen zwei besonders intensiv erarbeitete und gestaltete Konzeptionen für die Städte Erding und Schrobenhausen vorgestellt werden. Hinzu kommt eine ausgedehnte Untersuchung, die seinerzeit in der städtebaulichen Fachwelt große Beachtung gefunden hat – die von der Stadt München in Auftrag gegebene »Hochhausstudie« aus dem Jahr 1975. Wie so oft galt auch hier der Prophet zu Zeiten, als diese wegweisende Arbeit schon vorlag, aber in amtlichen Schubladen verschwand, wenig im eigenen Land. So konnte es passieren, daß Münchens Hochhausverwirrung fortbestand bis hin zu unübersehbaren Fehlleistungen und zuletzt, Jahrzehnte später, bis zum peinlich hilflosen Ausweg, Hochhäuser auf eine Maximalhöhe von hundert Metern zu beschränken. Dazu hätte es nicht kommen dürfen, liegt doch seit Jahren die Schreibersche »Hochhausstudie«, die von ihm 1995 noch vertiefend bearbeitet wurde, auf den Tischen. Doch davon später.

tent to carry out urban and structural planning. It received commissions over a period of 30 years to work on plans of varying degrees of radicality for small and middle-sized towns.

Land use, structural and landscape plans, in other words guidelines for the future, were drawn up, and when in 1982 commissions went out for old town redevelopments down to detailed plans for street spaces, the Schreiber practice was an important address.

The 1971/76 urban development promotion act, together with the so-called village renewal plan had set aside lavish funds for enterprising local authorities that could submit the required basic and structural plans for consideration by the higher authorities. Townscapes came into being everywhere exuding lucid, traditional unity. Sometimes on closer consideration they looked post-historical because they had never before achieved such density and beauty at the same time. Schreiber's work sought to set radical research, establishing and securing historical values and traces of what is genuine and typical of the place against this often superficial pleasantness.

But efforts of this kind, made up of many small steps and correct decisions, in fact have a considerable disadvantage when one tries to report about them. Unlike architecture, they can be presented fluently, readably and pictorially only through extensive documentation. The method of presenting sensible design by juxtaposing »before and after« has its limits. Interventions in the townscape usually show up only inadequately, even if documentary material is able to show the difference between the previous state of affairs and that after redevelopment. In the context of such presentations, it is important to emphasize the fact that a complete change of function and significance has taken place almost everywhere, and that the former complexity, the contradictory features of life and the historical processes, have now developed into a more or less convincing snapshot.

The examples

Two particularly intensively developed and designed concepts for the towns of Erding and Schrobenhausen have been chosen to be presented from the considerable number of plans and drafts. There follows an extended study that made a considerable impact in the urban development world in its day. The »Hochhausstudie« was commissioned by the City of Munich in 1975. As so often, here too the prophet was without honour in his own country when this momentous work was already available, but disappeared into officials' filing cabinets. So Munich's confusion about high-rise buildings continued, leading to conspicuous mistakes, and finally, decades later, to the embarrassingly helpless recourse of restricting high-rise building to a height of 100 m. It should not have come to this, as Schreiber's »Hochhausstudie« – high-rise building study –, which he revised and extended in 1995, was on everyone's desk. But we will come back to this.

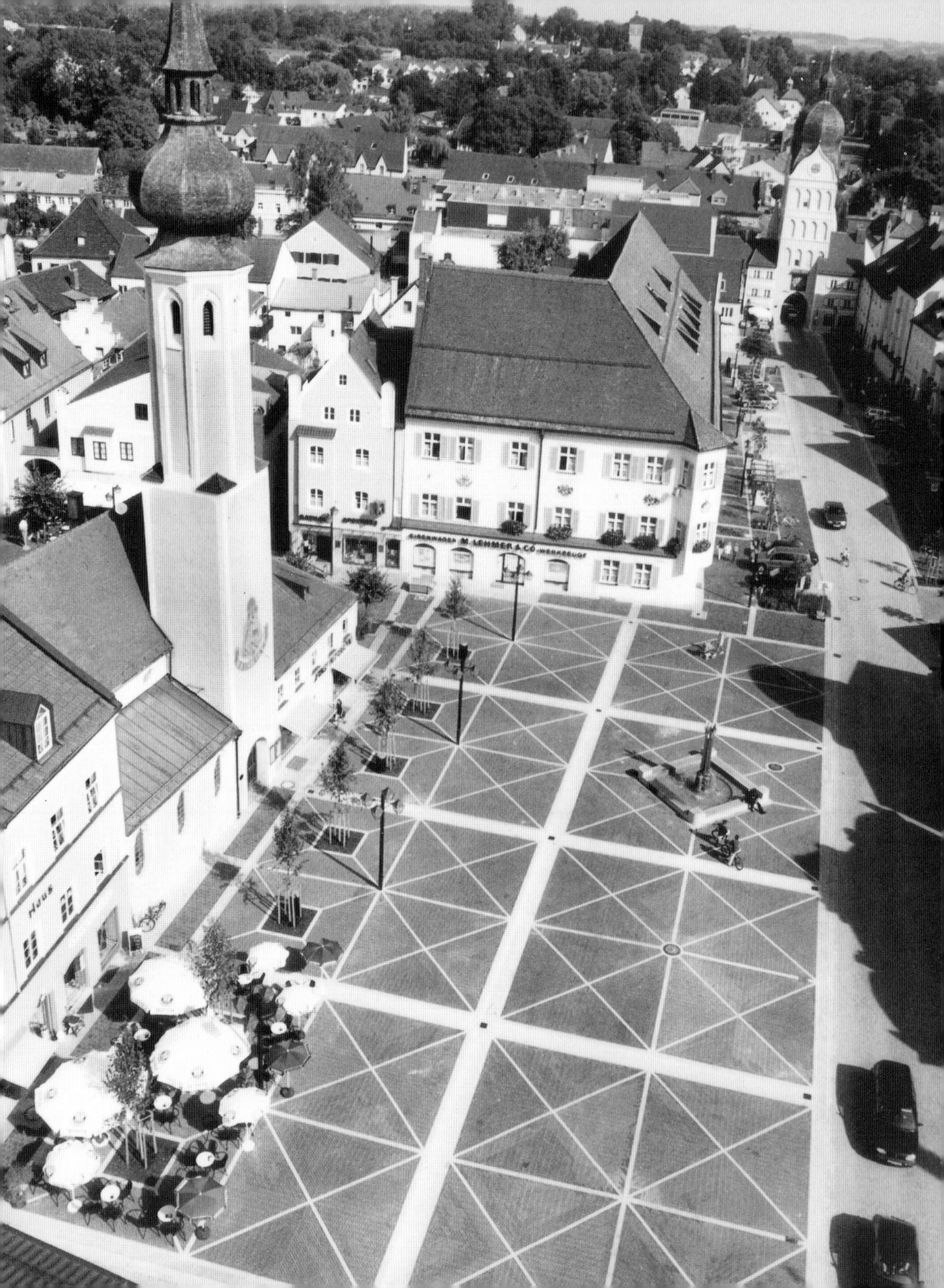
M. LEHMER & CO.

Erding

Im November 1986 konnten der Stadt Erding die vorbereitenden »Untersuchungen zur Sanierung der Altstadt« übergeben werden. Das Büro Schreiber hatte eine gründliche und interessante Studie geliefert.

Erding war in den Blickpunkt geraten, weil sich nach langem Hin und Her der neue Großflughafen München 2 unweit der kleinen, traditionreichen Landstadt im Bau befand. Diese riesige Baumaßnahme – sie war in der zweiten Hälfte der 1980er Jahre die größte in der ganzen damaligen Bundesrepublik – sollte in Zukunft Auswirkungen auf den gesamten europäischen und Weltluftverkehr haben und hatte die Abseite der Haupt- und Residenzstadt, den Münchner Norden, das unbekannte Erdinger Land, aus seiner Erstarrung gerissen.

Im Zuge der großflächigen Flächennutzungsplanung war von einschlägigen Fachleuten ein Gesamt-Verkehrskonzept erarbeitet worden, und nun erhielt Detlef Schreiber den Auftrag, die historische Altstadt samt den vorgelagerten »Vorstädten« – das sind die Münchner, die Haager sowie die Landshuter und Freisinger Vorstadt, lauter kleine Quartiere – verkehrszuberuhigen und für die Altstadtsanierung Vorschläge zu erarbeiten.

Zunächst gingen umfängliche Bestandserhebungen voraus, die im Verlauf des Planungsprozesses immer wieder diskutiert und abgestimmt wurden. Das Verkehrsberuhigungskonzept mußte ja, wo möglich, zum neuen Gesamtverkehrskonzept der Gegend passen. Im Juli 1986 wurde dem Stadtrat das Ergebnis vorgestellt, und etwas später gelangte es zur aufsichtführenden Regierung von Oberbayern.

Zur Geschichte der Stadt

Erding liegt in einem seit Jahrtausenden besiedelten Landstrich. Der Ort wurde erstmals im späten 8. Jahrhundert als Sitz eines bayerischen Edlen mit Namen Ardeo erwähnt. Dessen Siedlung lag allerdings auf dem Grund des heutigen Altenerding, und zum Bestand gehörte die Hofmark eines karolingischen Königsguts. Das heutige Erding war um 1430 eine Gründung des Herzogs Otto von Bayern. Man hatte durch Umleitung der Sempt und des Fehlbachs eine kleine Insel gewonnen und diese befestigt. Sinn der Gründung war es, dem damals übermächtigen Freisinger Hochstift mit seinen vielen Zollstationen nicht auf Schritt und Tritt Maut zahlen zu müssen. Deshalb legte man eine neue Handelsstraße an, welche über Schongau, München nach Landshut führte, und Erding war ein wichtiger Stützpunkt auf dieser Strecke.

Detlef Schreiber arbeitete die Merkmale und Vorgaben Erdings sorgfältig heraus, vernetzte die städtischen Räume miteinander, verdeutlichte Abfolgen und wurde so der alten Landstadt gerecht.

Der Ort mit seinen Plätzen und Marktstraßen – nichts war gewaltig, aber höchst vielfältig – war ein Handelsplatz für Getreide und Vieh, Standort zahlreicher Handwerker und lebte so vom und für das umliegende fruchtbare Bauernland.

Erding

The »Study for redevelopment of the old town« was available for submission to the town of Erding in November 1986. Schreiber's practice had delivered a thorough and interesting analysis.

Erding had become a focus of attention because after a great deal of toing and froing the new Munich 2 airport was under construction not far from the little country town. This immense building operation – it was the largest in the then Federal Republic in the 1980s – was to affect air travel all over Europe and the world in future, and had wrested this remote northern area of Munich's territory as capital and residence city, the unknown Erdinger Land out of its state of paralysis.

An overall transport concept had been drawn up by the relevant experts as part of the wide-ranging land use plan, and now Detlef Schreiber was commissioned to calm the traffic in the whole of the historic Erding old town, and also in all the »suburbs« – the small districts on the Munich, Haag, Freising and Landshut sides of the town – and to compile some suggestions for redeveloping the old town.

First of all came extensive surveys of existing conditions; these were constantly discussed and matched up in the course of the planning process. It was essential that if possible the traffic calming concept should fit in with the new overall transport concept for the area. The results were presented to the town council in July 1986, and a little later they came before the supervisory government of Upper Bavaria.

About the history of the town

Erding is in a region that has been settled for thousands of years. The place was first mentioned in the late 8th century as the seat of a Bavarian nobleman called Ardeo. However, his settlement was on the territory of the present Altenerding, and included a royal Carolingian estate. Today's Erding was founded by King Otto of Bavaria in about 1430. A little island had been created by diverting the Sempt and the Fehlbach, and was then fortified. It was founded to prevent the then unduly powerful bishopric of Freising with its many customs stations from levying tolls at every end and turn. For this reason a new trade route was established leading to Landshut via Schongau and Munich, and Erding was an important base on it.

Detlef Schreiber carefully worked out Erding's characteristic features and requirements, linked the urban spaces with each other, clarified sequences and thus did justice to the old country town.

Links: Blick vom Schönen Turm auf den neu gestalteten Schrannenplatz

Left page: view from »Schöner Turm« (beautiful tower) showing the newly designed Schrannenplatz

Die Geschichte der Stadt gleicht jener vieler kleiner Landstädte. Man war bayerisch-landshutisch, kam 1808 als Stadt und Sitz eines Landgerichts zum von Montgelas nach französischem Muster neu gebildeten Isarkreis und war seit 1837 bis in die Zeiten des neuen Großflughafens eine in Münchens Norden gelegene Kreisstadt, in jenem Norden, welchen die stets nach Süden tendierenden Münchner nicht recht zur Kenntnis nahmen.

Um 1800 hatte die Altstadt etwa 1700 Bewohner (ohne Dienstboten, die wurden nicht mitgezählt). Um 1900 sollen es rund 3800 und 1939 4500 gewesen sein. Als Bayern, durchaus zu seinem Heil, die gewaltigen Flüchtlingsströme nach 1945 aufnehmen mußte, wuchs Erding bis 1950 auf 8600 Einwohner im damaligen Stadtgebiet an. 1986, zu Zeiten der Schreiberschen Sanierungsuntersuchung, waren es nach Eingemeindung der Orte Altenerding und Langengeisling 24.000 Einwohner. Heute, im Jahr 2005, nach weiteren Eingemeindungen, sind es rund 33.000 und im Großraum (was etwa dem Landkreis entsprechen dürfte) 122.500 Einwohner geworden.

Erding hat heute die Funktion eines wichtigen Mittelzentrums. Die Stadt ist Einkaufs-, Versorgungs- und Wohnort, dazu Verwaltungszentrum eines ausgedehnten Landkreises und Schulort.

Der minutiös eingreifenden, gestaltenden oder bisweilen auch nur anleitenden Bemühung der Schreiberschen Planung ist es gelungen, den alten Stadtgrundriß hervorzuheben, auch wenn an dessen einstige unterschiedliche Funktionen nur noch die Namen der Straßen und Plätze erinnern.

Detlef Schreiber:

»Neben dem Konzept der Verkehrsberuhigung war das eigentliche Ziel die sinnvolle Nutzung und Gestaltung der Straßen- und Platzräume.

Diese sollten dabei als Bewegungs- und Aufenthaltsraum für den Fußgänger, als Spielfläche für Kinder und als elementarer Bestandteil von Ortsbild und Stadtgestalt wiedergewonnen werden. Für die Straßen- und Platzräume in der Erdinger Altstadt waren daher sowohl Maßnahmen zur Verringerung der Fahrgeschwindigkeit des Autoverkehrs als auch zur Verdeutlichung der Aufenthaltsfunktion durch Gestaltung der Räume notwendig.

Für die Altstadt von Erding gilt in weiten Bereichen der Ensembleschutz. Aus denkmalpflegerischen Gründen sollte deshalb ein altstadtgerechtes Granitpflaster aus Großsteinen in Verbandzeilen und aus Kleinsteinen in Segmentbögen zur Verlegung kommen […]

Für die Seitengassen wurde eine Pflasterung mit gebrauchten, glatt gefahrenen Großpflastersteinen in Verbandzeilen, diagonal verlegt, vorgeschlagen. Die Pflasterung geht stufenlos, aber im Dachgefälle profiliert, von Hauswand zu Hauswand mit Anpassungsstreifen aus Kleinsteinpflaster bei Gebäudevor- und -rücksprüngen. Von den Gebäuden führt ein Gefälle zu den im Straßenraum liegenden Entwässerungsrinnen.

Der Granitstein als Kleinsteinpflaster in Segmentbögen in erster Qualität wurde vor allem aus Gründen des Schallschutzes für die Alt-

The little town with its squares and market streets – nothing was on a grand scale, but it was all very varied – was a place where cereals and cattle were traded; it had numerous craftsmen, and thus lived from and for the fertile agricultural land around it.

The history of the town is like that of many small country towns. The people were Landshut Bavarians, and in 1808, as a town and seat of a district court, Erding became part of the new Isar district formed by Montgelas on the French pattern. From 1837 to the time of the new airport it was a district capital to the north of Munich, in that northern area that the people of Munich, who tend to look south always, did not pay any attention to.

In about 1800 the old town had about 1,700 inhabitants (excluding servants, who were not counted). In 1900 there were said to be about 3,800 and in 1939 4,500. When Bavaria, entirely to its benefit, had to take in massive streams of refugees after 1945, Erding's population rose to 8,600 in the town area as it was then by 1950. In 1986, at the time of Schreiber's redevelopment study, it had risen to 24,000, after Altenerding and Langengeisling had officially become part of it. Now, in the year 2005, after other communities have been absorbed, it has about 33,000 and in the greater area (roughly corresponding to the rural district), about 122,500 inhabitants.

Erding is now an important centre. The town offers shopping, services and accommodation, and is also the centre of an extensive rural district, and has schools.

Schreiber succeeded in his planning efforts, which intervened in minute detail, creating or simply offering guidance, in emphasizing the old town ground plan, even if only the names of the streets and squares now remind us of the former variety of functions.

Detlef Schreiber:

»Alongside the traffic calming plan, the actual aim was to use and design the street and squares meaningfully.

These were to be won back as spaces where pedestrians could move and linger, where children could play, and they were to be a key component of the image and shape of the town. For this reason, measures had to be taken for the streets and square in old Erding to reduce the traffic speed and to make it clear that people were intended to linger there by designing the spaces.

Buildings are protected as ensembles in large areas of Erding old town. So for reasons of monument preservation, granite paving suitable for an old town was to be laid, consisting of large slabs laid in lines and small stones in segment arcs. […]

For the side alleys, the proposition was a paving with used large pavement slabs that had been worn smooth, laid in lines, offset diagonally. The paving runs without steps, but sloped like a roof, from house wall to house wall, with compensation strips of small-stone paving where the buildings are set forward or back. The pavement slopes away from the buildings to the drainage gutters in the street.

Granite in the form of small-stone paving in segment arcs of the highest quality was used above all for noise control in the old town

stadtstraßen des Hauptachsenkreuzes Lange Zeile/Friedrich-Fischer-Straße/Haager Straße und Münchner Straße/Schrannenplatz/Landshuter Straße verwendet. Für diese Sammelstraßen, die auch weiterhin einen hohen Anteil an Quell- und Zielverkehr aufzunehmen haben, wurde die Trennung der Verkehrsarten mit einem Flachbord hinter straßenbegleitenden Parkplätzen beibehalten.

Mit Zustimmung des Landesamts für Denkmalpflege sind die Bürgersteige auf beiden Seiten der Langen Zeile mit rotbunten quadratischen Klinkerplatten mit gliedernden Granitpflasterzeilen belegt worden. Dieser Oberflächenbelag findet sich auch vor dem Rathaus in der Landshuter Straße und im Heiliggeisthof. Die Klinkerplatten stellen inzwischen ein wesentliches Merkmal des Erscheinungsbildes der Altstadt dar, zumal große Flächen an prominenter Stelle in Erscheinung treten und die reinen Fußgängerflächen hervorheben.

Auch der Kleine Platz und die bereits neugestaltete Nagelschmidgasse, die als Fußgängerzonen ausgewiesen werden, erhalten einen Oberflächenbelag aus Klinkerplatten mit gliederndem Granitmosaik, während der Schrannenplatz durch eine dekorative Oberfläche im Fischgrätenverband aus Straßenklinkern mit Granitrinnen hervorgehoben wird. […]

Zur Verwirklichung der Ziele zur Verkehrsberuhigung wie Verlangsamung des Fahrverkehrs und Aufwertung der Straßenräume als Bewegungs- und Aufenthaltsraum für Fußgänger und Radfahrer ist neben der Wahl und Verteilung der Oberflächenmaterialien auch die Wahl von Möblierungselementen und deren Standorten von hoher Bedeutung. Genauso wie sich die Gestaltung der Straßenoberfläche in der Erdinger Altstadt auf einfache, der historischen Situation angemessene Mittel beschränkt, sollten auch die gewählten Ausstattungselemente, wie Bäume, Leuchten, Bänke usw., zu einem einheitlichen und ruhigen Erscheinungsbild beitragen.

Aus diesem Grund sind mit dem Gestaltungskonzept für die Straßen, Plätze und Gassen auch verschiedene, auf die kleinteilige Bebauungsstruktur abgestimmte Möblierungselemente wie Leuchten, Bänke, Fahrradständer, Poller und Fahnenmasten entwickelt worden.«

Die Sehnsucht nach Urbanität und Kommunikation, dazu nach Gemeinschaft, bereitet Stadträume auf, in denen sich heute, gemessen an den alten Zeiten, ein gänzlich verändertes Stadtleben abspielt. Wo ehemals, man sieht dies am schönen Plan des Urkatasters von 1811, weder Baum noch Strauch geduldet worden wären – im öffentlichen Bereich würden wir heute sagen –, finden sich jetzt kleinkronige Bäume. Wo einst Obstbäume hinter Mauern und Zäunen hervorlugten, entstanden Privatparkplätze, und jedermann beglückwünscht sich zur Verkehrsberuhigung des öffentlichen Raumes.

streets on the main axis intersections Lange Zeile/Friedrich-Fischer-Straße/Haager Straße and Münchner Straße/Schrannenplatz/Landshuter Straße. Different traffic types were separated in these local distributor roads, which still have to carry a high proportion of origin and destination traffic, by a shallow kerb behind the parking spaces running along the streets.

The pavements on both sides of the Lange Zeile were laid with square red clinker slabs with structuring lines of granite paving, with the agreement of the local monument preservation department. This surface covering is also found in front of the town hall in Landshuter Straße and in Heiliggeisthof. The clinker slabs are now a key feature of the old town's appearance, especially as large areas are in evidence in conspicuous places, emphasizing the areas for pedestrians only.

Kleiner Platz and Nagelschmidgasse, which had already been redesigned and designated pedestrian areas, also acquired a new surface of clinker slabs with structuring granite mosaic, while Schrannenplatz is picked out by a decorative surface in a herringbone pattern made up of road clinker with granite gutters. […]

Choosing and siting street furniture items was very important as well as choosing and distributing the surface materials in achieving the aims for traffic calming and also slowing it down and enhancing the quality of the streets for pedestrians and cyclists in terms of movement and spending time there. Just as the design of the street surface in Erding old town was restricted to simple resources appropriate to the historical situation, the furnishing elements like trees, lamps, benches etc. were also intended to help to make the town look calm and unified.

For this reason, various furniture items like lamps, benches, bike stands, bollards and flagpoles were developed to match the intricate development structure.«

The longing for urban quality and communication, and also for community, leads to urban spaces where a completely different kind of urban life exists today compared to the past. Where formerly, and this can be seen on the fine plan for the original land register in 1811, neither trees nor shrubs were tolerated – in public areas, we would say today – there are now trees with small crowns. Where once fruit trees peeped out behind walls and fences there are now private parking spaces, and the whole town is congratulating itself on traffic calming in public places.

Vorbereitende Untersuchungen
zur Sanierung der Altstadt
Karte »Stadtlandschaft Zustand
vor den Sanierungen«

Preparatory investigations for the
refurbishment of the old town
Map »Urban landscape, situation
before refurbishment«

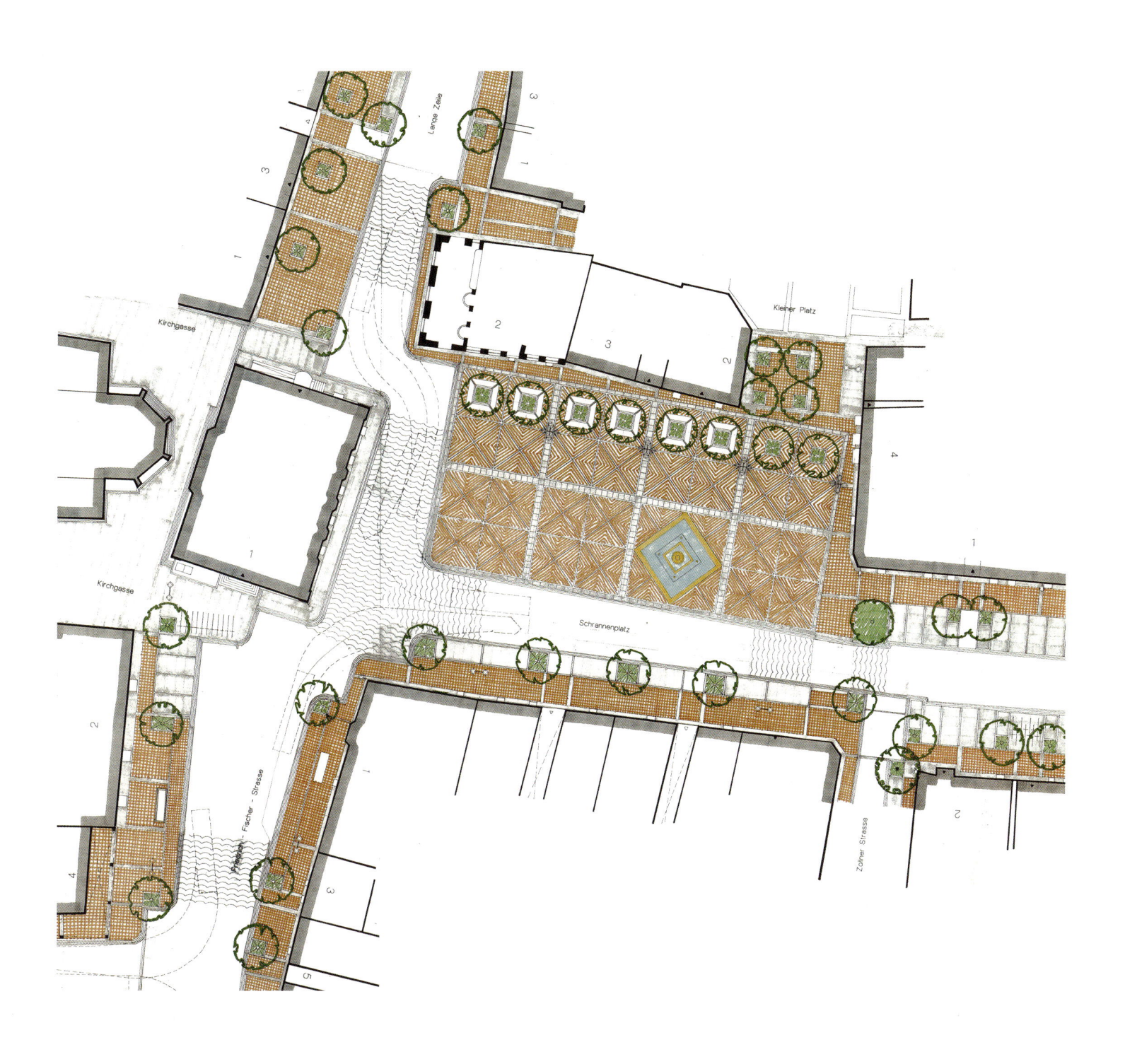

Gestaltungsvorschlag für Lange Zeile,
Schrannenplatz und Kleiner Platz

Design proposal for Lange Zeile,
Schrannenplatz and Kleiner Platz

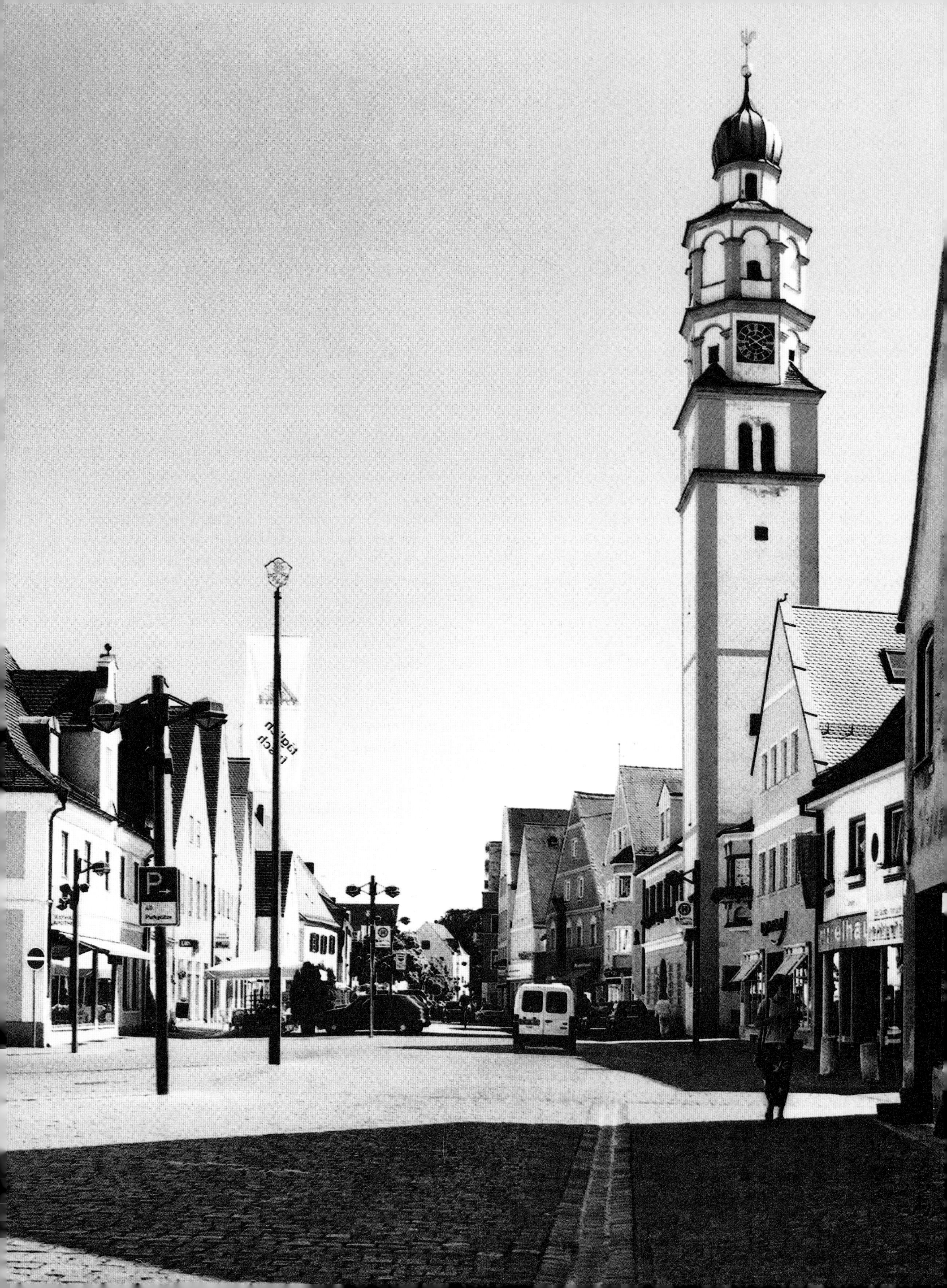
P

Schrobenhausen

Seit 1971 und fortentwickelt seit August 1976, gab es das Städtebauförderungsgesetz, welches den Kommunen bau- und bodenrechtliche Möglichkeiten für Entwicklungs- und Sanierungsmaßnahmen einräumte. Der Bund leistete hierfür, das war der Anreiz, Finanzhilfen an die Länder, welche diese nach Bedarf und Planungsstand auf die Kommunen verteilten.

Orte, die auf sich hielten, faßten damals die notwendigen Beschlüsse und ließen sich Unterlagen erarbeiten, um die Bedingungen für eine Aufnahme ins bundesdeutsche Städtebauförderungsprogramm zu erfüllen, so auch Schrobenhausen. 1982 wurde die Stadt ins Programm aufgenommen.

In den Jahren 1983 und 1984 erarbeitete das Büro Schreiber die umfangreichen Unterlagen und konnte bis 1984 die Recherche abschließen. Parallel dazu fanden laufend intensive Beratungen mit den städtischen Fachleuten statt. Baumaßnahmen wurden beurteilt, und ebenso überprüfte man Bauvorhaben, die Einfluß auf die Altstadtsanierung haben würden. Im Juli 1984 konnte der Stadtrat mit der Schreiberschen Arbeit vertraut gemacht werden.

Ziel der Sanierung war es, die Altstadt, den diese umgebenden Grünraum, wo einst die Befestigung verlief – in diesem Bereich bestanden schon Stadtratsbeschlüsse für die Aufstellung von Bebauungsplänen – sowie einzelne Straßenzüge in einen guten Zustand zu versetzen. Das galt vor allem auch für die Lenbachstraße und den Lenbachplatz, die beiden signifikanten Stadträume. Mit diesen Zielvorstellungen stimmte man überein.

Bevor indes dargelegt wird, was die Sanierung erbrachte und was für die alte, nördlich von der Paar umflossene Landstadt aus intensiver Zuwendung herauskam, wird ein Blick in die Geschichte nützlich sein.

Schrobenhausen wurde als Schenkung in den hochstiftlich freisingischen Annalen zur Regierungszeit des Bischofs Atto (783–811) erstmals namentlich erwähnt.

Kaiser Ludwig der Bayer verhalf zur Errichtung der ersten Ringmauer und gewährte 1333 wichtige, Einkünfte bewirkende Rechte. Nach der Zerstörung 1388 – das mächtige Augsburg hatte im bayerischen Städtekrieg Schrobenhausen geschleift – förderten die Ingolstädter Herzöge den Wiederaufbau und verliehen weitreichende Handelsrechte bis hin zum Salzhandelsrecht, das mehr wert war als Gold.

Handel, Handwerk und Gewerbe florierten im 16. Jahrhundert. Dann kam im nächsten Jahrhundert der dreißigjährige Krieg mit schwedischer Besatzung und der Pest. Im 18. Jahrhundert gab es erneut Krieg, Brandschatzungen und Epidemien, dazu Hochwässer, Stadtbrände und eine gewaltige Heuschreckenplage. 1803 hat die Stadt durch die Säkularisation mit der Aufhebung der Klöster schweren Schaden erlitten. Später wurden, vor allem nach 1860, viele für die Stadt konstituierende Bauwerke abgerissen. Es verschwanden die Stadttore samt Mauer und Türmen, Wall und Graben ebnete man ein, und das Rathaus wurde unter Mitwirkung von Lenbach und Gabriel von Seidl modernisiert.

Schrobenhausen

The urban development promotion act was passed in 1971 and developed further from August 1976. It gave local authorities possibilities in terms of building and land law for development and refurbishment measures. The Federal government, and this was the attractive feature, was offering money to the individual states to be distributed to the local authorities according to their needs and the state of their planning.

Places that thought something about themselves took the necessary decisions at that time and had documents drawn up to meet the conditions for being accepted for the urban development promotion programme, and these included Schrobenhausen. The town was admitted to the programme in 1982.

The Schreiber practice drew up the searching, extensive documents in 1983 and 1984, concluding their research by 1984. Intensive discussions with the municipal experts took place at the same time. Building measures were assessed, and building projects that would influence the old town redevelopment were also examined. By July 1984 the point had been reached to present the town council with Schreiber's work, which had expanded in the meantime.

The aim of the redevelopment was to restore good condition to the old town, the green space around it where the fortifications used to be – the town council had already passed resolutions for drawing up development plans here – and also individual streets. This applied above all to Lenbachstraße and Lenbachplatz, both of which are significant urban spaces. These aims were accepted.

But a glance at history will be useful before explaining what the redevelopment produced and what the old country town with the Paar running round the north of it gained from intensive attention.

Schrobenhausen was first named as a gift in the annals of the bishopric of Freising under Bishop Atto, who was in office from 783 to 811.

Emperor Ludwig the Bavarian helped to build the first ring wall and granted important rights providing income in 1333. After being destroyed in 1388 – mighty Augsburg had razed Schrobenhausen in the War of the Bavarian Cities – the Dukes of Ingolstadt funded rebuilding and granted extensive trade rights, including the salt trade, that were worth more than gold.

Trade, crafts and commerce flourished in the 16th century. Then in the next century came the Thirty Years' War, bringing Swedish occupation and plague. In the 18th century, there was more war, pillage and epidemics, and also floods, town fires and a massive plague of locusts. The town suffered severe damage under secularization and the dissolution of the monasteries in 1803. Later, above all after 1860, many buildings constituting the town were pulled down. The town gates disappeared, along with

Links: Blick in die neu gestaltete, verkehrsberuhigte Lenbachstraße

Left page: view of the newly designed Lenbachstrasse with its lower traffic volume

In den 1940er Jahren und den darauffolgenden Jahrzehnten begann der Umbau der Stadt mit harten, unmaßstäblichen Eingriffen in die Altstadtsubstanz. Man baute, wo es sich gerade ergab, und ohne Verständnis für das Wesentliche.

Genau diese baulichen Achtlosigkeiten der letzten Jahrzehnte machten die Arbeit für Detlef Schreiber und sein Büro nicht leicht. Der an sich mit großer Klarheit konzipierte, schon aus der Frühzeit der Stadt stammende, bis heute deutlich hervortretende Stadtgrundriß gab vor, was unbedingt erhalten, herzurichten und gegebenenfalls herauszuarbeiten sei.

Der alte Stadtgrundriß hatte die Gestalt eines Schildes. Eine breite Straße, die heutige Lenbachstraße, verläuft senkrecht etwa mittig von Süd nach Nord und teilt die Altstadt in eine Ost- und eine Westhälfte. Auf halbem Weg zeigt sich in der Osthälfte – von der Hauptstraße durch eine Häuserzeile, die Zugänge freiläßt, getrennt – der Marktplatz vor dem Rathaus. Östlich hinter dem Rathaus ragt die gotische Pfarrkirche St. Jakob mit ihrem barockisierten Turm auf. In der Osthälfte findet sich auch das Pflegschloß. Dieser wesentlichen Bebauung gegenüber, in der Westhälfte, finden sich große Bauwerke und markant die Kirche Unserer lieben Frau.

So sind im Stadtkern, der Durchgangsstraße zugeordnet, die Hauptbauwerke der Stadt versammelt, die Silhouette steigert sich also zur Mitte hin. Die übrige Bebauung war einst kleinteilig und überragte die Ringmauer kaum. Dieser folgte früher innen das Grün der innerstädtischen Gärten. Sie waren, wie sich leider zeigen sollte, Landreserve und ehemals Versorgungsbasis zugleich. Mehrere vom Fluß abgeleitete Bäche durchzogen die Stadt parallel zur Hauptstraße; sie erbrachten die Wasserversorgung, das Löschwasser und ermöglichten wasserabhängiges Gewerbe, insgesamt also eine sehr gescheite Anlage.

Einst muß die Altstadt – darin unterscheidet sie sich nicht von ähnlichen Städten – intensiv bewohnt und belebt gewesen sein. Zur Zeit der Untersuchung wohnten dort noch etwa 800 Schrobenhausener.

Wie schon angedeutet, wurde nach 1866 mehr als die Hälfte aller Gebäude der Stadt abgerissen und meist größer und wuchtiger wiedererrichtet. Nach 1942 erlitt die Westhälfte der Stadt den schlimmsten Einbruch. An der Liebfrauengasse wurde die kleinteilige Wohnbebauung durch einen alle Maßstäbe sprengenden Neubau des Englischen Instituts ersetzt. Bis 1985 wurde weiter abgerissen und in zu großem Maßstab neu gebaut. Die letzten der alten Gerinne, die als Bäche die Stadt belebt hatten, legte man damals trocken.

Detlef Schreiber: Das Gestaltungskonzept für die Altstadt

»Erhaltung der Wall- und Grabenbereiche als stadtnahe Erholungsflächen – das sind rund vier Hektar oder 27 % der Gesamtfläche von ca. 15 Hektar. Die Bauflächen belaufen sich auf acht Hektar oder 53 %, die öffentlichen Verkehrsflächen haben einen Anteil von 20 % oder rund drei Hektar.

wall and towers, rampart and moat were levelled and the town hall was modernized, with Lenbach and Gabriel von Seidl working on the project.

In the 1940s and subsequent decades the town started to be expanded, involving severe interventions with no regard to scale into the old town building stock. Buildings went up wherever people felt like it, and without any understanding of the essentials.

It was precisely this careless building in recent decades that made the work of Detlef Schreiber and his colleagues much more difficult. The urban ground plan, conceived with great lucidity, dating from the town's earliest days and still very clearly discernible today, showed what had to be retained at all costs, restored and where necessary made conspicuous.

The old town ground plan was in the shape of a shield. A wide street, now Lenbachstraße, runs vertically from north to south roughly in the middle, dividing the old town into an eastern and a western half. Half way up in the eastern half – separated from the main street by a row of houses leaving access free – the market place can be seen in front of the town hall. To the east beyond the town hall the Gothic parish church of St. Jakob towers up with its baroque tower. The Pflegschloss is in the eastern half. Opposite this major development, in the western half, are large buildings, with the Church of Our Lady as a striking feature.

Thus the main buildings are sited in the town centre, relating to the through road, and so the silhouette increases in impact towards the middle. The other buildings used to be small and scarcely protruded above the town wall. This was formerly accompanied on the town side by the green of the town gardens. They were, as was unfortunately to appear, reserved land, and formerly a supply base at the same time. Several streams diverted from the river ran through the town parallel with the main street; they provided a water supply and water for extinguishing fires, and made it possible to ply water-dependent trades, so all in all a very clever set-up.

The old town – and here it is no different from similar towns – must once have been densely populated and very lively. At the time of the study about 800 people of Schrobenhausen lived there.

As has already been indicated, after 1866 over half all the buildings in the town were pulled down and rebuilt, usually in a larger and weightier form. The western half of the town suffered the worst intrusion after 1942. The intricate housing in Liebfrauengasse was replaced by a new building for the English Institute that was completely out of scale. It was pulled down again by 1985 and rebuilt, again in too large a scale. The last of the old gullies that used to feed the town streams was drained at this time.

Detlef Schreiber: The design concept for the old town

»Retaining the rampart and moat areas as recreational areas close to the town – that entails about 4 ha or 27 % of the total area of about 15 ha. The building areas run to about 8 ha or 53 %, public transport has a share of 20 % or about 3 ha.

Daraus wird der große Wert der Straßen und Plätze als Freiräume und Aufenthaltsräume deutlich. Deshalb wurde der Gestaltung dieser öffentlichen Räume bei der Realisierung der Sanierung Priorität eingeräumt. Logische Folgerung daraus war der Vorschlag, die Stadträume mit den Grünräumen von Wall und Graben zu verbinden, um so mehr als die Hälfte der Gesamtfläche als qualitätvolle Freiräume zu übergeben.

Zwangsläufig erhob sich auch die Forderung, die Altstadt vom Durchgangsverkehr zu befreien und die Mischverkehrsnutzung mit Verkehrsberuhigung einzuführen: Weit über hundert Verkehrsschilder waren entbehrlich. Die Einführung von Kurzparkzeiten erhöhte die Verfügbarkeit von Stellplätzen bei gleichzeitiger Reduzierung der Parkierungsflächen. Schrobenhausen hat den flächenmäßig größten Bereich dieser Art in Bayern.

Durch die Zurücknahme von ungenutzten und unter Wert genutzten Bauflächen in den Rückarealen können wieder wertvolle innere Grünbereiche zurückgewonnen werden, um die Wohnfunktionen in der Altstadt zu begünstigen. Neben den gestalterischen Ordnungsvorstellungen wurden frühzeitig Ziele für die Nutzung der Bauflächen entwickelt und später im Rahmenplan präzise definiert.

Die Ermittlungen für Art und Maß der Nutzung ergaben, daß in der Altstadt noch gut 44 % Geschoßflächen für Wohnen, 41 % für Dienstleistung und Gewerbe und 14 % für Gemeindbedarf vorhanden waren. Die Grundflächenwerte (GRZ) erreichen im Mittel 0,53 GRZ, allerdings sind ein Drittel der Grundstücke fast zu 100 % überbaut. Die Geschoßflächenzahlen liegen z. T. weit über 1,0. Sie können nur hingenommen werden, wenn man die großen Freiflächen der Straßen und Plätze zur Berechnung heranzieht – sie liegen dann im Mittel bei 0,9 GFZ.

Dies macht deutlich, welche Bedeutung den öffentlichen Straßen und Plätzen zuwächst. Sie sind in ihrer verkehrsberuhigenden Funktion wertvolle Räume für das Wohnumfeld.

Das Nutzungskonzept sieht vor, daß die Wohnnutzung in der Altstadt nicht nur erhalten bleibt, sondern trotz Auflockerung gefördert wird, daß die Mischgebietsnutzungen entlang der Lenbachstraße vor allem in den Erdgeschoßzonen günstige Standortbedingungen finden und die Gemeindebedarfseinrichtungen zur Wahrung der Mittelpunktsfunktion der Stadt zentral angeordnet werden.

Mit diesem Plan wurden die Vorstellungen für die Sanierung der Altstadt anhand einer bildhaften Darstellung von Gebäudegrundrissen formuliert [...] Das Kernstück der Sanierungsziele, die Verkehrsberuhigung und die Aufwertung der öffentlichen Stadträume, konnte in Schrobenhausen weitgehend verwirklicht werden. Die unverwechselbare Raumfolge von Lenbachstraße und Lenbachplatz wurde in ihrer neuen Gestaltung als erste Maßnahme in mehreren Baustufen geplant und gebaut.

Der Ausbau der Seitenstraßen, zum Beispiel der Metzger-/Tuchmachergasse, folgte in weiteren Schritten. Inzwischen ist der überwiegende Teil mit wenigen Ausnahmen fertiggestellt. Das Gestaltungsprinzip war in allen Bereichen darauf abgestellt, die stadträumlichen Qualitäten durch Pflastergliederungen zu unterstreichen und die Straßenräume in Platzfolgen aufzulösen, um den Verkehrsfluß zu bremsen und die Aufenthaltsfunktion zu unterstreichen.«

This makes clear the great value of streets and squares as open spaces and areas in which to spend time. Hence top priority was allocated to the design of these public spaces when realizing the redevelopment. The logical consequence of this was the proposal that the urban spaces should be connected with the rampart and moat green areas, so that more than half the overall area could be handed over to the people of the town as high-quality open spaces for meaningful use.

Inevitably there was also a demand to free the old town of through traffic and introduce mixed traffic use with traffic calming: well over 100 traffic signs were superfluous to needs. Introducing short parking periods increased the availability of parking spaces while at the same time reducing parking areas. In terms of area, Schrobenhausen had the largest land use of this kind in Bavaria.

It is possible to regain valuable inner green spaces to benefit residential areas in the old town by reclaiming unused and underused building land in the rear areas. Targets were set at an early stage for the use of building land alongside the creative ideas for an overall pattern, and later defined precisely in the outline plan.

Surveys of the type and scale of use showed that in the old town a good 44 % of floor area was still used for dwellings, 41 % for services and 14 % for community purposes. The ground space values are 0.53 on average, though 1/3 of the plots are built on to almost 100 %. The floor space figures are well over 1 at present. They can only be accepted if the large open spaces of the streets and squares are added in – then the average is 0.9 for the ground space.

This makes it clear how important the streets and squares are. When the traffic has been calmed, they provide valuable space for the residential areas around them.

The use concept provides that residential use in the old town is not just to be maintained, but that despite thinning encouragement is to be given for mixed area uses along Lenbachstraße, above all in ground floor zones, to meet favourable location conditions, with communal facilities arranged centrally to maintain the town's function as a centre.

This plan formulated ideas for redeveloping the old town using a pictorial representation of building ground plans. [...] It proved large possible in Schrobenhausen to realize the core section of the redevelopment aims successfully, i.e. the traffic calming and the enhancement of public urban space. The unmistakable spatial sequence of Lenbachstraße and Lenbachplatz was planned and built in its new form as the first measure, in several building phases.

The side streets, for example Metzger-/Tuchmachergasse, were developed in subsequent stages. In the meantime the majority of the work has been completed, with a very few exceptions. The design principle was intended everywhere to underline urban qualities by structuring pavements and to break the street spaces down into sequences of squares, to slow down the traffic flow and underline the value of spending time there.«

Vorbereitende Untersuchungen
zur Sanierung der Altstadt
Karte »Gestaltungskonzept mit
Dachaufsicht«

Preparatory investigations for the
refurbishment of the old town
Map »Design concept with view
looking down on the roof«

Städtebaulicher Rahmenplan
Karte »Altstadtgrundriß mit
Darstellung der Veränderungen«

Urban development zoning plan
Map »Layout of the old town,
showing the changes«

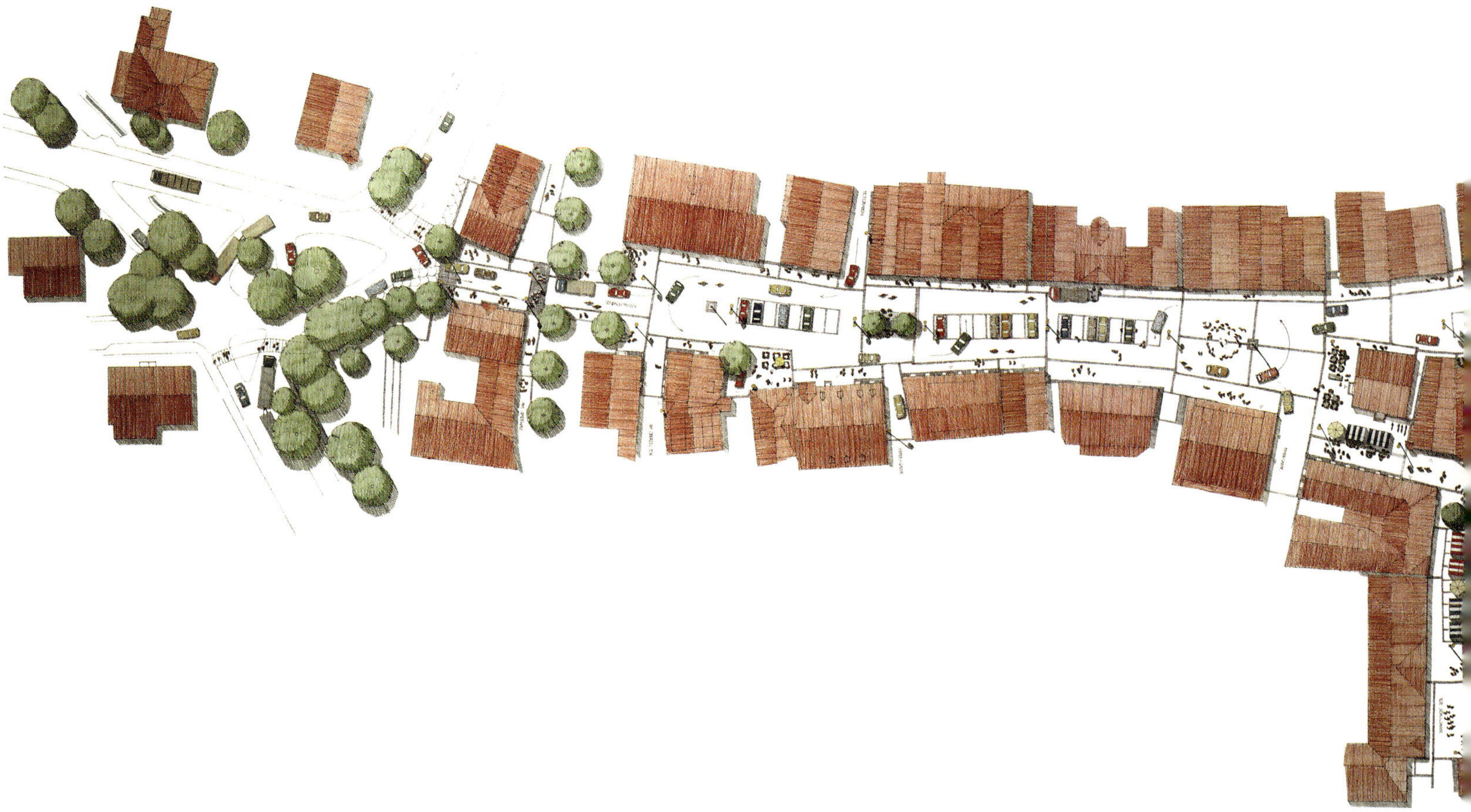

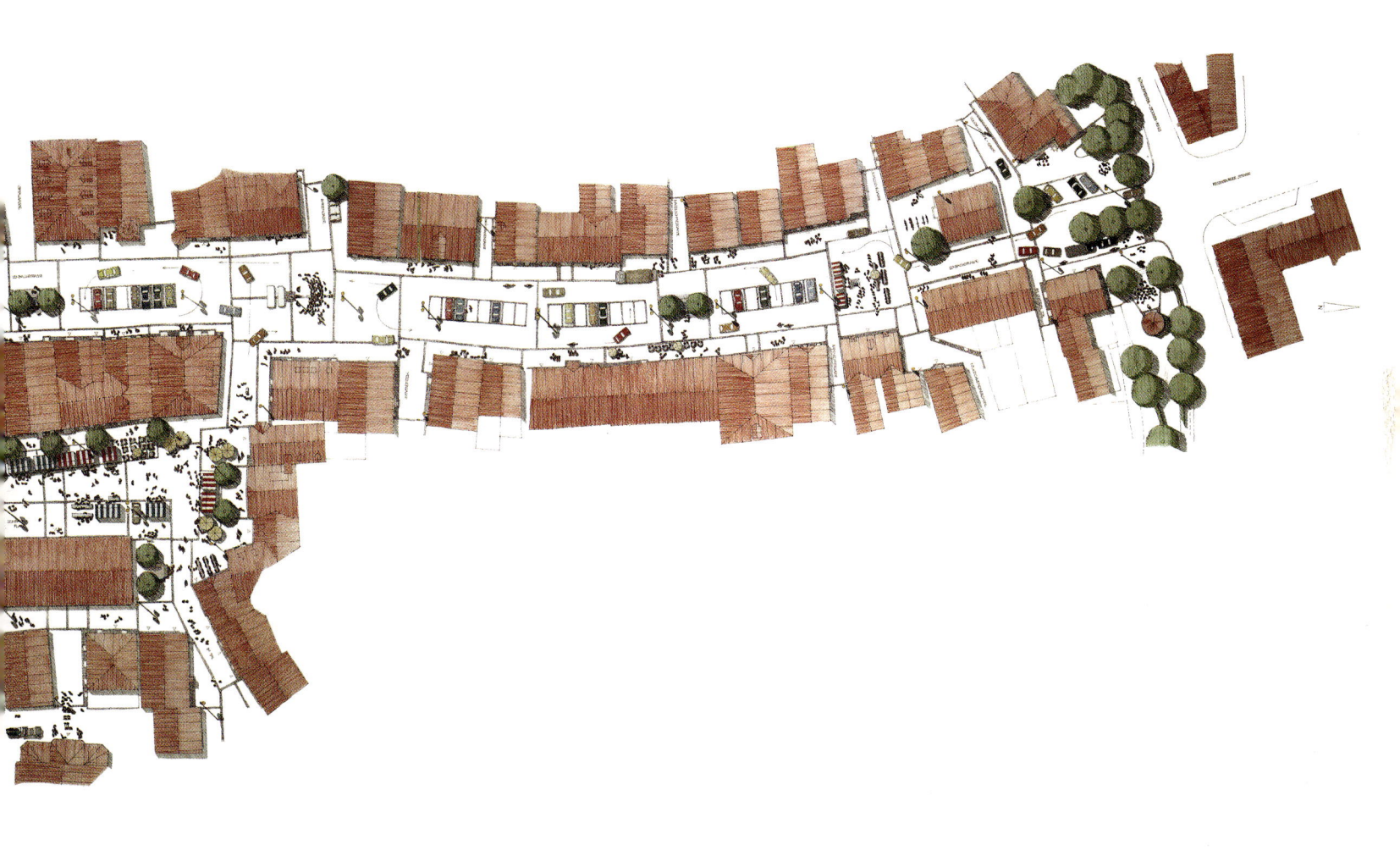

Neugestaltung der Lenbachstraße
und des Lenbachplatzes

New design of Lenbachstrasse
and Lenbachplatz

205

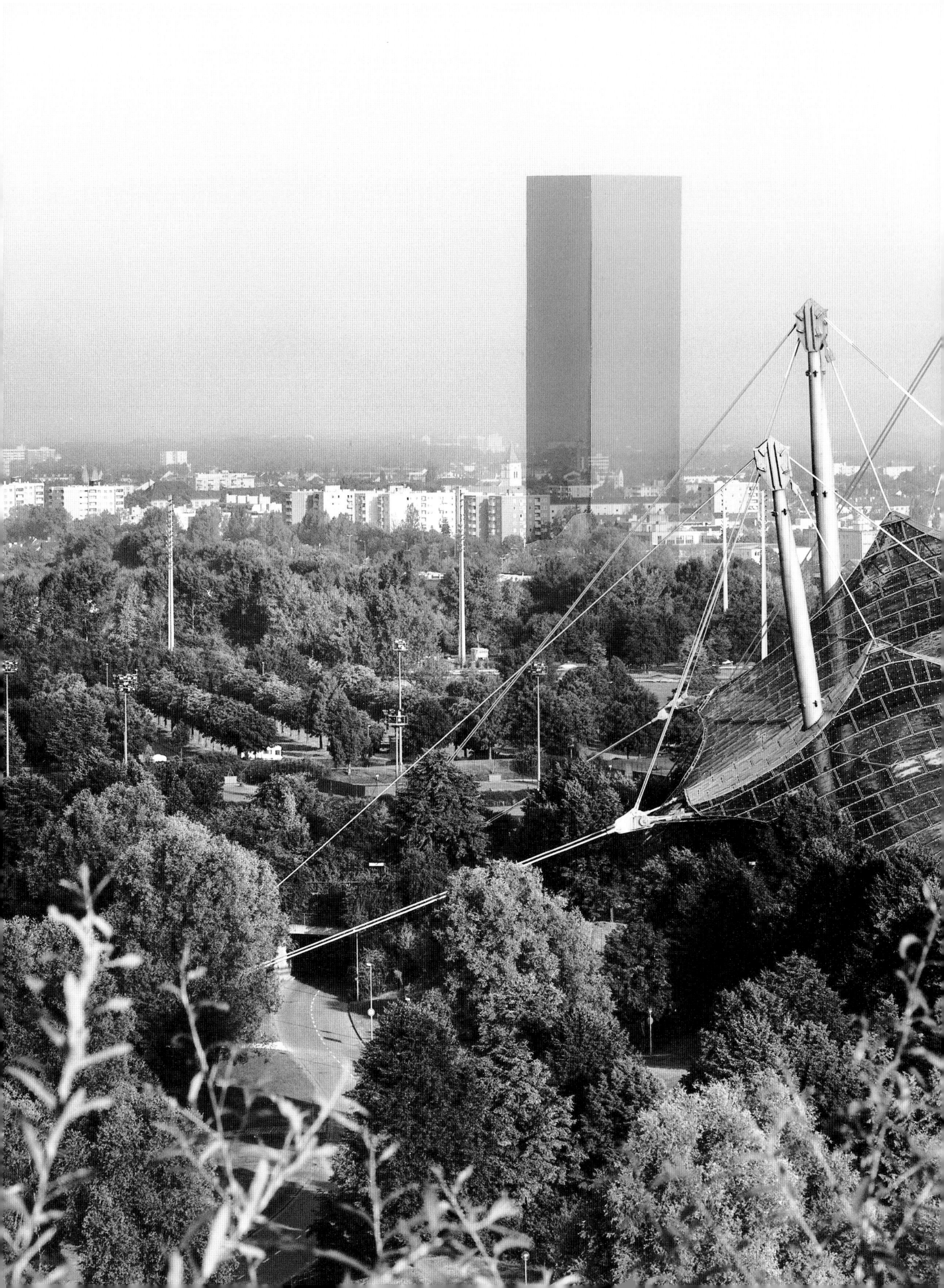

München. Untersuchung der Hochhausstandorte

Ausgangslage

Auch München war schwer getroffen von den nächtlichen Flächenbombardements und gezielten Tagesangriffen, als der totale Krieg 1945 in einer ebenso totalen Niederlage endete.

Im Gegensatz zu anderen deutschen Großstädten hatte man sich nach einigen interessanten Überlegungen und Planungsvorschlägen dafür entschieden, den Wiederaufbau, wenn auch in vielem vom Vorbestand abweichend, ohne allzu große Experimente, und vor allem im gewohnten Maßstab, so wie ihn die Prinzregentenzeit bewirkt hatte, in Angriff zu nehmen. Betrachtet man die Silhouette, wurde die Münchner Innenstadt trotz allen Lästerns und Kopfschüttelns bis auf einige nicht wiedergutzumachende Abrißsünden, etwa des Verkehrsministeriums mit seiner bedeutenden Kuppel, pfleglich behandelt. Maß der Höhenentwicklung waren nach wie vor die beiden Frauentürme, so daß zumindest, was hohe Bauwerke im Bereich der Innenstadt und ihrer tradionellen Randbereiche anging, alles beim Altvertrauten blieb.

Wo möglich erhalten – fortentwickeln

Dies mag einer der Gründe für die allgemeine Beliebtheit des ab den 1960er Jahren als sogenannte »heimliche Hauptstadt« der Bundesrepublik apostrophierten München gewesen sein.

Trotz solcher Sorgfalt war in der Wiederaufbauphase, vor allem während der bisweilen wenig bedachtsam ablaufenden Stadterweiterungen an den Rändern, eine Anzahl von hohen, profilbedeutsamen Bauten entstanden, die nunmehr die Silhouette der Gesamtstadt mit beeinflußten und leider gelegentlich sogar ärgerlich beeinträchtigten. Dies fiel um so mehr auf, als solche Bauten nicht in großer Anzahl, sondern eben besonders markant, vereinzelt auftraten.

Man sah rasch ein, daß man derartige »Zeichen«, seien es Hochhäuser, Kamine, Heizwerke, nicht weiterhin beliebig nur nach Grundstücksverfügbarkeit und Gutdünken errichten konnte, ohne dem wohlgeordneten und im allgemeinen sorgsam beachteten Profil der Landeshauptstadt Abbruch zu tun.

Die Verantwortlichen versuchten also, Leitlinien zur übergeordneten Beurteilung möglicher Standorte bzw. Schutzzonen zu definieren, wo dominierend hohes Bauen unbedingt zu unterlassen sei.

Neuformulierung des Vertikalen

Das in Bauangelegenheiten als stockkonservativ beleumundete München war übrigens die erste deutsche Großstadt, die solche Ordnungsvorstellungen entwickelte und hierfür Unterlagen erarbeiten ließ. Die Gruppe Stadtplanung führte zu Anfang der 1970er Jahre die ersten Untersuchungen durch, die dem Stadtrat und der Kommission für Stadtgestaltung vorgelegt wurden.

Munich. A study of high-rise building locations

Starting position

Munich too had been seriously affected by nocturnal carpet bombing and targeted daylight raids when total war ended in equally total defeat in 1945.

Unlike other major German cities, Munich decided, after a few interesting periods of reflection and sets of proposals, to tackle rebuilding without any unduly large experiments, though deviating in many respects from the previous building pattern, and above all to rebuild on the accustomed scale, as created in the period of the Prince Regency. Despite all the criticism and head-shaking, if one looks at the silhouette of central Munch, it has been caringly treated, with the exception of a few demolitions that cannot be made good like the Ministry of Transport with its important dome. As before, the two towers of the Frauenkirche set the height scale, so that everything remained in its old, familiar form at least as far as tall buildings in the city centre and its traditional peripheral areas are concerned.

Retain where possible – develop further

This may be one of the reasons for the general popularity of Munich, which has been mentioned as the so-called »secret capital« of Germany since the 1960s.

Despite the fact that all this care was taken in the rebuilding phase, a number of tall buildings with significant profiles appeared, above all during the city's expansion in the outskirts, which was handled less circumspectly, which then made an impact on the silhouette of the city as a whole, and indeed even affected it deleteriously in places. This was all the more striking because such buildings did not occur in large number, but were particularly striking as isolated structures.

It was quickly realized that »signs« of this kind, whether they were high-rise buildings, chimneys, district heating plants, could not continue to be built simply because plots were available and as people saw fit without damaging the Bavarian capital's well-ordered and generally solicitously treated profile.

So those responsible tried to define guidelines for higher judgements about possible sites or to establish protected zones where dominant tall buildings were not permitted.

Links: Untersuchung zur Stadtbildverträglichkeit des Hochhauses (155 m) am Georg-Brauchle-Ring 1998, Standort Olympiaberg. Die Fotomontage zeigt die Sichtüberschneidung des monolithischen Turms mit der filigranen Olympiadachkonstruktion.

Left page: investigation of the compatibility of the high-rise building (155 m) at Georg-Brauchle-Ring with the urban environment, 1998; Olympiaberg site. The photomontage shows the visible overlap of the monolithic tower with the filigree Olympic roof structure.

Um das den Planern wichtige, aber sonst wohl nicht für notwendig angesehene Regelwerk weiterzuentwickeln, beauftragte das Baureferat im Oktober 1975 Detlef Schreiber mit der Ausarbeitung der sogenannten »Hochhausstudie«, welche von ihm zwanzig Jahre später, 1995, aktualisiert und fortgeschrieben wurde.

Gedanken zur neuen Sicht

Sinn und Ziel der ›Hochhausstudie‹ war es, zu klären und eine Methode zur Beurteilung zu entwickeln:

»1. wo zusätzliche profilüberragende Gebäude auszuschließen sind,
2. in welchen Bereichen sie unter bestimmten Voraussetzungen möglich und
3. wo sie als zusätzliche profilüberragende Gebäude wünschenswert sind.

Der Begriff Hochhaus wurde durch den des profilüberragenden Gebäudes ersetzt, weil mögliche Konflikte mit dem gleichen baurechtlichen Begriff vermieden werden sollten.

Man wagte sich in München auf neue Wege. Ähnliche oder vergleichbare Studien anderer Städte gab es nicht. Es gab damals aber den neuen Flächennutzungsplan und den zur Beachtung empfohlenen und vom Stadtrat beschlossenen Stadtentwicklungsplan. Dieser formulierte auch die Ziele zu unserem Thema:

Berücksichtigung des Maßstabs der bestehenden Bebauung, Vermeidung von überzogenen Maßstäben bei Neubauten, Vermeidung von Wohnhochhäusern, Ausarbeitung eines Höhenentwicklungsplans als Grundlage der Bauleitplanung.

Die Zielvorstellungen des Stadtrats für einen Höhenentwicklungsplan entsprangen einerseits dem Wunsch, die derart erkennbar gemachten Konflikte zwischen alter und neuer Höhenprofilierung zu vermeiden und andererseits Vorsorge für die Zeit nach dem Auslaufen der Münchner Staffelbauordnung im Jahr 1980 zu treffen.

Die Staffelbauordnung aus dem Jahr 1904, von Theodor Fischer geformt, ging vom Leitbild einer geschlossenen, straßen- und platzbegleitende Stadträume bildenden Bebauung aus, die sich von der Stadtmitte zu den Stadträndern hin abflachen, niedriger werden und schließlich in eine offene Bebauung übergehen sollte. Die Traufhöhen waren bei 22 Metern limitiert. Man folgte dem historischen Leitbild der Stadtkrone im Zentrum der Stadt. Nach diesen Ordnungsvorstellungen ist die Stadtstruktur in München auch heute noch weitgehend geprägt.

Die großflächigen Stadterweiterungen und neue städtebauliche Leitbilder offener städtebaulicher Strukturen mit fließenden Räumen und differenzierten Höhen – vom erdgeschossigen Haus bis zum Hochhaus – verdeutlichen eindrucksvoll die Vorzüge dieser neuartigen Stadträume (siehe beispielsweise die Siemenssiedlung in Obersendling), die allerdings nur aufgrund der Befreiung von der Münchner Staffelbauordnung mit deren limitierter Traufhöhe möglich waren. Das Hochhaus war durch die Öffnung der Staffelbauordnung auch in München ›hoffähig‹ geworden.

Die Methode der städtebaulichen Befreiung basierte auf den Planungsprinzipien von ›trial and error‹. Dort wo neue städtebauliche

Reformulation of the vertical

Munich was considered to be thoroughly conservative and was incidentally the first major German city to develop regulations of this kind and make documents and forms available. The town planning group carried out the first studies in the early 70s, and they were presented to the city council and the urban design commission.

In order to develop this set of regulations, which was important for planners but probably not otherwise seen as necessary, in October 1975 the building department commissioned Detlef Schreiber to produce the so-called »Hochhaus-studie«, which he brought up to date and continued 20 years later, in 1995.

Thoughts about a new view

The ›Hochhausstudie‹ was intended to explain and devise method for making judgements about the following matters:

»1. where further buildings rising above the profile should be excluded,
2. in what areas they are possible under certain conditions,
3. where they are desirable as additional buildings above the profile.

The term high-rise building was replaced by building rising above the profile to avoid possible conflict with the same term in building law.

Munich took the risk of exploring a new path. No other city had produced a similar or comparable study. But at the time there was the new land use plan and the urban development plan, recommended for attention, that had been drawn up by the city council. This also formulated aims that are relevant to our subject:

Respecting the scale of existing building, avoiding exaggerated scale for new buildings, avoiding high-rise housing, developing a height development plan as a basis for a general development plan.

The city councils ideas for a height development plan came from a desire to avoid the conflicts between old and new height profiling that this identified, and also through concern about what would happen when the Munich ›Staffelbauordnung‹ (staggered building regulations), a set of guidelines, ran out in 1980.

They date from the year 1904, and were drawn up by Theodor Fischer. They are based on the model of closed development forming urban spaces accompanying streets and squares, levelling out and becoming lower, or staggered, as one moves from the city centre to the outskirts, and finally ending up in an open development. The eaves height was limited to 22 m. This followed the historical pattern of the upper city in the city centre. The urban structure of Munich is still largely shaped by these ordering ideas.

Untersuchung zur Stadtbildverträglichkeit des Hochhauses (155 m) am Georg-Brauchle-Ring 1998, Standort Nymphenburger Schloß Terrasse. Die Bildmontage zeigt den kompakten Turm in seiner ungünstigen Übereckform.

Investigation of the compatibility of the high-rise building (155 m) at Georg-Brauchle-Ring with the urban environment 1998; Nymphenburger Palace terrace site. The photomontage shows the compact tower in its less flattering corner form.

Konzepte mit ›profilüberragenden Bauten‹ sich mit traditionellen städtischen Strukturen trafen, waren Konflikte unvermeidlich, der ›error‹ offensichtlich. Ein Beispiel war die Sichtüberschneidung des hohen Blocks des Heizkraftwerkes an der Theresienstraße mit den Doppeltürmen der Ludwigskirche vom Monopteros aus und das andere die Überdeckung des Altstadtprofils durch das Europäische Patentamt, vom Aussichtspunkt Nockerberg her gesehen.

Es gab aber auch das Prinzip von ›trial and success‹, und dazu zählt in erster Linie das Ensemble des Olympiaparks mit Olympiaturm, BMW-Hochhaus und Olympiabauten. Dies ist eines der stattlichsten Beispiele des modernen Städtebaus mit fließenden Räumen und ausdrucksvollen Höhenprofilierungen. Auf die große Bedeutung dieses Ensembles wurde immer wieder hingewiesen. Es wird als gleichwertig mit dem Erlebnis der Altstadtsilhouette, vom Englischen Garten aus, angesehen.

Diese beiden Beispiele machen für München deutlich, daß neben der Erhaltung traditioneller Stadtbilder auch konfliktfrei neue städtebauliche Qulitäten entwickelt werden können. Sie verdeutlichen aber auch, daß es eine Stadt als Gesamtkunstwerk, gestützt durch einen Höhenentwicklungsplan, nicht geben kann und daß wir uns vom Leitbild des ›Stadthügels mit seiner Krone‹ lösen müssen – es sei denn, wir lassen dem Druck der Entwicklung freien Lauf und bauen München um, so wie es in den meisten amerikanischen Städten vollzogen wurde – mit einem Gebirge in der Mitte.

München hat dank der behutsamen Stadtentwicklungskonzepte eine intakte Stadtstruktur, die im positiven Sinn als Stadtlandschaft bezeichnet werden kann. Sie berücksichtigt Wertmaßstäbe für eine geordnete Entwicklung und eine sinnvolle Gestaltung des städtischen Lebensraums. Diese intakte Struktur war auch Grundlage für unsere ›Hochhausstudie‹ von 1977 und 1995, nämlich:
– Natur und Landschaft müssen als Lebensgrundlage und als Erholungsräume in der Stadt gesichert sein.
– Die stadträumlichen Qualitäten der Stadt müssen vor unmaßstäblichen Veränderungen bewahrt werden. Es müssen aber auch neue städtebauliche Qualitäten gefördert werden.

Urban expansion over large areas and new urban development models for open urban structures with fluid spaces and differentiated heights – from the single-storey building to the high-rise block – impressively illustrate the advantages of these innovative urban spaces (see for example the Siemens estate in Obersendling), though this only became possible after the end of the Munich staggered building regulations with their restricted eaves height. The high-rise building had also become ›acceptable at court‹ because the staggered building regulations had been relaxed.

The urban development liberation method was based on the planning principles of ›trial and error‹. Where the new urban development concepts with ›buildings rising above the profile‹ met traditional urban structures, conflicts were inevitable, and the ›error‹ obvious. One example was the way the view of the high district heating plant block in Theresienstraße clashed with the twin towers of the Ludwigskirche when seen from the Monopteros, and another is the way the profile of the old town is blocked by the European Patent Office when seen from the Nockerberg.

But there was also the principle of ›trial and success‹. First here comes the Olympic Park ensemble with the Olympic Tower, BMW skyscraper and the Olympic buildings. This is one of the most handsome examples of modern urban development with fluid spaces and expressive height profiling. The great importance of this ensemble has never been underestimated. It is seen as being just as good as the silhouette of the old town seen from the Englischer Garten.

These two examples make it clear that Munich can develop new urban qualities as well as retaining traditional cityscapes, without conflict. But it also makes it clear that there can be no such thing as a city as a complete work of art, supported by a height development plan, and that we must detach ourselves from the model of the ›town hill with its upper town‹ – unless we allow the pressure of development free rein and rebuild Munich as happened in most American cities – with a mountain range in the middle.

Thanks to careful urban development concepts, Munich has an intact urban structure that can be called an urban landscape in the

– Die Menschen müssen in privaten und öffentlichen Stadträumen eine erlebnisreiche und gesunde Umwelt finden.

Können solche Ziele eines ausgewogenen Gleichgewichts in Übereinstimmung mit der uralten Sehnsucht der Menschen, Türme zu bauen und Macht zu demonstrieren, gebracht werden? Ich glaube, daß es legitim ist, mit dem Bau von Häusern in der Stadt:

– die besondere Auszeichnung einzelner und gesellschaftlich bedeutender Institutionen darzustellen und
– vor allem die gestalterische Potenz und das technisch-konstruktive Können einer Zeit zu beweisen.

Daraus leitet sich aber auch folgerichtig ab, daß die überdurchschnittliche Inanspruchnahme des visuellen Luftraumes einer Stadt die Ausnahme und nur außergewöhnlichen gestalterischen Höchstleistungen vorbehalten sein sollte.

Es gibt aber auch praktische Überlegungen bei der Hochhausdiskussion:

– Städtebauliche Entwicklungen gehen Hand in Hand mit Verdichtungen. Will man die erdnahe flächenhafte Verdichtung und das Zubauen der Freiräume vermeiden, so muß man eine Vermehrung der Flächen durch Stapelung suchen.
– Es gibt Nutzungen, für die höhere Gebäude günstiger sind als niedrigere mit einer größeren Flächenausbreitung.
– Es gilt aber immer wieder darauf hinzuweisen, daß größere Bauhöhen a priori keine höheren Dichten erzeugen – zumindest nicht bei unseren planungsrechtlichen Regeln. Das Hochhaus ist also nicht das Mittel der Wahl, wenn man es zur Verdichtung allein heranziehen will.
– Vielmehr sind es städtebauliche Überlegungen, welche höhere Gebäude rechtfertigen. Das hohe Gebäude ist im Stadtraum als Stadtzeichen und als Orientierungsmerkmal unverzichtbar.

Die Bewertung des Stadtraums und seiner Merkmale hat in der ›Hochhausstudie‹ drei Bereiche ergeben:

1. Grünräume, die das Stadtgebiet gliedern und Anschlüsse an den landschaftlichen Außenraum herstellen und dem natürlichen Gleichgewicht im Stadtgefüge und der Erholung der Stadtbewohner gleichermaßen dienen – diese sollen ungestört erhalten bleiben;
2. vorrangig schützenswerte Stadträume, die durch hohe stadträumliche Qualitäten ein hohes Maß an ausgewogenen baulichen Profilierungen, differenzierte Nutzungsmischungen, wirtschaftliche städtische Dichten, hohe Zentralität und günstige Erschließung durch den öffentlichen Personen-Nahverkehr (ÖPNV) sowie eine vielfältige Ausstattung mit Baudenkmälern geprägt sind;
3. Stadträume, die, umschlossen von Grünräumen, in einer Art Satellitenposition zur Innenstadt liegen und in denen entwicklungsfähige Flächenpotentiale in Zonen günstiger Erreichbarkeit mit dem ÖPNV liegen und die auch Defizite in ihrer Stadtgestalt und dem Stadtprofil aufweisen.

Hier bieten sich Entwicklungsmöglichkeiten für zusätzliche Verdichtungen und höhere Gebäude an. An ausgewählten Standorten sind neue Stadtzeichen in der Form höherer Gebäude wünschenswert und auch detailliert nachgewiesen.

positive sense of the expression. It considers ordered development values, and sensible design of the city as a place to live. This intact structure was also the basis for our ›Hochhausstudie‹ in 1977 and 1995, as follows:

– Nature and landscape must be secured in the city as a basis for life and as recreation spaces.
– The city's urban qualities must be protected against changes that are not true to scale. But new urban development qualities must be promoted.
– People must be able to find a healthy environment that is rich in experience in private and public urban spaces.

Can such aims for balanced equilibrium be made to fit in with man's ancient longing to build towers and demonstrate power? I think it is legitimate when erecting building in a city:

– to represent the particular distinction of individually and societally important institutions and
– above all to prove the creative potency and technical and structural skill of an age.

But it follows from this that above average appropriation of the airspace above a city should be the exception and retained for extraordinary creative achievements of the highest order.

But there are practical considerations within the highrise building argument:

– Urban development goes hand in hand with greater density. If one wants to avoid undue density at lower levels, and does not want to build on open spaces, then area must be increasing by stacking.
– There are uses for which tall buildings are better than lower ones covering a large area.
– But it should be pointed out at regular intervals that greater building heights do not a priori create greater density – at least not under our planning laws. So the highrise building is not the means of choice if it is intended to increase density alone.
– On the contrary, it is urban development considerations that justify taller buildings. Tall buildings are essential in urban space as symbols of the city and as landmarks.

Three distinct spheres emerged when evaluating urban space and its characteristics:

1. green spaces that structure the urban space and create connections with the landscape outside and serve natural balance in the urban structure and the city-dwellers' recreation equally – these should be retained undisturbed;
2. urban spaces that are worth protecting as a matter of priority, whose high qualities as urban spaces are characterized by a high degree of balanced architectural profiling, sophisticated use mixtures, economical urban density, that are very central and easy to reach by public transport and are to have a large number of building monuments;
3. urban spaces that are surrounded by green spaces, placed in a kind of satellite position to the city centre and which contain areas that are capable of development in zones that are easy to reach by public transport and that also leave something to be desired in terms of the urban form and the city profile.

Aus diesen Überlegungen wurde mit der ›Hochhausstudie‹ ein Stadtmodell entwickelt, das Ordnungskomponenten enthält, die sich an zentralen Orten mit günstiger Erreichbarkeit orientieren und dort auch diesen Sachverhalt durch höhere bauliche Profilierung unterstreichen.

Profil im Stadtraum kann aber nicht beliebig angeordnet sein. Ein wichtiger Teil der Aufgabe waren auch die Entwicklung und der Anwendungsnachweis einer Prüfungsmethode zur Beurteilung von Hochhäusern im Stadtgebiet von München. Diese Methode konnte bereits bei mehreren konkreten Fällen mit Erfolg angewandt und auf seine umfassende Eignung überprüft werden. Diese Art der Einzeluntersuchung wird für jeden Einzelfall im gesamten Stadtraum empfohlen.

Das Ergebnis

Die wesentlichen Erkenntnisse, die sich bei der vorliegenden Fortschreibung der ›Hochhausstudie‹ ergeben haben, können abschließend wie folgt zusammengefaßt werden:

1. Der Stadtraum ist als Gesamtheit nicht mehr erfaßbar. Statt dessen entwickelt sich eine Stadtlandschaft, die Täler und Höhen, Mitten und Ränder aufweist.
2. Stadträume und Grünräume, die in ihrer besonderen Qualität erhaltenswert erscheinen, dürfen keinem Druck zur Profilveränderung ausgesetzt werden. Sie müssen auch von äußeren Einwirkungen unbeeinflußt bleiben.
3. In den Bereichen, in denen das vorhandene Stadtprofil hohe Defizite aufweist, ist eine zusätzliche Profilierung wünschenswert. Dort sollen die Standorte mit hoher Erschließungsgunst Nachverdichtungen und, verbunden damit, Profilaufwertungen erfahren.
4. Je nach Standort sollte die Höhenentwicklung differenziert auf den räumlichen Zusammenhang abgestimmt werden – Quartier, Stadtteil, Gesamtstadt.
5. Neben der punktförmigen und solitären Profilierung sollten vor allem auch lineare und flächige Profilanhebungen in Betracht gezogen werden.
6. Die unterschiedlichen Stadträume sollten verschiedenartige Erlebnisqualitäten in Form und Profil aufweisen. Neben kleinräumig geschlossenen und abgeblockten Stadträumen gibt es großräumige offene und fließende mit differenzierter Profilierung.
7. Die jeweilige Art der Nutzung muß auch die Erscheinungsformen von höheren Gebäuden bestimmen – Technik, Gewerbe, Wohnen und Mischformen.
8. Dem sparsamen Einsatz von Energie und der günstigen Verkehrsanbindung, vor allem mit dem ÖPNV, kommen eine erhöhte Bedeutung zu. Dabei sind vor allem Innovationen zur umweltfreundlichen Ausstattung hoher Gebäude zu nutzen.
9. Konstruktion und Gliederung profilüberragender Bauwerke müssen zu gestalterischen Höchstleistungen in Bautechnik und Architektur führen. Nur dann ist der für den Luftraum einer Stadt beherrschende Anspruch gerechtfertigt.«

Here there are development possibilities for additional density and taller buildings. New urban symbols in the form of taller buildings are desirable on selected sites, and have been identified in detail.

Using these ideas, the ›Hochhausstudie‹ developed an urban model containing components relating to order based on central areas that are easy to reach, here too underline this state of affairs with taller building profiles.

But profile cannot be arranged at random in the city. An important part of the work was also to develop, and to prove the efficacy of, a test method for assessing high-rise buildings in the Munich urban area. This method was applied successfully in several concrete cases and checked for its general suitability. This kind of individual study is recommended for each individual case in the city as a whole.

The result

The key insights gained from the present continuation of the ›Hochhausstudie‹ can ultimately be summarized as follows:

1. The city can no longer be grasped as a whole. Instead an urban landscape is developing with hills and vales, centres and peripheries.
2. Urban space and green spaces that seem to be worth keeping because of their particular quality must not be put under pressure to change their profile. They must also not be subjected to outside influences.
3. In areas where the existing urban profile leaves a great deal to be desired, it is desirable to raise the profile. Here locations with good access by public transport should have their density increased and their profile raised at the same time.
4. Height should be matched to the spatial context according to location – quarter, district, city as a whole.
5. Linear profile raising in particular, and area profile raising, should be considered as well as point and solitaire profiling.
6. The different urban spaces should demonstrate a variety of experience qualities in form and profile. Small-scale closed and blocked off urban spaces exist alongside large-scale open and fluid areas with differentiated profiling.
7. The particular use intended must also determine the appearance of taller buildings – technology, commerce, housing and mixed forms.
8. Increased importance is given to economical energy use and good transport connections, above all by public transport. Here above all innovations for environment-friendly equipment for tall buildings should be exploited.
9. The structure and articulation of buildings rising above the general urban profile must lead to the highest possible creative performance in terms of engineering technology and architecture. Only then is the claim to a city's air-space justified.«

Die Würdigung einer großen Konzeption

Was Detlef Schreiber in seinem Vortrag vom 18. 5. 2001 übersichtlich und zusammenfassend zum Ausdruck bringt, enthält das Wesentliche einer ausgezeichneten, der städtischen Entwicklung weite Perspektiven aufzeigenden Studie, die im Ergebnis ein Leitfaden ist. Ohne starre Regeln aufzustellen, ordnet er mögliche Entwicklungen dem großen Gedanken einer Einheit in Vielfalt, die nichts überwuchert, sondern einzig der Gesamtheit dient, diese entfaltend, unter.

Es ist begreiflich, daß es einige Zeit brauchte und einiges an Umdenken, an Verzicht auf gewohnte Verfahren und Sichtweisen, bis sich solche Gedanken durchsetzen.

Die Staffelbauordnung Theodor Fischers aus dem Jahr 1904, eine höchst achtbare und für ihre Zeit und darüber hinaus gültige Leistung, der die werdende Großstadt München viel an Ordnung und Stadtgestalt verdankt, hat den neuen, sich ständig beschleunigenden Anforderungen heutiger pluraler Großstadtentwicklung nicht mehr genügen können. Sie gehörte einer anderen Lebenswelt, der bürgerlichen, an und war dabei – dies ist keine Kritik an Fischers Leistung, sondern historische Erkenntnis –, unter den veränderten Verhältnissen der Nachkriegs- und Wiederaufbauzeit formalistische Erstarrung zu bewirken, nichts Lebendiges mehr zu fördern.

Die Fortentwicklung

Die Schreibersche »Hochhausstudie«, die nun schon seit dreißig Jahren vorliegt und vor zehn Jahren aktualisiert wurde, ermöglicht Zukunft oder, um vorsichtig zu sein, würde Zukunft ermöglichen, wenn sie mit der vom Verfasser gewünschten und erhofften Sorgfalt und Gründlichkeit eingesetzt und als unabdingbare Voraussetzung regelhaft angewandt werden würde.

Stadt zu bauen, dazu noch aktuelle, heutige, plurale Stadt mit all ihren Anforderungen, den unterschiedlichen Bürgerinteressen Rechnung tragend, gehört zu den schwierigsten kulturellen Leistungen, die man sich zumuten kann. Dazu bedarf es ausgewogener Verfahren, die klug konzipiert und, wenn möglich, für alle einsichtig sind. Solche regelhaften Verfahren führen zu Werthierarchien, ohne die ordnende Freiheit nicht auskommen kann.

Das Finden und Durchsetzen geordneter Wertigkeit ist im Alltag ein hartes Geschäft. Große und viele kleine Schritte gehören dazu. Es muß, wie Detlef Schreiber in seiner Studie bewiesen hat, jede nach den Regeln als wichtig geltende Situation einzeln und mit aller Sorgfalt untersucht werden. Die Rechtzeitigkeit solcher Recherche ist ebenso wichtig wie die eigene Bemühung. Es geht darum, nichts Erhebliches mehr zu bauen, bevor nicht alle Umstände geklärt sind.

Was nützt es, »nach dem Essen« festzustellen, daß ein architektonisch durchaus gelungenes Hochhaus eine der großen Veduten des nördlichen München verpatzt, wenn nichts mehr an der entstandenen Realität zu verändern ist.

Acknowledging a great concept

What Detlef Schreiber said in his lecture on 18. 5. 2001, drawing the threads together comprehensibly, contains the essence of an excellent study indicating the development of broad vistas, which turns out to provide a clear guide. Without setting up rigid rules, he subjects possible development to the great idea of unity in diversity, which does not permit excessive growth, but simply serves and develops the whole.

It is understandable that it took some time, and some rethinking, some abandoning of habitual procedures and ways of looking at things, before such ideas could be accepted.

Theodor Fischer's 1904 plan for staggered building (»Staffelbauordnung«), a highly estimable achievement, and one that is way ahead of its times, and also valid. The city of Munich owes it a great deal in terms of order and urban form, but it was no longer able to meet the constantly accelerating demands of today's plural urban development in major cities. It belonged to a different world, the bourgeois world, and was starting – this is not a criticism of Fischer, but a historical insight – to produce nothing but formalistic paralysis under the changed circumstances of the post-war rebuilding period, and no longer promoting lively development.

Further developments

Schreiber's »Hochhausstudie«, which has now been available for 30 years and was updated ten years ago, makes a future possible, or to be cautious, would make a future possible if it is used with the care and thoroughness its author wished and hoped for and applied regularly, as an essential requirement.

Building something that can be called city, and on top of that up-to-date, plural city with all its demands, meeting the needs of a variety of citizens' interests, is one of the most difficult cultural achievements that one can impose on oneself. It needs balanced processes that are well conceived and if possible comprehensible to all. Regulated procedures like this lead to the hierarchies of values without which ordering freedom cannot survive.

Finding and implementing ordered values is a hard job for every day. It needs large steps, and a lot of small ones. As Detlef Schreiber has shown in his study, every situation that is seen as important under the rules must be examined individually and with due care. The fact that such research is done at the appropriate time is as important as one's own efforts. It means not building anything else significant until every circumstance has been examined.

What use is it to find out »after dinner« that a high-rise building that is entirely successful architecturally has messed up one of the best city views in north Munich, if there is nothing that can be changed about the reality that has emerged.

It is almost axiomatic that we learn nothing from history. For example in Munich, and this is not very long ago, a tall commercial building clad in black glass that spoiled almost the same situation

Es ist fast ein Axiom, daß aus der Geschichte nichts gelernt wird. So hat man in München, das ist noch gar nicht so lange her, ein fast die gleiche Situation verderbendes, mit schwarzem Glas verkleidetes, hohes Geschäftshaus, welches jahrzehntelang ein Ärgernis war, abgerissen – und nun trotzdem da capo.

Man muß Geduld haben. Regeln, noch dazu solche, die differenzierte Verfahren nach sich ziehen, sind nicht leicht einzuführen, zumal wenn sie munterem Draufloshandeln entgegenstehen. Da wird Lehrgeld bezahlt oder gar, wie in München beim Hochhaus-Volksentscheid unter dem Druck des Mißlingens, mit Mehrheit überreagiert.

Das ist verständlich, aber kontraproduktiv für die Stadt, wenn man sie als Kulturleistung sieht. Klüger wäre es, sich den Vordenkern anzuschließen, welche Schwierigkeiten und Komplexität zu bewältigen und in die Reihe zu bringen fähig sind.

Detlef Schreiber war mit seiner »Hochhausstudie« für München ein gründlicher Vordenker. Es wird sich herausstellen, daß er sich für Stadt im allgemeinen und um München besonders verdient gemacht hat.

and that had been annoying for years was pulled down and now is being repeated nevertheless.

One must be patient. Rules, and particularly those that give rise to sophisticated procedures, are not easy to introduce, especially when they resist just cheerfully getting cracking. Then you have to learn the hard way, or as in Munich in the case of the high-rise building referendum under the pressure of failure, you overreact by a majority.

That is understandable, but counterproductive for the city seen as a cultural achievement. It would be more intelligent to take up the ideas of earlier thinkers who are capable of mastering difficulties and complexity and setting things right.

Detlef Schreiber's »Hochhausstudie« for Munich showed that he was a thorough earlier thinker. It will become clear that he has done a great service to cities in general and to Munich in particular.

Untersuchung zur Stadtbildverträglichkeit des Hochhauses (155 m) am Georg-Brauchle-Ring 1998; Standort Petuelring/Riesenfeldstraße. Die Bildmontage zeigt die Vorteile der Gruppierung von BMW-Hochhaus, Olympiaturm und deren Ergänzung durch den neuen Turm im Straßenraum des Mittleren Rings.

Investigation of the compatibility of the high-rise building (155 m) at Georg-Brauchle-Ring with the urban environment 1998; Petuelring/Riesenfeldstrasse site. The photomontage shows the advantages of the group: the BMW high-rise building, the Olympic tower and the supplementary new tower seen in the street environment of Mittlerer Ring.

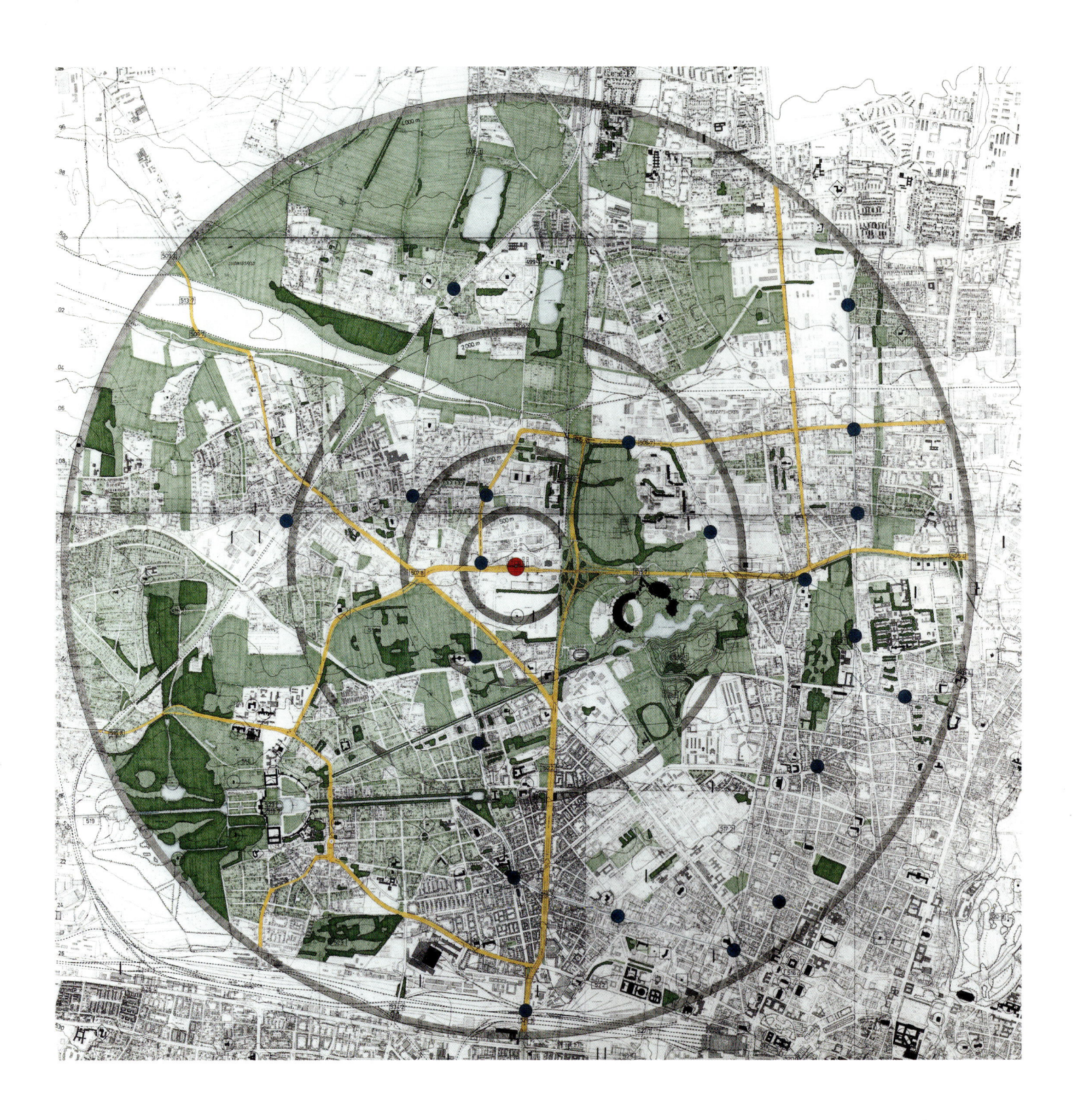

Untersuchung zur Stadtbildverträglichkeit
des Hochhauses (155 m) am Georg-Brauchle-Ring 1998
Karte »Grünflächen und Verkehrserschließung«
rot = Standort Hochhaus am Georg-Brauchle-Ring
schwarz = U-Bahn Haltepunkte

Investigation of the compatibility of the high-rise
building (155 m) at Georg-Brauchle-Ring with the urban
environment, 1998
Map »green spaces and traffic access«
red: site of the high-rise building on Georg-Brauchle-Ring
black: underground stations

Karte »Höhenlinien (in Zwei-Meter-Schritten) mit profilüberragenden Gebäuden«
rot = Standort Hochhaus (508,8 m ÜNN)

Map »Altitude lines (in 2 metre increments) with buildings which protrude above the profile«
red: site of a high-rise building (508.8 m above sea level)

Untersuchung zur Stadtbildverträglichkeit des Hochhauses
(155 m) am Georg-Brauchle-Ring 1998
Karte »Beobachtungsstandorte, Stadtteil und Stadtraum«
rot = Standort Hochhaus am Georg-Brauchle-Ring

Investigation of the compatibility of the high-rise building
(155 m) at Georg-Brauchle-Ring with the urban environment, 1998
Map »Observation locations, urban district and urban region«
red: site of the high-rise building on Georg-Brauchle-Ring

Fortschreibung der Hochhausstudie 1995
Karte »Schutzwürdige Grünräume und schutzwürdige Bauräume«

Continuation of the high-rise building study, 1995
Map »Green areas deserving protection and built areas deserving protection«

Fortschreibung der Hochhausstudie 1995;
Karte »Entwicklungsbereiche«

Continuation of the high-rise building study,
1995; Map »Development areas«

■ Schutzwürdige Grünräume
Green areas deserving protection

■ Schutzwürdige Bauräume
Built areas deserving protection

○ Günstige Bereiche für zukünftige höherprofilierte
Gebäude als Quartierszeichen
Favourable areas for future high-profile buildings
which will be landmarks for the district

● Günstige Bereiche für zukünftige höherprofilierte Gebäude als Stadtzeichen
Favourable areas for future high-profile buildings which will be landmarks for the city

▬ Profilüberragende Gebäude
Buildings which project beyond the profile

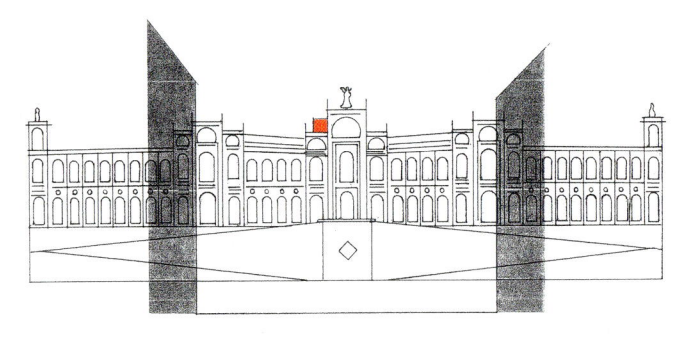

Gebäudehöhe 90 Meter

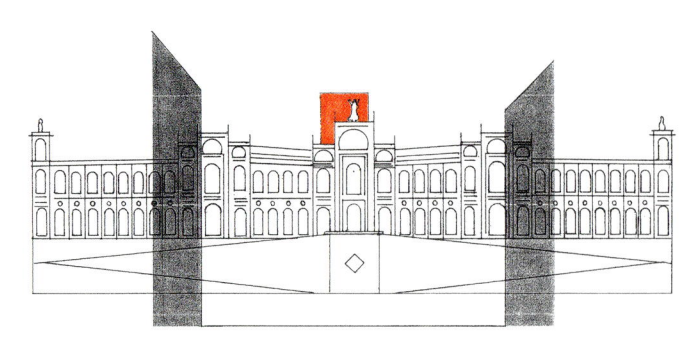

Gebäudehöhe 120 Meter

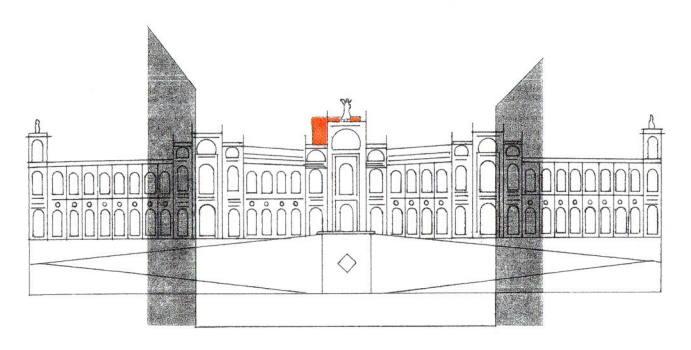

Gebäudehöhe 100 Meter

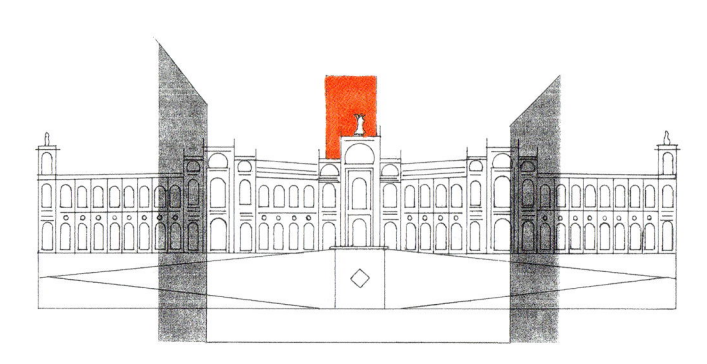

Gebäudehöhe 150 Meter

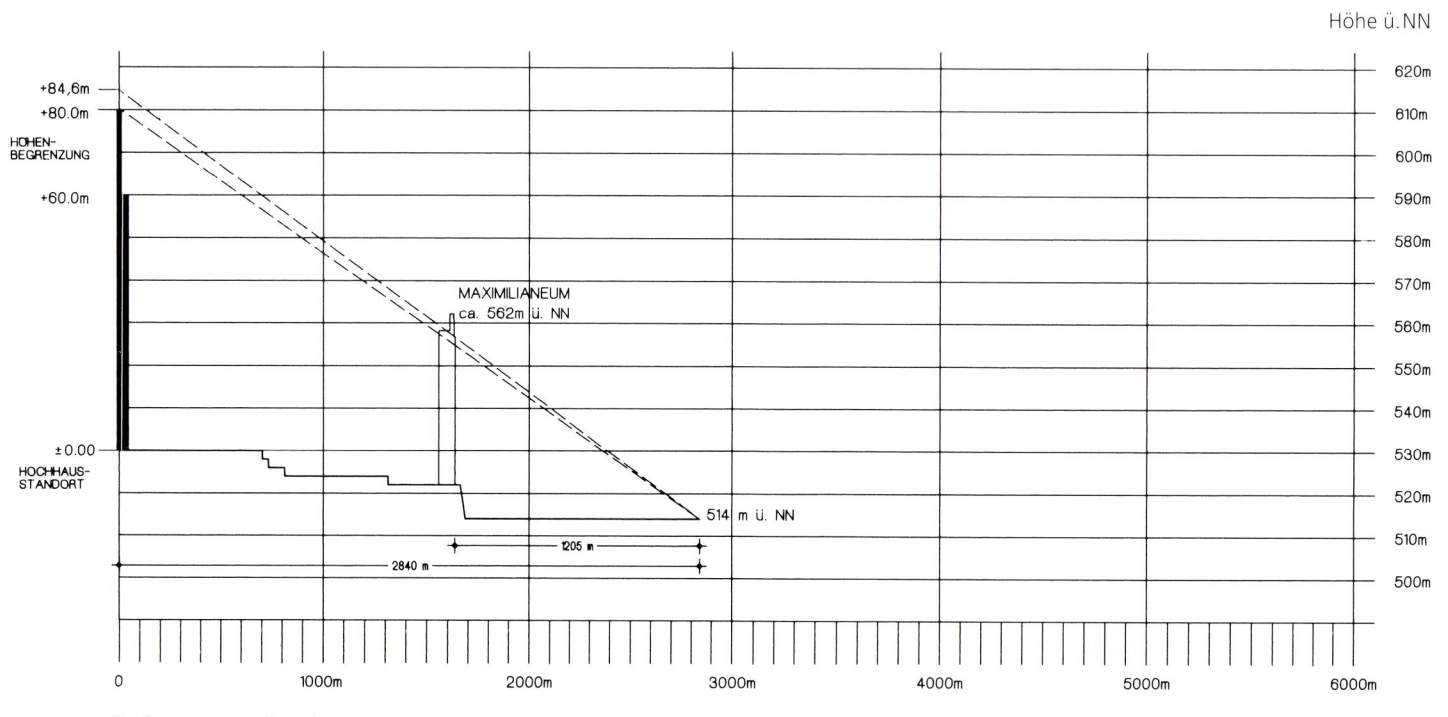

Höhe ü. NN

Entfernung vom Standort

Untersuchung der Stadtbildverträglichkeit
des Hochhauses an der Dingolfinger Straße 1996,
Standort Max-Joseph-Platz/Maximilianstraße

Links oben: Der geplante Standort liegt genau in der
Verlängerung einer der wichtigsten historischen Achsen
der Stadt München, der Maximilianstraße.
Diese empfindliche Lage führte zu einer deutlichen
Höhenzäsur des Hochhauses.

Links unten: Geländeschnitt mit Höhenlage des
Beobachtungspunktes und des profilüberragenden
Gebäudes mit absoluter Höhe

Investigation of the compatibility of the high-rise building
at Dingolfinger Strasse with the urban environment, 1996,
Location: Max-Joseph-Platz/Maximilianstrasse

Left page, top: the planned site is situated exactly in the
extension of one of the most important historical axes of
the city of Munich, Maximilianstrasse.
This sensitive location led to a significant limitation of
the height of the high-rise building.

Left page, bottom: sectional view of the land with contour
lines of the observation and the building which projects
beyond the profile, with absolute height

Oben: Maximilianstraße mit
Maximilianeum als Begrenzung

Above: Maximilianstrasse,
bounded by the Maximilianeum

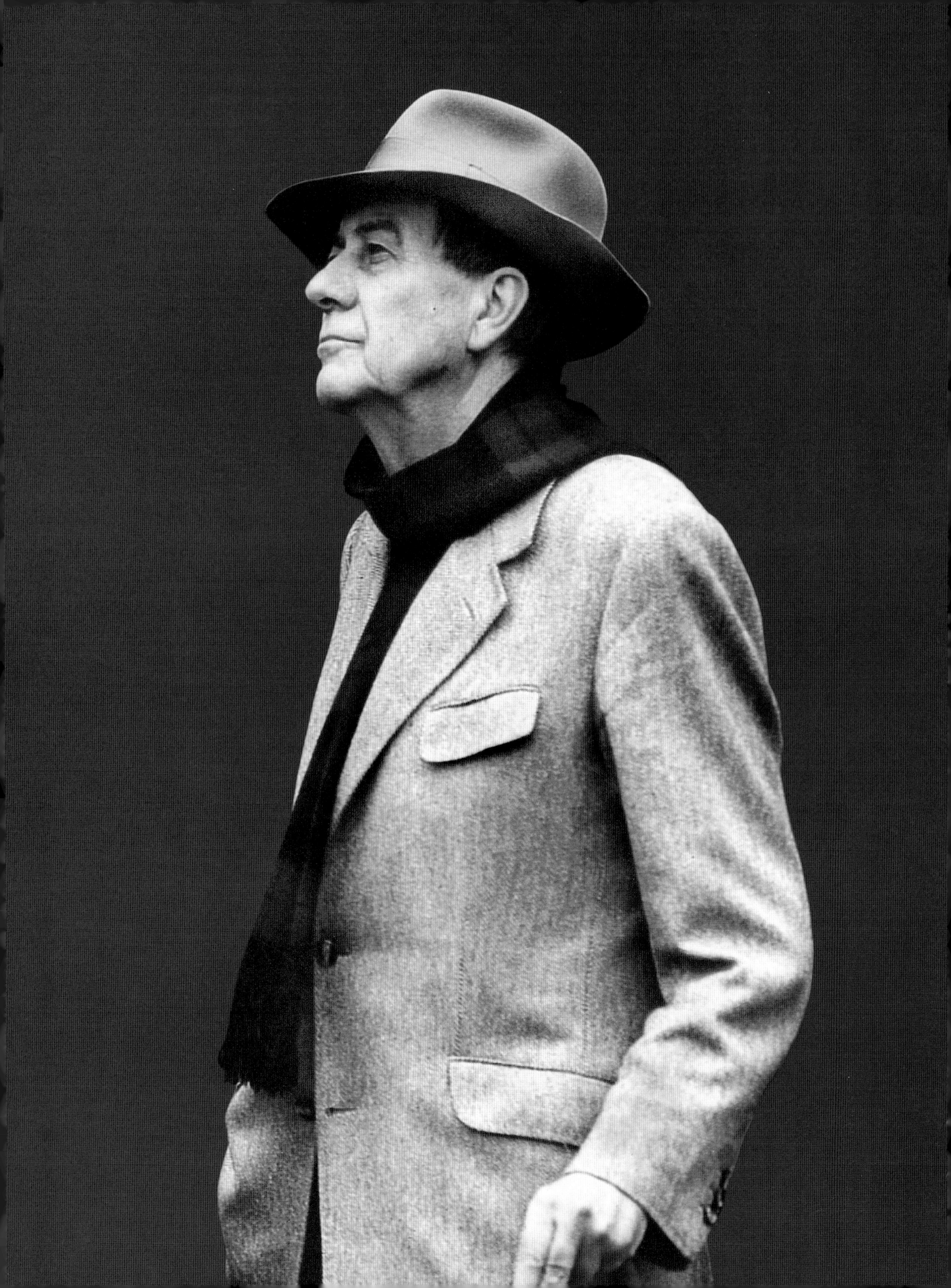

Biographie

6.10.1930
geboren im badischen Gailingen am Hochrhein als zweites von vier Kindern, Vater Architekt

1946–1949
Die Familie lebt in Ebenhofen im Allgäu, Besuch des Gymnasiums in Kaufbeuren

1949
Umzug nach München

1950
Abitur an der Luitpold-Oberrealschule in München

1950–1956
Studium der Architektur an der Technischen Hochschule in München, nebenbei Gastschüler an der Kunstakademie bei Professor Franz Nagel

1956
Diplom

1956–1957
Mitarbeit bei Professor Franz Hart

1957–1958
einjähriges Forschungsstipendium des British Council London, Studien bei Professor Sir William Holford am University College London und bei Professor Arthur Korn der Architectural Association London (AA); während dieses Studienaufenthalts ausschließliche Beschäftigung mit Stadt- und Landesplanung

1958
Certificate in Town and Country Planning, University College London

ab 1958
Mitglied der Architectural Association

1958–1960
Vorbereitungsdienst als Baureferendar bei der Bayerischen Staatsbauverwaltung

1960
Staatsprüfung

1960
Heirat mit Ulrike Lohan, vier Kinder – Markus, Claudia, Lukas und Julia

1960–1961
Mitarbeit bei der Arbeitsgemeinschaft Stadtentwicklungsplan München

ab 1961
freier Architekt in München

ab 1961
Mitglied im Bund Deutscher Architekten, BDA

ab 1961
Mitglied im Deutschen Werkbund Bayern, DWB

1962
gemeinsames Büro mit Herbert Groethuysen (bis 1974) und Gernot Sachsse (bis 1966) in der Südlichen Auffahrtsallee in München; Realisierung zahlreicher Bau- und Stadtplanungsprojekte

1966
Umzug nach Widdersberg bei Herrsching

1966–1974
Mitglied in der Plan Gesellschaft für Regional-, Architektur- und Ingenieurplanung mbH, Plan GmbH

1966
Staatlicher Förderpreis des Freistaats Bayern für Junge Künstler

1966
zusammen mit Peter C. von Seidlein Fernsehfilm über Mies van der Rohe, Dreharbeiten und Interviews in den USA

ab 1971
Mitglied der Deutschen Akademie für Städtebau und Landesplanung

1972
Studienaufenthalt in New York und Chicago

ab 1974
alleiniger Inhaber des Büros in der Südlichen Auffahrtsallee, 12–15 Mitarbeiter

1982/1984/1990
Auszeichnungen Deutscher Stahlbaupreis

1991
Auszeichnung Europäischer Constructa Preis

1993
Auszeichnung Deutscher Architekturpreis

1998
Honory Fellow of the American Institute of Architects, AIA, Hon. FAIA

19.8.2003
gestorben in München

Detlef Schreiber, 2001

Biography

6.10.1930
Born in Gailingen (Baden) on the Upper Rhine as the second of four children, father architect

1946–1949
Family lives in Ebenhofen/Allgäu, Attended the grammar school in Kaufbeuren

1949
Family moved to Munich

1950
Abitur (school leaving and university entrance qualification) in Luitpold-oberrealschule in Munich

1950–1956
Study of Architecture at the Technical University of Munich, also a visiting student at the Academy of Art under Professor Franz Nagel

1956
»Diplom« degree

1956–1957
Collaboration with Professor Franz Hart

1957–1958
One-year research grant from the British Council, London, Study under Professor Sir William Holford at University College, London and under Professor Arthur Korn of the Architectural Association, London (AA), during this period of study abroad, he worked exclusively on town and country planning.

1958
Certificate in Town and Country Planning from University College, London

From 1958
Member of the Architectural Association

1958–1960
Preparatory service as a building trainee at the Bavarian State Building Authority

1960
State examination

1960
Marriage to Ulrike Lohan, four children – Markus, Claudia, Lukas and Julia

1960–1961
Collaboration with the working group for the Munich urban development plan

From 1961
Freelance architect in Munich

1961
Member of the Association of German Architects (BDA)

1961
Member of the German Werkbund Bavaria, DWB

1962
Joint with Herbert Groethuysen (until 1974) Gernot Sachsse (until 1966) in Südliche Auffahrtsallee in Munich; Implementation of numerous construction and town planning projects

1966
Moved to Widdersberg near Herrsching

1966–1974
Member of the regional, architectural and engineering planning company Plan Gesellschaft für Regional-, Architektur- und Ingenieurplanung mbH, Plan GmbH

1966
State promotion prize of the Free State of Bavaria for young artists

1966
Production of a TV film about Mies van der Rohe together with Peter C. von Seidlein, filming work and interviews in the USA

From 1971
Member of the German Academy for Urban Development and Regional Planning

1972
Study periods in New York and Chicago

From 1974
Sole owner of the office in Südliche Auffahrtsallee, 12–15 employees

1982/1984/1990
Awarded the German Steel Construction Prize

1991
Awarded the European Constructa Prize

1993
Awarded the German Architecture Prize

1998
Honorary Fellow of the American Institute of Architects, AIA, Hon.FAIA

19.8.2003
Died in Munich

Werkverzeichnis
List of works

1958 **Museum-Münster** Wettbewerb	1958 **Museum – Münster** Competition
1960 **Wohnsiedlung Neuburg** Wettbewerb – engere Wahl	1960 **Residential estate – Neuburg** Competition – shortlisted
1960–62 **Sozialer Wohnungsbau 5 Blöcke – Fürstenried West, München** Bauherr: Baugenossenschaft München von 1871 Architekten: Oswald Schreiber + Detlef Schreiber	1960–62 **Social housing project, 5 blocks – Fürstenried West, Munich** Building owner: Baugenossenschaft München von 1871 Architects: Oswald Schreiber + Detlef Schreiber
1960 **Entlastungsstadt Dönche-Kassel** Wettbewerb	1960 **Overspill town Dönche-Kassel** Competition
1961 **St. Peters Church – Regent Square, London** Bauherr: Deutsche Evangelisch-Lutherische Kirche London (Projekt)	1961 **St. Peters Church – Regent Square, London** Building owner: german Lutheran church, London (Project)
1962 **Wohnsiedlung – Coburg** Wettbewerb – engere Wahl	1962 **Residential estate – Coburg** Competition – shortlisted
1962–69 **Bebauungsplan für 39 Wohnhäuser »Deutschbausiedlung« und Bauausführung – Lilienthalstraße, Oberschleißheim bei München** Bauherr: privater Verein Architekten: Groethuysen + Schreiber + Sachsse Entwurf und Projektleitung: Detlef Schreiber	1962–69 **Development plan for 39 residential buildings »Deutschbausiedlung« and construction – Lilienthalstrasse, Oberschleißheim near Munich** Building owner: private association Architects: Groethuysen + Schreiber + Sachsse Design and project leadership: Detlef Schreiber
1962 **Bürogebäude – Falkenturmstraße, München** Bauherr: Dr. Ernst Bullmer Architekten: Groethuysen + Schreiber + Sachsse (Projekt)	1962 **Office building – Falkenturmstrasse, Munich** Building owner: Dr. Ernst Bullmer Architects: Groethuysen + Schreiber + Sachsse (Project)

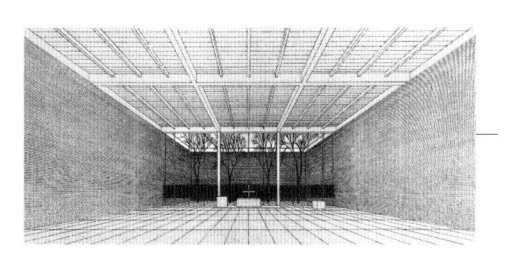

1962
Wohnhausgruppe – Zschokkestraße, München
Bauherr: Gemeinnützige Bayerische
Wohnungsbaugesellschaft AG
Architekten: Groethuysen + Schreiber + Sachsse
Entwurf: Detlef Schreiber (Projekt)

1962–64
Einfamilienhaus – Krailling bei München
Bauherr: Leo Leidner
Architekten: Groethuysen + Schreiber + Sachsse
Entwurf und Projektleitung: Detlef Schreiber

1963–64
24 Wohnungen – Schmalkaldener Straße, München
Bauherr: Aufbau Bayern
Architekten: Groethuysen + Schreiber + Sachsse

1963
Polytechnikum – München
Architekten: Groethuysen + Schreiber + Sachsse
Entwurf: Detlef Schreiber (Wettbewerb)

1963–70
Verwaltungsgebäude für den Süddeutschen Verlag
Färbergraben 23, München
Bauherr: Süddeutscher Verlag GmbH
Architekten: Groethuysen + Schreiber + Sachsse
Entwurf und Projektleitung: Detlef Schreiber

1963–70
Institut für Tierernährung – Weihenstephan bei München
Bauherr: Universitätsbauamt München
Architekten: Groethuysen + Schreiber + Sachsse
Entwurf und Projektleitung: Detlef Schreiber

1963–67
Kirchenzentrum St. Mauritius – Moosach, München
Bauherr: Erzbischöfliches Ordinariat München
Architekten: Groethuysen + Schreiber + Sachsse

1964–65
12 Wohnungen – Milbertshofener Straße, München
Bauherr: B.+ G. Huber
Architekten: Groethuysen + Schreiber + Sachsse

1962
Group of residential buildings – Zschokkestrasse, Munich
Building owner: Gemeinnützige Bayerische
Wohnungsbaugesellschaft AG
Architects: Groethuysen + Schreiber + Sachsse
Design: Detlef Schreiber (Project)

1962–64
Single house – Krailling near Munich
Building owner: Leo Leidner
Architects: Groethuysen + Schreiber + Sachsse
Design and project leadership:
Detlef Schreiber

1963–64
24 apartments – Schmalkaldener Strasse, Munich
Building owner: Aufbau Bayern
Architects: Groethuysen + Schreiber + Sachsse

1963
Polytechnikum – Munich
Architects: Groethuysen + Schreiber + Sachsse
Design: Detlef Schreiber (Competition)

1963–70
Administration building for the publisher Süddeutschen Verlag
Färbergraben 23, Munich
Building owner: Süddeutscher Verlag GmbH
Architects: Groethuysen + Schreiber + Sachsse
Design and project leadership:
Detlef Schreiber

1963–70
Institute for Animal Nutrition – Weihenstephan near Munich
Building owner: University building office Munich
Architects: Groethuysen + Schreiber + Sachsse
Design and project leadership:
Detlef Schreiber

1963–67
Church centre St. Mauritius – Moosach, Munich
Building owner: Archbishop's offices, Munich
Architects: Groethuysen + Schreiber + Sachsse

1964–65
12 apartments – Schmalkaldener Strasse, Munich
Building owner: B.+ G. Huber
Architects: Groethuysen + Schreiber + Sachsse

1965
Wohnungsbau für die Feuerwache 2 Aidenbachstraße, München
Bauherr: Stadt München
Architekten: Groethuysen + Schreiber + Sachsse

1967–71
Im Rahmen der Plan GmbH Gebietsentwicklungsplan Stadt Ingolstadt Strukturplan Stadt Ingolstadt
Auftraggeber: Stadt Ingolstadt
Verantwortlicher Architekt:
Detlef Schreiber

1967–71
Umbau Zeitungssetzerei und Technikgebäude, Sendlinger Straße Rgb, München
Bauherr: Süddeutscher Verlag GmbH
Architekten: Groethuysen + Schreiber

1967–69
Privatschwimmbad – Harthauser Straße, München
Bauherr: privat
Architekten: Groethuysen + Schreiber
Entwurf und Projektleitung:
Detlef Schreiber

1968
Wohnungsbau – Knorrstraße, München
Bauherren: B.+G. Huber
Architekten: Groethuysen + Schreiber

1968
Wohngebiet – Zorneding Ost
Architekten: Groethuysen + Schreiber
Wettbewerb

1969
Pfarrzentrum Heilige Familie – Gartenberg
Architekten: Groethuysen + Schreiber
Entwurf: Detlef Schreiber
Wettbewerb: 1. Preis

1969–73
Pfarrzentrum Heilige Familie mit Kindergarten Johannisplatz, Gartenberg
Bauherr: Erzbischöfliches Ordinariat München
Architekten: Groethuysen + Schreiber
Entwurf und Projektleitung:
Detlef Schreiber

1969
Ökumenisches Pfarrzentrum – Olympisches Dorf München
Architekten: Groethuysen + Schreiber
Wettbewerb: 2. Preis

1965
Residential building for fire brigade 2 Aidenbachstrasse, Munich
Building owner: city of Munich
Architects: Groethuysen + Schreiber + Sachsse

1967–71
In the framework of Plan GmbH District development plan for the municipality of Ingolstadt Structure plan for the municipality of Ingolstadt
Client: municipality of Ingolstadt
Responsible architect: Detlef Schreiber

1967–71
Conversion of newspaper typsetting centre and technical building
Sendlinger Strasse Rgb, Munich
Building owner: Süddeutscher Verlag GmbH
Architects: Groethuysen + Schreiber

1967–69
Private swimming pool – Harthauser Strasse, Munich
Building owner: private
Architects: Groethuysen + Schreiber
Design and project leadership:
Detlef Schreiber

1968
Residential building – Knorrstrasse, Munich
Building owner: B.+G. Huber
Architects: Groethuysen + Schreiber

1968
Residential area – Zorneding East
Architects: Groethuysen + Schreiber
Competition

1969
Holy Family church centre – Gartenberg
Architects: Groethuysen + Schreiber
Design: Detlef Schreiber
Competition: 1st prize

1969–73
Holy Family church centre with kindergarten Johannisplatz, Gartenberg
Building owner: Erzbischöfliches Ordinariat München
Architects: Groethuysen + Schreiber
Design and project leadership: Detlef Schreiber

1969
Ecumenical church centre – Olympic Village Munich
Architects: Groethuysen + Schreiber
Competition: 2nd Price

1970
Verwaltungsgebäude Bayerische Rückversicherung – München
Architekten: Groethuysen + Schreiber
Entwurf: Detlef Schreiber
Wettbewerb

1970
Pfarrzentrum St. Jakobus – München Perlach
Architekten: Groethuysen + Schreiber
Wettbewerb: Ankauf

1972 – 83
Herrsching – Entwicklungs- und Strukturplan, mehrere Bebauungspläne
Auftraggeber: Gemeinde Herrsching

1972
Bebauungsplan Gutachten – Perlach Süd, München
Architekten: Groethuysen + Schreiber
Entwurf: Detlef Schreiber
Wettbewerb

1972 – 82
Peißenberg – Flächennutzungsplan und Landschaftsplan, mehrere Bebauungspläne
Auftraggeber: Markt Peißenberg

1972
Wörthzentrum – Markt Peißenberg
Groethuysen + Schreiber
Entwurf: Detlef Schreiber (Projekt)

1973
Wohnhaus Hiebler – Widdersberg
Projekt

1973 – 81
Neubiberg – Flächennutzungsplan
Auftraggeber: Gemeinde Neubiberg

1973 – 76
Erkersreuth – Entwicklungs- und Strukturplan
Auftraggeber: Gemeinde Erkersreuth

1974 – 77
Laborbau – Internats- und Ganztagsschule, Landheim, Schondorf am Ammersee
Bauherr: Stiftung Landheim Schondorf

1974
Gemeindezentrum mit Wohnbebauung – Rödenthal
Wettbewerb

1970
Administration building, Bayerische Rückversicherung – Munich
Architects: Groethuysen + Schreiber
Design: Detlef Schreiber
Competition

1970
St. Jakobus church centre – Munich Perlach
Architects: Groethuysen + Schreiber
Competition: purchase

1972 – 83
Herrsching – development and structure plan, several development plans
Client: local community of Herrsching

1972
Expert's report on the development plan – Perlach south, Munich
Architects: Groethuysen + Schreiber
Design: Detlef Schreiber
Competition

1972 – 82
Peissenberg – land use plan and landscape plan, several development plans
Client: market town of Peissenberg

1972
Wörthzentrum – market town of Peissenberg
Groethuysen + Schreiber
Design: Detlef Schreiber (Project)

1973
Residential building Hiebler – Widdersberg
Project

1973 – 81
Neubiberg – land use plan
Client: local community of Neubiberg

1973 – 76
Erkersreuth – development and structure plan
Client: local community of Erkersreuth

1974 – 77
Laboratory building – boarding and day school, Landheim Schondorf am Ammersee
Building owner: Landheim Schondorf foundation

1974
Local community centre with residential buildings – Rödenthal
Competition

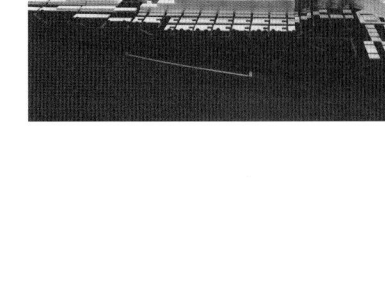

1974–76
Einfamilienhaus – Im Ginsterbusch,
Hamburg
Bauherr: Dr. Wolfgang Nolde

1974–78
Bebauungsplan Lena-Christ-Straße –
Neubiberg
Auftraggeber: Gemeinde Neubiberg

1974–79
Ortszentrum – Peißenberg
Auftraggeber: Markt Peißenberg
Projekt

1974–76
Künstleratelier – Muttenthaler Straße,
München
Bauherr: Rupprecht Geiger

1974–75
Einfamilienhaus – Kesselweg, Frieding
Bauherr: Herbert Schambeck

1974–76
Schäftlarn – Entwicklungs- und Strukturplan
Auftraggeber: Gemeinde Schäftlarn

1975–77
Einfamilienhaus – Burgstraße,
Widdersberg
Bauherr: Dr. Armbruster

1975
Schwimmbad – Markt Peißenberg
Wettbewerb

1975–76
Kindergarten – Lena-Christ-Straße,
Neubiberg
Bauherr: Gemeinde Neubiberg

1975–77
Bad Reichenhall – Altstadtsanierung
Obere Stadt
Sanierung und Gestaltung Sebastiansgasse
Auftraggeber: Bad Reichenhall

1975–92
Ingolstadt – Vorbereitende
Untersuchungen zur Altstadtsanierung
Strukturplan, Nord-West Ast
Flächennutzungsplan/Landschaftsplan
Auftraggeber: Stadt Ingolstadt

1975
Parkhaus – Altstadt Ingolstadt
Wettbewerb: 1. Preis

1974–76
Single house – Im Ginsterbusch,
Hamburg
Building owner: Dr. Wolfgang Nolde

1974–78
Development plan Lena-Christ-Strasse –
Neubiberg
Client: local community of Neubiberg

1974–79
Town centre, Peissenberg
Client: market town of Peissenberg
Project

1974–76
Artist's studio – Muttenthaler Strasse, Munich
Building owner: Rupprecht Geiger

1974–75
Single house – Kesselweg, Frieding
Building owner: Herbert Schambeck

1974–76
Schäftlarn – development and
structure plan
Client: local community of Schäftlarn

1975–77
Single house – Burgstrasse,
Widdersberg
Building owner: Dr. Armbruster

1975
Swimming pool – market town
of Peissenberg
Competition

1975–76
Kindergarten – Lena-Christ-Strasse, Neubiberg
Building owner: Local community of
Neubiberg

1975–77
Bad Reichenhall – refurbishment of
old centre of the upper town
Refurbishment and design of Sebastiansgasse
Client: Bad Reichenhall

1975–92
Ingolstadt – preparatory surveys for the
refurbishment of the old town centre
Structure plan, north-west branch
Land use plan/landscape plan
Client: municipality of Ingolstadt

1975
Indoor car park – old town of Ingolstadt
Competition: 1st prize

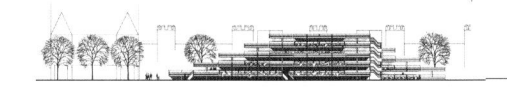

1975
Nutzungs- und Gestaltungsvorschlag –
Sanierung Markt Pförring
Wettbewerb

1976 – 02
Untersuchung Hochhausstandorte,
München
Fortschreibung 1995
Stadtbildverträglichkeitsstudien
zu Einzelstandorten
Auftraggeber: Landeshauptstadt München

1976
Wohn- und Bürohaus – Umbau und
Renovierung
Bavariaring, München
Bauherr: Horst G. Schreiber

1976
Stadtteilzentrum Arabellapark –
München
Wettbewerb

1976
Gemeinbedarfszentrum – Gemeinde
Planegg
Wettbewerb

1976
Pfarrzentrum St. Hedwig – Stadt Kempten
Wettbewerb

1976 – 77
Gaimersheim – Sanierungsgutachten
Auftraggeber: Markt Gaimersheim

1976 – 79
Kindergarten St. Nikolaus an der Stadtmauer
Bad Reichenhall
Auftraggeber: Erzbischöfliches Ordinariat
München

1976 – 77
Freising – Vorbereitende Untersuchung
zur Altstadtsanierung
Auftraggeber: Stadt Freising

1977 – 78
Volksschulerweiterung mit Neubau
einer Turnhalle
Rathausplatz, Neubiberg
Bauherr: Gemeinde Neubiberg

1977 – 82
Um- und Anbau mit Mehrzweckhalle
Grund- und Hauptschule
Nikolausweg, Herrsching
Bauherr: Gemeinde Herrsching

1975
Use and design proposal – refurbishment
of the market town of Pförring
Competition

1976 – 02
Study of high-rise building sites, Munich
Continuation 1995
Studies of the compatibility with the urban
environment in individual locations
Client: federal state capital of Munich

1976
Residential and office building –
conversion and renovation
Bavariaring, Munich
Building owner: Horst G. Schreiber

1976
Suburban centre Arabellapark –
Munich
Competition

1976
Local community centre – local community
of Planegg
Competition

1976
St. Hedwig church centre – town of Kempten
Competition

1976 – 77
Gaimersheim – refurbishment survey
Client: market town of Gaimersheim

1976 – 79
St. Nikolaus kindergarten in the town wall
Bad Reichenhall
Client: Archbishop's offices, Munich

1976 – 77
Freising – preparatory survey for the
refurbishment of the old town centre
Client: town of Freising

1977 – 78
School extension and new sports hall building
Rathausplatz, Neubiberg
Building owner: Local community of
Neubiberg

1977 – 82
Conversion and extension of primary
and general secondary school with a
multi-purpose hall
Nikolausweg, Herrsching
Building owner: local community of
Herrsching

1977–82
Freilassing – Struktur- und Entwicklungsplan
Auftraggeber: Verwaltungsgemeinschaft
Freilassing, Ainring, Saaldorf, Surheim

1978–82
**Haus für Bildung und Freizeit –
Rathausplatz, Neubiberg**
Bauherr: Gemeinde Neubiberg

1978–82
**Umbau Rathaus mit Anbau einer
Bibliothek – Gaimersheim**
Bauherr: Markt Gaimersheim

1978–81
**Büro- und Laborgebäude GRS I
Forschungsgelände, Garching**
Bauherr: Gesellschaft für Anlagen- und
Reaktorsicherheit mbH

1979–80
**Lager-, Ausstellungs- und Bürogebäude
Landsberger Straße 400, München**
Bauherr: Süddeutscher Verlag GmbH (Projekt)

1979–83
**Bad Wörishofen – Gestaltung
verkehrsberuhigter Bereich**
Auftraggeber: Bad Wörishofen

1979–81
**Ausstellungs- und Lagerhalle –
Gewerbegebiet Herrsching**
Bauherr: Bauwaren Haas

1980
**Plangutachten – Wohnbebauung,
Unterföhring Süd**
Wettbewerb: 1. Preis

1980–82
Wohnhaus – Buchendorf
Bauherr: Michael Haas

1980–82
**Wohnhaus – Am Haselnußstrauch,
München**
Bauherr: Professor Dr. Franz Mayinger

1980–86
Bebauungsplan Unterföhring Süd
Auftraggeber: Gemeinde Unterföhring

1981–85
**Bauhof und Recycling-Station
mit Wohnung
Gewerbegebiet, Herrsching**
Bauherr: Gemeinde Herrsching

1977–82
Freilassing – structure and development plan
Client: joint administrative community
of Freilassing, Ainring, Saaldorf, Surheim

1978–82
**Education and leisure building –
Rathausplatz, Neubiberg**
Building owner: local community
of Neubiberg

1978–82
**Conversion of town hall and addition
of a library – Gaimersheim**
Building owner: market town of Gaimersheim

1978–81
**Office and laboratory building GRS I
Research campus, Garching**
Building owner: Gesellschaft für Anlagen-
und Reaktorsicherheit mbH

1979–80
**Warehouse, exhibition and office building
Landsberger Strasse 400, Munich**
Building owner: Süddeutscher Verlag GmbH
(Project)

1979–83
**Bad Wörishofen – design of a reduced
traffic area**
Client: Bad Wörishofen

1979–81
**Exhibition and warehouse building –
Herrsching commercial estate**
Building owner: Bauwaren Haas

1980
**Planning survey for residential building
project, Unterföhring south**
Competition: 1st prize

1980–82
Residential building – Buchendorf
Building owner: Michael Haas

1980–82
**Residential building –
Am Haselnussstrauch, München**
Building owner: Professor Dr. Franz Mayinger

1980–86
Development plan Unterföhring south
Client: local community of Unterföhring

1981–85
**Building yard and recycling station
with apartment
Commercial estate, Herrsching**
Building owner: local community of Herrsching

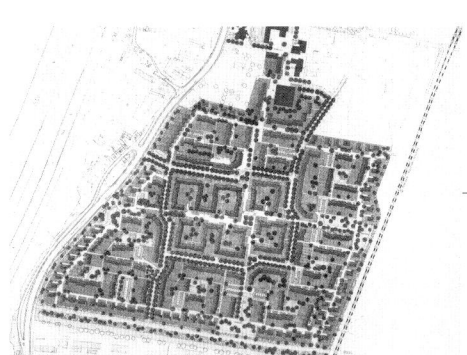

1981 Städtebauliches Gutachten – Poing bei München Wettbewerb: 1. Preis	1981 Urban development survey – Poing near Munich Competition: 1st prize
1981–82 Gesamtplanung Arkade – Verlagsgelände – München Bauherr: Süddeutscher Verlag GmbH Projekt	1981–82 Overall planning for an arcade – publishing house complex – Munich Building owner: Süddeutscher Verlag GmbH Project
1982–84 Fachklassenanbau Volksschule – Herrsching Bauherr: Gemeinde Herrsching	1982–84 Extension building for specialist classes at general school – Herrsching Building owner: local community of Herrsching
1982–83 Spielhäuser – Westpark München IGA 83 Bauherr: Landeshauptstadt München	1982–83 Play houses – Westpark Munich IGA 83 Building owner: federal state capital of Munich
1982–85 München – Städtebauliches Strukturkonzept Münchner Westen und Münchner Osten Auftraggeber: Landeshauptstadt München	1982–85 Munich – urban development structure concept West and east of Munich Client: federal state capital of Munich
1982 Bayerische Staatskanzlei – München Wettbewerb	1982 Bavarian State Chancellery – Munich Competition
1982–90 Schrobenhausen – Vorbereitende Untersuchungen zur Sanierung Sanierung und Gestaltung von Altstadtstraßen und -plätzen; verschiedene Bebauungspläne Auftraggeber: Stadt Schrobenhausen	1982–90 Schrobenhausen – preparatory surveys for refurbishment Refurbishment and design of streets and squares in the old town Various development plans Client: town of Schrobenhausen
1983 Ortszentrum – Gemeinde Gilching Wettbewerb	1983 Town centre – local community of Gilching Competition
1983 Wohnbebauung Oßwaldstraße – Stadt Starnberg Wettbewerb: 1. Preis	1983 Residential development, Osswaldstrasse – town of Starnberg Competition: 1st prize
1983 Kirche St. Nikolaus – Herrsching Wettbewerb	1983 St. Nikolaus church – Herrsching Competition
1984–87 Lagerhalle Firma Josef Gartner – Gundelfingen Bauherr: Josef Gartner GmbH	1984–87 Warehouse for Josef Gartner company – Gundelfingen Building owner: Josef Gartner GmbH
1984 Wohnbebauung Riemerfeld II – Stadt Garching Wettbewerb: 1. Preis	1984 Residential development, Riemerfeld II – town of Garching Competition: 1st prize

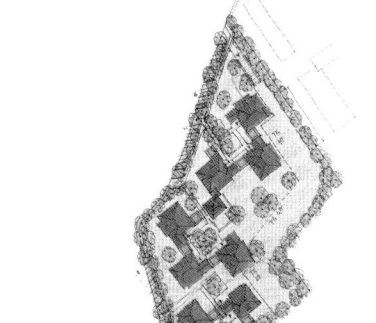

1984–86
Bebauungsplan Riemerfeld II – Garching
Auftraggeber: Stadt Garching

1984
Rathaus – Markt Pförring
Wettbewerb

1985–88
Umbau und Renovierung Redaktionsgebäude für Süddeutsche Zeitung – Sendlinger Straße, München
Bauherr: Süddeutscher Verlag GmbH

1985–89
Hohenwart – Städtebauliche Grobanalyse zur Sanierung Gestaltung des Marktplatzes
Auftraggeber: Markt Hohenwart

1985
Landesgartenschau – Dinkelsbühl
Wettbewerb

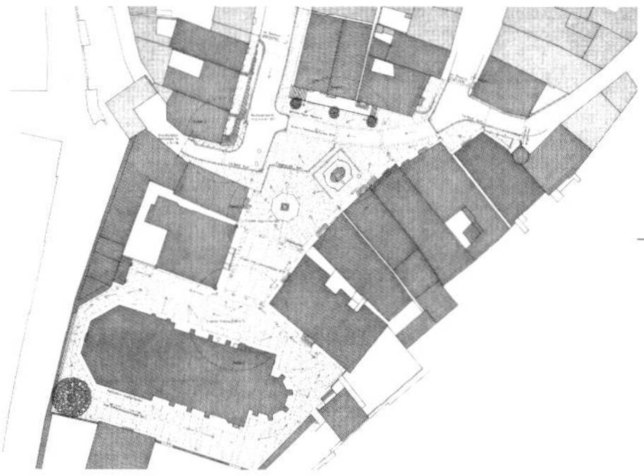

1985–88
Kronach – Vorbereitende Untersuchungen zur Altstadtsanierung
Gestaltung Otto-Melchior-Platz mit Treppenanlagen
Auftraggeber: Stadt Kronach

1985–90
Geisenfeld – Grobanalyse zur Sanierung des Ortskerns
Gestaltung Stadt-, Rathaus- und Kirchplatz
Feinplanung und Gestaltung Rosenstraße
Auftraggeber: Stadt Geisenfeld

1985–87
Jugendzentrum – Neu-Ulm
Bauherr: US Army Engineer Division, Europe

1985–86
Manching – Grobanalyse zur Sanierung des Ortskerns
Gestaltung Schulstraße
Auftraggeber: Markt Manching

1985–95
Erding – Vorbereitende Untersuchungen zur Sanierung der Altstadt
Ausbau und Gestaltung verschiedener Straßen, Gassen und Plätze
Auftraggeber: Stadt Erding

1986–92
Sanierung und teilweiser Neubau einer 700 Jahre alten Burgmauer und Burgtor – Vohburg
Bauherr: Stadt Vohburg

1984–86
Development plan, Riemerfeld II – Garching
Client: town of Garching

1984
Town hall – market town of Pförring
Competition

1985–88
Conversion and renovation of editorial building for Süddeutsche Zeitung – Sendlinger Strasse, Munich
Building owner: Süddeutscher Verlag GmbH

1985–89
Hohenwart – outline urban development analysis for refurbishment
Design of the market place
Client: market town of Hohenwart

1985
Garden Show of the federal state – Dinkelsbühl
Competition

1985–88
Kronach – preparatory surveys for the refurbishment of the old town centre
Design of Otto-Melchior-Platz with staircases
Client: town of Kronach

1985–90
Geisenfeld – outline analysis for the refurbishment of the town centre
Design of Stadtplatz, Rathausplatz and Kirchplatz
Fine planning and design, Rosenstrasse
Client: town of Geisenfeld

1985–87
Youth centre – Neu-Ulm
Building owner: US Army Engineer Division, Europe

1985–86
Manching – outline analysis for the refurbishment of the town centre
Design of Schulstrasse
Client: market town of Manching

1985–95
Erding – preparatory surveys for the refurbishment of the old centre of the town
Improvement and design of various roads, alleys and squares
Client: town of Erding

1986–92
Refurbishment and partial reconstruction of a 700 year old castle wall and castle gate – Vohburg
Building owner: town of Vohburg

1986
Gestaltungsvorschlag – Ortsmitte
Markt Peiting
Wettbewerb

1986–89
Büro- und Laborgebäude GRS II –
Forschungsgelände Garching
Bauherr: Gesellschaft für Anlagen- und
Reaktorsicherheit mbH

1986–89
Gestaltung Ulrich-Steinberger-Platz –
Vohburg
Auftraggeber: Stadt Vohburg

1986
Platzgestaltung – Stadt Münster
Wettbewerb

1986
Wohnbebauung Riemerfeld III –
Stadt Garching
Wettbewerb: 1. Preis

1986–89
Montagehalle – Firma Josef Gartner
Stonehouse/Bristol UK
Bauherr: Josef Gartner GmbH

1987–89
Institut für Luft- und Raumfahrt TU
Forschungsgelände Garching
Bauherr: Bauamt TU München

1987–89
Prüfinstitut für Radioaktivität in Technik
und Umwelt
Forschungsgelände Garching
Bauherr: Bayerisches Staatsministerium
für Umwelt und Landesplanung
Projekt

1987–89
Kindergarten – Markt Peißenberg
Bauherr: Markt Peißenberg

1988–90
Kindergarten – Angererstraße, München
Bauherr: Landeshauptstadt München

1988–89
Gestaltung Marktplatz und Marktstraße –
Gaimersheim
Auftraggeber: Markt Gaimersheim

1986
Design proposal – centre of the market
town of Peiting
Competition

1986–89
Office and laboratory building GRS II –
Garching research campus
Building owner: Gesellschaft für Anlagen-
und Reaktorsicherheit mbH

1986–89
Design of Ulrich-Steinberger-Platz – Vohburg
Client: town of Vohburg

1986
Design of the square – town of Münster
Competition

1986
Residential development, Riemerfeld III –
town of Garching
Competition: 1st prize

1986–89
Assembly building for Josef Gartner company
Stonehouse/Bristol UK
Building owner: Josef Gartner GmbH

1987–89
Institute for Air and Space Travel,
Technical University
Garching research campus
Building owner: Building Department of
the Technical University of Munich

1987–89
Test Institute for Radioactivity in
Technology and the Environment
Garching research campus
Building owner: Bavarian State Ministry
of the Environment and Regional Planning
Project

1987–89
Kindergarten – market town of Peissenberg
Building owner: market town of Peissenberg

1988–90
Kindergarten – Angererstrasse, Munich
Building owner: federal state capital of
Munich

1988–89
Design of the market place and Markt-
strasse – Gaimersheim
Client: market town of Gaimersheim

1988–91
Bebauungsplan Riemerfeld III – Garching
Auftraggeber: Stadt Garching

1989–92
Wolfratshausen – Vorbereitende
Untersuchungen zur Sanierung
Auftraggeber: Stadt Wolfratshausen

1989–90
Kindergarten – Riemerfeld, Garching
Bauherr: Stadt Garching

1989–92
Produktionshalle – Schöneberg
im Allgäu
Bauherr: Xaver Rampp Maschinenbau KG

1990–92
Büro- und Gewerbegebäude –
Bayerwaldstraße, München
Bauherr: Anneliese Tieber

1990–92
Bürokomplex – Freisinger Landstraße,
München
Bauherr: Leander B.V. Amsterdam
Kyrein GmbH + Co. Baubetreuungs KG
Projekt

1990–93
Studentenwohnheim – Riemerfeld,
Garching
Bauherr: Studentenwerk München

1991
Fußgängerbrücke über den Fehlbach –
Erding
Bauherr: Stadt Erding

1991
Gestaltungsvorschlag Autobahntunnel –
Eching a. Ammersee
Wettbewerb

1991–95
Büro mit Werkstatt für Werft –
Stegen am Ammersee
Bauherr: Bayerische Seenschiffahrt GmbH

1991
Stahlbauhalle, Lackierstraße und Kantine
auf dem Firmengelände der Firma Gartner –
Gundelfingen
Bauherr: Josef Gartner GmbH
Projekt

1988–91
Development plan, Riemerfeld III – Garching
Client: town of Garching

1989–92
Wolfratshausen – preparatory surveys
for refurbishment
Client: town of Wolfratshausen

1989–90
Kindergarten – Riemerfeld, Garching
Building owner: town of Garching

1989–92
Production building – Schöneberg
im Allgäu
Building owner: Xaver Rampp Maschinenbau KG

1990–92
Office and commercial building –
Bayerwaldstrasse, Munich
Building owner: Anneliese Tieber

1990–92
Office complex – Freisinger Landstrasse,
Munich
Building owner: Leander B.V. Amsterdam
Kyrein GmbH + Co. Baubetreuungs KG
Project

1990–93
Student hostel – Riemerfeld, Garching
Building owner: student welfare organisation
Munich

1991
Pedestrian bridge over the Fehlbach – Erding
Building owner: town of Erding

1991
Design proposal for motorway tunnel –
Eching a. Ammersee
Competition

1991–95
Office with workshop for shipyard –
Stegen am Ammersee
Building owner: Bayerische Seenschiffahrt
GmbH

1991
Steel construction building, paint line
and canteen on the factory complex of
the Gartner company – Gundelfingen
Building owner: Josef Gartner GmbH
Project

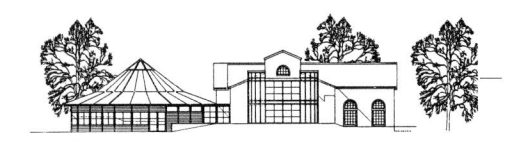

1991
Bürogebäude – Pettenkoferstraße,
München
Wettbewerb

1991
Bürgerhaus am Tiefstollen – Peißenberg
Bauherr: Markt Peißenberg
Projekt

1992 – 96
Geisenfeld – Feinuntersuchung des
historischen Ortskerns
Auftraggeber: Stadt Geisenfeld

1992
Städtebaulicher Ideenwettbewerb –
Gemeinde Putzbrunn
Wettbewerb

1992 – 95
Aussegnungshalle an der historischen
Burgmauer – Vohburg
Bauherr: Stadt Vohburg

1992
Bayerische Vereinsbank – Stadt Leipzig
Wettbewerb

1992
Verkehrsberuhigung der Altstadt mit
Hauptplatzgestaltung Stadt Landsberg
Wettbewerb

1993 – 94
Umbau und Renovierung einer
alten Villa – GRS Moskau
Umbau und Renovierung eines Büros
und Wohnungen – GRS Kiew
Bauherr: Gesellschaft für Anlagen- und
Reaktorsicherheit mbH

1993
Altenwohnheim Caritas – Gemeinde
Baldham
Wettbewerb

1993
Jungendgästehaus – Stadt Dachau
Wettbewerb

1994 – 95
Seniorenstift – Lochschwab, Herrsching
Bauherr: Seniorenstift in Herrsching GmbH
Projekt

1991
Office building – Pettenkoferstrasse, Munich
Competition

1991
Town house by Tiefstollen mine – Peissenberg
Building owner: market town of Peissenberg
Project

1992 – 96
Geisenfeld – detailed survey of the
historical town centre
Client: town of Geisenfeld

1992
Urban design competition – local community
of Putzbrunn
Competition

1992 – 95
Chapel of rest by the historical castle wall –
Vohburg
Building owner: town of Vohburg

1992
Bayerische Vereinsbank – city of Leipzig
Competition

1992
Traffic reduction in the old town centre
and design of the town square
Town of Landsberg
Competition

1993 – 94
Conversion and renovation of an old villa –
GRS Moscow
Conversion and renovation of an office
and apartments – GRS Kiev
Building owner: Gesellschaft für Anlagen-
und Reaktorsicherheit mbH

1993
Caritas old people's home –
local community of Baldham
Competition

1993
Youth guest house – town of Dachau
Competition

1994 – 95
Old people's home – Lochschwab, Herrsching
Building owner: Seniorenstift in
Herrsching GmbH
Project

1994
Umbau und Neubau einer Villa –
Wartaweil, Herrsching
Bauherr: Sabine Sten
Projekt

1994 – 96
Bürogebäude GRS III und Gesamtplan
Forschungsgelände Garching
Bauherr: Gesellschaft für Anlagen- und
Reaktorsicherheit mbH

1995
Bebauungsplan Vivamus – Unterbiberg,
Neubiberg
Auftraggeber: Gemeinde Neubiberg

1996 – 97
Reihenhäuser, Stadthäuser, Geschoss-
wohnungsbau, Winkelhäuser – Vivamus,
Unterbiberg
Bauherr: Bauland GmbH

1996
Herz-Jesu-Kirche – München
Wettbewerb

1996
Nachverdichtung Wohnanlage
Lenbachallee – Ottobrunn
Wettbewerb: 1. Preis

1996 – 02
Parkwohnanlage – Lenbachallee,
Ottobrunn
Bebauungsplan für Nachverdichtung
Auftraggeber: Gemeinde Ottobrunn
Aufstockung, Neubau und Sanierung
Bauherr: Wohnanlage Ottobrunn GmbH

1996 – 98
Bebauungsplan Gewerbe- und Medien-
park – Agrob Gelände Ismaning bei
München
Auftraggeber: Agrob AG München

1996
Bürogebäude Antenne Bayern –
Medienpark, Ismaning
Bauherr: Antenne Bayern
Projekt

1997
Zweigleisiger Ausbau der S-Bahn
mit Bahnhofsgebäude
und Platzgestaltung – Gemeinde
Unterföhring
Wettbewerb: 1. Preis

1994
Conversion and reconstruction of a villa –
Wartaweil, Herrsching
Building owner: Sabine Sten
Project

1994 – 96
Office building GRS III and overall plan
Garching research campus
Building owner: Gesellschaft für Anlagen-
und Reaktorsicherheit mbH

1995
Vivamus development plan – Unterbiberg,
Neubiberg
Client: local community of Neubiberg

1996 – 97
Terraced houses, town houses, apartment
buildings, corner houses – Vivamus,
Unterbiberg
Building owner: Bauland GmbH

1996
Herz-Jesu church – Munich
Competition

1996
Increase in density of a residential complex
Lenbachallee – Ottobrunn
Competition: 1st prize

1996 – 02
Park residential complex – Lenbachallee,
Ottobrunn
Development plan for increase in density
Client: local community of Ottobrunn
Vertical extension, new building and
refurbishment
Building owner: Wohnanlage Ottobrunn
GmbH

1996 – 98
Development plan, industrial and media
estate – Agrob complex
Ismaning near Munich
Client: Agrob AG Munich

1996
Office building Antenne Bayern –
media estate, Ismaning
Building owner: Antenne Bayern
Project

1997
Extension of the urban railway (S-Bahn) for
two-track operation, with station building
and square design – local community of
Unterföhring
Competition: 1st prize

1998–01	1998–01
Kindergarten am Hallstattfeld – Vivamus, Unterbiberg	**Kindergarten am Hallstattfeld – Vivamus, Unterbiberg**
Bauherr: Gemeinde Neubiberg	Building owner: local community of Neubiberg
1998–00	1998–2000
Erweiterung und Aufstockung Volksschule – Herrsching	**Horizontal and vertical extension of main school – Herrsching**
Bauherr: Gemeinde Herrsching	Building owner: local community of Herrsching
1998	1998
Marktplatzgestaltung – Pfaffenhofen an der Ilm	**Market square design – Pfaffenhofen an der Ilm**
Wettbewerb	Competition
1998–01	1998–01
Zweifachsporthalle – Internats- und Ganztagsschule, Landheim, Schondorf am Ammersee	**Dual sports hall – boarding and day school, Landheim Schondorf am Ammersee**
Bauherr: Stiftung Landheim Schondorf	Building owner: Landheim Schondorf foundation
Architekten: Detlef Schreiber und Peter Gradl	Architects: Detlef Schreiber and Peter Gradl
Entwurf und Projektleitung: Detlef Schreiber	Design and project leadership: Detlef Schreiber
1998	1998
Grundschule Panzerwiese West – Stadt München	**Primary school Panzerwiese West – city of Munich**
Wettbewerb	Competition
1998	1998
Parkhaus Messestadt Riem – München	**Indoor car park, trade fair town of Riem – Munich**
Wettbewerb	Competition
1999	1999
U-Bahnhofplatz Gestaltungsvorschlag – Stadt Garching	**Design proposal for square by underground station – town of Garching**
Wettbewerb	Competition
2001	2001
Umbau Andreaskirche zum Rathaus – Vohburg	**Conversion of Andreas church for use as the town hall – Vohburg**
Bauherr: Stadt Vohburg	Building owner: town of Vohburg
Projekt	Project
2001–02	2001–02
Marienkapelle, Gundelfingen	**St. Mary's Chapel, Gundelfingen**
Bauherr: Fritz und Heidi Gartner	Building owner: Fritz und Heidi Gartner
2001	2001
Schiffahrtsmuseum – Stegen am Ammersee	**Shipping museum – Stegen am Ammersee**
Bauherr: Förderverein Südbayerisches Schifffahrtsmuseum e.V.	Building owner: Förderverein Südbayerisches Schifffahrtsmuseum e.V.
Projekt	Project

Mitarbeiter
Staff and collaborators

Diese Aufzählung erhebt keinen Anspruch auf Vollständigkeit. Nach 42 Jahren war es nicht mehr möglich, sich an alle Namen zu erinnern.

This list does not claim to be complete. After 42 years it was not possible to remember all the names.

Norbert Achatz
Richard Adam
Ulrich Arndt
Ute Aschenborn

Alexander Bachmann
Stefan Bader
Peter Baer
Heinrich Bauer
Karin Bastl
Ellen Bender
Norbert Bicherl
Christine Böhm
Barbara Brumberger
Karl Brunner
Peter Buchert

Birgit Dellinger
Christiane Dettinger
Ursula Diesch
Richard Dirnberger

Christof Eckert

Andrea Fellmeth
Brigitte Feuerherdt
Michael Feuerherdt
Dieter Fischer
Thomas Frick
Michael Friede
Thomas Fuchs
Sabine Fuderer

Barbara Glöß
Horst Grüner
Renate Grünwald

Hans Hammer
Christine Haslberger
Hanne Höllerer
Kurt Holley
Angela Horak
Paul Horn
Helmut Huber
Hubert Hübner
Birgit Hüttl

Werner Junghans
Regina Junker

Hanno Kapfenberger
Josef Karg
Antonia Kasten
Wilhelm Kasten
Anette Kastner
Peter Kazek
Markus Keck
Eva Kohler
Bernd Krämer

Susanne Lang
Karin Larsson
Valentina Laus
Rainer von Linden
Klaus Lindner
Ralf Löw

Ulrike Mädge
Ingrid Maiser
Lutz Mahnkopf
Stefanie Meinicke
Oliver Mehl
Detlev Moldmann
Lore Mühlbauer

Heide Nocolaus
Angelika Nögel
Dietmar Oehler
Hilmar Ordelheide
Martin Ostenrieder

Günther Pauly
Christian Peter
Eva Pielmaier
Diane Plum
Sabine Pohl
Albrecht Puffert

Xaver Rauch
Markus Reischböck
Susanne Rentsch
Ralf Resele
Regina Rieder
Klaus Riemer
Alexander Rietzler
Gertrud Rottner
Klaus Rüssmann

Dietmar Sagmeister
Norbert Schachtner
Ulrich Schaflitzel
Ronald Scherzer
Christian Schittich
Peter Schneider
Robert Scholz
Hubert Schraud
Claudia Schreiber
Ulrike Schreiber
Klaus Schröder
Ursula Schubert
Harald Sigrist
Heiner Stengel
Christoph Strasser
Malgorzata Sylka

Sabine Thiede

Olga Vorlickowa

Domenik Wach
Peter Weilnböck
Claudia Weinhart
Dieter Wild
Sabine Wilhelm

Markus Zimmermann

Copyright 2006 by Junius Verlag GmbH
© für Fotos, Zeichnungen und Texte: bei den Fotografen, beim Autor und Herausgeber
Alle Rechte vorbehalten

Herausgegeben von Ulrike Schreiber

Fotonachweis/Photo credits:
Sigrid Neubert, München S. 22–24, 29, 35, 36–38, 39–41, 42, 45, 48, 49, 54–55, 62, 65–68, 72–75, 228, 230 (Mitte), 233 (oben)
Ingrid Voth-Amslinger, München S. 78, 82–84, 86–88, 95–98, 101–105, 116, 120–124, 128–131, 150, 152, 154–157, 180, 183, 185, 229 (Mitte)
Julia Schambeck, München S. 50, 158, 163, 165, 167, 169, 171, 198, 206, 209, 213, 221, 229 (oben), 231 (unten), 235 (Mitte oben), 238 (oben)
Christoph Franke, Schondorf a. Ammersee S. 106, 112–115, 172, 176–179, 235 (Mitte unten), 235 (unten)
Richard Bryant, London S. 146, 148–149
CL Fotojournalisten, Hamburg S. 56, 59–61
Werkphoto Firma Josef Gartner, Gundelfingen S. 76–77, 85, 132, 138–141, 143, 145, 147, 230 (unten), 235 (oben)
Hans Krakowitzer, Vohburg S. 236 (unten)
Gisela Buddeberg, München S. 21
Foto Baumann-Schicht, Bad Reichenhall S. 230 (oben)
Prof. Mayinger, München S. 231 (Mitte unten)
Detlef Schreiber, München S. 226 (unten), 233 (unten), 234, 238 (unten)
Luftbildverlag Hans Bertram GmbH, München S. 18
Studio Bauernsachs, Erding S. 192
Adelheid Gernhardt S. 222

Umschlag: Werkphoto Firma Josef Gartner, Gundelfingen
Detail Tragwerk, Halle Gundelfingen

Übersetzung: Michael Robinson, London; Victor Dewsbery, Berlin
Gestaltung: Büro Sieveking, München

Digitale Bildbearbeitung, Druck und Bindung:
Druckhaus Dresden GmbH, Dresden
Printed in Germany

ISBN-10 3-88506-576-2
ISBN-13 978-3-88506-576-0

1. Auflage 2006

Bibliografische Information der Deutschen Nationalbibliothek:
Die Deutsche Nationalbibliothek verzeichnet diese Publikation in der Deutschen Nationalbibliografie; detaillierte bibliografische Daten sind im Internet über http://dnb.ddb.de abrufbar.